Understanding Maths 1

Junior Certificate

Owen McConway
John McGuinness

Edco

First published 2007

The Educational Company
Ballymount Road
Walkinstown
Dublin 12

A member of the Smurfit Kappa Group

Editor: Kristin Jensen
Interior design concept: Design Image
Layout: Compuscript
Illustrations: Brian Fitzgerald
Cover design: Design Image
Printed in Ireland by ColourBooks

0 1 2 3 4 5 6 7 8 9

The paper used in this book comes from Managed Forests in Northern Europe For every tree felled, at least one new tree is planted

Acknowledgements

Thanks to Casio Computer Co. Ltd for permission to reproduce images and key references of the fx-83ES calculator. Photographs are courtesy of Alamy, Corbis, Imagefile, The Irish Image Collection, Photocall Ireland and Sportsfile.

The authors would like to thank the teachers of the mathematics department of Carndonagh Community School, both past and present, for their untold help and assistance over the past 22 years, and whose experience and support shaped a large amount of the content and direction of this book. We are also indebted to the editor, Kristin Jensen, and to Ruth Smyth and all at Edco. A special thanks also to Maurice Maxwell for his expertise, comments and suggestions, which were greatly appreciated and substantially improved the quality of the final textbook. A special word of thanks to our colleagues and friends Joe English, Peter Tiernan, Tom O'Connor, Cammie Gallagher, Anne McNamara and Anne Brosnan.

Dedication

We dedicate this book to our wives, Anne McConway and Mari O'Donovan.

Contents

Introduction

Understanding Maths 1 covers the syllabus for Junior Certificate Ordinary Level. Higher Level students would also use the book for the first year at secondary level.

The authors hope that you find the book useful in your studies. Our rationale in writing this book is to create a textbook which is accessible to all, including those who find mathematics challenging. We hope that the book goes some way towards explaining the 'why' of problems and not just the 'how'. Therefore, simple, clear language is used throughout the book and a visual approach is taken to examples, focusing on explaining why a particular method is being used. Text boxes are used in examples to aid understanding and enable the book to be used as a teaching aid in the classroom, rather than just a reference for questions. Colour is used extensively throughout the book to appeal to the visual learner and further aid understanding. The use of colour will also help the teacher to explain the 'why' in examples, rather than just seeing solutions as a list of procedures or algorithms. It is intended that the examples will become another teaching methodology and not just an indication of the type and nature of the questions in the exercise following them. 'Remember' text boxes are also used in the book to emphasise important terms or concepts.

There are plenty of carefully graded questions in the book, allowing all students to experience success while still challenging the more able student towards the end of exercises. This is as a result of feedback from teachers who want easy access to enough carefully graded questions to cover class work, homework and revision. We feel that the book caters for all situations and the time spent on each exercise should be at the teacher's discretion. Answers are provided to all questions (where possible) to facilitate quick access for the busy teacher and student. This is an acknowledgement that mathematics is more about 'method' than 'answer' and that encouraging students to show their work is more important than 'getting an answer'. A Chapter Summary exercise is provided at the end of each chapter which contains questions examining the topics covered in the entire chapter.

The book incorporates most recent developments in Irish mathematics education: the increased emphasis on active learning methodologies; the 'natural display' calculator; the use of the space instead of the comma for large numbers; and the multiplication sign is used to indicate multiplication.

A unique aspect of the book is a visual guide to the calculator used throughout the textbook and a separate calculator guide included at the back of the book, which will be very useful in teaching calculator skills to students.

The CD which accompanies this textbook is provided to schools. The CD contains sample examination papers, the Department of Education and Science syllabus and Teachers' Guidelines, some templates and activities which have proved successful in the classroom and a worksheet on each of the chapters in the book. The exercises on the CD are intended as reinforcement of material already covered in class and include a range of problems covering the entire chapter concerned.

The material on the CD is additional to the material in the book and would be suitable for class work, homework or revision. It would also be suitable as part of a portfolio of work which could be kept by the teacher as a record of work attempted.

A lot of time, effort, consultation and experience went into the writing of this book and we hope that it engages the student and encourages a positive attitude towards the subject.

Owen McConway
John McGuinness

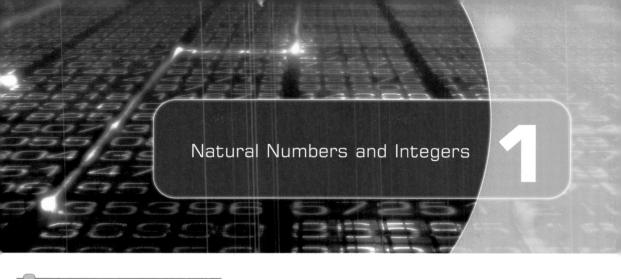

Natural Numbers and Integers

1

Natural numbers

The natural numbers are the ordinary counting numbers. Naturals do not include fractions, decimals or minus numbers. We use the capital letter **N** when talking about natural numbers. The natural numbers are coloured in green on the line below.

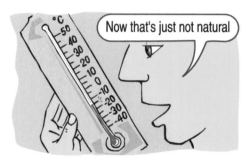

Example 1.1

(a) Why is −7 not a natural number?

Answer: Because it is a minus number.

(b) Why is 6.3 not a natural number?

Answer: Because it is not a whole number.

(c) Why is $-\frac{2}{3}$ not a natural number?

Answer: Because it is a minus number and also because it is not a whole number.

1

Factors (divisors)

Factors (or divisors) are numbers that divide in evenly to a number.

1. *How many children are there?*
2. *How many teams of 6 players could the children be divided into?*

Example 1.2

Write out all the factors of 32.

1 is a factor of every number. Every number is a factor of itself.

Solution

To do this, find all the numbers that divide in evenly to 32.

The factors of 32 are 1, 2, 4, 8, 16, 32.

Example 1.3

Write out the factors of 28 and 42 and hence find the highest common factor (HCF) of 28 and 42.

HCF stands for the highest common factor. This means the highest factor common to both lists.

Solution

Factors of 28 are 1, 2, 4, 7, 14, 28.

Factors of 42 are 1, 2, 3, 6, 7, 14, 21, 42.

$\Rightarrow$ HCF = 14

HCF

REMEMBER

NOTE: 1 is not itself considered to be a prime number.

A prime number is one that no other number will divide into, except 1 and itself. 13 is prime because only 1 and 13 will divide in evenly. 9 is *not* a prime number because 3 will divide in evenly.

Example 1.4

Write 1540 as a product of prime factors.

Solution

The red circles below are all prime numbers. Try each one in turn (starting with the lowest) to see if it divides in evenly. Keep doing this until you reach the final two red circles.

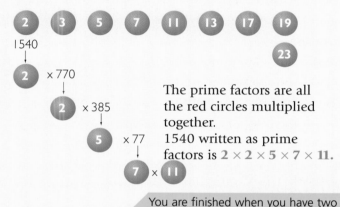

The prime factors are all the red circles multiplied together.

1540 written as prime factors is $2 \times 2 \times 5 \times 7 \times 11$.

You are finished when you have two red circles at the end, i.e. they cannot be broken up any more.

Exercise 1.1

1. List all the factors of the following: (a) 6 (b) 12 (c) 17 (d) 18 (e) 24 (f) 60 (g) 56 (h) 120.
2. List the factors of 30 and 42 and hence find the HCF of 30 and 42.
3. List the factors of 28 and 36 and hence find the HCF of 28 and 36.
4. List the factors of 15 and 20 and hence find the HCF of 15 and 20.
5. List the factors of 26 and 39 and hence find the HCF of 26 and 39.
6. List the factors of 12, 18 and 21 and hence find the HCF of 12, 18 and 21.
7. List the factors of 15, 45 and 60 and hence find the HCF of 15, 45 and 60.
8. List the factors of 18, 48 and 56 and hence find the HCF of 18, 48 and 56.
9. Write each of the following as a product of prime factors: (a) 8 (b) 12 (c) 18 (d) 45 (e) 90 (f) 100 (g) 72.
10. Write each of the following as a product of prime factors: (a) 120 (b) 150 (c) 196 (d) 500 (e) 225 (f) 2500 (g) 10 000.

Multiples

The multiples of a number is a list of bigger numbers that it will divide into. Multiples are sometimes called tables.

Example 1.5

(a) List the first five multiples of 13.
(b) List the first six multiples of 12 and 16 and hence find the LCM.

Solution

(a) Multiples of 13 are 13, 26, 39, 52, 65.
(b) Multiples of 12 are 12, 24, 36, 48, 60, 72.
Multiples of 16 are 16, 32, 48, 64, 80, 96.

The LCM of 12 and 16 is 48.

> LCM stands for the lowest common multiple. This means the lowest number that both will divide into.

Exercise 1.2

1. List the first five multiples of the following: (a) 3 (b) 7 (c) 8.
2. List the first five multiples of the following: (a) 20 (b) 19 (c) 17 (d) 24 (e) 31.
3. List the first eight multiples of each of 4 and 5 and hence find the LCM of 4 and 5.
4. List the first eight multiples of each of 8 and 14 and hence find the LCM of 8 and 14.
5. List the first eight multiples of each of 3 and 12 and hence find the LCM of 3 and 12.
6. List the first nine multiples of each of 16 and 18 and hence find the LCM of 16 and 18.
7. List the first eight multiples of each of 12 and 20 and hence find the LCM of 12 and 20.
8. List the first eight multiples of each of 14 and 21 and hence find the LCM of 14 and 21.
9. List the first eight multiples of each of 21 and 28 and hence find the LCM of 21 and 28.
10. List the first eight multiples of each of 14 and 35 and hence find the LCM of 14 and 35.

Integers

Integers are the plus and minus whole numbers, including 0. The capital letter Z is used when talking about integers. The integers are coloured in green in the line below. The integers do not include fractions or decimals. Plus numbers are written without the plus in front.

Integers on the number line:

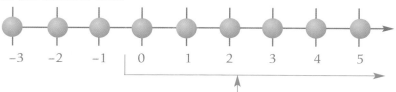

Remember, some of these integers are also natural numbers. From zero upwards are naturals *and* integers.

Example 1.6

Copy the following table into your exercise book and complete it.

Number	Natural	Reason	Integer	Reason
−7				
$\frac{3}{2}$				
5.2				
300				
6.0				

Solution

Number	Natural	Reason	Integer	Reason
−7	No	Minus number	Yes	Whole number
$\frac{3}{2}$	No	Fraction	No	Fraction
5.2	No	Decimal	No	Decimal
300	Yes	Plus, whole number	Yes	Whole number
6.0	Yes	Plus, whole number	Yes	Whole number

6.0 is a whole number. You can put '.0' after any whole number – it's just another way of writing it.

Adding and subtracting integers

The blue arrow means getting smaller (− means DOWN the line)

The orange arrow means getting bigger (+ means UP the line)

Example 1.7

Calculate the following: (a) $3 + 4$ (b) $-5 - 4$ (c) $2 - 6$ (d) $-5 + 8$ (e) $-1 - 5$.

Solution

The green arrow is the starting point.
The red arrow is the finishing point.

(a) $3 + 4$

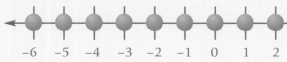

Answer: $3 + 4 = 7$

(b) $-5 - 4$

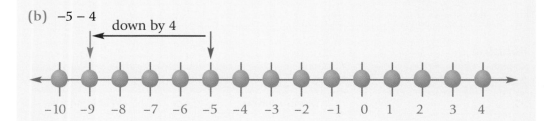

Answer: $-5 - 4 = -9$

(c) $2 - 6$

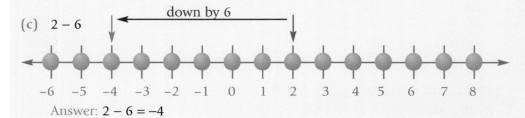

Answer: $2 - 6 = -4$

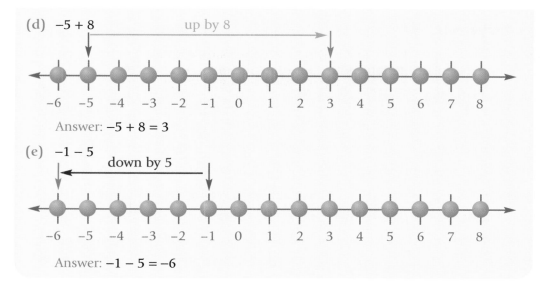

(d) −5 + 8   up by 8

Answer: −5 + 8 = 3

(e) −1 − 5   down by 5

Answer: −1 − 5 = −6

Rules for adding or subtracting integers:
1. If the signs are the same, add and use the common sign.
2. If the signs are different, subtract and use the sign of the bigger number.

Example 1.8

Calculate the following: (a) 7 + 9 − 8 + 3 − 9 − 1 + 2 (b) −3 + 5 − 6 + 3 − 5 − 2.

Solution

(a) 7 + 9 − 8 + 3 − 9 − 1 + 2
    7 + 9   + 3   + 2 = 21
       − 8 − 9 − 1 = −18
                = 3

(b) − 3 + 5 − 6 + 3 − 5 − 2
    + 5 + 3 = 8
  − 3 − 6 − 5 − 2 = −16
           = −8

Pick out all the plus numbers and add them. Then total all the minus numbers and get a final answer.

OR

(a) 7 + 9 − 8 + 3 − 9 − 1 + 2
  7 + 9   = 16
  − 8   = 8
  + 3   = 11
  − 9   = 2
  − 1   = 1
  + 2   = 3

(b) − 3 + 5 − 6 + 3 − 5 − 2
  −3 + 5 = 2
  − 6 = −4
  + 3 = −1
  − 5 = −6
  − 2 = −8

Take each of the numbers one by one. The original question is in black and the running total is in green.

Exercise 1.3

1. Copy the following table into your exercise book and complete it.

Number	Natural	Reason	Integer	Reason
21				
−21				
32				
$4\frac{2}{5}$				
16.0				
$\frac{3}{1}$				

Calculate each of the following.

2. −5 + 2	**10.** 3 + 2	**18.** −5 − 5	**26.** 0 − 5
3. −3 − 2	**11.** −7 − 4	**19.** −7 + 7	**27.** −5 + 0
4. −3 + 1	**12.** −9 − 8	**20.** 1 − 6	**28.** −5 + 5
5. 3 − 6	**13.** −9 + 9	**21.** 13 − 7	**29.** 5 − 5
6. −2 − 5	**14.** −3 + 3	**22.** −13 − 7	**30.** 0 + 6
7. −1 + 7	**15.** −3 − 8	**23.** 21 − 9	**31.** 0 − 6
8. 3 − 8	**16.** 0 − 7	**24.** −9 − 21	
9. −4 + 6	**17.** 0 + 5	**25.** −9 + 21	

Exercise 1.4

Calculate each of the following.

1. 8 − 10	**10.** 10 − 19	**19.** 12 − 7 − 9 + 3 + 4
2. 8 + 10	**11.** −12 − 4	**20.** −9 − 3 − 12 − 8 − 14
3. −8 − 10	**12.** 4 − 4	**21.** 9 + 3 + 12 + 8 + 14
4. −8 + 10	**13.** −3 + 7 + 2 − 3	**22.** −21 − 3 − 5 + 17
5. −7 + 2	**14.** 5 + 7 − 3 − 8 − 4	**23.** 34 − 71 − 45
6. 14 − 10	**15.** 6 − 3 + 5 − 9 + 1	**24.** −36 − 17 − 18 − 6 + 100
7. −14 + 10	**16.** 20 − 8 − 36 + 12 − 5	**25.** 37 − 63 + 28 − 32 − 19
8. −6 + 6	**17.** 16 − 18 − 20 − 16 + 13	**26.** −5 + 6 + 6 + 9 − 21
9. −6 − 6	**18.** −15 − 20 + 28 − 6 − 1	**27.** 13 − 17 + 16 − 18 − 1

28. On Monday the temperature was recorded at −1°C. On Tuesday the temperature went down by 3°C. What was the temperature on Tuesday?

29. On Friday the temperature was recorded at −2°C. On Saturday the temperature went up by 5°C. What was the temperature on Saturday?

30. One day the temperature was recorded at 9°C. Two days later it was recorded at −3°C. By how much had it gone down?

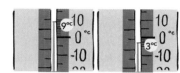

31. In July the average temperature was 19°C. In January the average temperature was 23°C below this. What was the average temperature in January?

32. Mary owes the bank €350. This shows in her bank statement as −350. Based on this starting point, what would happen if she did one of the following (each part from (a) to (e) is separate and should be worked out independently, taking the −350 as the starting point for each): (a) she spent another €40 (b) she spent another €80 (c) she paid in €60 to her account (d) she paid off half of what she owes (e) she paid in €350.

33. Goal difference is calculated by taking the goals 'against' away from the goals 'for'. Copy the following table into your exercise book and complete it.

Team	Goals For	Goals Against	Goal Difference
Brazil	18	7	
Germany	16	20	
Italy	12	12	
Greece	10	14	
Luxembourg	12		−7

34. Kate has €270 left in her bank account. Based on this starting point, what would happen if she did one or other of the following (each part from (a) to (d) is separate and should be worked out independently, taking 270 as the starting point for each): (a) she put in €140 (b) she spends €150 (c) she spends €300 (d) she spends €540.

Multiplying and dividing integers

The rules for multiplying and dividing are the same.

REMEMBER

When **multiplying** and **dividing**:
- The same signs give +.
- Different signs give −.

Multiplying	Dividing
+ multiplied by + gives + $8 \times 2 = 16$ $8 \cdot 5 = 40$ $6(2) = 12$ (There is an invisible plus sign in front of any number when no sign is visible)	**+ divided by + gives +** $8 \div 2 = 4$ $\dfrac{8}{4} = 2$ $6 \div 2 = 3$
− multiplied by − gives + $-8 \times -2 = 16$ $-1 \cdot -1 = 1$ $-6(-2) = 12$ (NOTE: A number outside a bracket means multiply)	**− divided by − gives +** $-6 \div -2 = 3$ $-8 \div -2 = 4$ $-1 \div -1 = 1$
+ multiplied by − gives − $8 \times -2 = -16$ $1 \cdot -4 = -4$ $6(-2) = -12$	**+ divided by − gives −** $8 \div -2 = -4$ $\dfrac{12}{-3} = -4$ $6 \div -2 = -3$
− multiplied by + gives − $-8 \times 2 = -16$ $-5 \cdot 3 = -15$ $-6(2) = -12$	**− divided by + gives −** $-8 \div 2 = -4$ $\dfrac{-24}{8} = -3$ $-6 \div 2 = -3$

Exercise 1.5

Calculate the following.

1. 3(4)
2. −3(−4)
3. 3(−4)
4. −3(4)
5. 12 ÷ 6
6. −12 ÷ −6
7. 12 ÷ −6
8. −12 ÷ 6
9. −4 × −8
10. 5 × −7
11. −6 × 4
12. 3 × 6
13. 4 . 7

14. −4 . 7
15. −4 . −7
16. $\dfrac{-12}{2}$
17. $\dfrac{-12}{-2}$
18. $\dfrac{12}{-2}$
19. −20 ÷ 4
20. 30 ÷ −5
21. 18 ÷ −6
22. −24 ÷ 2
23. −36 ÷ −6

24. 25 ÷ −5
25. 10 . 2
26. −10 . −2
27. −10 ÷ −2
28. 10 . −2
29. 10 ÷ 2
30. 3(2)(−4)
31. 5(−4)(−2)
32. −6(−2)(−3)
33. −4(3)(−5)
34. (−1)(−1)(−1)

Exercise 1.6

This exercise is a mixture of adding, subtracting, multiplying and dividing integers. Calculate each of the following.

1. −7 − 3
2. −7 . −3
3. 9 − 10
4. 9(−10)
5. −12 − 6
6. −12(−6)
7. −12 ÷ −6
8. −12 + 6
9. −12 ÷ −6
10. 8 − 10 − 3
11. 8(−10)(−3)

12. −60 . −3
13. $\dfrac{-60}{-3}$
14. −60 − 3
15. −60 + 3
16. −1 − 1 − 1
17. −4 − 4 + 8
18. −4(−4)(8)
19. 5(−4) − 2(−3)
20. −3(5) + 5(−3)
21. −2(3) + (−5)(−2) − (−3)(4)

Powers

Indices, powers and exponents all mean the same thing. The table below shows how they work.

Power (Index) (Exponent)	Means	Answer
7^2	7×7	49
7^3	$7 \times 7 \times 7$	343
3^4	$3 \times 3 \times 3 \times 3$	81
$(-4)^2$	-4×-4	16
$(-4)^3$	$-4 \times -4 \times -4$	-64
$(-2)^5$	$-2 \times -2 \times -2 \times -2 \times -2$	-32

Exercise 1.7

1. Copy the following table into your exercise book and complete it.

Power (Index) (Exponent)	Means	Answer
8^2		
8^3		
2^4		
$(-6)^2$		
$(-9)^3$		
$(-2)^5$		

Calculate each of the following.

2. 5^4

3. 0^2

4. 12^2

5. $(-12)^3$

6. $(-5)^2$

7. 16^2

8. $(-16)^2$

9. $(-11)^3$

10. 1^2

11. $(-1)^2$

12. $(-1)^3$

BEMDAS

In maths you must do the calculations in a particular order. This order is called

BEMDAS

Write down this question on a piece of paper: $6 + 9 \div 3$

Ask five or six people for the answer. The correct answer is **9**, but chances are that some people (even teachers!) may get it wrong and think the answer is 5. The reason that some people get it wrong is that they forget the order of doing mathematical calculations. This order is called BEMDAS and is explained in the table below.

Letter		Means
B	1	If there are brackets, you must calculate inside the brackets first.
E	2	If there are powers (also called exponents or indices), you must do them next.
MD	3	If there is multiplying or dividing, you must do them next. (If **both** multiplying and dividing are in a question, you must do whatever is furthest to the left first.)
AS	4	Finally, you do adding or subtracting.

Example 1.9

Calculate each of the following: (a) $12 - 2 \div 2$ (b) $(12 - 2) \div 2$ (c) $3(5 - 1)^2$
(d) $10 - 12 \div 3 \times 4$.

Solution

(a) $12 \boxed{- 2 \div 2} = 12 - 1 = 11$

> BEMDAS means that the dividing must be done before the subtracting.

(b) $\boxed{(12 - 2)} \div 2 = 10 \div 2 = 5$

> This time, BEMDAS means that we must do the brackets before the division.

(c) $3 \boxed{(5 - 1)^2} = 3(4)^2 = 3(16) = 48$

> BEMDAS means that we must do inside the brackets first, then the squaring and finally multiplying by the 3.

(d) $10 - 12 \div 3 \times 4 = 10 - 4 \times 4 = 10 - 16 = -6$

> Contains both multiplying and dividing, but we do the dividing first, since it is the furthest to the left.

Exercise 1.8

Calculate each of the following.

1. $18 + 2 \times 3$
2. $(18 + 2) \cdot 3$
3. $3(2)^2$
4. $6(4)^3$
5. $2(-3)^2$
6. $5(3 - 4)^5$
7. $24 \div 8 - 2$
8. $24 - (8 - 2)$
9. $8 - 3 \times 2 - 1$
10. $-5(7 - 9)$
11. $4(-2)^2 - 5(-2) + 7$
12. $3(4)^3 - 6(4) - 8$
13. $18 - 3 \times 4 - 6$
14. $16 + 4 \div 2 - 2$
15. $5(6 - 2 - 3)$

In questions 16 to 23, get an answer for the top first, then an answer for the bottom, and then finally do the dividing.

16. $\dfrac{8 + 16}{-12}$
17. $\dfrac{6 - 2 \times 5}{(4)^2 - 18}$
18. $\dfrac{18 + 2 \div 2}{3(-3)^2 - 8}$

19. $\dfrac{(3 - 7)^2}{-1 - 1}$
20. $\dfrac{20 - 12(2)}{2(-1)^2}$
21. $\dfrac{8^2 - 2^2}{(-2)^2 - (-6)}$

22. $\dfrac{6^2 - (-3)^2}{-3(3)}$
23. $\dfrac{2(3)^2 - 3(2 - 5)^2}{5 - 8}$

Exercise 1.9 (Chapter summary)

1. List the factors of 60 and 80 and hence find the HCF of 60 and 80.
2. List the factors of 52 and 78 and hence find the HCF of 52 and 78.
3. Write the following as a product of prime factors: (a) 36 (b) 70 (c) 68 (d) 140 (e) 300.
4. List the first nine multiples of 5 and 9 and hence find the LCM of 5 and 9.
5. List the first eight multiples of 14 and 12 and hence find the LCM of 14 and 12.

Calculate:

6. $3 - 12$
7. $-14 + 6$
8. $-9 + 2$
9. $5(-7)$
10. $5(7)$
11. $-5(-7)$
12. $-2(-4)(-3)$
13. On Friday the temperature was recorded at 5°C. On Saturday the temperature was down by 7°C. What was the temperature on Saturday?

14. On Monday the temperature was recorded at –2°C. The next day the temperature was up by 7°C. What was the temperature on the next day?

15. Draw the number line above three times in your exercise book. Then shade the following in red: (a) the natural numbers below 5 (b) the integers below 5 (c) the integers greater than –4.

16. Evaluate $\dfrac{3^3 - 5^2}{(-4)^2 - 3(5)}$

17. Copy the diagram below into your exercise book and fill in the missing numbers. Each box is the result of adding together the two numbers beneath it.

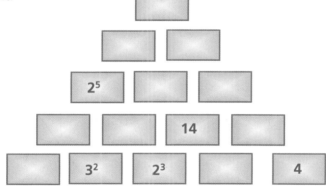

18. Each of the symbols below represents a number. The symbols are multiplied together and the totals for each row and column are shown. Find what number each symbol stands for.

$$❋ \times ▲ \times ♣ = 60$$
$$✳ \times ✳ \times ✳ = 8$$
$$▧ \times ✳ \times ❋ = 70$$
_____
70 12 40

Hint: ✳ is less than 10

Fractions and Decimals 2

In this chapter, you will learn about:

- Equivalent fractions.
- Simplifying fractions.
- Mixed numbers and improper fractions.
- Multiplying fractions.
- Addition and subtraction of fractions.
- Powers of fractions.
- Order of operation.
- Decimals.

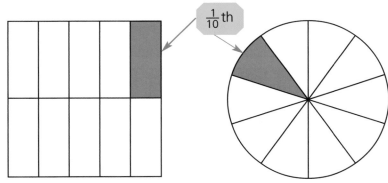

- Both the circle and square have been divided into 10 equal parts.
- Each part is called one-tenth of the circle or square, which means that fractions are always a part of something or a bit of something.
- Each part is called $\frac{1}{10}$th.
- The number below the line is called the **denominator** and tells us the number of equal parts there are (in this case, 10).
- The number on the top is called the **numerator** and tells us how many equal parts to take (in this case, 1).
- Fractions in the form of $\frac{a}{b}$ where a and b are integers and b is not 0 are called rational numbers. The symbol for the collection of rational numbers is Q.

Equivalent fractions

REMEMBER

The value of the fraction does not change when we multiply or divide both the top and the bottom by the same number. Any fraction generated by multiplying both parts by the same number is an **equivalent** fraction.

Example 2.1

Write three fractions equivalent to $\frac{1}{3}$.

Solution

$\frac{1}{3} \times \frac{2}{2} = \frac{2}{6}$

$\frac{1}{3} \times \frac{3}{3} = \frac{3}{9}$

$\frac{1}{3} \times \frac{4}{4} = \frac{4}{12}$

Example 2.2

Write the fraction equivalent to $\frac{3}{4}$ with 20 as the denominator.

Solution

$20 \div 4 = 5$

$\Rightarrow \frac{3}{4} \times \frac{5}{5} = \frac{15}{20}$

20 divided by 4 is 5. Now multiply both parts by 5.

Exercise 2.1

For part (a) of questions 1 to 10, list three equivalent fractions.

1. (a) $\frac{1}{2}$

   (b) Write the fraction equivalent to $\frac{1}{2}$ with 26 as the denominator.

2. (a) $\frac{3}{5}$

   (b) Write the fraction equivalent to $\frac{3}{5}$ with 50 as the denominator.

3. (a) $\frac{2}{7}$

   (b) Write the fraction equivalent to $\frac{2}{7}$ with 42 as the denominator.

4. (a) $\frac{5}{8}$

   (b) Write the fraction equivalent to $\frac{5}{8}$ with 56 as the denominator.

5. (a) $\frac{3}{9}$

   (b) Write the fraction equivalent to $\frac{3}{9}$ with 81 as the denominator.

6. (a) $\frac{9}{27}$

   (b) Write the fraction equivalent to $\frac{9}{27}$ with 3 as the denominator.

7. (a) $\frac{1}{5}$

   (b) Write the fraction equivalent to $\frac{1}{5}$ with 45 as the denominator.

8. (a) $\frac{5}{6}$

   (b) Write the fraction equivalent to $\frac{5}{6}$ with 36 as the denominator.

9. (a) $\frac{2}{3}$

   (b) Write the fraction equivalent to $\frac{2}{3}$ with 27 as the denominator.

10. (a) $\frac{15}{25}$

    (b) Write the fraction equivalent to $\frac{15}{25}$ with 5 as the denominator.

Simplifying fractions

REMEMBER

$\frac{3}{6}$ and $\frac{4}{8}$ are equivalent fractions. If we wish to write them in their simplest form, we must find a number that will divide into both the top and the bottom evenly.

$\frac{3}{6} = \frac{1}{2}$ Divide the top and bottom by 3.

$\frac{4}{8} = \frac{1}{2}$ Divide the top and bottom by 4.

Example 2.3

Simplify the following.

(a) $\frac{9}{27}$ (b) $\frac{4}{16}$ (c) $\frac{35}{55}$ (d) $\frac{21}{49}$

Solution

(a) $\frac{9}{27} = \frac{1}{3}$ Divide above and below by 9. (c) $\frac{35}{55} = \frac{7}{11}$ Divide above and below by 5.

(b) $\frac{4}{16} = \frac{1}{4}$ Divide above and below by 4. (d) $\frac{21}{49} = \frac{3}{7}$ Divide above and below by 7.

Exercise 2.2

Simplify the following.

1. $\frac{2}{8}$

2. $\frac{4}{10}$

3. $\frac{10}{15}$

4. $\frac{6}{14}$

5. $\frac{9}{15}$

6. $\frac{14}{21}$

7. $\frac{12}{18}$

8. $\frac{24}{56}$

9. $\frac{45}{60}$

10. $\frac{8}{64}$

11. $\frac{39}{66}$

12. $\frac{210}{320}$

13. $\frac{42}{63}$

14. $\frac{19}{57}$

15. $\frac{45}{81}$

16. $\frac{27}{72}$

17. $\frac{9}{108}$

18. $\frac{36}{144}$

19. $\frac{121}{1100}$

20. $\frac{180}{720}$

Mixed numbers and improper fractions

 REMEMBER

A mixed number is a whole number followed by a fraction, e.g. $2\frac{1}{3}$. This means $2+\frac{1}{3}$.

Improper fractions are fractions that have the numerator (top number) larger than the denominator (bottom number), e.g. $\frac{34}{4}$.

Example 2.4

Change the following mixed numbers to improper fractions.

(a) $4\frac{1}{3}$ (b) $7\frac{2}{5}$

Solution

(a) $4\frac{1}{3} = \frac{3\times4+1}{3} = \frac{13}{3}$

(b) $7\frac{2}{5} = \frac{5\times7+2}{5} = \frac{37}{5}$

Multiply the denominator by the whole number (in part (a) this is 4) and add the numerator to find the top line of the improper fraction. The denominator of the improper fraction is the same as the denominator in the mixed number.

Exercise 2.3

Change the following mixed numbers to improper fractions.

1. $4\frac{1}{4}$

2. $1\frac{2}{5}$

3. $5\frac{2}{3}$

4. $3\frac{3}{4}$

5. $3\frac{2}{7}$

6. $6\frac{4}{9}$

7. $2\frac{3}{8}$

8. $7\frac{5}{11}$

9. $3\frac{5}{6}$

10. $9\frac{8}{13}$

11. $7\frac{1}{4}$

12. $11\frac{2}{3}$

13. $13\frac{3}{16}$

14. $12\frac{3}{8}$

15. $17\frac{5}{8}$

16. $7\frac{3}{14}$

17. $3\frac{1}{7}$

18. $36\frac{3}{4}$

19. $25\frac{1}{5}$

20. $12\frac{7}{12}$

Multiplying fractions

Example 2.5

Multiply the following.

(a) $\frac{3}{4} \times \frac{5}{6}$ (b) $4 \times \frac{2}{7}$

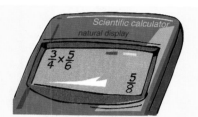

Solution

(a) $\frac{3}{4} \times \frac{5}{6} = \frac{3 \times 5}{4 \times 6} = \frac{15}{24} = \frac{5}{8}$

(b) $4 \times \frac{2}{7} = \frac{4}{1} \times \frac{2}{7} = \frac{4 \times 2}{1 \times 7} = \frac{8}{7}$

1. Multiply the numbers on the top.
2. Multiply the numbers on the bottom.
3. Simplify if possible, i.e. divide both the top and bottom by the same number. For example, 3 will divide into 15 and 24 in (a).

We can use the calculator to work out the answers to these questions. To input a fraction into the calculator, you must use the fraction button. In natural display calculators, this button will look like ▯. In DAL calculators, this button will look like a $\frac{b}{c}$.

To answer part (a), you must input the following way:

Now try using your calculator to check the answer in part (b) above.

Example 2.6

Divide the following fractions.

(a) $\frac{4}{7} \div \frac{5}{6}$ (b) $2\frac{2}{3} \div 1\frac{3}{4}$

Solution

(a) $\frac{4}{7} \div \frac{5}{6} = \frac{4}{7} \times \frac{6}{5}$

$= \frac{24}{35}$

(b) $2\frac{2}{3} \div 1\frac{3}{4} = \frac{8}{3} \div \frac{7}{4}$

$= \frac{8}{3} \times \frac{4}{7}$

$= \frac{32}{21}$

To divide by a fraction, you must turn it upside down and multiply.

REMEMBER

$\frac{4}{7} \div \frac{5}{6}$ could be written as $\dfrac{\frac{4}{7}}{\frac{5}{6}}$.

Exercise 2.4

Multiply the following fractions. Use your calculator to check your answer.

1. $\frac{3}{4} \times \frac{2}{5}$
2. $\frac{2}{3} \times \frac{2}{7}$
3. $\frac{1}{3} \times \frac{2}{5}$
4. $\frac{4}{3} \times \frac{4}{9}$
5. $\frac{3}{5} \times \frac{1}{3}$

6. $\frac{4}{7} \times \frac{3}{5}$
7. $2 \times \frac{4}{7}$
8. $1\frac{1}{2} \times \frac{2}{3}$
9. $\frac{21}{5} \times \frac{1}{2}$
10. $\frac{2}{5} \times 3\frac{1}{4}$

11. $3\frac{1}{2} \times 2\frac{2}{3}$
12. $4\frac{2}{3} \times 3\frac{1}{2}$
13. $4\frac{4}{5} \times 1\frac{1}{6}$
14. $\frac{9}{4} \times 1\frac{3}{5}$
15. $7\frac{1}{2} \times 1\frac{3}{5}$

Divide the following fractions. Use your calculator to check your answers.

16. $\frac{3}{4} \div \frac{1}{3}$
17. $\frac{8}{9} \div \frac{1}{2}$
18. $3\frac{1}{4} \div \frac{2}{3}$
19. $5\frac{1}{4} \div \frac{5}{9}$
20. $3\frac{2}{3} \div \frac{1}{3}$

21. $5\frac{3}{6} \div \frac{3}{4}$
22. $\frac{5}{3} \div 2\frac{1}{2}$
23. $3\frac{2}{3} \div 2\frac{1}{2}$
24. $16\frac{1}{4} \div 4$
25. $\frac{29}{5} \div \frac{7}{5}$

26. $9\frac{1}{3} \div 1\frac{3}{4}$
27. $\frac{6}{4} \div \frac{4}{6}$
28. $1\frac{5}{6} \div 2\frac{1}{3}$
29. $2\frac{2}{3} \div \frac{4}{9}$
30. $2\frac{2}{3} \div 1\frac{2}{3}$

Addition and subtraction of fractions

 REMEMBER

To add or subtract fractions, you must get a common denominator.

Example 2.7

Add the following.

(a) $\frac{3}{4}+\frac{2}{5}$ (b) $4\frac{1}{2}+\frac{3}{5}$

> $4 \times 5 = 20$ This will give you the common denominator.

Solution

(a) $\frac{3}{4}+\frac{2}{5}$

> Divide 4 into 20 to get the 5.

$$= \frac{3(5)+2(4)}{20}$$

> Divide 5 into 20 to get the 4.

$$= \frac{15+8}{20} = \frac{23}{20}$$

Using the calculator

> When inputting fractions with new calculators, use the arrow to get to the correct part of the fraction.

 $\Rightarrow \frac{23}{20}$

(b) $4\frac{1}{2}+\frac{3}{5}$

$$= \frac{9}{2}+\frac{3}{5}$$

> Change to top-heavy fraction.

$$= \frac{9(5)+3(2)}{10} \qquad = \frac{45+6}{10} = \frac{51}{10}$$

Using the calculator

 $\Rightarrow \frac{51}{10}.$

Example 2.8

Subtract the following fractions.

(a) $\frac{9}{4}-\frac{1}{3}$ (b) $2\frac{1}{2}-5\frac{1}{3}$

Solution

(a) $\frac{9}{4} - \frac{1}{3}$

$= \frac{9(3) - 1(4)}{12}$

$= \frac{27 - 4}{12}$ ← Common denominator is 3 × 4, the numbers on the bottom of the fractions.

$= \frac{23}{12}$

Check the answer using your calculator.

    $\Rightarrow \frac{23}{12}$.

(b) $2\frac{1}{2} - 5\frac{1}{3}$

$= \frac{5}{2} - \frac{16}{3}$

$= \frac{5(3) - 16(2)}{6}$

$= \frac{15 - 32}{6}$

$= \frac{-17}{6}$

Using the calculator

 $-\frac{17}{6}$.

Exercise 2.5

Calculate the following. Check your answers on the calculator.

1. $\frac{7}{12} + \frac{1}{3}$
2. $\frac{3}{4} + \frac{2}{5}$
3. $\frac{2}{3} + \frac{3}{4}$
4. $\frac{1}{2} + \frac{2}{3}$

5. $\frac{3}{4} + \frac{1}{2}$
6. $\frac{3}{5} + \frac{1}{2}$
7. $\frac{2}{3} + \frac{5}{8}$
8. $2\frac{1}{2} + 1\frac{1}{3}$

9. $3\frac{1}{3} + 4\frac{1}{5}$
10. $\frac{2}{3} + \frac{1}{2} + 1\frac{3}{4}$
11. $\frac{1}{5} + 2\frac{1}{4} + \frac{3}{10}$
12. $\frac{2}{3} + \frac{4}{6} + 4$

13. $1\frac{1}{3} + 2\frac{3}{4} + 1\frac{5}{6}$
14. $2\frac{1}{5} + 1\frac{4}{10} + \frac{7}{20}$

Subtract the following. Check your answers on the calculator.

15. $\frac{7}{6} - \frac{2}{3}$
16. $\frac{4}{5} - \frac{2}{7}$
17. $\frac{2}{3} - \frac{1}{2}$
18. $\frac{7}{9} - \frac{1}{3}$

19. $\frac{4}{5} - \frac{1}{2}$
20. $2\frac{3}{5} - \frac{4}{10}$
21. $6\frac{2}{3} - 5\frac{1}{2}$
22. $4\frac{1}{4} - 3\frac{1}{3}$

23. $4\frac{1}{3} - 2\frac{1}{2} - \frac{2}{3}$
24. $6\frac{2}{3} - 5\frac{1}{3} + 1\frac{1}{4}$
25. $6\frac{1}{4} - 2\frac{1}{2} - 1\frac{2}{5}$

26. $3\frac{5}{6} - \frac{1}{3} + 4$
27. $6\frac{1}{2} + 2\frac{1}{3} - 8\frac{1}{4}$
28. $1\frac{1}{5} - 3\frac{3}{10} + 2\frac{7}{15}$

Powers of fractions

 REMEMBER

$\left(\frac{1}{2}\right)^2$ means $\frac{1}{2} \times \frac{1}{2} = \frac{1}{4}$, i.e. multiply top by top and bottom by bottom.

 Example 2.9

Evaluate the following.

(a) $\left(\frac{2}{3}\right)^2$ (b) $\left(-\frac{4}{5}\right)^2$ (c) $\left(1\frac{2}{5}\right)^3$

Solution

(a) $\left(\frac{2}{3}\right)^2 = \frac{2}{3} \times \frac{2}{3} = \frac{4}{9}$

Using your calculator

$\boxed{} \; \boxed{2} \; \boxed{\downarrow} \; \boxed{3} \; \boxed{\rightarrow} \; \boxed{x^2} \; \boxed{=} \Rightarrow \frac{4}{9}$

(b) $\left(-\frac{4}{5}\right)^2 = -\frac{4}{5} \times -\frac{4}{5} = \frac{16}{25}$ ← $-4 \times -4 = 16$ Two minus numbers multiply to give a positive number.

(c) $\left(1\frac{2}{5}\right)^3 = \left(\frac{7}{5}\right)^3$ ←   Always change a mixed number to a top-heavy fraction first.

$\qquad = \frac{7}{5} \times \frac{7}{5} \times \frac{7}{5}$

$\qquad = \frac{343}{125}$

Exercise 2.6

Evaluate the following.

1. $\left(\frac{2}{4}\right)^2$ 4. $\left(\frac{1}{2}\right)^5$ 7. $\left(-\frac{1}{3}\right)^2$ 10. $\left(-2\frac{1}{2}\right)^2$

2. $\left(\frac{3}{5}\right)^2$ 5. $\left(2\frac{1}{3}\right)^2$ 8. $\left(-\frac{1}{2}\right)^5$ 11. $\left(3\frac{1}{3}\right)^2$

3. $\left(\frac{3}{4}\right)^3$ 6. $\left(1\frac{4}{3}\right)^3$ 9. $\left(-1\frac{3}{4}\right)^3$ 12. $\left(-4\frac{2}{5}\right)^2$

Order of operation

1st	Brackets	
2nd	Powers (exponent)	
3rd	Multiplication	Division
4th	Addition	Subtraction

(BEMDAS)

> If there are multiplication and division in the question, then whichever comes first when reading from left to right is worked out first,
> e.g. $16 \div 4 \times 4 = 4 \times 4 = 16$

Example 2.10

Evaluate the following.

(a) $\frac{1}{2} - \frac{2}{3} \times \frac{1}{4}$　　(b) $\left(3\frac{1}{3} + \frac{1}{2}\right) - \left(1\frac{1}{4}\right)^2$

Solution

(a) $\frac{1}{2} - \frac{2}{3} \times \frac{1}{4} = \frac{1}{2} - \frac{2}{12}$ (multiplication first)

$= \frac{1(6) - 2(1)}{12}$

$= \frac{6-2}{12} = \frac{4}{12} = \frac{1}{3}$

> Simplify by dividing above and below by 4.

Using the calculator

$\Rightarrow \frac{1}{3}$

(b) $\left(3\frac{1}{3} + \frac{1}{2}\right) - \left(1\frac{1}{4}\right)^2 = \left(\frac{10}{3} + \frac{1}{2}\right) - \left(\frac{5}{4}\right)^2$

$= \frac{10(2) + 1(3)}{6} - \frac{25}{16}$

$= \frac{20 + 3}{6} - \frac{25}{16}$

$= \frac{23}{6} - \frac{25}{16}$

$= \frac{23(8) - 25(3)}{48} = \frac{184 - 75}{48} = \frac{109}{48}$

> LCM of 6 and 16 is 48.

Using the calculator

$$\Rightarrow \frac{109}{48}$$

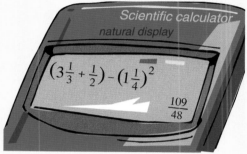

$$\left(3\tfrac{1}{3} + \tfrac{1}{2}\right) - \left(1\tfrac{1}{4}\right)^2$$

$$\frac{109}{48}$$

Exercise 2.7

Evaluate the following.

1. $\frac{1}{2} + \frac{1}{3} \times \frac{1}{5}$

2. $\left(3\frac{1}{2} - 1\frac{3}{4}\right) \times 2\frac{2}{3}$

3. $3\frac{1}{3} + 2\frac{1}{2} \times 1\frac{1}{4}$

4. $\left(2\frac{1}{4} + 3\frac{1}{3}\right) - 1\frac{2}{3}$

5. $\left(\frac{1}{2} + \frac{1}{6}\right) \times \frac{3}{5}$

6. $\left(5\frac{1}{2} - 3\frac{2}{3}\right) + 1\frac{1}{5}$

7. $\left(1\frac{3}{4} + 3\frac{1}{5}\right) \times 2\frac{2}{9}$

8. $\left(2\frac{2}{3} - 1\frac{5}{6}\right) \div \frac{2}{3}$

9. $\left(1\frac{1}{4} - \frac{3}{5}\right) \times 1\frac{2}{3}$

10. $\left(3\frac{1}{5} - 1\frac{2}{3}\right) \div 1\frac{3}{5}$

11. $3\frac{1}{5} \times \left(2\frac{1}{2} - 1\frac{5}{6}\right)$

12. $\left(2\frac{3}{4} - 1\frac{2}{3}\right) \times 1\frac{1}{3}$

13. $2\frac{1}{3} \div \left(1\frac{1}{3} - \frac{3}{4}\right)$

14. $5\frac{1}{4} \div \left(3\frac{1}{2} - 2\frac{1}{3}\right)$

15. $\left(2\frac{2}{3} - 1\frac{5}{6}\right) \div 1\frac{1}{5}$

16. $\left(3\frac{1}{2} - 1\frac{1}{4}\right) \times \left(2\frac{1}{3} - 1\frac{2}{9}\right)$

17. $\left(\frac{5}{6} - \frac{1}{4}\right) \times \left(3\frac{1}{2} - 1\frac{2}{5}\right)$

18. $\left(3\frac{1}{3} - 2\frac{2}{5}\right) \div \left(2\frac{1}{2} - 1\frac{5}{6}\right)$

Decimals

Place Value

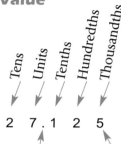

<table>
<tr><td>Tens</td><td>Units</td><td>Tenths</td><td>Hundredths</td><td>Thousandths</td></tr>
<tr><td>2</td><td>7 .</td><td>1</td><td>2</td><td>5</td></tr>
</table>

Decimal point   Any value after the decimal point forms a fraction of 1 unit.

Example: $.125 = \frac{125}{1000}$

Your calculator will convert fractions to decimals and decimals to fractions.

Example 2.11

Use your calculator to convert the following fractions to decimals.

  (a) $\frac{4}{5}$ (b) $2\frac{1}{4}$ (c) $-\frac{1}{4}$ (d) $-1\frac{1}{5}$

Solution

(a) $\boxed{\frac{\square}{\square}}$ $\boxed{4}$ $\boxed{\downarrow}$ $\boxed{5}$ $\boxed{\rightarrow}$ $=$ $\boxed{S \Leftrightarrow D}$ .8

(b) $\boxed{2^{nd}}$ $\boxed{\frac{\square}{\square}}$ $\boxed{2}$ $\boxed{\rightarrow}$ $\boxed{1}$ $\boxed{\downarrow}$ $\boxed{4}$ $\boxed{\rightarrow}$ $=$ $\boxed{S \Leftrightarrow D}$ 2.25

(c) $\boxed{\frac{\square}{\square}}$ $\boxed{-1}$ $\boxed{\downarrow}$ $\boxed{4}$ $\boxed{\rightarrow}$ $=$ $\boxed{S \Leftrightarrow D}$ −0.25

(d) $\boxed{2^{nd}}$ $\boxed{\frac{\square}{\square}}$ $\boxed{-1}$ $\boxed{\rightarrow}$ $\boxed{1}$ $\boxed{\downarrow}$ $\boxed{5}$ $\boxed{\rightarrow}$ $=$ $\boxed{S \Leftrightarrow D}$ −1.2.

Exercise 2.8

Write the following fractions as a decimal to three decimal places.

1. $\frac{3}{5}$

2. $\frac{3}{4}$

3. $\frac{1}{8}$

4. $\frac{1}{10}$

5. $\frac{7}{4}$

6. $\frac{4}{13}$

7. $\frac{13}{4}$

8. $\frac{14}{50}$

9. $\frac{1}{100}$

10. $\frac{1}{1000}$

11. $\frac{1}{75}$

12. $\frac{5}{8}$

13. $1\frac{3}{4}$

14. $2\frac{1}{3}$

15. $3\frac{4}{5}$

16. $10\frac{1}{5}$

17. $8\frac{1}{7}$

18. $\frac{19}{4}$

19. $\frac{12}{7}$

20. $\frac{41}{21}$

21. $-1\frac{1}{5}$

22. $-\frac{3}{7}$

23. $-4\frac{1}{6}$

24. $-3\frac{1}{7}$

25. $-\frac{8}{3}$

26. $-\frac{17}{5}$

27. $-\frac{1}{10}$

28. $-\frac{4}{100}$

29. $-2\frac{1}{10}$

30. $-\frac{15}{4}$

NOTE: To convert from decimals to fractions on your calculator, push the = button once the decimal is entered.

Calculations with decimals

Example 2.12

(a) In each part of (b), round off each value to the nearest whole number and estimate the expression.

(b) Evaluate the following:

    (i) 5.2(3.1) + 4.7

    (ii) $4.7(3.1 - 1.4)^2$ correct to two decimal places.

    (iii) $3\left(2.6 - 1\frac{1}{4}\right) + \sqrt{4.51}$ correct to three decimal places.

    (iv) $\dfrac{2.1(8.2 \times 3.14)}{\sqrt{5.45}}$ correct to one decimal place.

Solution

(a) (i) Estimate: $5(3) + 5$

$\quad = 15 + 5$

$\quad = 20$

> Multiplication

(b) (i) Answer: $5.2(3.1) + 4.7$

$\quad = 16.12 + 4.7$

$\quad = 20.82$

> Addition

(a)(ii) Estimate: $5(3 - 1)^2 = 5(2)^2$

$\quad = 5 \times 4 = 20$

(b)(ii) Answer: $4.7(3.1 - 1.4)^2$

$\quad = 4.7(1.7)^2$

$\quad = 4.7(2.89)$

$\quad = 13.583$

$\quad = 13.58$ correct to two decimal places, as the value after the second decimal is less than 5

> Brackets first
>
> Power next
>
> Multiplication

(a) (iii) Estimate: $3(3 - 1) + \sqrt{5}$

$\quad = 3(2) + 2$

$\quad = 8$

(b)(iii) Answer: $3\left(2.6 - 1\frac{1}{4}\right) + \sqrt{4.51}$

$\quad = 3(2.6 - 1.25) + \sqrt{4.51}$

$\quad = 3(1.35) + \sqrt{4.51}$

$\quad = 4.05 + 2.1237$

$\quad = 6.1737$

> Use your calculator to convert $1\frac{1}{4}$ to a decimal.
>
> Bracket
>
> Multiplication
>
> Addition

$\quad = 6.174$ correct to three decimal places, as the figure after the third decimal place is greater than 5

Using the calculator

$\boxed{3}\ \boxed{(}\ \boxed{2.6}\ \boxed{-}\ \boxed{2^{nd}}\ \boxed{\tfrac{\square}{\square}}\ \boxed{1}\ \boxed{\rightarrow}\ \boxed{1}\ \boxed{\downarrow}\ \boxed{4}\ \boxed{\rightarrow}\ \boxed{)}\ \boxed{+}\ \boxed{\sqrt{}}\ \boxed{4.51}\ \boxed{=}\ \boxed{S \Leftrightarrow D}$ 6.174

(a)(iv) Estimate: $\dfrac{2(8\times3)}{\sqrt{5}}$

$\sqrt{4}$ is an estimate for $\sqrt{5}$, i.e. $\sqrt{4}=2$.

$= \dfrac{48}{2}$

$= 24 \ (\text{estimate})$

Multiply inside bracket

(b)(iv) Answer: $\dfrac{2.1(8.2\times3.14)}{\sqrt{5.45}}$

$= \dfrac{2.1(25.748)}{\sqrt{5.45}}$

Multiply

$= \dfrac{54.0708}{2.3345}$

Find square root

$= 23.1616$

$= 23.2 \ \text{correct to one decimal place}$

Divide

Using the calculator

  2.1 (8.2 × 3.14) ↓ √ 5.45 → → = $\Rightarrow$ 23.16138598

Exercise 2.9

In each question, round off each value to the nearest whole number to find an estimate of the answer, then find the answer correct to two decimal places.

1. $5.4 \times 2.1 + 3.6$

2. $2.14 \times (3.2 - 1.4) + 2.1^2$

3. $3.14 \times 4.2^2 \times 2.7$

4. $(3.6 - 1.4)^2 \times 5.45$

5. $8.9 + 3.1 \times 4.6^2 - 38.13$

6. $(8.56 - 3.27)^2 + 3.7 \times \sqrt{4.5}$

7. $\dfrac{8.36 \times 3.75}{2.14}$

8. $\dfrac{5.368 + 10.83}{3.87}$

9. $\dfrac{38.231}{2.87 + 3.82^2}$

10. $\dfrac{36.81 - 17.13}{\sqrt{21.3}}$

11. $\dfrac{56.81 - 10.14}{2.68^2}$

12. $\dfrac{16.81 + 21.06}{7.31 - \sqrt{18.867}}$

13. $\dfrac{16.95 - 8.13}{8.06 - 1.87^2}$

14. $\dfrac{17.61 \times 2.84}{1.74 + 7.14}$

15. $\dfrac{\sqrt{27.61} \times (1.84)^2}{6.74 - 3.01}$

16. $\dfrac{(7.61)^2 \times \sqrt{4.84}}{18.24 - \sqrt{33}}$

17. $\dfrac{2.87^2 + 5.75^2}{1.88 + 6.75}$

18. $\dfrac{\sqrt{47.61} \times (2.14)^2}{(1.84)^2 - 1.14}$

19. $\dfrac{18.61 \times 5.68 + 2.3 \times (1.87)^2}{(5.74)^2 - (4.95)^2}$

20. $\dfrac{1}{0.04} + \dfrac{\sqrt{17.3}}{8.34} \times 25.8$

21. $\sqrt{16.3} + (3.18)^2 \times \dfrac{1}{0.375}$

22. $\dfrac{9.8^2 + \sqrt{65}}{4.2 \times 2.816}$

23. $\sqrt{91.6} \times \dfrac{4.18}{0.39} - (3.61)^2$

24. $\dfrac{1}{0.05} \times \sqrt{18.6} + \dfrac{(3.8)^2}{4.2}$

25. $(8.76)^2 \times \dfrac{1}{16.4} - \sqrt{12.8}$

26. $\dfrac{4.76 \times 3.86 - (1.97)^2}{\sqrt{11.8} - \sqrt{2.4}}$

27. $6.14^2 \times \dfrac{1}{0.4} + \sqrt{68.3}$

28. $\sqrt{39.6} \times \dfrac{1}{3.4} + (5.8)^2$

Exercise 2.10   (Chapter summary)

1. Simplify the following.

(a) $\dfrac{3}{9}$

(b) $\dfrac{12}{4}$

(c) $\dfrac{12}{15}$

(d) $\dfrac{33}{99}$

(e) $\dfrac{25}{75}$

(f) $\dfrac{16}{80}$

(g) $\dfrac{36}{54}$

(h) $\dfrac{27}{45}$

(i) $\dfrac{24}{60}$

(j) $\dfrac{12}{18}$

2. Change the following mixed numbers into top-heavy (improper) fractions.

(a) $1\frac{1}{5}$

(b) $3\frac{1}{3}$

(c) $1\frac{7}{8}$

(d) $5\frac{3}{4}$

(e) $2\frac{9}{11}$

(f) $4\frac{7}{8}$

(g) $12\frac{5}{8}$

(h) $9\frac{2}{3}$

(i) $6\frac{5}{12}$

(j) $8\frac{2}{13}$

3. Multiply the following.

(a) $\frac{5}{7} \times \frac{3}{4}$

(b) $\frac{5}{8} \times \frac{8}{5}$

(c) $\frac{1}{2} \times 4$

(d) $\frac{2}{5} \times \frac{4}{7}$

(e) $2\frac{1}{2} \times \frac{1}{4}$

(f) $3\frac{2}{3} \times 4\frac{3}{4}$

(g) $\frac{15}{7} \times \frac{3}{4}$

(h) $\frac{34}{4} \times \frac{5}{15}$

(i) $4\frac{1}{2} \times \frac{1}{10}$

(j) $\frac{4}{25} \times 20$

4. Divide the following.

(a) $\frac{21}{4} \div \frac{7}{2}$

(b) $\frac{1}{4} \div \frac{1}{2}$

(c) $\frac{3}{4} \div 2$

(d) $\frac{5}{4} \div \frac{2}{3}$

(e) $\frac{8}{9} \div \frac{1}{3}$

(f) $4\frac{1}{2} \div \frac{3}{4}$

(g) $5\frac{3}{7} \div 2\frac{1}{4}$

(h) $\frac{25\frac{1}{4}}{5\frac{1}{8}}$

(i) $\frac{12\frac{5}{9}}{4\frac{5}{12}}$

5. Add the following.

(a) $\frac{3}{4} + \frac{1}{10}$

(b) $\frac{2}{7} + \frac{5}{9}$

(c) $\frac{3}{5} + \frac{4}{9}$

(d) $\frac{2}{13} + \frac{5}{4}$

(e) $5\frac{1}{5} + 2\frac{1}{7}$

(f) $8\frac{3}{4} + 2\frac{1}{4}$

(g) $4\frac{5}{8} + \frac{1}{6}$

(h) $\frac{24}{5} + 2\frac{4}{9}$

(i) $\frac{25}{10} + \frac{10}{3}$

(j) $\frac{14}{3} + \frac{34}{12}$

6. Subtract the following.

(a) $\frac{45}{32} - \frac{1}{16}$

(b) $\frac{1}{4} - \frac{1}{8}$

(c) $1\frac{2}{3} - \frac{11}{15}$

(d) $2\frac{1}{2} - 1\frac{2}{3}$

(e) $\frac{5}{4} - \frac{4}{5}$

(f) $1\frac{5}{7} - \frac{4}{9}$

(g) $\frac{25}{10} - 1\frac{1}{5}$

(h) $7 - 3\frac{1}{5}$

(i) $\frac{27}{5} - \frac{3}{10}$

(j) $4\frac{1}{2} - 3\frac{1}{3}$

7. Evaluate the following.

(a) $\left(\frac{3}{4}\right)^2$

(b) $\left(\frac{2}{5}\right)^3$

(c) $\left(\frac{1}{2}\right)^5$

(d) $\left(-\frac{1}{2}\right)^3$

(e) $\left(\frac{1}{4}\right)^3$

(f) $\left(\frac{1}{3}\right)^3$

(g) $\left(1\frac{1}{4}\right)^3$

(h) $\left(-\frac{8}{9}\right)^2$

(i) $\left(\frac{5}{4}\right)^2$

(j) $\left(-\frac{2}{5}\right)^2$

8. Evaluate the following.

(a) $\left(3\frac{1}{2}+2\frac{2}{3}\right)-4\frac{5}{6}$

(b) $6\frac{1}{2}-\left(2\frac{1}{4}+3\frac{1}{3}\right)$

(c) $2\frac{1}{3}-\left(1\frac{1}{2}-\frac{1}{6}\right)$

(d) $\left(3\frac{1}{2}-2\frac{5}{6}\right)\times1\frac{1}{8}$

(e) $\left(5\frac{2}{3}+2\frac{1}{4}\right)\times4\frac{1}{5}$

(f) $\left(4\frac{2}{5}-3\frac{1}{4}\right)\div1\frac{1}{5}$

(g) $\left(2\frac{2}{3}-\frac{5}{6}\right)\div\left(2\frac{1}{2}+1\frac{2}{3}\right)$

(h) $\left(1\frac{3}{4}-\frac{11}{12}\right)\times\left(3\frac{1}{2}\div1\frac{1}{4}\right)$

9. (a) Estimate the value of each of the following by rounding off to the nearest whole number.

(b) Find the value of each correct to two decimal places.

(i) $(4.7\times3.8)^2\times\dfrac{1}{\sqrt{96.5}}$

(ii) $\dfrac{18.6+5.7\times1.2}{(2.86)^2}$

(iii) $\dfrac{7.7}{1.4}\times\sqrt{9.86+(8.93)^2}$

(iv) $\dfrac{19.81+13.14}{\sqrt{18.6-(1.66)^2}}$

(v) $\dfrac{21.6\times4.17}{13.6+7.86}$

(vi) $\dfrac{(20.16)^2-(3.84)^2}{\sqrt{61.5+(2.84)^2}}$

(vii) $\dfrac{(6.1\times2.13)^2}{\sqrt{41+3.14}}$

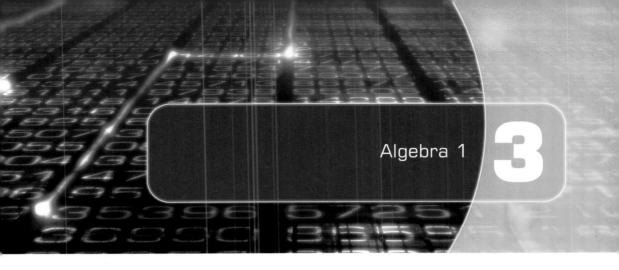

Algebra 1 **3**

In this chapter, you will learn about:

+ Adding and subtracting in algebra.
+ Multiplying in algebra.
+ Algebraic fractions.
+ Addition and subtraction of algebraic fractions.
+ Substitution.

Introduction

Algebra is an area of mathematics where letters take the place of numbers. The letters are called variables. If a number appears without a letter (variable), it is called a constant.

Algebra is used to keep the skies safe.

- 7 is a constant.
- x can also be written as $1x$ or $1x^1$ or x^1.
- $-x$ can also be written as $-1x$.
- $7x$ means 7 multiplied by x.
- $7 + x$ means 7 added to x.
- xy means x multiplied by y.
- xy is the same as yx.
- xyz means x multiplied by y multiplied by z.
- $7x^2$ means 7 multiplied by x multiplied by x.
- $(7x)^2$ means 7x multiplied by 7x.

Example 3.1

Above each arrow, write the operation used to produce the result in the next box. The operations will be addition, subtraction, multiplication or division. You must write what is being done to get into the next box.

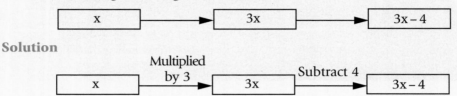

Solution

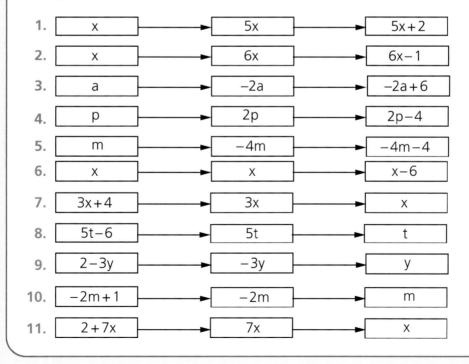

Exercise 3.1

Copy the questions into your exercise book. Complete the questions by writing the operation used to produce the result in the next box above each arrow. The operations will be addition, subtraction, multiplication or division. You must write what is being done to get into the next box. (See Example 3.1 above.)

1. x → $5x$ → $5x+2$
2. x → $6x$ → $6x-1$
3. a → $-2a$ → $-2a+6$
4. p → $2p$ → $2p-4$
5. m → $-4m$ → $-4m-4$
6. x → x → $x-6$
7. $3x+4$ → $3x$ → x
8. $5t-6$ → $5t$ → t
9. $2-3y$ → $-3y$ → y
10. $-2m+1$ → $-2m$ → m
11. $2+7x$ → $7x$ → x

Adding and subtracting in algebra

REMEMBER

In algebra, you can only add or subtract terms that are the same. In other words, you can only add or subtract x to x, x^2 to x^2, y^3 to y^3, a to a, and so on.

Example 3.2

Simplify the following.
(a) $5x + x$
(b) $5y + 3x$
(c) $6x^2 - 2x^2$
(d) $7x^2 + 8x - 3x^2 - x$
(e) $9x^3 + 4x^2 + 10x - 2x^3 - x^2 + 6x$
(f) $8y^3 - 4y^2 + 7y + 8 - y^3 - 3y^2 + 6y - 2$
(g) $2a^3 - a^2 + 3a - 5a^3 - 4a^2 + 6a - 7$
(h) $5ab + 3a - 2b + 4ab + 6b$

Solution
(a) $5x + x = 6x$ (x really means 1x. The 1 is usually invisible.)
(b) $5y + 3x$ cannot be added because they are not the same.
(c) $6x^2 - 2x^2 = 4x^2$
(d) $7x^2 + 8x - 3x^2 - x = 4x^2 + 7x$
(e) $9x^3 + 4x^2 + 10x - 2x^3 - x^2 + 6x = 7x^3 + 3x^2 + 16x$
(f) $8y^3 - 4y^2 + 7y + 8 - y^3 - 3y^2 + 6y - 2 = 7y^3 - 7y^2 + 13y + 6$
(g) $2a^3 - a^2 + 3a - 5a^3 - 4a^2 + 6a - 7 = -3a^3 - 5a^2 + 9a - 7$
(h) $5ab + 3a - 2b + 4ab + 6b = 9ab + 3a + 4b$

Terms that are the same and can be added or subtracted have been put in the same colour.

Exercise 3.2

Simplify the following.

1. $3x + 2x + 5x$
2. $x + x + x$
3. $4x + 2x + 3x + 6x$
4. $a + a + a + a$
5. $4y + 2y + 3y$
6. $2x + 3x + x$
7. $8y^2 + 2y^2 + 3y^2$
8. $5x^3 + 4y^3 + y^3 + 2y^3$
9. $2xy + 5xy + 3xy$
10. $2y + 4y + 6 + 3$
11. $a + 2a + 3a + 6y + 5y + 4 + 1$
12. $2x + 5y + 3 + 4y + 6x$
13. $4x^2 + 11x + x^2 + 6x$
14. $x^2 + 11x + 3 + 4x^2 + 2x + 5$
15. $2a^2 + 3a + 4 + 3a^2 + 6a$
16. $3x^3 + 2x^2 + 9x + 2x^3 + 6x^2 + x$
17. $2y^3 + 3y^2 + 3y + 5y^3 + 4y^2 + 6y$
18. $3x + 5y + 6x + 2y + 4$
19. $2x^2 + 11y + 8 + 3x^2 + 6y + 4$
20. $a + b + 4c + 2a + 6 + 3b + 2$
21. $3ab + 2a + 6ab + 5a + 2b + 3$
22. $5xy + 2y + 3xy + 4 + 6xy$
23. $10x - 2x$
24. $8y - 3y$
25. $5z - 2z$
26. $3x - x - x - x$

27. $6a - a$
28. $10x - 2x - 3x$
29. $8y^2 - 2y^2 - 3y^2$
30. $6x + 3y - 2x - y$
31. $4p^2 + 9p - 3p^2 + 2p$
32. $2y - 4y + 6 - 7$
33. $9x^2 + 11x - 2x^2 - 3x$
34. $7a^2 + 10a - a^2 - 2a$
35. $8x^2 + 9x + 1 - 4x^2 - 2x - 5$
36. $y^2 - 9y + 12 - 3y^2 - x - 2$
37. $5a^2 + 6a - 5 - 4a^2 - 4a - 6$
38. $2y^2 - 11y - 3 - 2y^2 - 8y - 9$
39. $6x^3 + 4x^2 + 9x - 2x^3 - 6x^2 - x$
40. $4p^3 + 6p^2 + 9p + 4 - p^3 - 6p^2 + x$
41. $5a^3 + 4a^2 + 3 - 4a^3 - 4a^2 + 3a^2 - 8$
42. $4p^3 + 2p^2 - 5p - 4p^2 - 6 - 2p$
43. $7x^2 + 2x - 13 + 6x^2 - 5x + 2 - 4x^2$
44. $10xy + 7x - 6 - 4xy - 9$
45. $3ab - 6b - 7ab - 8 - 4b$
46. $10xyz + 6xy + 3xz - 9xz - 3xy - xyz$
47. $2 - x^2 + 7x - 2 - 4x^2 + 2x + 2$
48. $7x^3 + 4x^2 + 10x + 5 + x^3 + 2x^2 + 6x + 3$
49. $2a^3 + 7a^2 + 8a + 3 + 2a^3 + 2a^2 + 3a + 5$
50. $3x^3 + 4y^2 + 3x + 5 + 2x^3 + 6y^2 + 2x + 1$
51. $x^3 + 4x^2 + 3x + 5x^3 + 3x^2 + x + 2$

Multiplying in algebra 1

REMEMBER

If there is a number outside the bracket,
multiply it by everything inside the bracket.

Example 3.3

Simplify the following.

(a) $3(2x + 5)$ (b) $5(2x^2 + 10x - 1)$ (c) $-4(3x^2 - 4x + 2)$

Solution

(a) $3(2x + 5) = 6x + 15$

REMEMBER

The rules for multiplying:

$+ \times + = +$

$- \times - = +$

$+ \times - = -$

$- \times + = -$

(b) $5(2x^2 + 10x - 1) = 10x^2 + 50x - 5$

(c) $-4(3x^2 - 4x + 2) = -12x^2 + 16x - 8$

Example 3.4

Simplify the following.

(a) $2(4x - 1) - 3(4x - 1)$

(b) $4(y^2 - 3y - 2) - 2(y^2 - 3y - 2)$

(c) $2(3x^2 + x - 1) - (x^2 - 4x - 5)$

Solution

(a) $2(4x - 1) - 3(4x - 1) = 8x - 2 - 12x + 3 = -4x + 1$

(b) $4(y^2 - 3y - 2) - 2(y^2 - 3y - 2) = 4y^2 - 12y - 8 - 2y^2 + 6y + 4 = 2y^2 - 6y - 4$

(c) $2(3x^2 + x - 1) - (x^2 - 4x - 5)$

$= 6x^2 + 2x - 2 - x^2 + 4x + 5$

$= 5x^2 + 6x + 3$

The minus sign outside the bracket changes all the signs inside.

Exercise 3.3

Simplify the following.

1. $2(3x + 4)$

2. $5(2y + 6)$

3. $6(2k + 4)$

4. $4(3x - 7)$

5. $5(7k - 6)$

6. $-3(4x + 5)$

7. $-4(2y - 3)$

8. $-6(3k - 2)$

9. $5(4x^2 + 2x + 5)$

10. $2(y^2 + 7y + 3)$

11. $3(2x + 4) + 5(3x + 2)$

12. $5(3y + 1) + 2(y + 7)$

13. $3(4k + 5) + 5(k + 3)$

14. $4(5x - 4) - 2(3x - 8)$

15. $3(2y + 8) - 6(5y - 2)$

16. $5(6x - 3) - (3x - 6)$

17. $8 - 2(5x - 3) - 6 + 3x$

18. $2(4x^2 + x + 2) + 3(2x^2 + 3x + 5)$

19. $4(2y^2 + 5y + 3) + 8(2y^2 + 2y + 4)$

20. $3(2x^2 - 11x + 3) - 5(4x^2 - 4x - 2)$

21. $2(y^2 - 3y - 4) - (2y^2 - 5y - 7)$

22. $x^2 + 11x + 9 - (4x^2 - 4x - 4)$

23. $2x^2 + x + 8 - (x^2 - 5x + 7)$

24. $6(4x^2 - 3x - 5) - 2(4x^2 - x - 7)$

25. $3(2y^2 + 3y + 2) - 4(2y^2 + 6y - 5)$

26. $5(y^2 - 6y - 1) - 3(4y^2 - 6y - 2)$

27. $6 - 3(2x^2 + x - 6) - 2x + 5$

28. $2(5x - 2) - 4(3x - 5) - 4(x + 4)$

29. $3(4y - 3) - 6(2y + 4) - 6(y - 2)$

30. $4(2k + 1) + 9(k - 4) - 3(5k - 5)$

31. $2(x^2 - 2x + 3) - (4x^2 - 4x) - 4(2x^2 - x - 4)$

32. $x^2 - 5x + 4 - (7x^2 + 5) - 2(3x^2 - 4x - 1)$

Multiplying in algebra 2

Term	Multiplied by	Term	Gives
y	×	y	y^2
a	×	a	a^2
y	×	y^2	y^3
x^2	×	x^3	x^5
3x	×	4x	$12x^2$
$5y^2$	×	3y	$15y^3$
$-3x^2$	×	2x	$-6x^3$
x	×	y	xy or yx
a	×	ab	a^2b
3k	×	2k	$6k^2$
ab	×	c	abc (or cba or bac or bca)
4xy	×	3xy	$12x^2y^2$

Example 3.5

Simplify the following.
(a) $4x(3x - 2)$
(b) $2y(3y^2 - y - 6) - 4(y^2 - 2y - 5)$

Solution

(a) $4x\,(3x - 2) = 12x^2 - 8x$

(b) $2y(3y^2 - y - 6) - 4\,(y^2 - 2y - 5) = 6y^3 - 2y^2 - 12y - 4y^2 + 8y + 20$
$$= 6y^3 - 6y^2 - 4y + 20$$

Exercise 3.4

1. Copy the table into your exercise book and complete it.

Term	Multiplied by	Term	Gives
x	×	x	
b	×	b	
k	×	k^2	
y^2	×	y^3	
4x	×	x	
$6y^2$	×	5y	
$-4x^2$	×	3x	
a	×	b	
b	×	3ab	
−5k	×	6k	
xy	×	z	
−2xy	×	−5xy	

Simplify each of the following.

2. $x(3x + 2)$

3. $y(y + 3)$

4. $2k(2k + 4)$

5. $4x(3x - 2)$

6. $4k(3k - 6)$

7. $-x(4x + 3)$

8. $-y(4y - 5)$

9. $-k(5k - 2)$

10. $x(2x^2 + 2x + 5)$

11. $2y(3y^2 + 4y + 3)$

12. $x(2x + 4) + 4(3x + 1)$

13. $2y(3y + 1) + 2(y + 3)$

14. $4k(2k + 5) + 3(k + 3)$

15. $2x(5x - 1) - 2(x - 8)$

16. $4y(2y + 5) - 3(5y - 2)$

17. $x(6x - 3) - (4x - 6)$

18. $3x(5x - 3) - 6 + 3x$

19. $3x(2x^2 + 3x + 2) + 2(x^2 + 3x + 5)$

20. $3y(2y^2 + 5y + 3) + 3(2y^2 + 2y + 4)$

21. $2x(x^2 - 11x + 3) - 3(4x^2 - 4x - 2)$

22. $3y(y^2 - 3y - 4) - 2(3y^2 - 5y - 7)$

23. $x^2 + 10x + 9 - x(4x^2 - 4x - 4)$

24. $2x(3x^2 - 3x - 2) - 2(3x^2 - x - 7)$

25. $2y(2y^2 + 4y + 2) - 2(2y^2 + 6y - 5)$

26. $3y(y^2 - 6y - 1) - 2(4y^2 - 6y - 2)$

27. $4x(2x^2 + x - 6) - 2x + 5$

28. $2x(2x - 2) - 4x(x - 5) - 4(x + 4)$

Multiplying in algebra 3

 REMEMBER

If there are brackets, multiply **everything** in the first set of brackets by **everything** in the second set.

Example 3.6

Multiply and simplify the following.
(a) $(5x + 3)(2x + 6)$
(b) $(2y − 4)(3y − 7)$
(c) $(4x − 2)(3x^2 + 2x − 4)$
(d) $(3x − 5)(7x^2 − 2x + 1)$
(e) $(4x − 3)^2$

Solution

(a) $(5x + 3)(2x + 6) = 10x^2 + 30x + 6x + 18 = 10x^2 + 36x + 18$

(b) $(2y − 4)(3y − 7) = 6y^2 − 14y − 12y + 28 = 6y^2 − 26y + 28$

(c) $(4x −2)(3x^2 + 2x − 4) = 12x^3 + 8x^2 − 16x − 6x^2 − 4x + 8 = 12x^3 + 2x^2 − 20x + 8$

(d) $(3x −5)(7x^2 − 2x + 1) = 21x^3 − 6x^2 + 3x − 35x^2 + 10x − 5 = 21x^3 − 41x^2 + 13x − 5$

(e) $(4x − 3)^2 = (4x − 3)(4x − 3) = 16x^2 − 12x − 12x + 9 = 16x^2 − 24x + 9$

Exercise 3.5

Multiply and simplify the following.

1. $(2x + 3)(x + 4)$
2. $(4x + 2)(2x + 1)$
3. $(5y + 3)(2y + 6)$
4. $(2k + 1)(2k + 3)$
5. $(2y - 3)(4y + 2)$
6. $(2x - 4)(3x - 3)$
7. $(4y + 4)(y - 5)$
8. $(x - 4)(x - 6)$
9. $(5x - 2)(3x - 1)$
10. $(2x - 5)(2x - 5)$
11. $(y + 2)(y + 2)$
12. $(6x - 3)(6x - 3)$
13. $(3a - 2)(4a - 3)$
14. $(5a + 3)(2a - 4)$
15. $(k - 1)(k - 1)$
16. $(2x - 2)(x^2 - 4x + 1)$
17. $(3y - 5)(7y^2 - 2y + 2)$
18. $(x - 1)(x^2 - 3x - 5)$
19. $(4y + 3)(7y^2 - 2y + 3)$
20. $(2x + 4)(3x^2 + 4x + 1)$

21. $(x - 3)(4x^2 + 3x - 6)$
22. $(3y - 4)(y^2 - 3x - 5)$
23. $(2x - 5)(3x^2 - 3x - 2)$
24. $(4y - 3)(3y^2 - 5y + 2)$
25. $(7x - 2)(x^2 + 2x - 1)$
26. $(2x + 3)(2x^2 - 3x - 5)$
27. $(x + 2)^2$
28. $(2x + 3)^2$
29. $(5x + 3)^2$
30. $(2y - 2)^2$
31. $(x + 5)^2$
32. $(5y + 2)^2$
33. $(3x - 2)^2$
34. $(3k + 1)^2$
35. $(x - 4)^2$
36. $(6x + 2)^2$
37. $(4x - 2)^2$
38. $(k - 3)^2$
39. $(5x - 1)^2$
40. $(3m - 1)^2$

Algebraic fractions

The basic rules are the same as those for ordinary fractions.

A fraction such as $\frac{21}{14}$ can be simplified by dividing above and below by the same number, i.e. by 7 ($21 \div 7 = 3$ and $14 \div 7 = 2$). Therefore, $\frac{21}{14} = \frac{3}{2}$.

$\frac{2x}{3x} = \frac{2\cancel{x}}{3\cancel{x}} = \frac{2}{3}$ divide above and below by x.

NOTE: $\frac{a}{a} = 1$ and $\frac{x+y}{x+y} = 1$

Term	Divided by	Term	Gives
y	÷	y	1
a	÷	a	1
y^2	÷	y	y
x^3	÷	x^2	x
$8x^4$	÷	4x	$2x^3$
$15y^2$	÷	3y	5y
$-12x^2$	÷	2	$-6x^2$
xy	÷	y	x
ab^3	÷	ab	b^2
3k	÷	$-2k$	$-\dfrac{3}{2}$
$-ab$	÷	$-c$	$\dfrac{ab}{c}$
$24x^4y$	÷	$-3xy$	$-8x^3$

Task: Copy the table into your exercise book and complete it.

Term	Divided by	Term	Gives
m	÷	m	
3k	÷	k	
x^2	÷	x	
x^3	÷	x^2	
$6x^3$	÷	2x	
$12x^2$	÷	4x	
$-20x^2$	÷	5	
ay	÷	a	
xy^3	÷	y	
10k	÷	$-5k$	
$-cd$	÷	c	
$16x^3y$	÷	$-4x^2y$	
$3x^2$	÷	$6x^5$	

Example 3.7

Simplify the following.

(a) $\dfrac{20ab}{5a}$ (b) $\dfrac{8a}{4a^2 - 12a}$

Solution

(a) $\dfrac{20ab}{5a} = \dfrac{20\,^4\,ab}{5\,a} = 4b$

20 divided by 5 is 4 and a divided by a is 1.

(b) $\dfrac{8a}{4a^2 - 12a}$

Divide the top and bottom by 4.

$= \dfrac{2a}{a^2 - 3a}$

Now factorise out the a on the bottom.

$= \dfrac{2a}{a\,(a - 3)}$

Divide the top and the bottom by a.

$= \dfrac{2}{a - 3}$

Exercise 3.6

Simplify the following.

1. $\dfrac{2a}{a}$

2. $\dfrac{4ab}{2a}$

3. $\dfrac{6bc}{3b}$

4. $\dfrac{8xyz}{4xy}$

5. $\dfrac{9ac}{3c}$

6. $\dfrac{25ghj}{5hj}$

7. $\dfrac{20x^2y}{4xy}$

8. $\dfrac{56x^3y^4z^5}{8xy^2z^3}$

9. $\dfrac{a}{a^2 - a}$

10. $\dfrac{2a}{a^2 + 2a}$

11. $\dfrac{4x}{6x^2 + 6x}$

12. $\dfrac{21mn^2}{7mn - 14mn^2}$

13. $\dfrac{6x - 3x^2}{9x^3}$

14. $\dfrac{36x - 24}{12}$

15. $\dfrac{24x^2 - 6xy}{18x}$

Addition and subtraction of algebraic fractions

The basic rules are the same as those for ordinary fractions.

REMEMBER

When adding fractions such as $\frac{2}{3}+\frac{5}{4}$, we must first find the common denominator, i.e. make the number on the bottom the same.

$$\frac{2}{3}+\frac{5}{4}=\frac{4(2)+3(5)}{12}=\frac{8+15}{12}=\frac{23}{12}$$

3 multiplied by 4 is 12, the common denominator.

Example 3.8

Simplify the following.

(a) $\frac{2x+5}{4}+\frac{3x-4}{6}$ (b) $\frac{2a+1}{3}-\frac{3a-4}{5}$

Solution

(a) $\frac{2x+5}{4}+\frac{3x-4}{6}=\frac{3(2x+5)+2(3x-4)}{12}=\frac{6x+15+6x-8}{12}=\frac{12x+7}{12}$

4 and 6 will divide evenly into 12. (You could use 4 x 6 = 24 as the common denominator. Try it and see.)

(b) $\frac{2a+1}{3}-\frac{3a-4}{5}=\frac{5(2a+1)-3(3a-4)}{15}=\frac{10a+5-9a+12}{15}=\frac{a+17}{15}$

3 and 5 will divide evenly into 15. With the minus sign, always put the top line in brackets.

Example 3.9

Simplify the following.

(a) $\frac{3a}{4}+\frac{5a}{6}$ (b) $\frac{7}{a^2}-\frac{8}{a}$ (c) $\frac{3x}{4}-2x$

Solution

(a) $\frac{3a}{4}+\frac{5a}{6}=\frac{3(3a)+2(5a)}{12}=\frac{9a+10a}{12}=\frac{19a}{12}$

4 and 6 will divide evenly into 12.

(b) $\dfrac{7}{a^2} - \dfrac{8}{a} = \dfrac{7(1)-8(a)}{a^2} = \dfrac{7-8a}{a^2}$

a^2 can be divided evenly by both a^2 and a.

(c) $\dfrac{3x}{4} - 2x = \dfrac{3x}{4} - \dfrac{2x}{1} = \dfrac{3x-4(2x)}{4} = \dfrac{3x-8x}{4} = \dfrac{-5x}{4}$

Exercise 3.7

Simplify the following.

1. $\dfrac{7}{2} + \dfrac{5}{3}$

2. $\dfrac{6}{5} + \dfrac{7}{2}$

3. $\dfrac{9}{4} + \dfrac{7}{3}$

4. $\dfrac{5}{2} + \dfrac{9}{2}$

5. $\dfrac{9}{2} - \dfrac{2}{3}$

6. $\dfrac{6}{5} - \dfrac{2}{3}$

7. $\dfrac{7}{12} - \dfrac{1}{3}$

8. $9 - \dfrac{4}{3}$

9. $\dfrac{5}{3} + 4$

10. $\dfrac{a+1}{2} + \dfrac{a-1}{3}$

11. $\dfrac{x+3}{4} + \dfrac{2x-1}{2}$

12. $\dfrac{3c-5}{3} + \dfrac{c-2}{7}$

13. $\dfrac{j+5}{5} + \dfrac{2j-2}{10}$

14. $\dfrac{2x-3}{4} + \dfrac{2x-1}{6}$

15. $\dfrac{2x+7}{5} - \dfrac{3x-5}{4}$

16. $\dfrac{x-5}{2} - \dfrac{3x-2}{5}$

17. $\dfrac{2x-5}{3} - \dfrac{x-3}{9}$

18. $\dfrac{4x+2}{6} - \dfrac{x+5}{4}$

19. $\dfrac{3m-4}{7} - \dfrac{5m+3}{4}$

20. $\dfrac{6}{x^2} - \dfrac{5}{x}$

21. $\dfrac{3y}{2} - 4y$

22. $\dfrac{3}{y^3} + \dfrac{2}{y^2}$

23. $\dfrac{5a}{3} - 6a$

24. $\dfrac{b-4}{2} + \dfrac{2b+3}{4}$

25. $\dfrac{2c-5}{5} + \dfrac{c-1}{2}$

Substitution

Substitution means replacing letters with numbers.

Margarine is a substitute for butter.

REMEMBER

When we substitute a number for a letter, it means that we replace the letter with the number and perform the same operation on the new number. For example, 3x means 3 multiplied by x. If we substitute x = 5, 3x means 3 multiplied by 5, so 3x = 3(5) = 15.

Example 3.10

If $x = 2$, find the value of the following.

(a) 6x　　　　(b) 3x – 8　　　　(c) $\frac{4x}{4}$

Solution

(a) $6x = 6(2) = 12$

Always replace the letter with brackets and the number that you want to substitute in its place.

(b) $3x - 8 = 3(2) - 8 = 6 - 8 = -2$

(c) $\frac{4x}{4} = \frac{4(2)}{4} = \frac{8}{4} = 2$

Example 3.11

If $x = 5$ and $y = -3$, find the value of the following.

(a) 4x + 5y　　　(b) 5x – 2y　　　(c) $\frac{3y + 2x}{3}$

Solution

(a) $4x + 5y = 4(5) + 5(-3) = 20 - 15 = 5$

Always replace the letter with brackets and the number that you want to substitute in its place.

(b) $5x - 2y = 5(5) - 2(-3) = 25 + 6 = 31$

Remember, when you multiply a minus by a minus, you get a plus ($- x - = +$).

(c) $\dfrac{3y + 2x}{3} = \dfrac{3(-3) + 2(5)}{3} = \dfrac{-9 + 10}{3} = \dfrac{1}{3}$

Exercise 3.8

1. If $a = 3$, find the value of the following.
   (a) $2a$　　(b) $5a$　　　　　　(c) $3a + 5$　　　　(d) $4a - 3$　(e) a^2　(f) $4a^2$
   (g) a^3　　(h) $6a^2 + 2a + 4$　(i) $2a^2 - 4a - 5$　(j) $2a^3$

2. If $x = 4$, find the value of the following.
   (a) $3x + 1$　　(b) $2x - 4$　　(c) $x - 5$　　(d) $4 - 3x$　　(e) $4x^2 + 3x$
   (f) $(x + 2)^2$

3. If $m = 2$ and $n = 1$, find the value of the following.
   (a) $3m + 2n$　　(b) $m + n$　　(c) $m - n$　　(d) $3n - 2m$　(e) mn
   (f) $5mn$　　　　(g) $m^2 + 4m$

4. If $x = 2$ and $y = -3$, find the value of the following.
   (a) $2x + y$　(b) $x - 2y$　(c) $-2x + 5y$　(d) $-x - y$　(e) $x^2 + 3x$　(f) $4y^2 + 3x$
   (g) $x + y$　　(h) xy　　　(i) $(x - 5)^2$　(j) $x^2 - 5$　(k) $y^3 + 2y$

5. If $a = -1$ and $b = 3$, find the value of the following.
   (a) $\dfrac{a}{b}$　(b) $\dfrac{3b - 2a}{2}$　(c) $\dfrac{a - 6b}{a}$　(d) $\dfrac{3b - a}{5}$　(e) $\dfrac{4b - 2}{5}$　(f) $\dfrac{b^2 + a}{2}$

6. If $a = -3$ and $b = 5$, find the value of the following.
   (a) $a + 4a$　　(b) $2a - 2a$　　(c) $5a + 7b$　　(d) $-3a - 5b$　(e) $a^2 + a - 2$
   (f) $b^2 + 6b + 3$　(g) $2a^2 + 4a - 2$　(h) $(a - 2)^2$　　(i) $(b - 3)^2$　　(j) a^3

7. If $x = 4$ and $y = -1$, find the value of the following.
   (a) $3x + 6y$　　(b) $4x - 5y$　　(c) $-5x + 3y$　(d) $-2x - 4y$　(e) $x^2 + 3x - 4$
   (f) $y^2 + 2y + 5$　(g) $4x^2 + 3x - 1$　(h) $(x - 7)^2$　(i) $(y - 1)^2$　　(j) x^3

8. If $a = 4$ and $b = -2$, find the value of the following.

   (a) $\frac{4a}{b}$ (b) $\frac{3b-2a}{5}$ (c) $\frac{2a-b}{2}$ (d) $\frac{3b-a}{5}$ (e) $\frac{4b-2}{6}$ (f) $\frac{b^2+a}{2}$

9. If $m = 5$ and $n = -3$, find the value of the following.

   (a) $m + 2n$ (b) $3m - n$ (c) $m - 5n$ (d) $5n - 6m$ (e) mn

   (f) $4mn$ (g) $m^2 + 4m$ (h) $m^2 + 6m$ (i) $n^2 + 3n + 4$ (j) $4n^2 - 3n - 6$

10. If $g = \frac{1}{4}$ and $h = -\frac{1}{2}$, find the value of the following.

   (a) $g + h$ (b) gh (c) $\frac{2g}{3h}$ (d) $\frac{4g-2h}{2}$ (e) $\frac{8g+10h}{7}$ (f) $\frac{6h-16g}{-1}$

Exercise 3.9   (Chapter summary)

Simplify the following.

1. (a) $4x^2 + 3x - 5 + x^2 + 7x - 4$ (b) $4x - 3 + 5x + 2 + 7y$
   (c) $6x^3 + 2x^2 + x - 3 - 4x^2 + 6x$ (d) $x^2 + 8x - 3 - x^2 + 6x$
   (e) $2y^2 + 6y + 8 + 4y^2 + 2y$ (f) $5y^2 + 4x - 5y^2 - 4x - 5$

2. (a) $3(4x + 3)$ (b) $5x(3x + 2)$ (c) $4(2x^2 - 4x - 1)$
   (d) $4x(5x^2 + 3x - 2)$ (e) $2(4y^2 + 3y - 3)$ (f) $2x(5x^2 - 2x - 6)$

3. (a) $(x + 2)(3x + 5)$ (b) $(2y + 6)(3y - 5)$ (c) $(4x - 2)(3x - 1)$
   (d) $(3x + 4)(2x^2 + 4x - 1)$ (e) $(3y + 2)(y^2 + 6y - 4)$ (f) $(5x - 6)(3x^2 - 2x - 3)$

4. (a) $(3x + 1)^2$ (b) $(5x - 4)^2$ (c) $(3y - 7)^2$
   (d) $(7x - 4)^2$ (e) $(2k - 3)^2$ (f) $(3m + 2)^2$

5. (a) $\frac{x-2}{3} + \frac{2x+5}{5}$ (b) $\frac{2y-6}{4} + \frac{3y+2}{2}$ (c) $\frac{5x-4}{6} - \frac{4x-3}{4}$

6. If $x = 3$, $y = -4$ and $z = -5$, find the value of the following.
   (a) $3x + 2y + 6z$ (b) $x^2 + y^2$ (c) $x^2 - z^2$ (d) y^3
   (e) $3z^2 - 4x^2 + 6$ (f) $\frac{x-1}{2} + \frac{2y+5}{3}$ (g) $\frac{6y}{4x}$ (h) $\frac{5x+3}{3} - \frac{2z+5}{5}$
   (i) $\frac{4z-2}{11} - \frac{7x+9}{16}$ (j) $x + y + z$ (k) xyz (l) $x^2 + (y - z)$

In this chapter, you will learn about:

+ The metric system – length, weight and volume.
+ Time and timetables.
+ Speed, distance and time.

▌▌▌The metric system

The metric system is based on the decimal system. We can convert from one unit of measurement to another by multiplying or dividing by a power of 10.

REMEMBER

From a big unit to a smaller unit, multiply.
From a small unit to a bigger unit, divide.

▌▌▌Length

Length is usually measured in millimetres (mm), centimetres (cm), metres (m) or kilometres (km).

REMEMBER

1 cm = 10 mm
1 m = 100 cm = 1000 mm
1 km = 1000 m

Example 4.1

Convert the following to metres.

(a) 300 cm   (b) 10 cm   (c) 5000 mm   (d) 4 km   (e) 3.25 km

Solution

cm → m = small to bigger → divide

(a) 300 cm = $\frac{300}{100}$ m = 3 m

(b) 10 cm = $\frac{10}{100}$ m = 0.1 m

(c) 5000 mm = $\frac{5000}{10}$ cm = 500 cm

$\quad = \frac{500}{100}$ m = 5 m

(d) 4 km ⇒ big to smaller ⇒ multiply
⇒ 4 km = 4 × 1000 m = 4000 m

(e) 3.25 km = 3.25 × 1000 m = 3250 m

Example 4.2

How many pieces of wood, each 15 cm long, can be cut from a length of wood 5.4 m long?

Solution

Change both lengths to the same units first.

5.4 m = 5.4 × 100 cm = 540 cm

Number of pieces = how many 15 cm in 540 cm = $\frac{540}{15}$ = 36 pieces of wood

Exercise 4.1

1. Write the following in millimetres (mm).
   (a) 12 cm   (b) 3 m   (c) 5.3 cm   (d) 1.65 m   (e) 3.26 cm

2. Write the following in metres (m).
   (a) 1450 cm   (b) 5 km   (c) 257 cm   (d) 37 600 mm
   (e) 25 cm   (f) 2.4 km   (g) 0.6 km   (h) 234 cm

3. Write the following in centimetres (cm).
   (a) 300 mm   (b) 3.2 m   (c) 0.45 km   (d) 2300 mm
   (e) 2.34 m   (f) 340 mm   (g) 0.045 km   (h) 4.045 m

4. Write the following in kilometres (km).
   (a) 3000 m   (b) 8500 m   (c) 15 600 cm   (d) 3264 m
   (e) 820 m   (f) 30 m   (g) 150 m   (h) 4300 cm

5. Write these measurements in metres (m) and give your answer in metres.
   (a) 1 km + 30 cm + 6 m
   (b) 450 cm + 5 km – 4500 cm
   (c) 274 cm – 3 km + 4500 m
   (d) 4700 mm – 85 cm + 2.4 m

6. One lap of a running track is 400 m long. How many laps must an athlete run to complete a 1500 m race?

7. When Mary walks the dog, each of her steps covers 60 cm, while the dog's step is only 20 cm long. If she walks the dog for 3 km, how many steps will (a) Mary take (b) the dog take?

8. Write each measurement in metres, then find the cost of the following lengths of cloth.
   (a) 3 m 75 cm at €8.60 per metre
   (b) 5 m 20 cm at €7.50 per metre
   (c) 380 cm at €5.95 per metre

9. Find the cost of laying tarmac on the following road lengths.
   (a) 3 km at €276 per km
   (b) 2 km 600 m at €310 per km
   (c) 10 km 30 m at €250 per km

10. A restaurant supplier stocks kitchen foil in two different roll lengths. One is of length 30 m at a price of €11.50 per roll, and the other of length 100 m at a price of €28 per roll.
    (a) How many of the shorter 30 m rolls will give the same length of foil as three of the longer rolls?
    (b) How much would be saved in buying three of the longer rolls rather than the equivalent length in 30 m rolls?

11. Laminate flooring is to be bought to cover the floors of three different rooms. In each case, one length of flooring measures 130 cm.
    Room 1 needs a total length of 18 m 30 cm at €38.40 per pack.
    Room 2 needs a total length of 24 m 70 cm at €45.90 per pack.
    Room 3 needs a total length of 30 m 14 cm at €62.50 per pack.
    (a) Calculate the number of lengths of the flooring needed to cover each floor to the nearest whole number.
    (b) Find the number of packs required for each room if each pack contains five lengths.
    (c) Calculate the cost of the flooring for each room (full packs only may be bought).

Weight and volume

When we ask how heavy something is, the answer is given in grams (g), kilograms (kg) or tonnes (t).

REMEMBER

1 kg = 1000 g
1 tonne = 1000 kg

If we ask how full a container is, the answer is given in millilitres (ml), centilitres (cl) or litres (l).

REMEMBER

1 cl = 10 ml
1 litre = 100 cl = 1000 ml

Medicine is measured in ml and some drinks are measured in cl. Milk and petrol, for example, are measured in litres.

Example 4.3

Write the following in kilograms.
(a) 3700 g   (b) 4 t   (c) $\frac{1}{2}$t   (d) 4500 g

Solution

(a) small → bigger → divide

$3700\,g = \frac{3700}{1000}\,kg = 3.7\,kg$

(b) big → smaller → multiply

$4\,t = 4 \times 1000\,kg = 4000\,kg$

(c) $\frac{1}{2}t = \frac{1}{2}(1000\,kg) = 500\,kg$

(d) small → bigger → divide

$4500\,g = \frac{4500}{1000}\,kg = 4.5\,kg$

Example 4.4

A drink pack is designed to hold 30 cl of juice. How many packs can be filled from a container filled with 4.5 litres of juice?

Solution

4.5 litres = 4.5 × 100 cl = 450 cl ← Change both to the same (smaller) units.

Number of packs = how many 30 cl in 450 cl $= \frac{450}{30} = 15$ packs

Exercise 4.2

1. Write the following in kilograms.
   (a) 5 t
   (b) 3200 g
   (c) $\frac{1}{4}$t
   (d) 2 kg 300 g
   (e) 3 kg 850 g
   (f) 1 t 450 kg
   (g) 3.12 t
   (h) 40 000 g

2. Write the following in tonnes (t).
   (a) 4000 kg
   (b) 4 t 300 kg
   (c) 35 000 kg
   (d) 400 kg
   (e) 5 t 16 kg
   (f) 3 t 700 kg
   (g) 4050 kg
   (h) 2 t 40 kg

3. Add the following.
   (a) 6 kg 800 g + 5.13 kg + 75 g; answer in kg.
   (b) 0.015 kg + 1 kg 63 g + 570 g; answer in g.
   (c) 765 kg + 2.15 t + 3 t 35 kg; answer in tonnes.
   (d) 0.35 kg + 360 g + 0.013 tonnes + 5.12 kg; answer in kg.

4. Calculate the following.
   (a) 5 kg 750 g – 3 kg 800 g; answer in g.
   (b) 4 t 600 kg – 3 t 750 kg, answer in tonnes.
   (c) 6 kg – (3.42 kg + 68 g); answer in kg.
   (d) (8142 g – 3 kg 82 g) – 3.4 kg; answer in kg.

5. Find the cost of the following loads.
   (a) 8 kg at €3.50 per kg.
   (b) 5.2 kg at €4.20 per kg.
   (c) 3600 g at €2.50 per kg.
   (d) 2 kg 20 g at €4.50 per kg.

6. One dose of medicine is 5 ml. How many doses can be taken from a bottle containing 15 cl?

7. A bottle contains 2 litres of water. How many glasses, each containing 40 cl, can be filled from this bottle?

8. A beaker holds 65 cl of water when full and is to be used to fill an empty fish tank with water. The tank is to hold 1.95 litres of water. How many times must the beaker be filled and emptied into the tank so that the tank is filled?

9. Small packs of sugar are to be filled with 2 g of sugar from a container holding 10 kg of sugar. How many packs can be filled from this container?

10. Fruit juice is sold in a packet of three cartons, costing €1.45. Each carton holds 200 ml. It is also sold in litre packs at €1.91 per pack.
    (a) Show that five packets, each containing three cartons, hold the same amount of juice as three of the 1-litre packs.
    (b) How much more would you pay in buying the five packets of three cartons rather than three of the 1-litre packs?

11. To create pastry for a tart, 400 g of flour has to be mixed with 300 g of margarine.
    (a) How many kg of flour and
    (b) How much margarine are needed to make the pastry for 40 of these tarts?

12. A bottle of a drink is designed to hold 300 ml. How many of these bottles can be filled from a container holding 6 litres?

13. A packet of wallpaper paste is to be mixed with 8 litres of water. All that is available as a measure is a cup which can hold 20 cl. How many times must this cup be filled to provide the right amount of water?

14. A bottle of washing-up liquid contains 50 cl of liquid. A family estimates that they use 2 ml of liquid each time the washing-up basin is filled. How many times can the washing-up basin be filled using this amount of liquid each time?

15. An elevator can carry up to six people but with a limit of 350 kg in total. Four people enter the lift, and these people weigh 105 kg, 117 kg, 125 kg and 110 kg. The elevator indicates that the weight limit has been exceeded. Who is the lightest person who should leave the elevator to solve the problem?

16. Packets of breakfast flakes are sold in four different sizes. A 30 g packet costs 50c, the 500 g packet costs €2.18, the 750 g packet costs €3.12 and the 1 kg packet costs €3.89.

(a) Calculate the price per gram for each packet.
(b) How much more will I pay if I buy 15 of the 30 g packets rather than one 750 g packet?

17. A soft drink is sold in four sizes – 15 cl, 33 cl, 35 cl and 1.25 litres. The prices are:
€4.79 per packet of 12 fun-size cans, each holding 15 cl.
€3.29 per packet of six cans, each holding 33 cl.
85c for each bottle containing 35 cl.
€1.89 for a 1.25 litre bottle.

(a) Calculate, to the nearest cent, the price per 10 cl bought in each size.
(b) Which is the best value?
(c) Show that three bottles at 85 cent each hold the same total amount as seven fun-size 15 cl cans.
(d) Joan buys 24 fun-size cans while Jim buys 12 cans, each holding 33 cl.
   (i) Who has more of the drink? (ii) Who pays more for their drinks?
   (iii) By how much?

|||Time and timetables

Time can be written in 12-hour clock time, with a.m. or p.m. following the figures, or in 24-hour clock time.

To convert from 12-hour to 24-hour time:

- Leave the numbers alone if it is a.m.
- Add 12 to the hour if it is p.m.

To convert from 24-hour time to 12-hour time:

- Subtract 12 from the hour if it can be subtracted and write the time as p.m.
- If 12 cannot be subtracted from the hour, write it as a.m.

Example 4.5

(a) Write the following in 24-hour clock time.
    (i) 3:45 a.m.   (ii) 9 p.m.   (iii) 1:45 p.m.
    (iv) 10:30 a.m.   (v) 11:10 a.m.   (vi) 8:12 p.m.

(b) Write the following in 12-hour clock time.
    (i) 13:00   (ii) 08:45   (iii) 17:42   (iv) 10:45

Solution

(a)   (i) 3:45 a.m. = 03:45
      (ii) 9 p.m. = 9 + 12 = 21:00
     (iii) 1:45 p.m. = 1:45 + 12 = 13:45
     (iv) 10:30 a.m. = 10:30
      (v) 11:10 a.m. = 11:10
     (vi) 8:12 p.m. = 8:12 + 12 = 20:12

(b)   (i) 13:00 = 1:00 p.m.
      (ii) 08:45 = 8:45 a.m.
     (iii) 17:42 = 5:42 p.m.
     (iv) 10:45 = 10:45 a.m.

Subtract 12 from the hour.

Example 4.6

(a) The film on a DVD lasts 112 minutes. If Kevin starts it at 14:15, what time will the film end? Give your answer in 12-hour clock time.

(b) He plays another DVD starting at 19:30 which ends at 21:08. How long was the DVD?

Solution

(a) 112 minutes = 1 hour 52 minutes ◄—— Subtract 60 minutes for hours.

14:15 + 1:52 = 15:67 = 16:07

= 16:07 = 4:07 p.m. ◄—— Change the 67 minutes into 1 hour 7 minutes.

(b) 21:08 → 20:68 ◄—— Change 1 hour into 60 minutes to help subtraction.

$$
\begin{array}{r}
20:68 \\
-\ 19:30 \\
\hline
1:38
\end{array}
$$

= 1 hour 38 minutes

Exercise 4.3

1. Write the following in 24-hour clock time.
   (a) 6 a.m.   (b) 3 p.m.   (c) 2:30 a.m.   (d) 4:50 a.m.   (e) 3:30 p.m.
   (f) 5:50 p.m. (g) 10:55 a.m. (h) 9:25 p.m.   (i) 11:05 p.m. (j) 10:07 a.m.

2. Write the following in 12-hour clock time using a.m. or p.m.
   (a) 07:00   (b) 09:30   (c) 13:00   (d) 18:00   (e) 10:30
   (f) 19:30   (g) 02:55   (h) 15:35   (i) 16:55   (j) 08:35

3. A bus journey takes 3 hours 20 minutes. What time should it arrive at its destination if it leaves the terminus at 08:45?

4. A train leaves Waterford at 15:25 and arrives in Kildare at 17:15. How long does this journey take?

5. A train leaves Dublin at 18:35 and takes 1 hour 38 minutes to get to Ballinasloe. What time should it arrive in Ballinasloe?

6. A plane leaves Shannon Airport at 13:45 and arrives in London at 15:18. How long does the flight last?

7. A bus leaves Dundalk at 13:35 and takes 35 minutes to travel to Newry. What time should it arrive in Newry?

8. A film lasts 122 minutes. If Pat starts watching the film at 3:50 p.m., what time will the film end?

9. A train takes 2 hours 47 minutes to travel from Dublin to Rosslare. It leaves Dublin at 17:25. What time should it arrive in Rosslare?

10. The table shows the bus timetable from Tralee to Rosslare.

Tralee	06:15	07:50	13:50	17:50
Farranfore	06:30	08:05	14:05	18:05
Killarney	06:55	08:30	14:30	18:30
Millstreet	07:30	09:05	15:05	19:05
Macroom	07:40	09:15	15:30	19:30
Cork	08:45	10:05	16:20	20:20
Youghal	10:30	11:30	17:30	21:30
Dungarvan	11:05	12:05	18:05	22:05
Waterford	11:55	12:55	18:55	22:55
Rosslare	13:40	14:40	20:50	00:40

(a) How long does the entire journey take on the 06:15 bus?

(b) On the 07:50 bus, how long does it take to travel from Waterford to Rosslare?

(c) On the 17:50 bus, how long does it take to travel from Millstreet to Dungarvan?

(d) John lives in Macroom and wishes to catch the 17:20 boat from Rosslare to France. He has to check in 1 hour before sailing time. Which bus should he catch from Macroom?

11. The timetable shows the bus timetable from Athlone to Belfast.

	Mon–Sat	Sun
Athlone	14:45	16:25
Longford	15:35	17:15
Cavan	16:35	18:15
Armagh	18:18	20:40
Portadown	19:00	21:22
Belfast	19:50	21:55

(a) How long does the journey take on a weekday?

(b) How long does the journey take on a Sunday?

(c) If you travelled from Longford to Portadown during the week, how long would it take?

(d) Which two towns on the route are closest to each other?

12. The timetable below shows a section of the rail timetable for Dublin to Belfast.

Dublin (Connolly)	07:35	09:35	13:20	19:00	20:45
Drogheda	08:05	10:06	13:50	19:31	21:15
Dundalk	08:30	10:30	14:15	19:55	21:40
Newry	08:48	10:48	14:33	20:13	21:58
Portadown	09:09	11:09	14:54	20:34	22:19
Belfast (Central)	09:45	11:45	15:30	21:10	22:55

(a) How long does each train take?

(b) How long does it take to travel from Drogheda to Portadown?

(c) Mary lives in Dundalk and is flying out from Belfast Airport at 19:45 on Saturday. She must check in 2 hours before her flight. It takes 30 minutes by taxi from the train station to the airport. Which train should she catch from Dundalk?

13. A plane takes $7\frac{1}{4}$ hours to fly from Dublin to New York. The plane leaves Dublin at 09:40.
    (a) In Irish time, what time should the plane arrive in New York?
    (b) If time in New York is 5 hours behind Irish time, at what time, in New York time, should the plane arrive?

14. The following shows a portion of the Westport to Dublin timetable.

Westport	07:30	13:40	18:20
Castlebar	07:44	13:54	18:34
Claremorris	08:08	14:20	19:05
Castlerea	08:39	14:50	19:35
Athlone	09:31	15:41	20:31
Dublin	11:00	17:15	22:10

    (a) How long is the journey from Westport to Castlebar?
    (b) Which train to Dublin is the slowest?
    (c) At what time, in 12-hour clock time, does the 13:40 train from Westport arrive in Dublin?
    (d) Jim travels on a bus from Louisburg, which arrives in Westport at 11:15 a.m. How long will Jim have to wait for the next train from Westport?

15. A plane leaves Dublin at 13:20 for Kathmandu. The journey takes $8\frac{1}{2}$ hours.

(a) What time is it in Dublin when the plane arrives in Kathmandu?

(b) If time in Kathmandu is $5\frac{3}{4}$ hours ahead of Dublin time, at what local time should the plane arrive in Kathmandu?

16. Part of a bus timetable from Dublin to Carlow is shown.

Dublin	07:30	10:15	13:10	17:45
Kildare	08:45	11:30	14:25	19:00
Carlow	09:25	12:10	15:15	19:50

(a) How long does the 13:10 bus take to make the journey from Dublin to Carlow? Is there a faster bus? If so, which one is it?

(b) At what time, in 12-hour clock time, does the last bus leave Dublin for Carlow?

(c) At what time, in 12-hour clock time, does the last bus arrive in Carlow?

(d) It is planned to add an extra bus to the timetable, leaving Dublin at 19:10. Assuming this bus takes the same time as the 17:45 bus, what time should it arrive in Carlow?

17. A plane leaves London at 11:25 for Buenos Aires. The journey takes 14 hours 20 minutes.

(a) What time is it in London when the plane arrives in Buenos Aires?

(b) The time in Buenos Aires is 3 hours behind London time. What is the local time in Buenos Aires when the plane arrives?

Speed, distance and time

Speed is the rate at which distance is covered in each unit of time. A speed of 60 km per hour – often written as 60 km/h – means that in each hour, a distance of 60 kilometres is covered.

$$\text{average speed} = \frac{\text{distance travelled}}{\text{time taken}}$$

$$\text{time taken} = \frac{\text{distance travelled}}{\text{speed}}$$

$$\text{distance travelled} = \text{speed} \times \text{time}$$

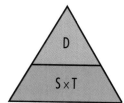

The triangle may help in remembering these formulas.

Example 4.7

A journey of 140 km was completed in $3\frac{1}{2}$ hours. Find the average speed for the journey.

Solution

$$\text{Average speed} = \frac{D}{T} = \frac{140}{3.5}\,\text{km/h} = 40\,\text{km/h}$$

Example 4.8

Adrian cycled for 10 seconds and covered a distance of 70 metres. Calculate his average speed in (a) m/s (metres per second) (b) km/h (kilometres per hour).

Solution

(a) $\text{Speed} = \frac{D}{T} = \frac{70}{10} = 7\,\text{m/s}$

(b) 7 m/s = 7 metres in 1 second

$\Rightarrow$ 7m $\times$ 60 sec $\Rightarrow$ 1 minute = 420 m

$\Rightarrow$ 420m $\times$ 60 min $\Rightarrow$ 1 hour = 25 200 m = 25.2 km in 1 hour

$\Rightarrow$ 7 m/s = 25.2 km/h

Example 4.9

A car is driven at an average speed of 65 km/h for 45 minutes. Calculate the distance travelled by the car.

Solution

distance = speed × time

$\qquad$ = 65 km/h × 45 minutes

$\qquad = 65 \times \dfrac{45}{60}$ ◄

$\qquad$ = 48.75 km

Note that the units in which we work must be similar. For example, a speed in km/h means time must be in hours; distance must be in km. In Example 4.9, the 45 minutes was changed to hours (by dividing by 60).

Example 4.10

A bus was driven for 375 km at an average speed of 75 km/h. How long did the journey take?

Solution

$\text{time} = \dfrac{\text{distance}}{\text{speed}}$

$\qquad = \dfrac{375}{75}$

$\qquad$ = 5 hours

Example 4.11

Josephine walks at an average speed of 8 km/h for 45 minutes and then cycles at an average speed of 30 km/h for 30 minutes.
(a) Find the distance she walked.
(b) Find the distance she cycled.
(c) Calculate her average speed for the entire distance travelled.

Solution

distance = speed × time (d = s × t)

(a) Walking: distance = $8 \times \dfrac{45}{60}$ ◄

$\qquad\qquad\qquad$ = 6 km

Note the time in hours.

(b) Cycling: distance = speed × time

$$= 30 \times \frac{30}{60}$$

$$= 15 \text{ km}$$

(c) Average speed $= \dfrac{\text{total distance}}{\text{total time}}$

$$= \frac{6 \text{ km} + 15 \text{ km}}{(45 + 30) \text{ minutes}}$$

$$= \frac{21 \text{ km}}{75 \text{ minutes}}$$

$$= \frac{21 \text{ km}}{1.25 \text{ hrs}}$$

$$= 16.8 \text{ km/h}$$

> 75 minutes = 1 hour 15 minutes and 1 hour 15 minutes = 1.25 hours, i.e. 15 minutes = $\frac{1}{4}$ hour = .25 hours.

Example 4.12

Calculate the speed of 45 km/h in m/sec.

Solution

45 km/h = 45 km in 1 hour = 45 000 m in 60 minutes

$$= \frac{45000 \text{ m}}{60 \text{ minutes}} \text{ in 1 minute}$$

$$= 750 \text{ m in 1 minute } (= 60 \text{ seconds})$$

$$= \frac{750 \text{ m}}{60 \text{ seconds}} \text{ in 1 second}$$

$$= 12.5 \text{ m/sec}$$

Exercise 4.4

1. Find the average speed in km/h for these journeys.
   (a) 120 km in 3 hours
   (b) 84 km in 2 hours
   (c) 150 km in $2\frac{1}{2}$ hours
   (d) 17 km in 30 minutes
   (e) 54 km in $2\frac{1}{4}$ hours

(f) 78 km in 3 hours 15 minutes

(g) 12 km in 20 minutes

(h) 20 km in 25 minutes

(i) 36 km in 1 hour 20 minutes

(j) 88 km in 3 hours 40 minutes

2. Find the distance covered in km in the following.

(a) Average speed of 20 km/h for 2 hours

(b) Average speed of 18 km/h for $3\frac{1}{2}$ hours

(c) Average speed of 36 km/h for 2 hours 30 minutes

(d) Average speed of 48 km/h for 3 hours 45 minutes

(e) Average speed of 24 km/h for 1 hour 10 minutes

(f) Average speed of 36 km/h for 2 hours 15 minutes

(g) Average speed of 27 km/h for 40 minutes

(h) Average speed of 30 km/h for 5 minutes

(i) Average speed of 4 km/h for 2 hours 15 minutes

(j) Average speed of 20 km/h for 1 hour 18 minutes

3. Find the time taken for the following journeys.

(a) 80 km at an average speed of 20 km/h

(b) 60 km at an average speed of 12 km/h

(c) 36 km at an average speed of 10 km/h

(d) 240 km at an average speed of 45 km/h

(e) 300 km at an average speed of 80 km/h

(f) 10 km at an average speed of 3 km/h

(g) 60 km at an average speed of 40 km/h

(h) 3 km at an average speed of 2 m/sec

(i) 5 km at an average speed of 8 m/s

(j) 200 m at an average speed of 36 km/h

4. Jack walks at an average speed of 12 km/h for 35 minutes. How far has he walked?

5. Máire walks 20 m in 5 seconds. Calculate her average speed in (a) m/s (b) km/h.

6. A cyclist covers a distance of 810 m in $1\frac{1}{2}$ minutes. Calculate the average speed in (a) m/s (b) km/h.

7. A car travels 30 m in 3 seconds. Calculate the average speed over this distance in (a) m/s (b) km/h.

8. A plane takes $7\frac{1}{2}$ hours to fly from Dublin to Boston at an average speed of 600 km/h. How far does the plane fly?

9. A plane travels 300 m in 2 seconds. How long would it take, at the same average speed, to travel 60 km?

10. Liam walked at an average speed of 8 km/h for 30 minutes and then cycled at an average speed of 24 km/h for $1\frac{1}{2}$ hours.
    (a) How far did he walk?
    (b) How far did he cycle?
    (c) Calculate his average speed for the entire journey.

11. Ann went by car from home to the airport to collect a friend and drove at an average speed of 78 km/h. The journey took $2\frac{1}{2}$ hours. She then returned home, which took her 3 hours.
    (a) Calculate the distance from her home to the airport.
    (b) Calculate her average speed for the journey home.
    (c) Calculate her average speed for the round trip from her home to the airport and back to the nearest km/h.

12. The distance from Galway to Dublin is 224 km. A car left Galway at 09:50 and arrived in Dublin 3 hours 15 minutes later.
    (a) What time did the car reach Dublin?
    (b) What was the car's average speed for this journey to the nearest km/h?

13. An athlete running 400 m covers the first
    200 m in 24 seconds and the second 200 m at
    an average speed of 36 km/h. Calculate:
    (a) The total time taken for the 400 m.
    (b) The average speed over the 400 m
        to the nearest km/h.

14. The first 80 km of a journey of 125 km took exactly 3 hours. The rest was
    covered at an average speed of 30 km/h due to heavy traffic.
    (a) How long did it take to travel the distance at 30 km/h?
    (b) Find the average speed, to the nearest km/h, for the entire journey.

15. A plane left Cork at 12:50 and landed in Paris at 14:40 Irish time.
    The plane flew at an average speed of 540 km/h during the journey.
    (a) Calculate the distance between the two airports.
    (b) The return trip from Paris to Dublin took $2\frac{1}{4}$ hours. What was the
        average speed for this trip?
    (c) Calculate the average speed of the plane for the round trip from
        Dublin to Paris and back to the nearest km/h.

Exercise 4.5   (Chapter summary)

1. Write the following in metres.
   (a) 1 km   (b) 0.75 km   (c) 450 cm
   (d) 1250 mm   (e) 1250 cm   (f) 90 mm
   (g) 180 cm   (h) 2450 cm   (i) 1.2 km + 23 m + 340 cm
   (j) 3.2 km + 240 m − 1.78 km
   (k) 450 cm + 2.3 m − 5500 mm
   (l) 4.56 m + 340 cm − 1200 mm

2. Write the following in kilograms.

(a) 3.12 t   (b) 3200 g   (c) 4 kg 25 g

(d) 4 t 35 kg   (e) 2 kg 575 g   (f) 4 t 10 kg

(g) 500 g + 300 g − 464 g   (h) 3.12 t + 34 kg

(i) 2 t 50 kg + 3 t 200 kg   (j) 5 t 40 kg − 3 t 800 kg

(k) 3.12 kg + 475 g   (l) 4 t 50 kg − 3 t 750 kg + 1 t 300 kg

3. Write the following in litres.

(a) 340 cl

(b) 3 litres 40 cl

(c) 5.4 litres + 45 cl

(d) 6(330 cl) + 12(150 cl)

4. Decorative garden stone is sold loose by the tonne and also in 25 kg sealed bags. If bought loose, it costs €85 per tonne, plus €20 for the container in which it is delivered. Each 25 kg sealed bag costs €11.50 with no delivery charge.

(a) How many sealed bags are needed to make up a tonne?

(b) How much more will I pay per tonne if I buy the sealed bags of stone rather than having it delivered loose?

5. Write the following in 24-hour clock time.

(a) 10:30 a.m.

(b) 9:45 p.m.

(c) 12 noon

(d) 12:04 a.m.

(e) 7:35 p.m.

6. Write the following in 12-hour clock time.

(a) 13:40

(b) 10:12

(c) 20:17

(d) 14:25

(e) 09:20

7. The following is part of a Waterford to Dublin rail timetable.

Waterford	06:00	07:40	10:50	15:25	18:15
Kilkenny	06:48	08:20	11:30	16:05	18:58
Carlow	07:20	08:53	12:07	16:41	19:35
Kildare	07:55	09:24	12:43	17:15	20:11
Newbridge	08:05	09:35	12:51	17:23	20:19
Dublin	08:30	09:55	13:20	17:50	20:50

(a) How long does it take for the 07:40 train to travel from Waterford to
   (i) Carlow (ii) Dublin?

(b) Calculate the total time taken for each train to travel from Waterford
   to Dublin.

(c) At what time, in 12-hour clock time, does the last train from Waterford
   arrive in Dublin?

8. The following is part of the bus timetable for buses from Cork to Dublin.

Cork	08:40	10:40	12:40	18:40
Fermoy	09:05	11:05	13:05	19:05
Mitchelstown	09:20	11:20	13:20	19:20
Cashel	10:05	12:15	14:20	20:05
Portlaoise	11:25	13:45	15:50	21:35
Kildare	12:30	15:00	17:00	22:40
Dublin	13:10	16:30	18:40	23:30

(a) How long does it take to travel from Cork to Dublin on the 10:40 bus?

(b) If Bridget gets on the bus at Cashel at 12:15, how long will it be
   before she arrives in Dublin?

(c) Which bus completes the journey in the least time?

(d) On the 08:40 service, how long does it take to travel from Fermoy to
   Portlaoise?

(e) If the 08:40 bus travels from Cork to Dublin at an average speed of
   56 km/h, how far does it travel in going from Cork to Dublin?

9. Find the average speed, in km/h, over the following distances.

(a) 84 km in 2 hours

(b) 196 km in $3\frac{1}{2}$ hours

(c) 31.25 km in $1\frac{1}{4}$ hours

(d) 150 km in 4 hours 10 minutes

(e) 80 m in 5 seconds

10. Calculate how long the following journeys take.

(a) 300 km at an average speed of 40 km/h

(b) 36 km at an average speed of 72 km/h

(c) 150 km at an average speed of 450 km/h

(d) 225 km at an average speed of 100 km/h

(e) 275 km at an average speed of 75 km/h

11. Calculate the distance, in km, travelled in the following journeys.

(a) Average speed of 20 km/h for $2\frac{1}{2}$ hours

(b) Average speed of 120 km/h for 2 hours 2 minutes

(c) Average speed of 30 km/h for 5 minutes

(d) Average speed of 70 km/h for $4\frac{1}{4}$ hours

(e) Average speed of 20 m/s for 2 hours

12. How long would the following journeys take?

(a) 1500 m at an average speed of 200 m per minute

(b) 350 m at an average speed of 10 m/s

(c) 15 km at an average speed of 10 m/s

(d) 150 km at an average speed of 15 m/s

(e) 88 km at an average speed of 20 m/s

13. Calculate the distance, in km, travelled in the following journeys.

(a) Average speed of 36 km/h for 10 seconds

(b) Average speed of 10 m/s for 55 minutes

(c) Average speed of 16 km/h for 45 minutes

(d) Average speed of 27 km/h for 10 minutes

(e) Average speed of 90 km/h for 3 hours 20 minutes

14. Find the average speed, in km/h, over the following distances.

(a) 140 km in $3\frac{1}{2}$ hours

(b) 400 km in 5 hours

(c) 35 m in 5 seconds

(d) 100 m in 10 seconds

(e) 1500 metres in $4\frac{1}{2}$ minutes

15. A bus travelled from Athlone to Galway at an average speed of 80 km/h for $1\frac{1}{2}$ hours. It then travelled another 90 km in 2 hours.

(a) Calculate the distance travelled from Athlone to Galway.

(b) Calculate the average speed after it left Galway.

(c) Calculate the average speed for the entire journey over the $3\frac{1}{2}$ hours.

16. A snail moved at an average rate of 20 cm per minute.

(a) At that rate, how far would it travel in $2\frac{3}{4}$ hours?

(b) How long would it take to move 1 km?

17. A plane flew from Rome to Paris at an average speed of 450 km/h. The journey took $1\frac{1}{2}$ hours. It flew from Paris to Dublin at an average speed of 550 km/h and that journey also took $1\frac{1}{2}$ hours.

(a) Calculate the distance flown from Rome to Paris.

(b) Calculate the distance flown from Paris to Dublin.

(c) The plane left Rome at 13:55 Irish time. At what time, in Irish time, did it arrive in Paris?

(d) If the plane landed in Dublin at 18:25, at what time did it leave Paris?

(e) Calculate the average flying speed of the plane in its journey from Rome to Dublin.

18. On a training run, Deirdre runs at an average speed of 20 km/h for 15 minutes and then walks at an average rate of 2 m/s for 30 minutes.

(a) Calculate the distance she runs.

(b) Calculate the distance she walks.

(c) Calculate her average speed over the training run to one decimal place.

Simple Equations and Inequalities $\quad$ **5**

CHAPTER SUMMARY

In this chapter, you will learn about:

+ Simple equations.
+ Equations with fractions.
+ Linear inequalities in one variable.

||| Simple equations

An equation **must** have an equals sign in it. An equation is all about **balance**. The left-hand side (LHS) is equal to the right-hand side (RHS).

A balanced equation:

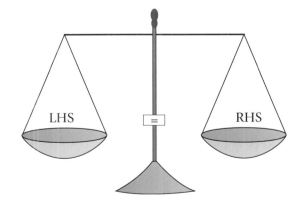

LHS $\quad$ = $\quad$ RHS

There is balance between the
LHS and the RHS.

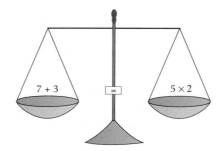

Without balance, there is no equation. In the diagram below, the LHS is not equal to
the RHS.

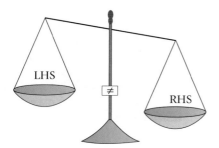

Not an equation – unbalanced

This scrum is balanced.

There is no balance between the LHS
and the RHS.

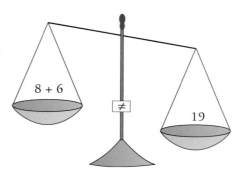

REMEMBER

Whatever you do to **one** side of an equation, you must do **exactly** the same to the **other side** to maintain the balance.

For example, if you add or subtract a number from one side, you must add or subtract the same number from the other side. If you multiply or divide one side by a number, you must multiply or divide the other side by the same number.

Solving a question: There are different answers (solutions) to different questions. To solve a question means to find the correct answer for **that particular** question.

Example 5.1

Solve the following for x.

(a) $x + 7 = 12$　　(b) $2x - 4 = 8$　　(c) $5x + 2 = 2x - 16$

Solution

(a) $x + 7 = 12$

$\quad\quad -7 \quad -7$ ← Take 7 away from both sides.

$\quad\quad x = 5$

(b) $2x - 4 = 8$

$\quad\quad +4 \quad +4$

$\quad\quad 2x = 12$

$\quad\quad \dfrac{2x}{2} = \dfrac{12}{2}$ ← Divide both sides by 2.

$\quad\quad x = 6$

(c) $5x + 2 = 2x - 16$

$\quad\quad -2 \quad\quad -2$ ← Take away 2 from both sides.

$\quad\quad 5x \quad = 2x - 18$

$\quad -2x \quad\quad -2x$ ← Take away 2x from both sides.

$\quad\quad 3x = -18$

$\quad\quad \dfrac{3x}{3} = \dfrac{-18}{3}$ ← Divide both sides by 3.

$\quad\quad x = -6$

REMEMBER

If you multiply both sides by -1, the signs will change from plus to minus or from minus to plus.

For example:

$-3x = 12$

$3x = -12$

$x = -4$

Multiply both sides by -1. Notice what happens to the 12.

Example 5.2

Solve the following for y.

$4y + 5 = 6y - 9$

Solution

$4y + 5 = 6y - 9$

$-5 = - 5$

$4y = 6y - 14$

$-6y -6y$

$-2y = -14$ (multiply both sides by -1)

$2y = 14$

$\dfrac{2y}{2} = \dfrac{14}{2}$

$y = 7$

REMEMBER

The rules for multiplying and dividing.

Multiplying:	Dividing:
$+ \times + = +$	$+ \div + = +$
$- \times - = +$	$- \div - = +$
$+ \times - = -$	$+ \div - = -$
$- \times + = -$	$- \div + = -$

Exercise 5.1

Copy the following diagrams into your exercise book and insert a number for the question mark that would make the equation balance.

(a)

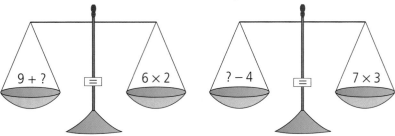

(b)

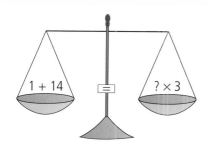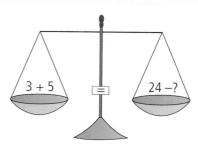

Solve for x or y in each of the following.

1. 3x = 6
2. 5x = −10
3. 2x = −14
4. 7x = 21
5. −3x = 15
6. −4x = −28
7. −6x = −24
8. −3y = 27
9. x + 6 = 13
10. x − 4 = 10
11. x + 2 = −9
12. x − 5 = −3
13. 2x + 5 = 11
14. 3x − 7 = 20
15. 5x + 4 = −26
16. 4x − 2 = 2x − 14
17. 3y + 6 = y − 8
18. 3x − 1 = 5 − 3x

19. 4x + 2 = 12 − x
20. 3x + 7 = x + 3
21. 4y + 1 = 3y + 5
22. 2y − 5 = y + 7
23. 3y − 2 = y + 4
24. 5y + 4 = 2y + 10
25. 2x − 8 = 6x + 12
26. 4x + 5 = 6x − 11
27. x − 2 = 4x + 10
28. x + 3 = 5x − 13
29. 2x − 9 = 5x + 12
30. 3 − 8y = 9y + 37
31. 5 − 2x = 6 − 3x
32. 4x + 2 = −8 − 16x
33. 3 − 5x = 2x + 9
34. 5x + 5 = 11 + 7x
35. 3x − 4 = 7x − 8

REMEMBER

If there is a number outside the brackets, multiply it by everything that is inside the brackets.

Example 5.3

Solve the following for x.

(a) $3(2x - 4) = 4(x - 1)$

(b) $4(2x + 1) - 4 = 32 - 2(3x + 2)$

Solution

(a) $3(2x - 4) = 4(x - 1)$

$6x - 12 = 4x - 4$

$6x - 4x = -4 + 12$

$2x = 8$

$\dfrac{2x}{2} = \dfrac{8}{2}$

$x = 4$

> The 3 outside the first set of brackets (and the 4 outside the second set of brackets) must be multiplied by **everything** that is inside the brackets.

> Letters to the left, numbers to the right. This is the same as adding 12 to both sides and subtracting 4x from both sides.

(b) $4(2x + 1) - 4 = 32 - 2(3x + 2)$

$8x + 4 - 4 = 32 - 6x - 4$

$8x = 28 - 6x$

$8x + 6x = 28$

$14x = 28$

$\dfrac{14x}{14} = \dfrac{28}{14}$

$x = 2$

> The 4 outside the brackets (and the −2 outside the other brackets) must be multiplied by **everything** that is inside the brackets. Also, remember that BEMDAS tells us to multiply by the −2 **before** subtracting on the RHS.

> When the −6x crosses over to the LHS, it becomes +6x. This is the same as adding +6x to both sides.

REMEMBER

When something crosses the equals sign, it changes sign. This is the same as adding the exact same thing to both sides.

$3x - 2 = x - 12$

$3x - x = -12 + 2$

$2x = -10$

$x = -5$

> This is the same as adding 2 to both sides and taking away x from both sides.

NOTE: The solution (answer) is not always a whole number. Sometimes you get a fraction or a decimal.

Example 5.4

Solve for x.

$3(2x - 5) - 7 + 2x = 6(3x + 2) - 8 - 5x$

Solution

$3(2x - 5) - 7 + 2x = 6(3x + 2) - 8 - 5x$

$6x - 15 - 7 + 2x = 18x + 12 - 8 - 5x$

$6x - 15 - 7 + 2x = 18x + 12 - 8 - 5x$

$8x - 22 = 13x + 4$

$8x - 13x = 4 + 22$

$-5x = 26$

$5x = -26$

$\frac{5x}{5} = \frac{-26}{5}$

$x = \frac{-26}{5}$

Simplify the x terms with the x terms and the numbers with the numbers on both sides at this stage.

If it doesn't work out evenly, you can just leave it like this.

or $x = -5\frac{1}{5}$

Exercise 5.2

Solve each of the following.

1. $3(x - 2) = 2(x + 1)$
2. $2(x + 1) = 4(x - 2)$
3. $3(x + 2) = 6(x - 3)$
4. $5(x + 2) = 3(x + 4)$
5. $2(4x + 1) = 5(x + 4)$
6. $5(3y - 2) = 2(y - 18)$
7. $3(2y + 3) = 4(2y - 1)$
8. $3(4x - 1) = 2(4x + 3)$
9. $4(2x - 1) - 3(3x + 4) = 2(x + 5) + 4$
10. $5(2 - x) - 3(5 - x) + 3x = 0$
11. $7(3x + 2) - 4(2x + 3) = 2$
12. $9(1 - 2y) = 5(2 - 5y) + 20$
13. $6(5x + 3) = 5(6x - 1) - 3(x - 10)$
14. $8(5y - 1) = 3(9y - 2) - 2$
15. $2(3x - 5) + 3(5x + 7) = 5(2x + 11)$

16. $5(3x - 4) = 4(2x - 3) + 6$
17. $4(3a - 1) = 6(2a + 5) - 2(4a - 3)$
18. $6(x - 3) + 5(2x - 3) - 3 = 7x$
19. $3(2x + 1) - 6(x + 2) = 1 - 5(3x - 1)$
20. $5(3y - 2) + 1 = 3(2y + 1) + 2(y + 1)$
21. $4(3x - 1) - 2(2x - 5) = 5(2x + 1) - 11$
22. $4(3y - 4) - (y - 3) - 3(2y - 1) = 3$
23. $5 - 3(x - 1) = 2(x + 3) - 3$
24. $3(x - 4) + 5 = 5(x - 1) - 6$
25. $6 = 2(x + 1) + 10$
26. $6 + 4(x - 1) = 4 + 2(x - 3)$
27. $3(2x - 2) + 5 = 8x - 9$
28. $4 - 2(3x - 6) = 3 + 2(x - 1)$
29. $3(2x - 1) + 4 = 4x$
30. $5x + 1 = 25 + 2(x - 3)$

Equations with fractions

REMEMBER

If you have an equation with fractions, you should multiply every part by the LCD of the numbers on the bottom. This will be easier to understand if you do it in a different colour (for example, **red**, as in the examples below).

NOTE: The box above is one of the most important and useful methods you will learn and use in maths. It makes equations easier to solve and you should practise it, as it's also used in other areas of maths.

LCD stands for lowest common denominator. It means the lowest number that all of the given numbers will divide into evenly. For example, the LCD of 2, 5 and 6 is 30.

Example 5.5

Solve for x: (a) $\frac{3x}{4} = -6$ (b) $\frac{3x}{4} - \frac{1}{3} = \frac{2x}{3}$ (c) $\frac{3x-1}{2} - 2 = \frac{2x-5}{3}$

Solution

(a) $4\left(\frac{3x}{4}\right) = 4(-6)$

$\cancel{4}\left(\frac{3x}{\cancel{4}}\right) = 4(-6)$

> Put brackets around every part and multiply every part by 4. The fours will cancel out on the LHS.

$3x = -24$

$x = -8$

(b) $12\left(\frac{3x}{4}\right) - 12\left(\frac{1}{3}\right) = 12\left(\frac{2x}{3}\right)$

> Put brackets around every part and multiply every part by 12, then cancel where possible.

$\overset{3}{\cancel{12}}\left(\frac{3x}{4}\right) - \overset{4}{\cancel{12}}\left(\frac{1}{3}\right) = \overset{4}{\cancel{12}}\left(\frac{2x}{3}\right)$

$3(3x) - 4(1) = 4(2x)$

$9x - 4 = 8x$

$9x = 8x + 4$

$9x - 8x = 4$

$x = 4$

> Letters to the left, numbers to the right.
> This is the same as adding 4 to both sides.
> This is the same as subtracting 8x from both sides.

(c) $6\left(\frac{3x-1}{2}\right) - 6(2) = 6\left(\frac{2x-5}{3}\right)$ ← Put brackets around every part and multiply every part by 6, then cancel where possible.

$3(3x - 1) - 6(2) = 2(2x - 5)$ ← Multiply the number outside the brackets by everything that is inside.

$9x - 3 - 12 = 4x - 10$

$9x - 15 = 4x - 10$

$9x - 4x = -10 + 15$ ← Letters to the left, numbers to the right.

$5x = 5$

$x = 1$

Exercise 5.3

Solve each of the following equations.

1. $\frac{x}{2} = 6$

2. $\frac{x}{5} = 9$

3. $\frac{2x}{3} = 8$

4. $\frac{5x}{4} = -10$

5. $\frac{-3x}{2} = 6$

6. $\frac{-5x}{3} = 10$

7. $\frac{1}{3}x = 8$

8. $\frac{2}{5}x = 4$

9. $\frac{1}{4}x = 9$

10. $\frac{x}{2} + \frac{x}{3} = 5$

11. $\frac{5x}{2} - \frac{x}{4} = -9$

12. $\frac{y}{2} + \frac{3y}{4} = 5$

13. $\frac{2x}{3} + \frac{x}{2} = 7$

14. $\frac{x}{2} + \frac{3x}{2} = -4$

15. $\frac{4x}{5} + x = 9$

16. $\frac{2x}{3} + 4 = 6$

17. $\frac{x}{4} + \frac{x}{5} = \frac{-1}{20}$

18. $\frac{x}{5} - 1 = 3 - \frac{3x}{5}$

19. $\frac{2x}{3} + \frac{5x}{7} = \frac{11x - 4}{7}$

20. $\frac{a+5}{3} - \frac{a}{4} = 2$

21. $\frac{5x+3}{2} + 1 = \frac{x-4}{5}$

22. $\frac{x+1}{3} = 5$

23. $\frac{2x-3}{5} = 7$

24. $\frac{x-3}{4} = \frac{x-2}{5}$

25. $\frac{2y-5}{3} = \frac{y+2}{6}$

26. $\frac{x-1}{2} = \frac{x-2}{3} + \frac{x-3}{4}$

27. $\frac{3a+2}{4} + \frac{1}{6} = \frac{2a+5}{3}$

28. $\frac{x-3}{2} - \frac{x-4}{3} = 1$

29. $\frac{3y-1}{2} - \frac{2y-5}{3} = 2$

30. $\frac{2x-3}{5} - \frac{x+9}{6} = 0$

31. $\frac{3x-8}{4} = \frac{3}{4} - \frac{3x-1}{6}$

32. $\frac{7}{6}(3x - 1) - \frac{3}{2}(2x - 5) = \frac{25}{3}$

33. $\frac{3}{4}(2x - 5) = \frac{2}{5}(3x + 2) - 2$

34. $\frac{1}{7}(3a + 5) - \frac{1}{3}(2a + 7) = \frac{3a}{5} - 10$

35. $\frac{1}{5}(x - 5) = \frac{1}{12}(5x - 3) - \frac{1}{3}(x - 3)$

Linear inequalities in one variable

> This symbol means 'greater than', e.g. $9 > 5$.

< This symbol means 'less than', e.g. $5 < 9$.

$\geq$ This symbol means 'greater than or equal to', e.g. $9 \geq 5$ and $9 \geq 9$.

$\leq$ This symbol means 'less than or equal to', e.g. $5 \leq 9$ and $5 \leq 5$.

Inequalities can be swapped around. For example, $8 > 2$ is the same as saying $2 < 8$.

NOTE: Solving inequalities is exactly the same as solving equations. In other words, put the letters to one side and the numbers on the other.

You also need to know what is meant by naturals, integers and reals.

−5 is smaller than 4.

N are the natural numbers. They are the plus whole numbers.

Z are the integers – these are plus and minus whole numbers.

R are the reals. This includes all numbers. The reals are plus and minus whole numbers as well as plus and minus fractions and decimals.

NOTE: $x \in N$ means x is one or more of the natural numbers. Similarly, $x \in Z$ and $x \in R$ means integers and real numbers, respectively.

Example 5.6

Graph the solution of the following on the number line.

(a) $3x - 4 \leq x + 8$, $x \in N$ (b) $3x - 4 \leq x + 8$, $x \in Z$ (c) $3x - 4 \leq x + 8$, $x \in R$

Solution

(a) $3x - 4 \leq x + 8$, $x \in N$

$3x - x \leq 8 + 4$

$2x \leq 12$

$\dfrac{2x}{2} \leq \dfrac{12}{2}$

$x \leq 6$

This is exactly as you would do with equations.

But remember, x ∈ N, therefore we're not allowed to have fractions or minus numbers.

$$x \leq 6, \, x \in N$$

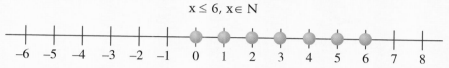

(b) $3x - 4 \leq x + 8$, $x \in Z$

$x \leq 6$

> This is the same as part (a) except that this time we're looking for integers. Only the number line will be different.

Remember, integers (Z) are plus **and** minus whole numbers.

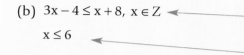

> This arrow means the numbers carry on forever.

(c) $3x - 4 \leq x + 8$, $x \in R$

$x \leq 6$

> This is also the same as part (a) except that this time we're looking for the reals. Only the number line will be different.

Remember, the reals are plus and minus whole numbers as well as plus and minus fractions. The reals are **all** numbers, so we colour **along** the line, rather than draw dots and use an arrow to show the values go on in that direction.

NOTE: There is one major difference between equations and inequalities. If we multiply both sides of an inequality by a minus number, then the direction of the inequality also changes. For example, −4 < 2, but +4 > −2.

REMEMBER

If you multiply both sides of an inequality by a minus number, then the direction of the inequality will change. See Example 5.7.

Example 5.7

Show the solution of the following on the number line.

$x + 2 \leq 4x + 8$, $x \in R$

$x - 4x \leq 8 - 2$

$-3x \leq 6$ ← Multiply both sides by −1. See how the direction of the inequality changed, from $\leq$ to $\geq$.

$3x \geq -6$ ←

$\dfrac{3x}{3} \geq \dfrac{6}{3}$

$x \geq -2$

Example 5.8

Show the solution of the following on the number line.

$5(2x - 3) - 3(x - 1) < 6(2x + 3) - 5$, $x \in R$

$10x - 15 - 3x + 3 < 12x + 18 - 5$

$7x - 12 < 12x + 13$

$7x - 12x < 13 + 12$

$-5x < 25$ ←

$5x > -25$

$x > -5$

Multiply the number outside the brackets by everything inside.
Simplify each side: put Xs to one side, numbers to the other.
Multiply both sides by −1. See how the direction of the inequality changed.

The empty circle around the −5 shows that it's not included.

Exercise 5.4

Graph the solution of each of the following on the number line. Draw a different number line for each solution.

1. $x \le 5$, $x \in N$
2. $x \le 5$, $x \in Z$
3. $x \le 5$, $x \in R$
4. $x \ge 4$, $x \in N$
5. $x > 4$, $x \in N$
6. $x > -3$, $x \in R$
7. $3x + 2 \le x - 10$, $x \in R$
8. $5x - 4 \ge 2x + 8$, $x \in R$
9. $4x + 7 \ge 3x + 10$, $x \in R$
10. $3k - 1 < k + 5$, $k \in N$
11. $2x + 7 \ge x + 9$, $x \in Z$
12. $3x - 1 > x + 7$, $x \in R$
13. $5t - 4 \ge t + 8$, $t \in N$
14. $8x + 7 \ge 6x + 13$, $x \in Z$
15. $3m - 1 \ge 13 - 4m$, $m \in N$
16. $5x - 18 > 6 - 3x$, $x \in R$
17. $4x + 7 \le 7 - 8x$, $x \in R$
18. $3x - 4 \ge 8 - 3x$, $x \in Z$

19. Write all the values of the solution of $3x < 12$, $x \in N$.
20. Write all the values of the solution of $2x + 1 < 11$, $x \in N$.
21. Write all the values of the solution of $3x + 1 < x + 9$, $x \in N$.
22. Write all the values of the solution of $5x + 2 \le 2x + 17$, $x \in N$.

From question 23 on, some of the questions will require you to multiply both sides of the inequality by a minus number. (See example 5.7 above.)

23. $3x + 7 < 4x + 3$, $x \in R$
24. $2x - 5 \le x - 1$, $x \in N$
25. $5x - 1 \ge 7x - 9$, $x \in Z$
26. $3x + 7 \le 5x + 11$, $x \in R$
27. $6t - 1 > 7t + 5$, $t \in Z$
28. $3x - 8 < 5x - 12$, $x \in N$
29. $4x - 1 \le 6x + 3$, $x \in Z$
30. $5k + 2 \ge 8k + 14$, $k \in R$
31. $3x - 1 \le 4x - 5$, $x \in N$
32. $6x - 3 > 2x + 9$, $x \in R$
33. $3x - 2 \le 5 + 7x$, $x \in Z$
34. $2(x + 3) < 3(2x - 4)$, $x \in Z$
35. $3(x + 1) > 4(3x + 3)$, $x \in R$
36. $3(2x + 4) > 2(x + 1) - 2$, $x \in R$
37. $4(x + 2) \le x - 1$, $x \in N$
38. $5(2x + 1) > 3(2x - 3) - 1$, $x \in R$
39. $4(2m - 5) - 3(m - 3) > 4$, $m \in R$
40. $3(x - 1) \ge 5(2x + 1) + 5$, $x \in R$
41. $5(3x + 2) + 4(2x - 3) \le 5(6x + 1)$,
    $x \in Z$

Exercise 5.5 (Chapter summary)

For questions 1 to 20, solve for x.

1. $x + 4 = 12$
2. $5x + 1 = 6$
3. $3x - 1 = 2x + 5$
4. $6x + 3 = x - 17$
5. $6x - 2 = 2x + 13$
6. $6x + 2 - x = 7 + 3x + 5$
7. $7x + 3 - 2x = 4x + 7$
8. $3x + 1 = 2x + 5$
9. $2x - 4 = 6x + 12$
10. $x + 6 = 6x - 9$
11. $3x - 1 = 6x + 11$
12. $5(3x - 2) = 4(x + 3)$
13. $2(3x + 1) = 4(x + 2)$
14. $2(3x - 4) = 3(x - 4) + 2$
15. $5(3x - 1) + 2 = 3(4x + 5)$
16. $2(3x - 1) - 5(x - 3) = 2x - 7$
17. $\frac{3x+1}{2} = 5$
18. $\frac{3x+1}{2} + \frac{4x-3}{3} = 8$
19. $\frac{2x-5}{3} - \frac{x+4}{2} = \frac{5x-14}{6}$
20. $\frac{4x-1}{3} - \frac{2(2x+1)}{5} = \frac{x+2}{3}$

Show the solution of each of the following on the number line.

21. $x \leq 7, x \in N$
22. $x \leq 7, x \in Z$
23. $x \leq 7, x \in R$
24. $5x + 2 < x + 18, x \in N$
25. $3x - 1 \geq 7x - 9, x \in Z$
26. $3(2x - 1) \leq 5 + 7x, x \in R$
27. $4(2x + 2) > 2(3x - 5), x \in R$
28. $6 - 5(x - 3) \leq 2(2x + 5) - 7, x \in R$
29. $\frac{2x-3}{5} < \frac{x+9}{6}, x \in Z$
30. $\frac{2x-1}{4} \geq \frac{x-1}{5} + 1, x \in R$

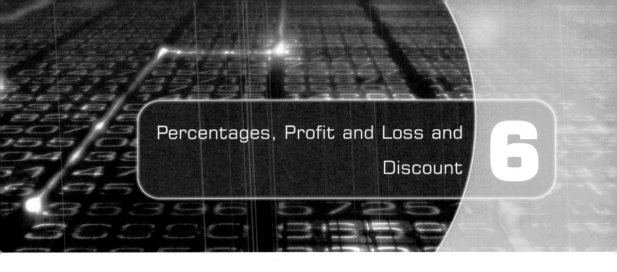

Percentages, Profit and Loss and Discount

6

CHAPTER SUMMARY

In this chapter, you will learn about:

+ Fractions, decimals and percentages.

+ Finding a percentage of a number.

+ Finding the number if you are given a percentage of it.

+ Expressing one number as a percentage of another.

+ Percentage increase and decrease.

+ Discount.

+ Percentage profit and loss.

||| Fractions, decimals and percentages

Fractions, decimals and percentages are three ways of writing the same number. For example, the decimal 0.5 is the same as the fraction $\frac{1}{2}$, which are both the same as the percentage 50%.

It is useful to be able to change from one form to another, i.e. from fractions to decimals or decimals to percentages. The table on the next page shows you how to convert from one form to the other.

0.5	
=	
$\frac{1}{2}$	
=	
50%	

To change from	To	What you must do
Percentage	Fraction	Put percentage over 100 and then cancel (if possible)
Percentage	Decimal	Divide by 100
Fraction or decimal	Percentage	Multiply by 100

Example 6.1

Write the following percentages as fractions: (a) 35% (b) 26.4%.

Solution

(a) 35%

Put over 100.

$= \dfrac{35}{100}$

$= \dfrac{7}{20}$

Cancel by dividing the top and bottom by 5. Remember, this fraction is simply another way of writing 35%.

(b) 26.4%

Put over 100.

$= \dfrac{26.4}{100}$

In this case, you must multiply the top and bottom by 10 to make the top a whole number.

$= \dfrac{264}{1000}$

Now cancel, more than once if you can.

$= \dfrac{33}{125}$

Example 6.2

Write the following percentages as decimals: (a) 48% (b) 62.5%.

Solution

(a) 48%

Put over 100.

$= \dfrac{48}{100}$

Now divide the bottom into the top.

$= 0.48$

(b) 62.5%

$= \frac{62.5}{100}$

Put over 100.

Now divide the bottom into the top.

$= 0.625$

Example 6.3

Write the following as percentages: (a) $\frac{7}{20}$ (b) $\frac{2}{3}$ (c) 0.54.

Solution

(a) $\frac{7}{20}$

Multiply by 100.

$= \frac{7}{\overset{1}{\underset{}{20}}} \times \overset{5}{100} = 35\%$

When you write a number as a percentage, you should write the % symbol after it.

(b) $\frac{2}{3}$

Multiply by 100.

$= \frac{2}{3} \times 100 = \frac{200}{3} = 66\frac{2}{3}\%$

(c) 0.54

Multiply by 100.

$= 0.54 \times 100$

$= 54\%$

Exercise 6.1

What percentage of the cake is shaded in black in each of the following?

1.

2.

3.

4. Copy the table below into your exercise book. Fill in one number from List B that matches each number from List A.

List A	(a)	(b)	(c)	(d)	(e)	(f)	(g)	(h)	(i)	(j)
	$\frac{1}{5}$	24%	0.4	0.36	1	0.1	3%	$\frac{1}{3}$	30%	$\frac{1}{30}$
Matching item										

List B:
   (a) $\frac{2}{5}$ (b) $3\frac{1}{3}$%   (c) 100%   (d) 0.3   (e) 0.2

   (f) $33\frac{1}{3}$%   (g) $\frac{9}{25}$ (h) 10%   (i) $\frac{3}{100}$ (j) $\frac{6}{25}$

For questions 5 to 8, write the percentages as fractions in their simplest form.

   5. (a) 70%   (b) 60%   (c) 45%   (d) 75%   (e) 40%   (f) 44%

   6. (a) 95%   (b) 62%   (c) 120%   (d) 150%   (e) 160%

   7. (a) $12\frac{1}{2}$%   (b) $33\frac{1}{3}$%   (c) $62\frac{1}{2}$%   (d) $66\frac{2}{3}$%

   8. (a) 200%   (b) $37\frac{1}{2}$%   (c) 5.8%   (d) 14.6%

For questions 9 to 11, write the percentages as decimals.

   9. (a) 40%   (b) 80%   (c) 55%   (d) 65%   (e) 30%   (f) 28% (g) 67%

   10. (a) 43%   (b) 142%   (c) 185%   (d) 160%   (e) 210%

   11. (a) $37\frac{1}{2}$% (b) 2.6%   (c) 24.8% (d) $12\frac{1}{2}$% (e) $33\frac{1}{3}$% (f) $66\frac{2}{3}$%

For questions 12 and 13, write the values as percentages.

   12. (a) $\frac{9}{20}$ (b) $\frac{3}{5}$ (c) $\frac{5}{8}$ (d) 0.47   (e) 0.28   (f) 0.6   (g) 0.2   (h) 0.02

   13. (a) $\frac{1}{4}$ (b) $\frac{2}{25}$ (c) $\frac{4}{5}$ (d) $\frac{1}{3}$ (e) $\frac{9}{40}$ (f) $\frac{4}{5}$ (g) $\frac{5}{4}$ (h) $1\frac{3}{8}$

   (i) 3.2   (j) $\frac{7}{8}$ (k) 0.24 (l) 0.024

Finding a percentage of a number

Sometimes you are given a number and asked to find a certain percentage of this number. To do this, you get 1% by dividing by 100, then you multiply by the percentage you want. The formula below will do these two steps at once.

 REMEMBER

$$\text{percentage required} = \frac{\text{total}}{100} \times \% \text{ you want}$$

Example 6.4

Find: (a) 15% of €60   (b) 32% of €180.

Solution

This gets us 1%.

(a) $15\% = \frac{60}{100} \times 15 = €9$

(b) $32\% = \frac{180}{100} \times 32 = €57.60$

This gets us up to 15%.

The formula above will work for **all** percentages. However, there are some percentages where you might find it easier to write the percentage as a fraction and use the fraction version instead. The table below explains some of these.

Percentage	Fraction	What to do (divide by the bottom and multiply by the top)
25%	$\frac{1}{4}$	Divide by 4.
10%	$\frac{1}{10}$	Divide by 10.
20%	$\frac{1}{5}$	Divide by 5.
30%	$\frac{3}{10}$	Divide by 10 and multiply by 3.
40%	$\frac{2}{5}$	Divide by 5 and multiply by 2.
50%	$\frac{1}{2}$	Divide by 2.
60%	$\frac{3}{5}$	Divide by 5 and multiply by 3.
75%	$\frac{3}{4}$	Divide by 4 and multiply by 3.

Percentage	Fraction	What to do (divide by the bottom and multiply by the top)
$33\frac{1}{3}\%$	$\frac{1}{3}$	Divide by 3.
$66\frac{2}{3}\%$	$\frac{2}{3}$	Divide by 3 and multiply by 2.
$12\frac{1}{2}\%$	$\frac{1}{8}$	Divide by 8.
$37\frac{1}{2}\%$	$\frac{3}{8}$	Divide by 8 and multiply by 3.
$62\frac{1}{2}\%$	$\frac{5}{8}$	Divide by 8 and multiply by 5.

Example 6.5

Find: (a) 75% of €640   (b) $37\frac{1}{2}\%$ of €130.

Solution

(a) $75\% = \frac{3}{4} \Rightarrow 4\overline{)640}$ $\quad 160 \times 3 = €480$ (b) $37\frac{1}{2}\% = \frac{3}{8} \Rightarrow 8\overline{)130.00}$ $\quad 16.25 \times 3 = €48.75$

OR

(b) This question could have been done using the same method as Example 6.4:

$37\frac{1}{2}\% = \frac{130}{100} \times 37\frac{1}{2} = 1.30 \times 37.5 = €48.75$

Exercise 6.2

In the following questions, find the required value.

1. 18% of €600
2. 25% of €600
3. 47% of €600
4. 20% of 400 km
5. $33\frac{1}{3}\%$ of €600
6. 8% of €600
7. 11% of €77
8. 11% of 300 km
9. 27% of €8

10. 10% of €850
11. 63% of €7
12. 25% of 120 km
13. 33% of 50 km
14. 84.5% of €500
15. $66\frac{2}{3}\%$ of €900
16. $37\frac{1}{2}\%$ of 336 kg
17. 40% of €90

18. 120% of €60
19. 115% of 400 km
20. 105% of €350
21. $62\frac{1}{2}\%$ of 1600 km
22. 78% of €650
23. 0.1% of €700
24. 2% of €5
25. 3.6% of €90

Finding the number if you are given a percentage of it

Sometimes you are just given a percentage (or fraction) of a number and are asked to find the number.

Example 6.6

27% of a number is 324. Find the number.

Solution
Layout 1
27% of a number is 324.

$$\frac{324}{27} \times 100 = 1200$$

To get back up to the number, multiply by 100.

324 is not the total, it is 27%. To get 1%, divide by 27.

OR

Layout 2
27% = 324

$$1\% = \frac{324}{27}$$

$$100\% = \frac{324}{27} \times 100 = 1200$$

Example 6.7

$\frac{3}{5}$ of a number is 51. Find the number.

Solution
Layout 1

$\frac{3}{5}$ of a number is 51.

51 is three-fifths. We need to get one-fifth first. Therefore, divide by 3.

$$3\overline{)51} \quad \frac{17}{}$$

17 is one-fifth. The whole number is five-fifths, therefore we must multiply by 5 to get the number.

17 × 5 = 85

OR

Layout 2
60% = 51

$$1\% = \frac{51}{60}$$

$$100\% = \frac{51}{60} \times 100 = 85$$

Exercise 6.3

In the following questions, find the number.

1. 6% of the number is 204.
2. 17% of the number is 850.
3. 20% of the number is 56.
4. 23% of the number is 46.
5. $\frac{2}{3}$ of the number is 44.
6. $\frac{3}{5}$ of the number is 21.
7. $\frac{5}{8}$ of the number is 30.
8. $\frac{4}{7}$ of the number is 36.
9. 18% of the number is 234.
10. 16% of the number is 80.
11. 58% of x is 1856. Find x.
12. 4.5% of the number is 63.
13. $\frac{5}{8}$ of the number is 105.
14. 23% of x is 345. Find x.
15. 15% of the number is 900.
16. 3% of x is 45. Find x.
17. $\frac{7}{16}$ of the number is 126.
18. 130% of a number is 72.8.
19. John spent 30% of his money. If he spent €15, how much money did he have to start with?
20. Mary saved $\frac{2}{9}$ of her wages. If she saved €40, what was her total wage?
21. The prize money in a draw was 40% of the total money collected. If the prize money was €800, how much money was collected in total?

Expressing one number as a percentage of another

Sometimes you will be asked to express one number as a percentage of another.

For example, if a girl scored 24 marks in an exam out of a total of 32 marks available, what was her percentage mark?

To solve a question like this, use the following formula:

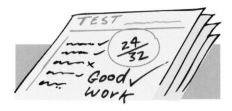

$$\% = \frac{\text{number}}{\text{total}} \times 100 \ = \ \frac{24}{32} \times 100 = 75\%$$

Example 6.8

A girl scored 53 marks in an exam out of a total of 180 marks available. What was her percentage mark? Give the answer correct to one decimal place.

Solution

$$\% = \frac{\text{number}}{\text{total}} \times 100$$

$$= \frac{53}{180} \times 100 = 29.4\%$$

Example 6.9

A race was 10 km long. An athlete ran 850 m and then stopped. What percentage of the race had been run?

Solution

This question cannot even be started until the measurements are all in the same units. Therefore, 10 km is converted to metres before starting the question.

(1 km = 1000 m)

10 × 1000 = 10 000 metres

$$\frac{\text{number}}{\text{total}} \times 100$$

Number

$$\frac{850}{10\ 000} \times 100 = 8.5\%$$

Total

REMEMBER

In maths, measurements must all be in the same unit before starting a question. If they are not, you will have to convert them so that they are all in one common unit, e.g. metres, centimetres, grams, cents, euro. (See Example 6.9 above.)

Exercise 6.4

1. Express the first number as a percentage of the second number.
   (a) 12, 50 (b) 15, 20 (c) 25, 75 (d) 18, 108 (e) 28, 28 (f) 15, 40 (g) 27, 36

2. Express the first number as a percentage of the second number.
   (a) 12 cm, 30 cm (b) 235 cm, 5 m
   (c) 45c, €3   (d) 540 ml, 2 litres
   (e) 25 mm, 6 cm   (f) 400 g, 5 kg

3. Adrian scored 77 marks in an exam out of a total of 350 marks available. What was his percentage mark?

4. An oil lorry delivered 750 litres out of the full tank, which held 5000 litres. What percentage of the full tank was delivered?

5. An oil lorry delivered 1200 litres out of the full tank, which held 5000 litres. What percentage of the tank was still left on the lorry?

6. John scored 69 marks in an exam out of a total of 150 marks available. What percentage did he get?

7. A family had a mortgage of €180 000. After five years they had paid off €41 400. What percentage of their original mortgage had they paid after the five years?

8. In a class of 24 pupils, 8 were girls. Find the percentage that were (a) girls (b) boys.

9. In a 5 km race, Joe completed 1350 m before stopping. What percentage of the race had he run at that time?

10. A football stadium can hold up to 80 000 people. If there were 24 800 people at a match, what percentage of the stadium was used?

11. In an election, a candidate got 3000 votes out of the total votes cast of 15 000. What percentage vote did the candidate get?

12. A family had a mortgage of €200 000. Their repayments were €1200 per month. Calculate (a) the amount they would have paid in after 10 years (b) the percentage that this amount is of their original mortgage.

13. An exam was made up of two papers, paper 1 and paper 2. Niamh got 60 marks on paper 1 and 80 marks on paper 2. If each paper was worth 150 marks, find the overall percentage that she got.

14. A holiday for a family of four cost €4500. If they paid €135 deposit per head, what percentage of the total holiday did they pay as deposit?

15. Kevin's wage was €700 per week. If he spent €80 on groceries, €40 on petrol and €20 on phone credit, calculate the percentage of his wages he spent in total.

16. As part of a training programme, a runner had to complete 200 km in a month. If she ran 50 km in week one and 30 km in each of weeks two, three and four, what percentage of her target remained?

Percentage increase and decrease

Problems that involve a percentage increase or a percentage decrease are calculated using the same formula as before.

$$\frac{\text{number}}{\text{total}} \times 100 = \frac{\text{change}}{\text{original total}} \times 100$$

(The amount of the change is found by subtracting the original total and the new total.)

Example 6.10

A salary was increased from €65 000 last year to €68 250 this year. Calculate the percentage increase in salary.

Solution

increase = new salary – old salary

increase = 68 250 – 65 000 = 3250 (increase)

$$\frac{\text{change}}{\text{original total}} \times 100 = \frac{\text{increase}}{\text{old salary}} \times 100 = \frac{3250}{65\ 000} \times 100 = 5\%$$

Example 6.11

In one year, the rainfall in a certain area was recorded as 260 cm. The following year it was recorded as 221 cm. Find the percentage decrease in rainfall the second year.

Solution

decrease = first year's rainfall – following year's rainfall

decrease = 260 – 221 = 39

$$\frac{\text{change}}{\text{original total}} \times 100 = \frac{\text{decrease}}{\text{first year's rainfall}} \times 100 = \frac{39}{260} \times 100 = 15\%$$

Example 6.12

A woman had a salary of €2600 per month. She is to be awarded a 4% rise. Calculate (a) the amount of the increase in salary (b) her new salary.

Solution

A woman had a salary of €2600 per month. She is awarded a 4% rise.

(a) $\frac{2600}{100} \times 4 = €104$ (amount of salary rise)

(b) old salary + increase = new salary

2600 + 104 = €2704

The wage before the increase is 100%. Therefore, to get 1%, divide by 100. To get the amount of the increase, multiply by 4. These two steps are done in one go here.

Example 6.13

Matt received a wage increase of 9%. If his wage after the increase was €708.50, find his wage before the increase.

Solution

$\frac{708.50}{109} \times 100 = €650$ (original wage)

> The wage before the increase was 100%. €708.50 is the wage **after** the increase. Therefore, it is 109%. To get 1%, divide by 109. To find the original wage, multiply by 100.

Discount

If something is on sale at a reduced price, the reduction in price is called a discount. For example, during a sale, a pair of shoes might be reduced from €50 to €40. The €10 reduction is called a discount. These questions are also solved using the previous formula.

$$\frac{\text{number}}{\text{total}} \times 100 = \frac{\text{discount}}{\text{original price}} \times 100$$

(The amount of the discount is found by subtracting the new price from the original price.)

Example 6.14

During a sale, a holiday was reduced from €2400 to €1800. Find the percentage discount.

Solution

discount = original price − sale price

discount = 2400 − 1800 = €600 (discount)

$\% = \frac{\text{discount}}{\text{original price}} \times 100 = \frac{600}{2400} \times 100 = 25\%$ (percentage discount)

Example 6.15

The price of a flight from Dublin to New York was reduced by €15 if it was booked online. If the percentage discount was 5%, calculate the original price of the flight.

Solution

$\frac{15}{5} \times 100 = €300$ (original price)

> The €15 is the discount. The 5% is also the discount. Therefore, 5% = 15. To get 1%, divide by 5. To find the full price, multiply by 100.

101

Exercise 6.5

1. The capacity of a tin of paint was increased from 1.2 litres to 1.5 litres. Calculate the percentage increase in the capacity.

2. The average temperature in June was recorded at 20°C. It was recorded at 23.5°C in July. Calculate the percentage increase.

3. A computer was reduced from €1550 to €1426 during a sale. Find the percentage reduction.

4. Bridget got a wage increase. Her wage rose from €780 per week to €819. Find her percentage increase in salary.

5. The price of a sandwich went from €3.50 to €3.57. What was the percentage increase in the price?

6. A house was bought for €580 000. Three years later, it was sold for €672 800. Calculate the increase in price as a percentage of the original price of the house.

7. During a sale, a table was reduced from €250 to €200. Find
   (a) the amount of the reduction in price during the sale (discount)
   (b) the percentage reduction.

8. A census revealed that the population of an area went down from 35 640 people to 33 858 people. What was the percentage reduction in population?

9. A holiday was reduced by 20%. If it was reduced by €250, calculate the original price of the holiday.

10. A school went from an enrolment of 650 to an enrolment of 780. Calculate the percentage increase in the school enrolment.

11. A magazine was priced at €5.40 before a price rise. If the price rise was 5%, find the new price of the magazine.

12. A new football stadium increased the capacity from 45 000 people to 60 000. What was the percentage increase in the capacity?

13. Last year, the average house price was €450 000. This year, the average price is €477 000.
    (a) How much did the average price go up?
    (b) What was the percentage increase?

14. The price of a football ticket was €30 last year. If it went up by 6% this year, what is the new price of the ticket?

15. The government was spending €5200 million on housing. It wanted to increase this spending by 12%. Find (a) the amount of the increase in spending (b) the new level of spending.

16. An apartment was priced at €280 000. A discount of 15% was offered. What was the new selling price?

17. An apartment was priced at €280 000. A year later, the value had increased by 5%. What was the new value?

18. An apartment was priced at €280 000. A discount of €16 800 was offered.
    (a) What was the new selling price?
    (b) Express the discount as a percentage of the original selling price.

19. A television was reduced from €450 to €324. Find (a) the amount of the discount (b) the percentage discount.

20. A DVD originally cost €18. If it was reduced by 30% during a sale, find (a) the amount of the discount (b) the new sale price.

21. Due to fuel price increases, the cost of a bus journey increased from €16 to €24. Find the percentage increase.

22. Maria was on a salary of €2300 per month. If she was given an increase of 8%, find her new salary.

23. A book is priced at €20. To clear the shelves, it is decided to reduce the price by 15%. Calculate (a) the amount of the discount (b) the new selling price.

24. Due to rising costs, the price of a book went up by 10%. If the new price is €15.40, find the original cost of the book before the increase.

25. A suite of furniture was reduced by €210, a discount of 30%. Find (a) the original price of the suite (b) the reduced price.

26. A holiday for five people (two adults and three children) was priced at €1360. If a discount was given of €40 per adult and €30 per child, find (a) the total amount of the reduction that the family would get (b) the percentage reduction that the family would get.

27. Airfares to America were reduced by 10% during September. If the reduced price of a flight to Florida was €450, find the original cost of the flight.

28. A computer was being sold at €1500 if you paid for it in instalments over one year. However, a discount of €50 was available if you ordered it before the end of the month and a further discount of €200 if you paid all the money immediately. Find the percentage discount for the following people: (a) Pat, who orders the computer before the end of the month, but pays in instalments over the year (b) Mary, who orders it before the end of the month and pays all the money immediately.

Percentage profit and loss

If someone sells something for less than they paid for it, then they have made a loss. If they sell it for more than they paid, then they have made a profit. Sometimes it is necessary to calculate the percentage profit or loss. Again, the same formula is used.

$$\% = \frac{\text{number}}{\text{total}} \times 100 = \frac{\text{profit/loss}}{\text{original price}} \times 100$$

(The amount of the profit/loss is obtained by subtracting the new price and the original price.)

Example 6.16

A house was bought for €300 000. Three years later, it was sold for €420 000. Find the percentage profit.

Solution

new price − original price = profit
420 000 − 300,000 = 120 000

$$\% = \frac{\text{profit}}{\text{original price}} \times 100 = \frac{120\ 000}{300\ 000} \times 100 = 40\% \text{ percentage profit}$$

Example 6.17

A factory bought a suite of furniture for €1600. The factory sold it at a profit of 20%. Find (a) the amount of the profit (b) the selling price.

Solution

(a) $\frac{1600}{100} \times 20 = €320$ (amount of profit)

(b) cost price + profit = selling price
    1600 + 320 = €1920

The cost price is always 100%. Therefore, to get 1%, divide by 100. To get the amount of profit, multiply this by 20. (NOTE: Another way to get 20% is to divide by 5.)

REMEMBER

The cost price is always 100%. The selling price may be higher or lower than this.
- If a profit is made, the selling price will be higher.
- If a loss is made, the selling price will be lower.

105

Example 6.18

A car was bought for a certain price. It was sold at a 12% loss. If the selling price was €6600, find the cost price.

Solution

$\frac{6600}{88} \times 100 = €7500$ cost price

The cost price is always 100%. This time, a loss of 12% was made. The 6600 is after the loss and must therefore be equal to 88%, i.e. 100% − 12%. Therefore, to get 1%, divide by 88. To find the cost price, multiply by 100.

Example 6.19

A garage bought a car for a certain price and sold it at a profit of 6%. If the selling price was €25 970, find what the garage paid for the car.

Solution

$\frac{25\ 970}{106} \times 100 = €24\ 500$ cost price

The cost price is always 100%. This time, a profit of 6% was made. The 25 970 includes the profit and must therefore be equal to 106%, i.e. 100% + 6%. Therefore, to get 1%, divide by 106. To find the cost price, multiply by 100.

Example 6.20

An electrical shop bought 20 DVD players for a certain price. It sold all of them at a profit of 18%. If it made a profit of €54 per DVD player, calculate (a) the cost price of one DVD player (b) the total cost of the 20 DVD players.

Solution

(a) $\frac{54}{18} \times 100 = €300$ cost of 1 DVD recorder

(b) $300 \times 20 = €6000$ cost of all 20 players

The profit is 18%. The amount of the profit is €54. Therefore, 18% = 54. To get 1%, divide by 18. To find the cost price, multiply by 100.

Exercise 6.6

1. A man bought a car for €8000. One year later, he sold it for €6000. Calculate (a) how much he lost on the sale (b) the percentage loss.

2. A house was built for €240 000. The builder then sold it for €283 200. Calculate the percentage profit.

3. A garage buys a car for €12 000 and sells it for €13 500. Calculate the percentage profit.

4. A shop buys Christmas trees for €20 each. Calculate the selling price if the shop makes a 30% profit on each tree.

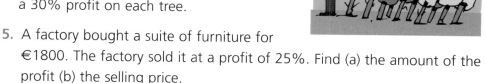

5. A factory bought a suite of furniture for €1800. The factory sold it at a profit of 25%. Find (a) the amount of the profit (b) the selling price.

6. A newsagent buys a magazine for €4 and sells it at 37.5% profit. Find the selling price of the magazine.

7. A woman buys a laptop computer for €1400 and sells it six months later for €1190. Calculate her percentage loss.

8. A mobile phone was bought for €180 and sold at a loss of 15%. Calculate (a) the amount of money lost (b) the selling price.

9. A car dealer sold a car for €6625, making a profit of 6%. Calculate (a) the cost price of the car (b) the amount of the profit.

10. A retailer buys 10 refrigerators at a total cost of €1400. Each fridge is sold at 12.5% profit. Calculate (a) the cost price of one fridge (b) the selling price of one fridge (c) the total amount of profit if all fridges are sold.

11. A jeweller buys a bracelet for €140 and sells it for €560. (a) How much profit was made? (b) What was the percentage profit?

12. A garage bought a car for €8000. The garage sold it at a profit of 20%. Calculate (a) the amount of the profit (b) the selling price.

13. A computer shop bought 20 computers, costing €37 000 in total. All the computers were sold for €2072 each. Find (a) the original cost of one computer to the shop (b) the profit made on one computer (c) the percentage profit made on each computer.

14. A house was bought for €400 000. Three years later, it was sold for €500 000. Calculate the percentage profit.

15. A DVD player was bought for €140 and sold at a profit of 15%. Calculate the selling price.

16. A car was bought for a certain price. It was sold for €9600, making the garage a profit of 20%. Calculate the cost price of the car.

17. An electrical shop bought 20 toasters for €360. The shop sells 15 of them for €30 each and is unable to sell any more of the toasters. Calculate (a) the total amount made from selling the toasters (b) the percentage profit made.

18. A TV was sold for €170, making a loss of 15%. Calculate the cost price of the TV.

19. An electric kettle was sold, making a profit of 15%. If the profit made was €3, calculate the cost price of the kettle.

20. A washing machine was sold at a profit of 20%. The profit made was €130. Calculate the cost price of the washing machine.

Exercise 6.7 (Chapter summary)

In questions 1 to 5, find the given percentage.

1. 15% of €600

2. 25% of €900

3. 47% of €500

4. 20% of 800 km

5. $66\frac{2}{3}\%$ of €1200

6. Write the following as percentages: (a) $\frac{3}{20}$ (b) $\frac{2}{5}$ (c) $\frac{7}{8}$ (d) 0.55 (e) 0.32.

7. If 10% of a number is 53, find the number.

8. If 24% of a number is 36, find the number.

9. James scored 160 marks in an exam out of a total of 250 marks available. What was his percentage mark?

10. A history exam is marked out of 260 marks. The pass mark is 40%. How many marks are needed to pass the paper?

11. A car is being sold for €15 500. A discount of 5% is offered if the car is bought before the end of the week. Calculate the cost of the car if sold before the week ends.

12. A family had a mortgage of €300 000. After six years they had paid off €50 000. What percentage of their original mortgage had they paid after the six years?

13. There were 5600 votes cast in an election. If a candidate received 35% of the votes cast, how many votes was this?

14. An exam was made up of two papers, paper 1 and paper 2. Ciara got 230 marks on paper 1 and 190 marks on paper 2. If each paper was worth 300 marks each, find her overall percentage mark.

15. During a sale, a table was reduced from €400 to €250. Find
(a) the amount of the reduction in price during the sale (discount)
(b) the percentage reduction.

16. A car was priced at €12 000. During a sale, a discount of $12\frac{1}{2}$ % was offered. Calculate the new selling price.

17. During a sale, an item was marked down by 20%. The sale price is €19.20. Calculate the original price of the item.

18. David bought a car for €9000. One year later, he sold it for €6000. Calculate (a) how much money he lost (b) the percentage loss.

19. Each symbol represents a fraction. Find the value of each symbol.

$✱ + ✱ + ✱ = 1$

$1 + ◆ + ◆ = 1\frac{1}{2}$

$● = ✱ + ✱$

$✱ + ■ + ● = 1\frac{1}{5}$

CHAPTER SUMMARY

In this chapter, you will learn about:

+ Compound interest.
+ Compound interest with changes.
+ Depreciation.
+ Value-added tax (VAT).

||| Compound interest

Compound interest is the extra amount of money that is paid for borrowing or investing money. Before starting, you should understand a few basic terms.

Term	What it means
Principal (P)	The sum of money borrowed or invested.
Interest (a)	The sum of money paid every month/year for borrowing or investing.
Rate (R)	The percentage charged every year.
Amount (A)	The total amount of money when the interest is added on.
Time (T)	The number of years and months that the money is invested/borrowed.
Per annum (p.a.)	Per year.

Compound interest questions will be easier to do if you understand the terms below and use them for each question.

Term	What it means
P_1	This is the money at the start of year 1.
I_1	This is the interest paid/earned during year 1.
P_2	This is the money at the end of year 1 and at the beginning of year 2, since the end of year 1 is the same as the start of year 2.
I_2	This is the interest paid/earned during year 2.
P_3	This is the money at the end of year 2 and at the beginning of year 3, since the end of year 2 is the same as the start of year 3.
I_3	This is the interest paid/earned during year 3.
P_4	This is the money at the end of year 3.

Example 7.1

€3000 was invested for three years at 5% per annum. Calculate (a) the total interest earned over the three years (b) the amount of the investment at the end of the three years.

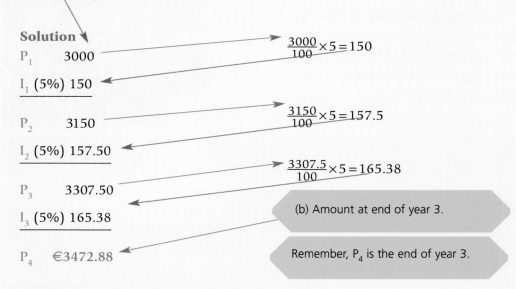

Solution

P_1 3000   → $\dfrac{3000}{100} \times 5 = 150$

I_1 (5%) 150

P_2 3150   → $\dfrac{3150}{100} \times 5 = 157.5$

I_2 (5%) 157.50

P_3 3307.50   → $\dfrac{3307.5}{100} \times 5 = 165.38$

I_3 (5%) 165.38   (b) Amount at end of year 3.

P_4 €3472.88   Remember, P_4 is the end of year 3.

(a) The total interest can be got by adding I_1, I_2 and I_3.
$$€150 + €157.5 + €165.38 = €472.88$$

OR

by taking P_1 away from P_4
$$€3472.88 - €3000 = €472.88$$

Exercise 7.1

1. €3000 was invested for one year at 6% interest. Calculate (a) the interest earned during the year (b) the amount of the investment at the end of the year.

2. €4000 was invested for one year at 5% interest. Calculate (a) the interest earned during the year (b) the amount of the investment at the end of the year.

3. €950 was invested for one year at 8% interest. Calculate (a) the interest earned during the year (b) the amount of the investment at the end of the year.

4. Kate took out a loan of €3000 at 4% interest for one year only. If she did not repay any of the loan during the year, how much did she owe at the end of the year?

5. Will put €6000 in a bank for one year at 7% interest. What was the investment worth at the end of the year?

6. Kelly put €9000 in a bank for one year at 6% interest. What was the investment worth at the end of the year?

7. €5000 was invested for three years at 5% compound interest. Copy the table below and use it to calculate (a) the interest earned during each of the three years (b) the amount of the investment at the end of the three years.

P_1

I_1 ——————————

P_2

I_2 ——————————

P_3

I_3 ——————————

P_4

8. €850 was invested for two years at 5% per annum (p.a.) compound interest. Calculate (a) the interest earned during the two years (b) the amount of the investment at the end of the two years.

9. €4000 was invested for two years at 8% p.a. compound interest. Calculate to the nearest cent (a) the interest earned during the two years (b) the amount of the investment at the end of the two years.

10. €6500 was invested for two years at 4% p.a. compound interest. Calculate (a) the interest earned during the two years (b) the amount of the investment at the end of the two years.

11. €7000 was invested for two years at 6.5% p.a. compound interest. Calculate (a) the interest earned during the two years (b) the amount of the investment at the end of the two years.

12. Michael took out a loan of €10 000 at 4.5% interest p.a. If he did not repay any of the loan during the year, how much did he owe at the end of the year?

13. €4000 was invested for three years at 7% p.a. compound interest. Calculate (a) the interest earned during the three years (b) the amount of the investment at the end of the three years.

14. €2000 was invested for three years at 9% p.a. compound interest. Calculate (a) the interest earned during the three years (b) the amount of the investment at the end of the three years.

15. €800 was invested for three years at 5% p.a. compound interest. Calculate (a) the interest earned during the three years (b) the amount of the investment at the end of the three years.

16. €5000 was invested for three years at 4.5% p.a. compound interest. Calculate (a) the interest earned during the three years (b) the amount of the investment at the end of the three years.

17. Ann borrowed €6000 from a building society at 6% p.a. compound interest each year. She decided to repay €5000 of the loan at the end of two years. How much of the loan remained after she made this payment?

18. Richard borrowed €10 000 from a bank at 4% p.a. compound interest each year. He decided to repay €8000 of the loan at the end of two years. How much of the loan remained to be paid after he made this payment?

19. Síobhan borrowed €4000 from a bank at 7% compound interest each year. She decided to repay €3000 of the loan at the end of two years. How much of the loan remained to be paid after she made this payment?

20. Eileen borrowed €5000 from a bank at 9% compound interest each year. She decided to repay nothing for two years. At the end of the two years she decided to pay off three-quarters of the total amount of the loan at that time. How much of the loan was left to pay after she made this payment?

Compound interest with changes

NOTE: Sometimes things change. The rate may change from year to year or money may be put in or taken out each year.

Example 7.2

€9500 was invested for three years. For the first year the rate was 5%, for the second year the rate was 6% and for the third year the rate was 7%. Calculate (a) the total compound interest earned (b) the value of the investment at the end of the three years.

Solution

P_1	9500	$\dfrac{9500}{100} \times 5 = 475$
I_1 (5%)	475	
P_2	9975	$\dfrac{9975}{100} \times 6 = 598.5$
I_2 (6%)	598.50	
P_3	10 573.50	$\dfrac{10\,573.5}{100} \times 7 = 740.15$
I_3 (7%)	740.15	
		(b) Amount at end of year 3.
P_4	€11 313.65	

(a) The total interest can be got by adding I_1, I_2 and I_3.

$$475 + 598.50 + 740.15 = €1813.65 \text{ (a)}$$

OR

by taking P_1 away from P_4

$$1_1\,313.65 - 9500 = €1813.65 \text{ (a)}$$

Example 7.3

€5000 was invested on the first of January each year for three consecutive years. During the first year the rate was 5%, during the second year it was 3% and during the third year it was 6%. Calculate (a) the total compound interest earned during the three years (b) the value of the investment at the end of the three years.

Solution

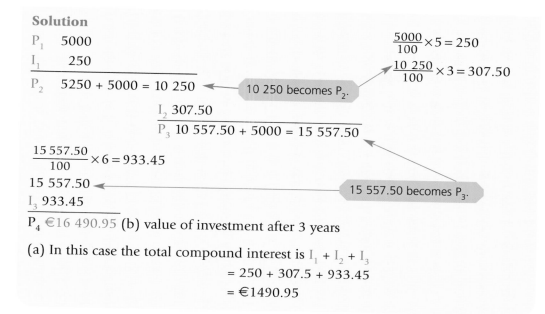

P_1 5000

I_1 250

P_2 5250 + 5000 = 10 250

$\dfrac{5000}{100} \times 5 = 250$

$\dfrac{10\,250}{100} \times 3 = 307.50$

10 250 becomes P_2.

I_2 307.50

P_3 10 557.50 + 5000 = 15 557.50

$\dfrac{15\,557.50}{100} \times 6 = 933.45$

15 557.50

I_3 933.45

15 557.50 becomes P_3.

P_4 €16 490.95 (b) value of investment after 3 years

(a) In this case the total compound interest is $I_1 + I_2 + I_3$

$$= 250 + 307.5 + 933.45$$
$$= €1490.95$$

Exercise 7.2

In this exercise, give your answers to the nearest cent.

1. €2000 was invested for three years. For the first year the rate was 4%, for the second year it was 5% and for the third year it was 6%. Calculate (a) the total compound interest earned (b) how much the investment was worth at the end of the three years.

2. €9000 was invested for two years. During the first year the rate was 8% and during the second year the rate was 6.5%. Calculate (a) the total compound interest earned (b) the value of the investment at the end of the two years.

3. €7400 was invested for three years. The first year the rate was 6%, the second year it was 5% and the third year it was 9%. Calculate (a) the total compound interest earned (b) the value of the investment at the end of the three years.

4. Calculate the compound interest on €6000 over three years if the interest rate was 6% during year 1, 8% during year 2 and 5% in year 3.

5. Calculate the compound interest on €900 over three years if the interest rate was 8% during year 1, 7% during year 2 and 5% during year 3.

6. Calculate the compound interest on €3500 over three years if the interest rate was 6% in year 1 and went up by 1% in year 2 and a further 1% in year 3.

7. Calculate how much €3000 amounts to in two years if the rate of interest is 4% in year 1 and 5% in year 2.

8. Calculate how much €800 amounts to in three years if the rate of interest is 4% in year 1 and year 2, and 5% in year 3.

9. €4000 was invested on the first of January each year for three consecutive years. During the first year the rate was 7%, during the second year it was 4% and during the third year it was 5%. Copy the table below and use it to calculate (a) the total compound interest earned (b) the value of the investment at the end of the three years.

P_1
I_1
_____

P_2
I_2
_____

P_3
I_3
_____

P_4

10. €9000 was invested on the first of January each year for three consecutive years. The rate of interest each year was 8%. Calculate
(a) the total compound interest earned (b) the total value of the investment at the end of the three years.

11. Calculate how much €5000 amounts to after three years if the rate of interest was 6% in year 1, 5% in year 2 and 4% in year 3.

12. Calculate how much €6500 amounts to after three years if the rate of interest was 5% in year 1, 4% in year 2 and 7% in year 3.

13. Anne-Marie borrows €3000 at 7% compound interest p.a. At the end of the first year she pays off €2000. How much does she have left to pay at the end of the first year?

14. Conor borrows €10 000 at 5% compound interest each year. At the end of the second year he pays off half of the value of the loan. How much is still owed on the loan at the end of the third year?

15. Liam borrows €8000 and is charged 6% compound interest the first year, 9% the second year and 5% the third year. He pays off €2500 at the end of year 1 and €3000 at the end of year 2. How much does he still have left to pay at the end of year 3?

16. Margaret borrows €15 000 and pays 5% compound interest the first year, 6% the second year and 7% the third year. She pays off €3500 at the end of year 1 and €6000 at the end of year 2. How much does she still have left to pay at the end of year 3?

17. Rita invests €12 000 and gets 5% interest during the first year. She puts in a further €2000 at the start of year 2, when the rate changes to 7% during this second year. She then invests a further €3000 at the start of year 3, when the rate is reduced to 4%. Calculate the value of the investment at the end of the three years.

18. Eamonn invests €20 000 and gets 4% interest during the first year. He puts in a further €3000 at the start of year 2, when the rate changes to 5%. He then invests a further €5000 at the start of year 3, when the rate is increased again to 7%. Calculate the value of the investment at the end of the three years.

19. Avril borrows €6000 at 5% compound interest per annum. At the end of each year she pays off €2000. How much does she have left to pay at the end of the third year?

20. David borrows €5000 at 4% compound interest p.a. At the end of each year he pays off €1000. How much does he have left to pay at the end of the third year?

Depreciation

If someone buys a car for, say, €20 000 this year, the car is worth less next year. The amount that the car decreases in value is called the depreciation, i.e. the decrease in value over time. For example, if this car was only worth €16 000 after one year, then the depreciation would be €4000. Similarly, if a factory buys a machine now for €70 000, it will be worth less than that next year and even less again the following year.

Depreciation works in exactly the same way as compound interest, except that with depreciation you take away the amount each year, since the value is going down rather than up.

Depreciation questions will be easier to do if you understand the terms below and use them for each question.

Term	What it means
P_1	This is the value of the item at the start of year 1.
D_1	This is the amount by which the item went down during year 1.
P_2	This is the value of the item at the end of year 1 (or the beginning of year 2, since the end of year 1 is the same as the start of year 2).
D_2	This is the amount by which the item went down during year 2.
P_3	This is the value at the end of year 2 (or the beginning of year 3, since the end of year 2 is the same as the start of year 3).
D_3	This is the amount by which the item went down during year 3.
P_4	This is the value of the item at the end of year 3 (or the beginning of year 4, since the end of year 3 is the same as the start of year 4).

Example 7.4

A printing machine for a factory was bought for €25 000. It depreciated by 20% during the first year, 15% the second year and 10% the third year. Find (a) the value of the machine at the end of the third year (b) the total amount of the depreciation over the three years.

Solution

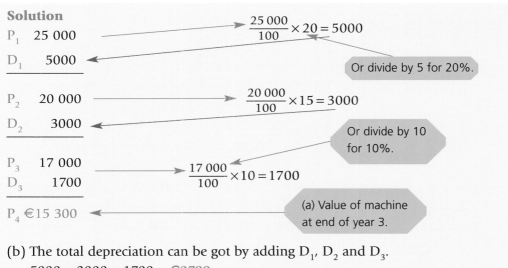

P_1 25 000

$\dfrac{25\ 000}{100} \times 20 = 5000$

D_1 5000

Or divide by 5 for 20%.

P_2 20 000

$\dfrac{20\ 000}{100} \times 15 = 3000$

D_2 3000

Or divide by 10 for 10%.

P_3 17 000

$\dfrac{17\ 000}{100} \times 10 = 1700$

D_3 1700

P_4 €15 300

(a) Value of machine at end of year 3.

(b) The total depreciation can be got by adding D_1, D_2 and D_3.

5000 + 3000 + 1700 = €9700

OR

by taking P_4 away from P_1

25 000 − 15 300 = €9700

Example 7.5

A machine cost €16 350. At the end of the year it was worth €15 369. Find (a) the amount of the depreciation during the year (b) the rate of depreciation during the year.

Solution (copy the table and fill in the information in the question)

P_1 16 350

D_1 ?

P_2 15 369

(a) The depreciation is got by subtracting $P_1 − P_2$

$D_1 = P_1 − P_2$

16 350 − 15 369 = €981 D_1

(b) rate = $\dfrac{\text{interest}}{\text{amount}} \times 100$ D_1 P_1

$\dfrac{981}{16\ 350} \times 100 = 6$ (b) Depreciation rate 6%

Exercise 7.3

1. A DVD recorder cost €250. It depreciated by 15% during the first year. What was the value of the DVD recorder at the end of the year?

2. A new car was bought for €48 000. It depreciated by 20% during the first year. What is the value of the car at the end of the first year?

3. A new lawnmower was bought for €2500. It depreciated by 20% during the first year and 10% during the second year. Calculate the value of the lawnmower at the end of the second year.

4. A suite of furniture cost €1850. It went down in value by 10% during each of two years. Find the value of the suite of furniture at the end of the second year.

5. A new motorbike was bought for €12 000. It depreciated by 20% during the first year and 10% during each of the following two years. Calculate the value of the motorbike at the end of the three years.

6. A set of table and chairs cost €300. It depreciated by 20% during the first year and 10% during the second year. Calculate the value of the table and chairs at the end of the two years.

7. A new car cost €32 000. It depreciated by 20% during each of three years. Calculate the value of the car at the end of the three years.

8. A new car cost €47 000. It depreciated by 20% during the first year, 16% during the second year and 10% during the third year. Calculate the value of the car at the end of the three years.

9. A family bought a computer for €2000. It depreciated by 30% during the first year, 10% during the second year and 5% during the third year. What was the value of the computer at the end of the third year?

10. A machine was bought for a factory for €12 500. It depreciated by 10% during the first year and 5% during the second and third year. Find the value of the machine at the end of the third year.

11. A new car cost €24 000 in January. At the end of the year the car was worth €20 400. Find (a) the amount of the depreciation during the year (b) the rate of depreciation.

12. A family bought a computer for €1400. It depreciated by 30% during the first year, 20% during the second year and 15% the third year. What was the value of the computer at the end of the third year?

13. A new suite of furniture cost €2400 in January. At the end of the year the suite was worth €2064. Find (a) the amount of the depreciation during the year (b) the rate of depreciation.

▌▌▌ Value-added tax (VAT)

VAT is a tax that is charged when goods and services are sold. The VAT is a percentage of the price of an item.

There are two ideas that you should understand before starting VAT questions.

1. 'Plus VAT' means that you must work out the amount of the VAT and add it onto the price to get the total price that you would have to pay.
2. 'VAT inclusive' means that the VAT has already been included and the price quoted is the total that you would have to pay.

Make out a table like the one below for VAT questions and fill in the information you are given in the problem. This will help you to understand the question.

> Before VAT: Before the VAT is added on, you have 100%.
> VAT: A percentage of the 'before VAT' price (usually 21%).
> VAT inclusive: Total price you will have to pay, including VAT (greater than 100%).

Example 7.6

A TV was priced at €180 plus VAT at 21%. Find (a) the amount of the VAT (b) the total price of the TV including the VAT. = 37.80

Solution

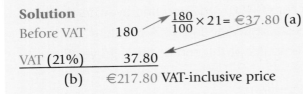

Before VAT   180 $\frac{180}{100} \times 21 =$ €37.80 (a)

VAT (21%)   37.80

(b)   €217.80 VAT-inclusive price

Exercise 7.4

For each of the questions in this exercise, it may help to make out and use a table like that in question 1.

1. A microwave is priced at €80 plus VAT at 21%. Calculate the total price including the VAT.

    Before VAT
      VAT
_____

                      VAT-inclusive price

2. A suite of furniture is priced at €1200 plus VAT at 21%. Calculate
   (a) the amount of the VAT (b) the VAT-inclusive price.

3. A watch costs €260 + VAT at 21%.
   Calculate the cost of the watch including
   VAT, to the nearest euro.

4. A restaurant bill came to €70 plus VAT.
   If the rate of VAT was 21%, find
   (a) the amount of the VAT (b) the total price including the VAT.

5. A garage bill came to €600 plus VAT. If the rate of VAT was 20%, find
   (a) the amount of the VAT (b) the total price including the VAT.

6. A radio costs €80 plus VAT at 12.5%. Calculate (a) the amount of the
   VAT (b) the price including the VAT.

7. A gas bill comes to €85 plus VAT of 16%. Calculate the total cost of the
   gas bill.

8. A car is priced at €30 000 plus VAT at 21%. Find (a) the amount of the
   VAT (b) the total price of the car inclusive of VAT.

9. A quote from a painter and decorator
   is for €640 plus VAT. If the rate of VAT
   is 15%, calculate the amount of the
   total quote.

10. A pair of jeans cost €40 + VAT. If the
    rate of VAT was 25%, calculate the
    total cost of the jeans.

11. A car is priced at €36 300 plus VAT at 18%. Find the VAT-inclusive price
    of the car.

12. A watch costs €90 + VAT at 21%. Calculate the cost of the watch,
    including VAT, to the nearest euro.

13. A garage bill was €1200. If the rate of VAT is 17%, calculate
(a) the amount of the VAT (b) the total bill.

14. A restaurant bill came to €23.50 plus VAT. If the rate of VAT was 21%,
calculate the total price of the bill to the nearest cent.

15. An electricity bill comes to €120 + VAT of 16.5%. Find the total cost of
the electricity bill.

16. An item was priced at €800 + VAT. If the rate of VAT is 24%, calculate
(a) the amount of the VAT (b) the total cost.

17. 2000 litres of oil were delivered to a house. The cost of one litre is 95c
plus VAT at 21%. Calculate (a) the amount of VAT on one litre of oil, to
the nearest cent (b) the total cost of one litre (c) the total cost of the
2000 litres.

18. A warehouse prices carpet at €18 per m² excluding VAT.
(a) If the rate of VAT is 21%, find the total price per square metre.
(b) How many square metres could you buy for €1089?

19. An oil bill came to €900 plus VAT. Find the difference in the total cost of
the oil if the rate of VAT was decreased from 21% to 17%.

20. In January, an electricity meter read
12 853 units. In March it read 14 291
units. Electricity costs 15c plus VAT
per unit. The VAT rate is 18%.
Calculate (a) the number of units used
between January and March (b) the cost
of these units before VAT (c) the amount
of the VAT, to the nearest cent (d) the
total cost of the bill including the VAT.

January

March

NOTE: Sometimes you are not asked to calculate the total price including the VAT.
You might be asked to calculate the rate of VAT or the price before the VAT was
added on, or you might just be given the amount of the VAT and work from that
figure. See the following examples.

Example 7.7

A car is priced at €26 000 inclusive of VAT. If the VAT rate is 21%, calculate
(a) the price of the car to the nearest euro before the VAT was added on
(b) the amount of the VAT.

Solution (using the table as in Example 7.6)

Before VAT   ?
VAT   ?(21%)
_____
26 000 VAT-inclusive price

26 000 already includes the 21% VAT and is therefore 121%.

(a) $\frac{26\,000}{121} \times 100 = 21\,487.60$

Price before VAT = € 21 488

(b) To get the amount of the VAT, simply subtract the 'before VAT' price from the 'VAT-inclusive' price.

26 000 − 21 488 = €4512 amount of VAT

Example 7.8

A table was priced at €420 plus VAT and at €495 inclusive of VAT. Calculate
(a) the amount of the VAT (b) the rate of VAT to the nearest whole number.

Solution

Before VAT 420
VAT ?
_____
495 VAT-inclusive price

(a) To get the amount of the VAT, simply subtract the 'before VAT' price from the 'VAT-inclusive' price.

495 − 420 = €75 amount of VAT

(b) rate = $\frac{VAT}{before\ VAT\ price} \times 100$ 420

rate = $\frac{75}{420} \times 100 = 17.86$ (b) Rate of VAT = 18%

Example 7.9

The VAT on a coat is €10.50. If the rate of VAT is 21%, calculate (a) the price before VAT (b) the price including VAT.

Solution

Before VAT   ?

VAT   10.50   (21%)

10.50 is 21%.

——————————

? VAT-inclusive price

(a) $\frac{10.50}{21} \times 100 = 50$ (a) Price before VAT = €50

(b) To get the total price, add the 'before VAT' price to the VAT.

50 + 10.50 = €60.50

Exercise 7.5

For each of the questions in this exercise, copy the table shown in question 1 and insert the money given into the correct place. Then use it to help you to answer the questions.

1. A quote for carpet is €242 inclusive of VAT at 21%. Calculate (a) the price before VAT (b) the amount of the VAT.

Before VAT

VAT   ————————

VAT-inclusive price

2. A new car is priced at €35 090 including VAT at 21%. Calculate (a) the price before VAT (b) the amount of the VAT.

3. A TV and DVD recorder combined is priced at €480 when the rate of VAT is 21%. Find the price before the VAT.

4. A table was priced at €650 plus VAT and at €760 inclusive of VAT. Calculate (a) the amount of the VAT (b) the rate of VAT to the nearest whole number.

5. The VAT on a pair of jeans was €5.25. If the rate of VAT is 21%, calculate (a) the price before VAT (b) the price including VAT.

6. A hi-fi system is priced at €859.10 inclusive of VAT at 21%. What would the price of the system be without the VAT?

7. A car was priced at €28 500 plus VAT and at €35 000 inclusive of VAT. Calculate (a) the amount of the VAT (b) the rate of VAT to the nearest whole number.

8. A quote for replacing windows was €508.20 including VAT at 21%. Find (a) the price before VAT (b) the amount of the VAT.

9. A table is priced at €625 VAT inclusive, when the VAT rate is 25%. Find the cost before VAT.

10. The VAT on a car was €12 180 when the rate of VAT was 21%. Calculate (a) the price of the car before VAT (b) the price including VAT.

11. A ring costs €230 including VAT at 21%. Find (a) the price before VAT to the nearest euro (b) the amount of the VAT.

12. A magazine costs €3.45 inclusive of VAT at 21%. Calculate the amount of the VAT to the nearest cent.

13. A quote for a new kitchen came to €3650 before VAT and to €4100 inclusive of VAT. Calculate (a) the amount of the VAT (b) the rate of VAT to the nearest whole number.

14. A car is priced at €36 300 VAT inclusive. Find the price of the car before the VAT at 21% was added on.

15. A magazine was priced at €4.30 before VAT and at €5.20 inclusive of VAT. Calculate (a) the amount of the VAT (b) the rate of VAT to the nearest whole number.

16. When the VAT rate was 18%, a woman paid VAT of €540 for an item. What was the total price of the item including the VAT?

17. A television is priced at €610 inclusive of VAT at 22%. What would be the price of the television without the VAT?

18. The VAT on a meal came to €12.60 when the rate of VAT was 21%. Find the total price of the meal.

Exercise 7.6 (Chapter summary)

1. €17 000 was invested for one year at 9% interest. Calculate
   (a) the interest earned during the year (b) the amount of the investment at the end of the year.

2. €400 was invested for one year at 5% interest. Calculate (a) the interest earned during the year (b) the amount of the investment at the end of the year.

3. A TV cost €200. It depreciated by 18% during the first year. What was the value of the TV at the end of the year?

4. €1500 was invested for two years at 7% compound interest. Calculate (a) the interest earned during the two years (b) the amount of the investment at the end of the two years.

5. €700 was invested for two years at 4% compound interest. Calculate (a) the interest earned during the two years (b) the amount of the investment at the end of the two years.

6. €2000 was invested on the first of January each year for three consecutive years. During the first year the rate was 5%, during the

second year it was 8% and during the third year it was 9%. Calculate (a) the total compound interest earned (b) how much the investment was worth at the end of the three years.

7. A new car cost €27 000. It depreciated by 15% each year for the first three years. Calculate the value of the car, to the nearest euro, at the end of the three years.

8. Robert invested €145 000. At the end of one year it was worth €156 600. Calculate (a) the amount of interest (b) the rate of interest.

9. Emma borrows €8000 at 4% compound interest p.a. At the end of each year she pays off €2000. How much, to the nearest cent, does she have left to pay at the end of the third year?

10. A new car cost €50 000. It depreciated by 25% the first year, 20% the second year and 10% the third year. Calculate the value of the car at the end of the three years.

11. Find the compound interest on €14 000 over three years if the interest rate was 5% in year 1 and went up by 1% in year 2 and a further 1% in year 3.

12. Aoileann bought a computer for €1600. It depreciated by 25% the first year, 20% the second year and 10% the third year. What was the value of the computer at the end of the third year?

13. A washing machine is priced at €400 plus VAT at 21%. Calculate the total price, including the VAT.

14. A suite of furniture is priced at €1800 plus VAT at 21%. Calculate (a) the amount of the VAT (b) the VAT-inclusive price.

15. A DVD costs €16 + VAT at 21%. Calculate the cost of the DVD, including VAT, to the nearest euro.

16. In April, a gas meter read 237 764 units. In June it read 238 540 units. Gas costs 35c plus VAT per unit. The VAT rate is 21%. Calculate
   (a) the number of units used between April and June
   (b) the cost of these units before VAT
   (c) the amount of the VAT, to the nearest cent
   (d) the total cost of the bill including the VAT.

17. A new car is priced at €25 955 including VAT at 21%. Calculate
   (a) the price before VAT to the nearest euro (b) the amount of the VAT.

18. A garage bought a new machine costing €9000. At the end of the year the machine was worth €7740. Find (a) the amount of the depreciation during the year (b) the rate of depreciation.

19. The VAT on a pair of glasses was €16.80. If the rate of VAT is 21%, calculate (a) the price before VAT (b) the price including VAT.

20. A necklace costs €950 including VAT at 21%. Calculate (a) the price of the necklace before VAT to the nearest euro (b) the amount of the VAT.

€950.

21. The VAT on a car was €9450 when the rate of VAT was 21%. Calculate (a) the price of the car before VAT (b) the price including VAT.

22. A magazine costs €8.47 inclusive of VAT at 21%. Calculate the amount of the VAT.

CHAPTER SUMMARY

In this chapter, you will learn about:

+ Ratio.

+ Exchange rates.

+ Income tax.

Ratio

Ratio is the comparison between the size of two or more values. A ratio will remain unchanged if each number is multiplied or divided by the same number.

Example 8.1

Express the following ratios in their simplest forms:
(a) 20 : 45 (b) 12 : 16 : 24 (c) $\frac{1}{2} : \frac{3}{4}$ (d) $\frac{2}{3} : 1\frac{3}{4}$ (e) 0.2 : 1.6.

Solution

(a) 20 : 45 ⟵   Divide each number by 5.

    = **4 : 9**

(b) 12 : 16 : 24 ⟵   Divide each number by 4.

    = **3 : 4 : 6**

(c) $\frac{1}{2} : \frac{3}{4}$ ← Multiply each number by 4.

= **2 : 3**

(d) $\frac{2}{3} : 1\frac{3}{4}$

$12\left(\frac{2}{3}\right) : \left(\frac{7}{4}\right)12$ ← Multiply each number by 12.

= **8 : 21**

Multiply each number by 10.

(e) 0.2 : 1.6 ←

2 : 16 ← Now divide each number by 2.

= **1 : 8**

Example 8.2

Write the following ratios in their simplest forms: (a) 300 m : 4 km (b) €3 : 48c.

Solution

(a) 300 m : 4 km ← 4 km must be changed to metres by multiplying by 1000.

300 : 4000 ← Now divide each number by 100.

= **3 : 40**

(b) €3 : 48c ← €3 must be changed to cent by multiplying by 100.

300 : 48 ← Now divide each number by 12.

= **25 : 4**

Exercise 8.1

Express the following ratios in their simplest forms.

1. (a) 5 : 15   (b) 30 : 27   (c) 3 : 21   (d) 12 : 18

2. (a) 20 : 30   (b) 15 : 12   (c) 28 : 36   (d) 24 : 30

3. (a) 120 : 200   (b) 175 : 275   (c) 250 : 400   (d) 360 : 420

4. (a) $\frac{2}{3} : \frac{3}{5}$ (b) $1\frac{1}{2} : 2\frac{1}{4}$ (c) $2\frac{1}{2} : 1\frac{1}{4}$

5. (a) $4 : \frac{2}{3}$ (b) $\frac{2}{5} : 1\frac{1}{8}$ (c) $3\frac{1}{2} : 2\frac{1}{4}$

6. (a) 0.3 : 0.6   (b) 1.2 : 0.36   (c) 0.08 : 0.16

7. (a) 10 : 15 : 20   (b) 12 : 24 : 40   (c) 3 : 6 : 36   (d) 16 : 40 : 60

8. (a) 20 : 35 : 55   (b) 120 : 72 : 60   (c) 28 : 35 : 63

9. (a) 2000 : 3500 : 6000   (b) 9000 : 12 000 : 15 000

10. (a) 20 cm : 2 m   (b) 50 cm : 3 m

11. (a) 3 years : 6 months   (b) 8 months : 2 years

12. (a) €8 : 80c   (b) €12 : 60c

13. (a) 40 minutes : 2 hours   (b) 36 minutes : 3 hours

14. (a) 600 m : 4 km   (b) 200 m : 3 km

15. (a) 4 days : 4 weeks   (b) 6 days : 6 weeks

16. (a) 4 kg : 800 g   (b) 2 kg : 500 g

17. (a) 20 mm : 3 cm   (b) 45 mm : 6 cm

For questions 18 to 23, give your answer in the simplest form.

18. During a football match, the home team had possession of the ball for 45 minutes and the away team had possession for 25 minutes. What is the ratio of the home team's possession to the away team's possession?

19. In a class of 24 pupils, there are 18 girls. What is the ratio of girls to boys in the class?

20. Owen studies maths for 45 minutes, Irish for 40 minutes and science for 1 hour. What is the ratio of time spent on each subject?

21. During the course of a day, Caitlín spends 45 minutes travelling to school, 2 hours studying and 5 hours in class. What is the ratio of time spent on each activity?

22. During a 24-hour period, John spends 6 hours at work, 2 hours exercising, 8 hours in bed, 2 hours eating and the rest at leisure. Express the ratio of time spent on these activities.

23. Mark spent one-third of his money on phone credit, one-quarter of his money on DVDs and five-twelfths on clothes. Express the ratio spent on each in its simplest form.

Example 8.3

(a) €240 is divided among three people in the ratio 2 : 3 : 5. Calculate how much each person gets.

(b) €280 is divided between two people in the ratio $\frac{1}{2} : \frac{2}{3}$. Calculate how much each person gets.

Solution

(a) Ratio 2 : 3 : 5

$2 + 3 + 5 = 10$

Add the ratios and divide the amount by the total to get the value of one part.

$240 \div 10 = 24$

$2(24) = €48$

$3(24) = €72$

Then multiply by each ratio to find the amount each gets.

$5(24) = €120$

Check total : $48 + 72 + 120 = 240$

(b) Ratio $\frac{1}{2} : \frac{2}{3}$

Multiply each of the ratios by 6.

$3 : 4$

This is the same ratio, but is easier to work with.

$280 \div 7 = 40$

$3(40) = €120$

$4(40) = €160$

This is the value of one part. Now multiply by each ratio.

Example 8.4

A certain sum of money was divided between John and Mary in the ratio 3 : 2. If John got €84, calculate (a) how much Mary got (b) the total amount of money.

Solution

€84 belongs to John and is therefore three parts.

$84 \div 3 = 28$ ← This is the value of one part.

$2(28) = €56$ (a) Mary's share

$56 + 84 = €140$ OR $5(28) = €140$ (b) Total amount

Exercise 8.2

1. €300 is divided between two people in the ratio 5 : 1. Calculate how much each person gets.

2. €216 is divided between Brian and Jeff in the ratio 4 : 5. Calculate how much each gets.

3. Divide 80 g in the ratio 3 : 5.

4. In a class of 24 students, the ratio of boys to girls is 5 : 3. Calculate how many boys and girls are in the class.

5. Divide €200 in the ratio 3 : 1.

6. A rope is 54 cm long. Divide it in the ratio 5 : 13.

7. Divide €720 between Anne and Owen so that Anne gets twice as much as Owen.

8. Copper and silver are mixed in an alloy in the ratio 3 : 5. How many grams of each metal are in an alloy of 960 g?

9. Two people together buy a ticket for €50. One person pays €30 and the other pays €20. If the ticket wins a cash prize of €80 000, how much should each person get?

10. Divide €480 among three people in the ratio 1 : 2 : 3.

11. Divide 56 minutes in the ratio 2 : 1 : 5.

12. Divide €800 in the ratio 7 : 19 : 24.

13. Divide €8000 among three people in the ratio 10 : 2 : 8.

14. Divide €170 among three people in the ratio $\frac{2}{3} : 2\frac{2}{3} : 2\frac{1}{3}$.

15. The sides of a triangle are in the ratio 3 : 2 : 4. If the length of the three sides of the triangle adds up to 117 cm, calculate the length of each side.

16. A line 160 cm long is divided in the ratio of 2 : 3 : 3. What length is each part?

17. Divide €1600 among three people in the ratio $1 : \frac{1}{2} : 2\frac{1}{2}$.

18. Three people are in business together. The profits are divided among the three in the ratio 2 : 3 : 7. If the business made a profit of €72 000, calculate how much profit each person gets.

19. In an election with 10 000 voters, three candidates received votes in the ratio 5 : 3 : 2. Calculate how many votes each candidate received.

20. Three people invest €3500, €2500 and €1500 in a business. If the business makes a profit of €12 000, calculate how much profit each should receive.

21. A certain sum of money was divided between Patrick and Claire in the ratio 5 : 2. If Patrick got €60, calculate (a) how much Claire got (b) the total amount of money.

22. Copper and silver are mixed in an alloy in the ratio 3 : 5. If there are 270 g of silver in an alloy, calculate (a) the amount of copper in the alloy (b) the total weight of the alloy.

23. A certain sum of money is divided between Kathleen and James in the ratio of 2 : 3. If James received €45, calculate (a) how much Kathleen received (b) the total amount of money.

24. A certain sum of money is divided among Joseph, Patrick and Eileen in the ratio 4 : 3 : 5. If Patrick received €240, calculate how much Joseph and Eileen each received.

25. A certain sum of money was divided between John and Mary in the ratio 5 : 2. If Mary got €60, calculate (a) how much John got (b) the total amount of money.

26. €800 is divided between Emily and Kate so that Emily receives 1.5 times the amount Kate receives. Calculate how much money each girl gets.

27. An alloy consists of zinc, tin and copper in the ratio 4 : 3 : 2. If there are 60 g of copper, calculate (a) how many grams each of zinc and tin are in the alloy (b) the total weight of the alloy.

28. €420 is divided among three people so that the first person gets twice as much as the second person and the third person gets twice as much as the first person. Calculate the amount of money each gets.

29. €300 is divided among three people so that the first person gets three times as much as the second person and the third person gets twice as much as the second person. Calculate the amount of money each gets.

30. Find x in the following: (a) 3 : 5 = 12 : x (b) 10 : x = 60 : 84 (c) 5 : x = 20 : 40 (d) $1\frac{1}{2}$: 3 = 12 : x (e) 4 : x = 28 : 35 (f) x : 5 = 100 : 60.

Exchange rates

An exchange rate is the amount of one currency that is given in exchange for one unit of another currency. For example, €1 = US$1.30 means that for every euro exchanged, US$1.30 will be given in return.

An exchange rate will always have one unit of one currency equal to a certain amount of another currency. Conversions from one currency to another are explained using the orange and **blue** arrows below.

The dotted arrow represents converting from the one-unit currency to the other currency.

The blue arrow represents changing from the other currency to the one-unit currency.

REMEMBER

To change from euro to yen, multiply by 350.

€1 = ¥350

To change from yen to euro, divide by 350.

Example 8.5

Chris changes €5000 to sterling before going to England. In England he spends £1500. If the exchange rate is €1 = £0.65, calculate (a) the amount he received originally in sterling (b) how much sterling he had left on his return (c) the value in euro of this sterling left over after converting it back to euro (round off to the nearest cent).

Solution

(a) €1 = £0.65   To change from euro to sterling, multiply by 0.65.

5000 × 0.65 = £3250 Original amount converted to sterling

(b) 3250 − 1500 = £1750 Amount of sterling remaining

(c) €1 = £0.65   To change from sterling to euro, divide by 0.65.

1750 ÷ 0.65 = €2692.31 Remainder converted to euro

Exercise 8.3

1. When the exchange rate is €1 = $1.50, convert the following:
   (a) €300 to dollars (b) $300 to euro.

2. When the exchange rate is €1 = $1.40, convert the following: (a) $5600 to euro (b) €5600 to dollars.

3. When the exchange rate is €1 = ¥300 (Japanese yen), convert the following: (a) €150 to yen (b) ¥15 000 to euro.

4. When the exchange rate is €1 = $2.30 (Canadian dollars), convert the following: (a) €30 000 to Canadian dollars (b) $20 000 to euro, to the nearest euro.

5. When the exchange rate is €1 = R2.60 (South African rand), convert the following: (a) R52 000 to euro (b) €520 to rand.

6. A football ticket costs £60. How much, to the nearest cent, will this cost in Ireland if the exchange rate is €1 = £0.70?

7. A book costs $36 on the internet, including postage. How much in euro will someone in Ireland pay if the exchange rate is €1 = $1.20?

8. An airline quotes the price of a flight to London as £130 return. Calculate how much someone in Ireland would pay if the exchange rate was €1 = £0.72 sterling. Answer to the nearest cent.

9. A flight from Belfast to Portugal is quoted at £250. The price from Dublin to Portugal is quoted at €360. Find out which flight is cheaper and by how much (in euro) if the exchange rate is €1 = £0.62.

10. Sally changes €800 to sterling before going to England. In England she spends £300. If the exchange rate is €1 = £0.61, calculate
    (a) the amount she received originally in sterling (b) how much sterling she had left on her return (c) the value of this sterling left over after converting it back to euro (round off to the nearest cent).

141

11. When the exchange rate is €1 = $2.60 Canadian dollars, how much would someone going on holiday to Canada get for €2500?

12. A tourist came to Ireland from South Africa with R7840 (rand). She spends €2100 in Ireland. If the exchange rate is €1 = R2.80, calculate (a) how much her original amount was worth in euro (b) how much euro she had left (c) how much this would be if she converted this remainder back into South African rand.

13. A car costs £16 000 in England plus an additional €8000 in transfer and registration costs. The same car costs €32 000 if bought in Ireland. If the exchange rate is €1 = £0.64, which is the cheaper option and by how much (in euro)?

14. Seán goes on holiday to the US. He exchanges €5000 for US dollars when the exchange rate is €1 = $1.20. He spends $4700 in America. How much does he have left in euro on his return if the exchange rate has changed to €1 = $1.30?

Income tax

In order to pay for services like education, health, social welfare, etc., the government needs money. Some of this money is in the form of a percentage of income earned by everybody in the country. This section shows how this system of income tax works.

You must know the following terms in order to deal with income tax:

- Gross income: This is the total income/salary earned before any deductions have been taken away. Gross income is the figure quoted when a job is advertised.
- Standard rate of tax and marginal rate of tax: There are two rates of tax, a lower rate and a higher rate. The lower rate is often called the standard rate. The higher rate is often called the marginal rate of tax.
- SRCP: Standard rate cut-off point – this the amount of income which is taxed at the lower rate of tax.
- Gross tax: This is the total tax calculated.
- Tax credits: This is the amount of discount/reduction in tax which a person is allowed.
- Net tax: This is the actual amount of tax paid to the government. It is calculated by subtracting the tax credits from gross tax.
- Net income/pay/salary: This is the amount of income left after the deductions have been taken away.

The template below can be used to calculate income tax and net income.

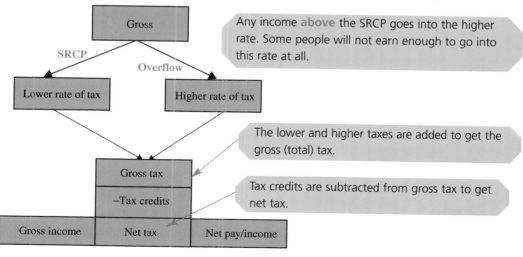

Net tax is then taken away from gross income to give net pay/salary/take-home pay.

Example 8.6

Dylan has a gross salary of €580 per week. The standard rate cut-off point is €18 000 per year. He has tax credits of €3500 per year. The standard rate of income tax is 20% and the marginal rate is 40%. Calculate his net income per year.

Solution

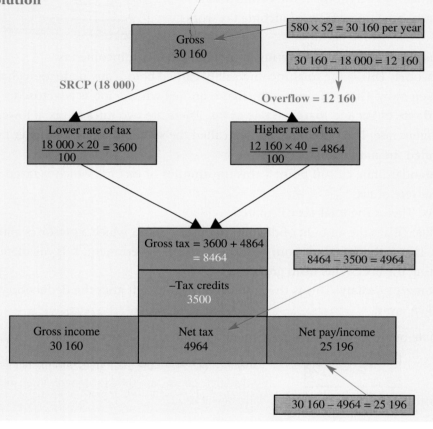

Example 8.7

A young person working part-time has a gross salary of €17 500 per year. The standard rate cut-off point is €19 000 per year. This person has tax credits of €2400. The standard rate of income tax is 20% and the marginal rate is 40%. Calculate the net income per year.

Solution

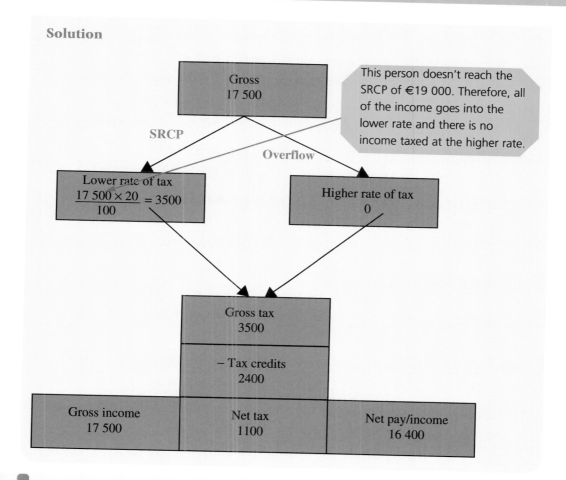

Gross
17 500

This person doesn't reach the SRCP of €19 000. Therefore, all of the income goes into the lower rate and there is no income taxed at the higher rate.

SRCP

Overflow

Lower rate of tax
$$\frac{17\ 500 \times 20}{100} = 3500$$

Higher rate of tax
0

Gross tax
3500

− Tax credits
2400

Gross income
17 500

Net tax
1100

Net pay/income
16 400

Exercise 8.4

For all of the questions in this exercise, the standard rate of tax is 20% and the higher rate of tax is 40%.

1. For these employees, calculate (i) gross tax (ii) net pay.

Employee	Gross income per year	SCRP	Tax credit
(a) Mary	€48 000	€18 000	€4000
(b) Joseph	€35 000	€16 500	€5000
(c) Áine	€28 000	€16 000	€3200
(d) Patrick	€32 600	€15 000	€2500

2. Dermot earns €650 per week. He has an SRCP of €20 000. His tax credits are €4200. Calculate (a) gross tax (b) net pay for the year.

3. Samantha earns €730 per week. She has an SRCP of €25 000. Her tax credits are €5600. Calculate (a) her gross tax (b) her net pay for the year.

4. Kate had a gross income of €16 000 for last year. She had an SRCP of €19 000 and tax credits of €1900. Calculate her net income for last year.

5. Joe had a gross income of €25 000 for last year. He had an SRCP of €20 000 and tax credits of €2100. Calculate his net income for last year.

6. Calculate the take-home pay for someone earning €28 000 per year who has tax credits of €3500, when the SRCP is €22 000.

7. Brian earns €700 per week. He has an SRCP of €15 000. His tax credits are €2300. Calculate his take-home pay (a) per year (b) per week, to the nearest cent.

8. Jack had a gross income of €19 000 last year. He had an SRCP of €21 000 and tax credits of €2100. Calculate his net income last year.

9. Calculate the take-home pay for someone earning €21 000 per year who has tax credits of €3000, when the SRCP is €23 000.

10. Patrick earns €850 per week. The SRCP is €20 000 and he has tax credits of €4000 per year. Calculate (a) gross tax per year (b) net tax per year (c) net tax per week, to the nearest cent.

11. Mary earns €900 per week. She has an SRCP of €18 000. Her tax credits are €2600. Calculate her take-home pay (a) per year (b) per week, to the nearest cent.

12. Eileen earns €1700 per fortnight. She has annual tax credits of €4000. John earns €800 per week and has annual tax credits of €3800. The SRCP for both people is €25 000. Who has the highest take-home pay and by how much?

13. Mark and Pat were comparing their take-home pay. Mark earns €2400 per month, while Pat earns €675 per week. Mark's tax credits are €5600. Pat's tax credits are €4300. The SRCP for both people is €21 000. Who has the highest take-home pay and by how much?

Exercise 8.5 (Chapter summary)

Express the ratios in questions 1 to 5 in their simplest forms.

1. (a) 15 : 65   (b) 60 : 54   (c) 24 : 18   (d) 6 : 10

2. (a) 250 : 300   (b) 40 cm : 2 m

3. (a) 2 years : 8 months   (b) 16 months : $2\frac{1}{2}$ years

4. (a) €5 : 75c   (b) 40c : €12

5. (a) 160 m : 3 km   (b) 560 m : 2 km

6. Divide €500 in the ratio 3 : 2.

7. Divide €600 among three people in the ratio 2 : 1 : 7.

8. A certain sum of money is divided between John, Mary and Eileen in the ratio 2 : 3 : 7. If Mary received €480, calculate how much John and Eileen each received.

9. When the exchange rate is €1 = $1.40, convert (a) $1246 to euro (b) €1246 to dollars.

10. When the exchange rate is €1 = $1.20, convert (a) €8400 to dollars (b) $8400 to euro.

11. An airline quotes the price of a flight to London as £180 return. Calculate how much, to the nearest euro, someone in Ireland would pay if the exchange rate was €1 = 63p sterling.

12. Shelia goes on holiday to the US. She exchanges €1200 for US dollars when the exchange rate is €1 = $1.40. She spends $1400 in America. How much, to the nearest cent, does she have left in euro on her return if the exchange rate has changed to €1 = $1.30?

13. Joan has a gross income of €49 000 per year. Her SRCP is €23 000 and her tax credits are €5800. Calculate her net income.

14. Joe earns €860 per week. He has an SRCP of €22 000. His tax credits are €4800. Calculate his net tax for the year.

15. Kate has a gross income of €19 700. She has an SRCP of €22 000 and tax credits of €3000. Calculate her net income per year.

In this chapter, you will learn about:

+ Indices, with and without the calculator.
+ Adding, subtracting, multiplying and dividing numbers in scientific notation.
+ Evaluating reciprocals.
+ Estimating an answer and obtaining the exact answer on the calculator.

Indices

Index is another word for power. For example, 3^4 is read as '3 to the power of 4'. The 4 is called the **index** (or power). The power indicates repeated multiplication. In this case, 3^4 means $3 \times 3 \times 3 \times 3$, which gives 81.

Examples

- 5^2 (called 5 squared) means 5×5, which gives 25.
- 6^3 (called 6 cubed) means $6 \times 6 \times 6$, which gives 216.
- 2^5 (2 to the power of 5) means $2 \times 2 \times 2 \times 2 \times 2$, which gives 32.

NOTE:

- 6 can be written as 6^1. The power of 1 is not normally written.
- $9^{\frac{1}{2}}$ is another way of writing $\sqrt{9}$, which is 3.

Powers on a calculator

The value of a number in index form can be obtained from a calculator by using the power button.

Example 9.1

Using your calculator, or otherwise, calculate 7^4.

Solution

Calculator method:

On your calculator, press: 7 $\boxed{x^\bullet}$ 4 = 2401

NOTE: In some calculators, the $\boxed{x^\bullet}$ button is $\boxed{\wedge}$.

Repeated multiplication method:

$7 \times 7 \times 7 \times 7 = 2401$

Example 9.2

Express the following as a single power:

(a) $7^3 \times 7^5$ (b) $\dfrac{8^6}{8^2}$ (c) $(3^5)^2$ (d) $64^{\frac{1}{2}}$

Solution

(a) $7^3 \times 7^5 = \underbrace{7 \times 7 \times 7}_{7^3} \times \underbrace{7 \times 7 \times 7 \times 7 \times 7}_{7^5} = 7^8$

> When multiplying indices of the same number, **add** the indices, e.g. $8 = 3 + 5$.

(b) $\dfrac{8^6}{8^2} = \dfrac{8 \times 8 \times 8 \times 8 \times 8 \times 8}{8 \times 8} = 8 \times 8 \times 8 \times 8 = 8^4$

> These will now cancel.

> When dividing indices of the same number, subtract the indices, e.g. $4 = 6 - 2$.

(c) $(3^5)^2 = 3^5 \times 3^5 = 3^{10}$

> Anything squared means the number multiplied by itself.

> When raising one power to another power, multiply the indices, e.g. $10 = 5 \times 2$.

(d) $64^{\frac{1}{2}} = \sqrt{64} = 8$

> The power of $\frac{1}{2}$ is another way of writing the square root.

149

Exercise 9.1

1. Use repeated multiplication to evaluate the following.
   (a) 9^2 (b) 15^2 (c) 2^4 (d) 8^3 (e) 10^3

2. Write the following as a single power.
   (a) $5^2 \times 5^4$ (b) $5^3 \times 5$ (c) 7×7 (d) $8^3 \times 8^3$ (e) $4^2 \times 4^6$

3. Write the following as a single power.
   (a) $7^2 \times 7^6$ (b) $8^3 \times 8^6$ (c) $3^7 \times 3^4$ (d) $4^3 \times 4^2 \times 4^5$ (e) $3 \times 3^2 \times 3^4$

4. Express the following as a single power.
   (a) $\dfrac{6^5}{6^3}$ (b) $\dfrac{7^6}{7^5}$ (c) $\dfrac{8^4}{8^2}$ (d) $\dfrac{3^5}{3}$ (e) $\dfrac{4^3}{4}$

5. Express the following as a single power.
   (a) $\dfrac{9^5}{9^2}$ (b) $\dfrac{2^6}{2}$ (c) $\dfrac{6^5}{6^2}$ (d) $\dfrac{3^8}{3}$ (e) $\dfrac{7^9}{7^4}$

6. Write the following as a single power.
   (a) $(4^3)^2$ (b) $(5^4)^3$ (c) $(6^2)^4$ (d) $\left(5^{\frac{1}{2}}\right)^2$ (e) $\left(8^{\frac{2}{3}}\right)^3$

7. Write the following as a single power.
   (a) $(9^2)^3$ (b) $(3^5)^4$ (c) $\left(7^{\frac{1}{2}}\right)^4$ (d) $(5^3)^3$ (e) $\left(12^{\frac{1}{3}}\right)^9$

8. Calculate the value of the following.
   (a) $16^{\frac{1}{2}}$ (b) $36^{\frac{1}{2}}$ (c) $3 \times 81^{\frac{1}{2}}$ (d) $5(49)^{\frac{1}{2}}$ (e) $2(25)^{\frac{1}{2}}$

9. Simplify the following and write your answer as a whole number.
   (a) $\dfrac{2^5 \times 2^3}{2^4}$ (b) $\dfrac{5^2 \times 5^4}{5^3}$ (c) $\dfrac{8^2 \times 8^5}{8^6}$ (d) $\dfrac{7^2 \times 7^4}{7^3}$ (e) $\dfrac{3^7 \times 3}{3^5}$

10. Evaluate the following.
    (a) $5^2 \times 100^{\frac{1}{2}}$ (b) $\sqrt{4} + \left(3^2\right)^2$ (c) $\dfrac{2^2 \times 9^{\frac{1}{2}}}{6}$ (d) $4 \times 2^3 + 3\sqrt{81}$ (e) $2\left(4 + 121^{\frac{1}{2}}\right)$

11. Given that $(3x)^3 = 3^3 \times x^3 = 27x^3$, simplify the following.
    (a) $(3y)^2$ (b) $(5x)^3$ (c) $(2y)^4$ (d) $(7x)^2$ (e) $(3y)^4$

12. Simplify the following, giving your answer in the form a^n, where $n \in N$.
    (a) $a^3 \times a^4$ (b) $a^6 \times a$ (c) $\dfrac{a^7}{a^2}$ (d) $\dfrac{a^6 \times a^4}{a \times a^3}$

Scientific notation

It may not be possible to display very large or very small numbers properly on your calculator. For example, the mass of the earth is 5 973 600 000 000 000 000 000 000 kg. It is not convenient to write such numbers in this form. Scientific notation is used as a more compact way of writing these numbers. In scientific notation, the earth's mass is written as 5.9736×10^{24} kg.

Earth's mass $= 5.9736 \times 10^{24}$ kg.

Scientific notation is also sometimes called standard index form.

There are two parts to any number written in scientific notation:
- **Part 1:** A number between 1 and 10 (but not 10).
- **Part 2:** Multiplied by 10 to the power of a number.

NOTE: Part 1 and Part 2 are written together in mathematical form as:
$a \times 10^n$, where $1 \le a < 10$ and $n \in \mathbb{N}$.

Example 9.3

Calculate the following and write your answer in the form

$a \times 10^n$, where $1 \le a < 10$ and $n \in N$.

(a) 32   (b) 58 000   (c) 6 752 000

Solution

(a) $32 = 3.2 \times 10$

The decimal point was moved one place. **Note**: $10 = 10^1$.

Place the decimal point so that the number is between 1 and 10.

(b) $58\,000 = 5.8 \times 10^4$

The decimal point was moved four places.

(c) $6\,752\,000 = 6.752 \times 10^6$

The decimal point was moved six places.

Place the decimal point so that the number is between 1 and 10.

Example 9.4

Write the following as a natural number.
(a) 4.6×10^3
(b) 3.21×10^4

The power indicates that the decimal point is to be moved three places.

Solution
(a) $4.6 \times 10^3 = 4600$

The power indicates that the decimal point is to be moved four places.

(b) $3.21 \times 10^4 = 32\,100$

Addition and subtraction in scientific notation

Example 9.5

Simplify the following: $(3.85 \times 10^5) - (4.6 \times 10^4)$.

Solution

There are two methods of adding or subtracting numbers in scientific notation.

Natural number method

$(3.85 \times 10^5) - (4.6 \times 10^4)$

$= 385\ 000 - 46\ 000$

Step 1: Change the numbers to natural numbers.

$= 339\ 000$

Step 2: Subtract the numbers.

$= 3.39 \times 10^5$

Step 3: Change the number back to scientific notation.

Calculator method

Input the following:

Right arrow of replay button.

$\boxed{(}\ 3.85\ \boxed{\times}\ 10\ \boxed{x^\blacksquare}\ 5\ \boxed{\rightarrow}\ \boxed{)}\ \boxed{-}\ \boxed{(}\ 4.6\ \boxed{\times}\ 10\ \boxed{x^\blacksquare}\ 4\ \boxed{\rightarrow}\ \boxed{)}\ \boxed{=}$

This is the 'power' button. It may look like $\boxed{\wedge}$ or $\boxed{y^x}$ or $\boxed{x^y}$.

The calculator will display the number in this form.

$= 339\ 000$

$= 3.39 \times 10^5$

Change to scientific notation.

153

Multiplication and division in scientific notation

Example 9.6

(a) $(3.1 \times 10^3) \times (2 \times 10^5)$ (b) $2.4 \times 10^4 \div 1.2 \times 10^3$

Solution

(a) Method 1

$$10^3 \times 10^5 = 10^{3+5} = 10^8$$

$$(3.1 \times 10^3) \times (2 \times 10^5) = 6.2 \times 10^8$$

$$3.1 \times 2 = 6.2$$

Right arrow of replay button.

Method 2: Calculator method

(3.1 × 10 $x^{\blacksquare}$ 3 →) × (2 × 10 $x^{\blacksquare}$5 →) =

The calculator will display the number in this form. ⟶ $= 620\,000\,000$

Change to scientific notation. ⟶ $= 6.2 \times 10^8$

This question could have been written as $\dfrac{2.4 \times 10^4}{1.2 \times 10^3}$

(b) $(2.4 \times 10^4) \div (1.2 \times 10^3)$

Method 1

$$10^4 \div 10^3 = 10^{4-3} = 10^1 = 10$$

$$(2.4 \times 10^4) \div (1.2 \times 10^3) = 2 \times 10$$

$$2.4 \div 1.2 = 2$$

Method 2: Calculator method

(2.4 × 10 $x^{\blacksquare}$ 4 →) ÷ (1.2 × 10 $x^{\blacksquare}$ 3 →) =

Calculator display. ⟶ $= 20$

$$= 2 \times 10$$

REMEMBER

It is good practice to write a number in scientific notation within brackets. For example, $6.4 \times 10^4 + 3 \times 10^2$ is better written as $(6.4 \times 10^4) + (3 \times 10^2)$.

Exercise 9.2

1. Write the value of n in the following.
   (a) $650 = 6.5 \times 10^n$ (b) $48\,000 = 4.8 \times 10^n$ (c) $31 = 3.1 \times 10^n$
   (d) $42\,000\,000 = 4.2 \times 10^n$ (e) $4600 = 4.6 \times 10^n$

2. Write the value of n in the following.
   (a) $95 = 9.5 \times 10^n$ (b) $35\,800 = 3.58 \times 10^n$ (c) $580\,100 = 5.801 \times 10^n$
   (d) $75\,350 = 7.535 \times 10^n$ (e) $885\,524 = 8.85524 \times 10^n$

In questions 3 to 10, express the numbers in the form $a \times 10^n$, where $1 \le a < 10$ and $n \in N$, without using a calculator. Only check your answers on the calculator.

3. (a) 8000   (b) 19 000   (c) 285 000

4. (a) 470   (b) 562   (c) 7500

5. (a) 480 000   (b) 903   (c) 7005

6. (a) 320 000 000   (b) 92 000 000   (c) 9 000 000 000

7. (a) 762 000 000 000   (b) 5 000 000 000   (c) 56 789 420

8. (a) 52   (b) 502   (c) 50 002

9. (a) 607   (b) 67 800   (c) 8 570 000

10. (a) 168   (b) 168 000   (c) 1 680 000 000

In questions 11 to 14, write the numbers as natural numbers.

11. (a) 4.5×10^3 (b) 6.1×10^2 (c) 5.3×10^4

12. (a) 3.6×10^5 (b) 2.2×10^4 (c) 9.37×10^3

13. (a) 6.25×10^4 (b) 4.92×10^5 (c) 3.79×10^3

14. (a) 2.83×10^2 (b) 4.3×10^5 (c) 6.39×10^4

15. Write the following numbers in ascending order (from smallest to largest).
     (a) 6.95×10^3 (b) 3.8×10^2 (c) 900 (d) 1.2×10^6 (e) 4.2×10^2
     (f) $42\ 000$ (g) 4.2×10^3

16. Write the following numbers in ascending order (from smallest to largest).
     (a) 6.5×10^3 (b) $12\ 000$ (c) 8.97×10^2 (d) 2.3×10^5 (e) 6.5×10^4
     (f) 8000 (g) 1.3×10^3

In questions 17 to 22, write the numbers as natural numbers. Add or subtract as required, then change back to scientific notation again. Check your answer on the calculator.

17. $(1.4 \times 10^3) + (3.7 \times 10^2)$

18. $(8.5 \times 10^4) + (2.3 \times 10^3)$

19. $(4.9 \times 10^2) + (5 \times 10^3)$

20. $(7.2 \times 10^4) - (2.5 \times 10^2)$

21. $(5.5 \times 10^3) - (1.4 \times 10^3)$

22. $(3.65 \times 10^5) - (1.42 \times 10^4)$

In questions 23 to 32, write your answer in the form $a \times 10^n$, where $1 \le a < 10$ and $n \in N$.

23. (a) $(6.4 \times 10^4) + (3 \times 10^2)$ (b) $(9.1 \times 10^5) + (4 \times 10^3)$
     (c) $(5.34 \times 10^4) + (7.3 \times 10^2)$

24. (a) $(5.89 \times 10^3) + (2.134 \times 10^2)$ (b) $(3.84 \times 10^5) + (6.4 \times 10^4)$
     (c) $(3.75 \times 10^6) + (6.7 \times 10^5)$

25. (a) $(9.2 \times 10^5) + (4.1 \times 10^4)$ (b) $(2.7 \times 10^5) + (4.9 \times 10^4)$
     (c) $(1.36 \times 10^4) + (5.5 \times 10^4)$

26. (a) $(5.2 \times 10^3) - (1.1 \times 10^2)$ (b) $(8.5 \times 10^3) - (5.4 \times 10^3)$
     (c) $(3.5 \times 10^3) - (2.4 \times 10^4)$

27. (a) $(4 \times 10^4) \times (3 \times 10^3)$ (b) $(5 \times 10^3) \times (2 \times 10^4)$
    (c) $(2.3 \times 10^5) \times (1.2 \times 10^2)$

28. (a) $(5 \times 10^6) \times (2 \times 10^4)$ (b) $(3.4 \times 10^4) \times (1.8 \times 10^5)$
    (c) $(8.21 \times 10^3) \times (4.16 \times 10^3)$

29. (a) $(1.4 \times 10^5) \times (4.7 \times 10^3)$ (b) $(4.6 \times 10^4) \times (3.1 \times 10^2)$
    (c) $(3.1 \times 10^6) \times (2.4 \times 10^2)$

30. (a) $(6.4 \times 10^5) \div (3.2 \times 10^4)$ (b) $(7.8 \times 10^3) \div (1.2 \times 10^2)$
    (c) $(4.8 \times 10^6) \div (9.6 \times 10^3)$

31. (a) $(2.4 \times 10^6) \div (1.2 \times 10^3)$ (b) $(7 \times 10^5) \div (3.5 \times 10^3)$
    (c) $(2.8 \times 10^4) \div (1.4 \times 10^4)$

32. (a) $(6.3 \times 10^5) \div (2.1 \times 10^2)$ (b) $(8.8 \times 10^6) \div (2.2 \times 10^4)$
    (c) $(9.6 \times 10^6) \div (3.2 \times 10^3)$

33. Light travels at approximately 290 000 km per second.
    (a) Write this number in scientific notation.
    (b) How far would it travel in a minute?
    (c) How far would it travel in an hour?
    (d) How far would it travel in a day?

34. The following table gives the approximate average distance of each planet from the sun. Copy the table in your exercise book and complete it.

Planet	Average distance from sun in km (natural number)	Average distance from sun in km (scientific notation)
Mercury	58 000 000	
Venus		1.08×10^8
Earth	150 000 000	
Mars		2.28×10^8
Jupiter	778 000 000	
Saturn	1 427 000 000	
Pluto		5.9×10^9

||| Reciprocals

The reciprocal of a number is 1 over the number, i.e. $\dfrac{1}{\text{number}}$.

The reciprocal of 5 is $\dfrac{1}{5}$ (or 0.2 as a decimal by dividing 1 by 5).

Example 9.7

Evaluate the following correct to two decimal places, where necessary.
(a) The reciprocal of 7 (b) The reciprocal of $\dfrac{2}{3}$

Solution
(a) The reciprocal of $7 = \dfrac{1}{7} = 0.1428571429$

$\qquad = 0.14$ correct to two decimal places

(b) The reciprocal of $\dfrac{2}{3}$

Method 1: Non-calculator method

Reciprocal of $\dfrac{2}{3} = \dfrac{1}{\frac{2}{3}} = \dfrac{1}{1} \times \dfrac{3}{2} = \dfrac{3}{2}$

The reciprocal of the fraction $\dfrac{a}{b}$ is $\dfrac{b}{a}$.

To divide by $\dfrac{2}{3}$, multiply by $\dfrac{3}{2}$.

Method 2: Calculator method

$1 \boxed{\div} \boxed{\blacksquare \atop \square} 2 \boxed{\downarrow} 3 \boxed{=} \dfrac{3}{2}$ or 1.5

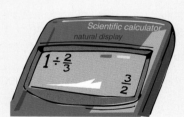

Scientific calculator natural display

$1 \div \dfrac{2}{3}$

$\dfrac{3}{2}$

Exercise 9.3

Evaluate the following correct to two decimal places, where necessary.

1. (a) $\frac{1}{8}$ (b) $\frac{1}{3}$ (c) $\frac{1}{12}$ (d) $\frac{1}{9}$ (e) $\frac{1}{15}$

2. (a) $\frac{1}{6}$ (b) $\frac{1}{14}$ (c) $\frac{1}{2.5}$ (d) $\frac{1}{22}$ (e) $\frac{1}{3.4}$

3. Without using a calculator, write the following as a fraction.

   (a) The reciprocal of $\frac{4}{5}$

   (b) The reciprocal of $\frac{1}{3\frac{3}{8}}$

   (c) The reciprocal of $\frac{1}{1\frac{1}{6}}$

4. Using a calculator or otherwise, evaluate the following to two decimal places.

   (a) The reciprocal of $\frac{4}{7}$.

   (b) The reciprocal of 11.

   (c) $\frac{1}{5}+\frac{1}{3.9}$

   (d) $\frac{1}{1.2}-\frac{1}{5.6}$

   (e) $\frac{1}{(3.2)^2}$

Estimation and approximation

If you press the wrong number on a calculator, you can get an answer that is far from correct. By rounding off each number in a question to the nearest whole number, we can estimate the answer and tell if an error has been made on the calculator.

Example 9.8

$\approx$ means approximately equal to.

Estimate the following and then obtain the exact answer from the calculator, correct to two decimal places.

(a) $\frac{1}{4.5}$

(b) $\frac{1}{(3.4)^2}$

(c) $\sqrt{29}$

(d) $\frac{25.62 - 12.43}{6.6}$

(e) $\sqrt{65.61} \times \frac{3.14}{0.47} - (2.42)^2$

Solution

(a) Estimate $\frac{1}{4.5} \approx \frac{1}{5} = 0.2$

This rounds up to 5.

Calculator $\frac{1}{4.5} = 0.2222 = 0.\dot{2}$

A dot above a digit means this digit repeats indefinitely.

The estimate 0.2 is almost identical to the exact answer $0.\dot{2}$.

(b) Estimate $\frac{1}{(3.4)^2} \approx \frac{1}{3^2} = \frac{1}{9} = 0.1$

This rounds to 3^2.

Calculator $\frac{1}{(3.4)^2} = \frac{1}{11.56} = 0.08650519031 = 0.09$ correct to two decimal places

The estimate 0.1 is near the exact answer 0.09.

(c) Estimate $\sqrt{29} \approx \sqrt{25} = 5$

Square roots should be rounded off so that the estimated square root is a natural number.

Calculator $\sqrt{29} = 5.385164807 = 5.39$ correct to two decimal places

The estimate 5 is very near the exact answer, 5.39.

(d) $\frac{25.62 - 12.43}{6.6}$

Estimate $\frac{26 - 12}{7} = \frac{14}{7} = 2$

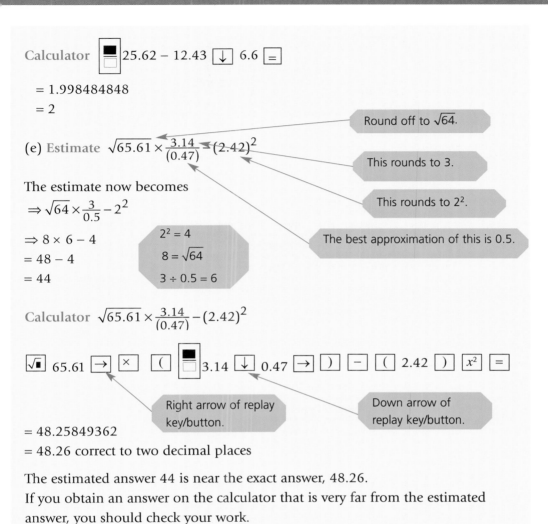

Calculator ▣ $25.62 - 12.43$ ⬇ 6.6 ▭

$= 1.998484848$

$= 2$

> Round off to $\sqrt{64}$.

(e) Estimate $\sqrt{65.61} \times \dfrac{3.14}{(0.47)} - (2.42)^2$

> This rounds to 3.

The estimate now becomes

$\Rightarrow \sqrt{64} \times \dfrac{3}{0.5} - 2^2$

> This rounds to 2^2.

$\Rightarrow 8 \times 6 - 4$

$2^2 = 4$

> The best approximation of this is 0.5.

$= 48 - 4$

$8 = \sqrt{64}$

$= 44$

$3 \div 0.5 = 6$

Calculator $\sqrt{65.61} \times \dfrac{3.14}{(0.47)} - (2.42)^2$

√▣ 65.61 → × ((▣ 3.14 ⬇ 0.47 →)) − ((2.42)) x^2 ▭

> Right arrow of replay key/button.

> Down arrow of replay key/button.

$= 48.25849362$

$= 48.26$ correct to two decimal places

The estimated answer 44 is near the exact answer, 48.26.
If you obtain an answer on the calculator that is very far from the estimated
answer, you should check your work.

Exercise 9.4

1. Estimate the value of the following by rounding off each number to the
   nearest whole number. Then obtain the exact answer using the calculator.
   (a) $3.7 + 14.4$ (b) $16.58 - 7.38$ (c) $20.34 - 8.22$
   (d) $43.26 + 15.35 - 6.2$ (e) $38.21 + 16.8 - 6.4$

2. Estimate the following and then obtain the exact answer using the calculator.
   (a) $3.24 \times (18.3 - 8.7)$
   (b) $6.78 \times (10.8 - 2.4)$
   (c) $\dfrac{16.48 - 7.3}{2.7}$
   (d) $\dfrac{28.57 + 6.8}{4.7 + 2.5}$

3. Estimate the answer of the following, then obtain the correct answer using the calculator, correct to two decimal places.
   (a) $(2.6)^2$ (b) $(3.8)^2$ (c) $\sqrt{80}$ (d) $\sqrt{40}$

4. Estimate the following, then check the answer on the calculator, correct to two decimal places.
   (a) $\dfrac{1}{8.7}$

   (b) $\dfrac{1}{(2.6)^2}$

   (c) $\sqrt{52} \times \dfrac{1}{7.8}$

   (d) $\sqrt{5} \times \dfrac{4.3}{1.2} - (1.5)^2$

5. Estimate the following, then check the answer on the calculator.
   (a) $\sqrt{46} + \dfrac{1}{(2.8)^2}$

   (b) $\dfrac{\sqrt{5} + \sqrt{8}}{(1.2)^2 + (1.8)^2}$

   (c) $\dfrac{\sqrt{18} - \sqrt{10}}{(3.1)^2 - 7.6}$

6. Gráinne is paid an hourly wage of €12.60. Estimate the total pay if she works 7 hours 45 minutes.

7. Liam earns €10.30 per hour. Estimate his total pay if he works 6 hours 20 minutes.

8. A household uses 860 litres of home heating oil. Estimate the cost of the oil if the price is 95c per litre.

9. A household uses 321 units of electricity at a cost of 15.12c per unit. Estimate the total cost of the electricity. Use your calculator to obtain the true cost to the nearest cent.

10. Ken buys two bottles of orange at €1.30 each. He also buys three bags of crisps at 58c each and two ice cream cones at €1.20 each. Estimate the total cost of his bill.

11. Maeve uses her mobile phone for 389 minutes at a cost of 5.7c per minute. By rounding the minutes to the nearest 100 and the cost to the nearest cent, estimate the total cost of the calls.

12. Owen uses his mobile phone for 438 minutes. The cost of the first 300 minutes was 6.2c per minute and the cost for any time above this was 4.8c per minute. Estimate the total cost of the calls.

13. Maria has €23.70 credit left on her mobile phone. Calls cost her 7.8c per minute. By rounding off the credit to the nearest euro and the cost to the nearest cent, estimate how many minutes she will get using her remaining credit.

14. A school is intending to raise money to buy a new computer suite. There are 24 computers in the full suite. The cost of each computer is €570. Estimate, to the nearest thousand, how much the school will need to raise to cover the total cost of the computer suite. (Hint: Round off the cost of one computer to the nearest 100.)

Exercise 9.5 (Chapter summary)

1. Use repeated multiplication to evaluate the following.
   (a) 7^2 (b) 3^3 (c) 10^3 (d) 4.5^2

2. Write the following in the form 6^n, $n \in N$.

   (a) $6^2 \times 6^5$ (b) 6×6^4 (c) $\dfrac{6^5}{6^2}$ (d) $\dfrac{6^3 \times 6^5}{6^2 \times 6^4}$

3. Write the following as a single power.

   (a) $(7^2)^4$ (b) $(6^3)^2$ (c) $(8^4)^2$ (d) $\left(13^{\frac{1}{2}}\right)^4$

4. Simplify the following.

   (a) $144^{\frac{1}{2}}$ (b) $1^{\frac{1}{2}}$ (c) $3 \times 25^{\frac{1}{2}}$ (d) $2(36)^{\frac{1}{2}}$

5. Write the value of n in the following.
   (a) $78 = 7.8 \times 10^n$ (b) $6200 = 6.2 \times 10^n$ (c) $36\,000 = 3.6 \times 10^n$
   (d) $3\,875\,000 = 3.875 \times 10^n$

6. Express the following in the form $a \times 10^n$, where $1 \le a < 10$ and $n \in N$.
   (a) $14\,000$ (b) 2684 (c) 39 (d) 475

7. Write the following as natural numbers.
   (a) 2.8×10^2 (b) 3.2×10^5
   (c) 6.215×10^3 (d) 1.8×10

8. Write the following numbers in ascending order.
   (a) 8000 (b) 3.4×10^7 (c) 7.8×10^4 (d) 4.56×10^2 (e) 7.8×10
   (f) $25\,000$ (g) 7800

9. Evaluate the following and write your answer in scientific notation.
   (a) $(3.4 \times 10^3) + (1.2 \times 10^2)$ (b) $(5.6 \times 10^2) + (1.4 \times 10)$
   (c) $(1.6 \times 10^4) - (1.2 \times 10^3)$ (d) $(8.5 \times 10^3) - (3.6 \times 10^2)$

10. Evaluate the following and write your answer in scientific notation.
    (a) $(1.2 \times 10^4) \times (2.3 \times 10^2)$ (b) $(3.6 \times 10^3) \times (4.3 \times 10^2)$
    (c) $(4.8 \times 10^3) \div (2.4 \times 10^2)$ (d) $(1.2 \times 10^7) \div (6 \times 10^3)$

11. Light travels at approximately 290 000 km/sec. How far does it travel in one year?

12. In the table, column A lists seven countries. Column B gives a clue about the population of each country. The population of each country is listed below the table. Using the clues in column B, match each population with the correct country and write it into column C. Write your answers as natural numbers.

Country	Clue	Population
Greece	Just under 10 m	
Ireland	Between 3 m and 4 m	
Italy	Between 55 m and 60 m	
Norway	Just over 4 m	
Portugal	Just over 10 m	
Spain	Between 35 m and 40 m	
United Kingdom	Between 55 m and 60 m but less than Italy	

1.02×10^7 m, 5.7×10^7 m, 5.6×10^7 m, 9.9×10^6 m, 3.8×10^7 m, 4.2×10^6 m, 3.55×10^6 m

13. Evaluate the following (correct to two decimal places where necessary).
    (a) The reciprocal of 20.
    (b) The reciprocal of 14.
    (c) The reciprocal of $\frac{3}{8}$.
    (d) The reciprocal of $\frac{11}{2}$.

14. Estimate the value of the following by rounding each number to the nearest whole number.
    (a) $6.2(5.8 + 4.1)$
    (b) $6.2 \times 5.8 + 4.1$
    (c) $\frac{43.8 - 3.6}{1.2 + 3.6}$
    (d) $\frac{(3.7)^2 + 1.8}{(1.7)^2}$

15. Estimate the following by rounding each number inside the square root to the nearest square number. (a) $\sqrt{23}$ (b) $\sqrt{53}$ (c) $\sqrt{84}$ (d) $\sqrt{110}$

16. Estimate the following.

(a) $(6.8)^2 - \sqrt{17}$

(b) $\sqrt{46} + \frac{(4.7)^2}{5} - \frac{1}{3.9}$

(c) $\frac{6.2 + \sqrt{40}}{(2.1)^2 + 2.7}$

(d) $\sqrt{18} \times \frac{8.03}{2.09} - (2.3)^2$

17. Use your calculator to find the true value of each part of question 16 correct to two decimal places.

18. Matt is paid €14.35 per hour. If he works 6 hours 10 minutes on Monday and 8 hours 40 minutes on Tuesday, estimate his total pay.

19. Niamh has €23.65 credit left on her mobile phone. If calls cost 3.8c per minute, estimate how many minutes credit she has left.

20. The meter on a home heating tank read 1250 litres in December. By the end of January it read 873. The cost of the oil is 73c.

(a) Estimate how many litres of oil were used by rounding the January reading to the nearest 100.

(b) Estimate the total cost of the oil by rounding the cost of the oil to the nearest 10c.

(c) Calculate the exact cost of the oil.

In this chapter, you will learn about:

✦ Expressions with a common factor.
✦ Factorising expressions with four terms.
✦ Factorising quadratic expressions of the form $x^2 + ax + b$.
✦ Factorising the difference of two squares.
✦ Using the difference of two squares in calculations.

REMEMBER

Factors are sets of numbers and/or variables that multiply together to give another number or algebraic expression, e.g. $12 = (3)(4)$; 3 and 4 are the factors of 12.

$12 = (2)(6)$; 2 and 6 are the factors of 12.
$a^2 = (a)(a)$; a and a are the factors of a^2.
$ab = (a)(b)$; a and b are the factors of ab.

Expressions with a common factor

Example 10.1

Factorise the following.

(a) $7x + 21$
(b) $2y^2 + 4y$
(c) $6a^2 - 12a$
(d) $3a^2b - 12ab^2$

Solution

(a) $7x + 21$
$= 7(x + 3)$

Look at the numbers and take out any common factor (in this case, 7).
Remember, 7 multiplied by x is 7x and 7 multiplied by 3 is 21.

(b) $2y^2 + 4y$

$= 2y(y + 2)$ ← The common factor for 2 and 4 is 2. Now look at the variables and see if there are any common variables (in this case, y).

(c) $6a^2 - 12a$

$= 6a(a - 2)$

(d) $3a^2b - 12ab^2$ ← The common factor for 3 and 12 is 3. Common variables are a and b. Remember, $a^2 = (a)(a)$ and $ab = (a)(b)$.

$= 3ab(a - 4b)$

Exercise 10.1

Factorise the following.

1. $2a + 8$
2. $3b + 9$
3. $5x - 25$
4. $10y + 8$
5. $12a + 18$
6. $15b + 30$
7. $4x + 18$
8. $28y + 49$
9. $14c + 21$
10. $9c^2 + 27c$
11. $12d^2 + 36d$
12. $8x^2 - 16$
13. $4y^2 + y$
14. $4m - 16m^2$

15. $24p^2 + 10p$
16. $35m^2 + 42m$
17. $45n^2 + 90n$
18. $18a - 24a^2$
19. $b - b^2$
20. $2xy + x$
21. $bd - 3bd^2$
22. $15ac - 10c^2$
23. $7xy + 14xy^2$
24. $20w^2 - 30wxy$
25. $7c^3d^2 - 14c^2d^3$
26. $x^2y - xy^2$
27. $3mn^2 - 7m^2n$
28. $30yb + 42b^2$

29. $20pq - (pq)^2$
30. $-6p^2q + 9pq$
31. $3ab - 9ad + 6ac$
32. $-18uv^2 + 6uv - 12v$
33. $xy - y - yxz$
34. $-a^2 - a + ab$
35. $6y^2 + 4y - 2yp$
36. $9x^2 - 12x + 3x^3$
37. $2x^2y + 8xy - 12xy^2$
38. $25a^2b + 5ab - 10a^2b^2$
39. $2p^2q + 3pq^2 + 5pq$
40. $5a^2b + 15ab^2 - 200a^2b^2$

Factorising expressions with four terms

Many expressions consisting of four terms may be factorised by grouping the four terms into two pairs, where each pair has a common factor.

Example 10.2

Factorise the following.

(a) $2ac + ad + 2bc + bd$ (b) $3m + ck + cm + 3k$

(c) $4a^2 - 8a + ab - 2b$ (d) $xy + x - y^2 - y$

Solution

(a) $2ac + ad + 2bc + bd$

| Break the four terms into two pairs. Take out the common terms from each pair. The terms inside the two brackets should be identical. Factorise out the common bracket. |

$= a(2c + d) + b(2c + d)$

$= (2c + d)(a + b)$

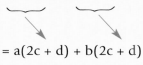

(b) $3m + ck + cm + 3k$

pair

| When picking a pair of terms at the start, it will not always be possible to take the first two terms. When this happens, try to pair any of the other terms together. |

$= 3(m + k) + c(m + k)$

$= (m + k)(3 + c)$

(c) $4a^2 - 8a + ab - 2b$

$= 4a(a - 2) + b(a - 2)$

$= (a - 2)(4a + b)$

| Be careful when you have a minus sign outside the bracket, as this will change the sign of the terms inside the bracket. |

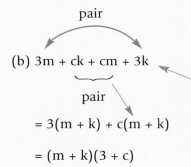

(d) $xy + x - y^2 - y$

$= x(y + 1) - y(y + 1)$

$= (y + 1)(x - y)$

Exercise 10.2

Factorise the following.

1. $2x + bx + 2y + by$
2. $xy + px - by - bp$
3. $3a^2 + 3ab + 8a + 8b$
4. $5x^2 + 10a + 2ab + bx^2$
5. $y^2 + 2yb + 4b + 2y$
6. $p^2 - 3p + 2pq - 6q$
7. $mn + 2pn + 3m + 6p$
8. $y^2 + y + vy + v$
9. $2a^2 - 3b - a + 6ab$
10. $ab - a + b - 1$
11. $xy + x + y + 1$
12. $3x^2 - 15x + 2ax - 10a$
13. $2p^2 + 4p + qp + 2q$
14. $x^2 + x + ax + a$
15. $14b^2 + 7b + 2bc + c$

16. $4y^2 - 8y + yp - 2p$
17. $4a^2 + 28a + 3ab + 21b$
18. $3m - 6n + xm - 2nx$
19. $2a - 4 + 4ax - 8x$
20. $2x - 8y + x^2 - 4xy$
21. $p + 1 + pq + q$
22. $m - mn + 1 - n$
23. $2p^2 + 3a + ap + 6p$
24. $ap - bq - aq + bp$
25. $2ac - 3bd - ad + 6bc$
26. $-ab - mc - mb - ac$
27. $p^2q + 2pq^2 - 3pr - 6qr$
28. $4a^3 + 8a^2 + 4a + 8$
29. $5x^3y + 10xy^3 - 18x^2 - 36y^2$
30. $k^2p + k^2q + l2p + l2q$

Factorising quadratic expressions of the form x² + ax + b

Method 1

Factorise trinomials by breaking the linear term into two different terms and then factorise by grouping.

Example 10.3

Factorise $x^2 + 5x + 4$.

Solution

$x^2 + 5x + 4$

$$4 \times 1 \qquad -4 \times -1$$

$$2 \times 2 \qquad -2 \times -2$$

$x^2 + 4x + 1x + 4$

$x(x + 4) + 1(x + 4)$

$(x + 4)(x + 1)$

> Write all the factors of 4. Only one of these sets will add up to give the middle term (in this case, 4 + 1 = 5). Now break the 5x into 4x + x.

> Factorise this expression by breaking it up into two groups, as in Example 10.2.

Example 10.4

Factorise $x^2 - 5x + 6$.

Solution

$x^2 - 5x + 6$

$$6 \times 1 \qquad -6 \times -1$$

$$2 \times 3 \qquad -2 \times -3$$

$x^2 - 2x - 3x + 6$

$x(x - 2) - 3(x - 2)$

$(x - 2)(x - 3)$

> Write all the factors of 6.
> $-2 + -3 = -5$, the middle term.

> Remember to watch for the minus sign outside the bracket, as this will change the signs inside the bracket.

Example 10.5

Factorise $x^2 + 2x - 8$.

$x^2 + 2x - 8$

$$-1 \times 8 \qquad 1 \times -8$$
$$-2 \times 4 \qquad 2 \times -4$$

Write all the factors of -8.
$-2 + 4 = 2$, the middle term.

$x^2 - 2x + 4x - 8$
$x(x - 2) + 4(x - 2)$
$(x - 2)(x + 4)$

Exercise 10.3

Factorise the following.

1. $x^2 + 3x + 2$
2. $x^2 + 5x + 6$
3. $a^2 + 7a + 10$
4. $y^2 + 10y + 21$
5. $b^2 + 7b + 12$
6. $y^2 + 14y + 40$
7. $x^2 + 2x + 1$
8. $a^2 + 8a + 15$
9. $y^2 + 10y + 9$
10. $p^2 + 9p + 14$
11. $a^2 + 7a + 10$
12. $p^2 + 14p + 45$
13. $q^2 + 9q + 18$
14. $m^2 + 10m + 21$
15. $n^2 + 5n + 4$
16. $y^2 + 9a + 14$
17. $b^2 + 15b + 14$
18. $a^2 + 10a + 21$

19. $c^2 + 6c + 9$
20. $d^2 + 17d + 42$
21. $x^2 - 6x + 5$
22. $y^2 - 7y + 12$
23. $y^2 - 8y + 15$
24. $m^2 - 11m + 18$
25. $p^2 + 10p + 25$
26. $x^2 - 13x + 30$
27. $b^2 - 8b + 7$
28. $d^2 - 12d + 27$
29. $c^2 - 13c + 42$
30. $a^2 + a - 2$
31. $x^2 + 2x - 15$
32. $b^2 - 14b + 33$
33. $a^2 - a - 20$
34. $x^2 - 10x + 24$
35. $p^2 - 7p - 18$
36. $y^2 - 6y - 40$

37. $c^2 - 2c - 3$
38. $a^2 - 9a - 36$
39. $x^2 - 6x - 16$
40. $y^2 - 16$ (Hint: This could be written as $y^2 + 0y - 16$)
41. $x^2 - x - 12$
42. $a^2 - a - 2$
43. $b^2 - 3b - 70$
44. $d^2 - 4d - 5$
45. $y^2 - 4y - 12$
46. $g^2 - 6g - 16$
47. $h^2 - 7h - 8$
48. $x^2 - 5x - 6$
49. $y^2 + 13y - 30$
50. $a^2 + 7a - 18$

The difference of two squares

Before you begin to factorise this type of expression, you must be able to recognise the square numbers.

$1^2 = 1$	$6^2 = 36$	$11^2 = 121$	$16^2 = 256$
$2^2 = 4$	$7^2 = 49$	$12^2 = 144$	$17^2 = 289$
$3^2 = 9$	$8^2 = 64$	$13^2 = 169$	$18^2 = 324$
$4^2 = 16$	$9^2 = 81$	$14^2 = 196$	$19^2 = 361$
$5^2 = 25$	$10^2 = 100$	$15^2 = 225$	$20^2 = 400$

The formula for factorising the difference of two squares is:

$$a^2 - b^2 = (a + b)(a - b)$$

Multiply $(a + b)(a - b) = a^2 - ab + ab - b^2$
$$= a^2 - b^2$$

Any expression of the form $a^2 - b^2$ is called the difference of two squares, i.e. one variable squared minus another variable squared.

Example 10.6

Factorise $x^2 - 25$.

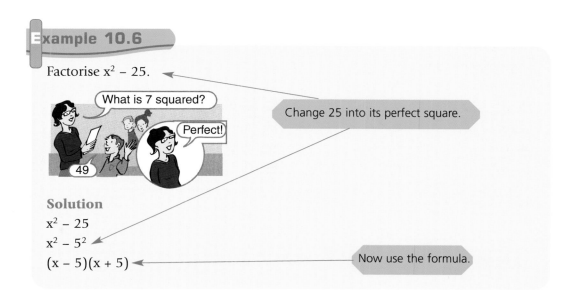

What is 7 squared?

Perfect!

49

Change 25 into its perfect square.

Solution
$x^2 - 25$
$x^2 - 5^2$
$(x - 5)(x + 5)$

Now use the formula.

173

Example 10.7

Factorise $9 - y^2$.

Solution

$9 - y^2$

$3^2 - y^2$

$(3 - y)(3 + y)$

Change 9 to its perfect square.

Example 10.8

Factorise $4a^2 - 121$.

Solution

$4a^2 - 121$

$(2a)^2 - 11^2$

$(2a - 11)(2a + 11)$

Change both 4 and 121 to their perfect squares.

Exercise 10.4

Factorise the following.

1. $x^2 - 81$
2. $a^2 - 64$
3. $b^2 - 100$
4. $y^2 - 225$
5. $m^2 - 144$

6. $49 - p^2$
7. $196 - x^2$
8. $25 - p^2$
9. $36 - c^2$
10. $121 - d^2$

11. $25x^2 - 81$
12. $16y^2 - 169$
13. $4p^2 - 1$
14. $16v^2 - w^2$
15. $9a^2 - 25b^2$

16. $1 - x^2$
17. $1 - 49y^2$
18. $16k^2 - 1$
19. $400r^2 - 1$
20. $1 - 324y^2$

Using the difference of two squares in calculations

$$a^2 - b^2 = (a - b)(a + b)$$

Example 10.9

Find the value of $25^2 - 20^2$ by using factors.

Solution
$25^2 - 20^2$
$(25 - 20)(25 + 20)$
$(5)(45) = 225$

Example 10.10

Calculate $1001^2 - 999^2$ by using factors.

Solution
$1001^2 - 999^2$
$(1001 - 999)(1001 + 999)$
$(2)(2000) = 4000$

Exercise 10.5

Use the difference of two squares to calculate the following.

1. $11^2 - 9^2$
2. $101^2 - 99^2$
3. $999^2 - 1001^2$
4. $25^2 - 5^2$
5. $1000^2 - 900^2$
6. $799^2 - 801^2$
7. $6.3^2 - 0.7^2$
8. $9.1^2 - 0.9^2$
9. $6.4^2 - 5.6^2$
10. $10\ 000 - 9^2$
11. $6561 - 6241$
12. $36^2 - 36$

Exercise 10.6 (Chapter summary)

1. Factorise the following.
   (a) $9x + 15$ (b) $20y + 50$ (c) $8m + 32$ (d) $2a^2 + 8a$
   (e) $14b^2 - 35b$ (f) $xy - ax$ (g) $54 - 45a^2$ (h) $21b^2 - 42b$
   (i) $cd^2 - cd$ (j) $27 - 12m$

2. Factorise the following.
   (a) $3a^2 - 15a + 2ab - 10b$ (b) $b^2 + b + bc + c$
   (c) $d^2 - d + de - e$ (d) $xy + px - yq - pq$
   (e) $3a^2 - 15a + 2ba - 10b$ (f) $x^2 - 2x - xy + 2y$
   (g) $m^2 + m + mn + n$ (h) $4x^2 + 4xy + 7x + 7y$
   (i) $px - qx + pb - bq$ (j) $cd + 2gc + 3d + 6g$

3. Factorise the following.
   (a) $a^2 + 13a + 42$ (b) $b^2 + 7b + 6$ (c) $c^2 + 19c + 88$
   (d) $d^2 - 4d + 4$ (e) $e^2 - 8e + 15$ (f) $f^2 - 16f + 64$
   (g) $g^2 + 14g + 24$ (h) $h^2 + 6h - 7$ (i) $k^2 + 4k - 32$
   (j) $m^2 - 9m - 70$

4. Factorise the following.
   (a) $x^2 - 49$ (b) $4y^2 - 25$ (c) $9a^2 - 36b^2$
   (d) $225m^2 - 196n^2$ (e) $100p^2 - 1$ (f) $1 - 64q^2$
   (g) $4x^2 - 144y^2$ (h) $49y^2 - 100x^2$ (i) $a^2 - 169b^2$
   (j) $9e^2 - 1$

Algebra 2 **11**

In this chapter, you will learn about:

✦ Solving simultaneous equations.

✦ Solving quadratic equations with two terms.

✦ Solving quadratic equations with three terms.

Solving simultaneous equations

Equations with two or more variables are called simultaneous equations.

Example 11.1

Solve the simultaneous equation:

$x + y = 5$

$x - y = 3$

Solution

$x + y = 5$

$\underline{x - y = 3}$ ← Eliminate one variable by adding both equations.

$2x \quad = 8$

$\Rightarrow x = \frac{8}{2}$

$\Rightarrow x = 4$

$x + y = 5$ ← Choose any one of the two equations and substitute your new value for x.

Substitute $x = 4$

$\Rightarrow (4) + y = 5$

$\Rightarrow y = 5 - 4$

$\Rightarrow y = 1$

$x = 4$ and $y = 1$

177

Example 11.2

Solve the simultaneous equations:

$2x + 3y = 13$

$x - 2y = 3$

To eliminate the variable y in this example, we must multiply **all** the parts of each equation by a number that will make both coefficients the same.

Solution

$[2x + 3y = 13] \, (\times 2) \; \Rightarrow \; 4x + 6y = 26$

$[x - 2y = 3] \, (\times 3) \; \Rightarrow \; 3x - 6y = 9$

$ 7x = 35$

Adding both equations.

$\Rightarrow \quad x = \dfrac{35}{7}$

$\Rightarrow \quad x = 5$

$2x + 3y = 13$

Substitute $x = 5$

Pick either of the two original equations.

$2(5) + 3y = 13$

Substitute in the new value for x.

$\Rightarrow 10 + 3y = 13$

$\Rightarrow \quad\quad 3y = 13 - 10$

$\Rightarrow \quad\quad 3y = 3$

$\quad\quad\quad\; y = 1$

$\quad\quad x = 5 \text{ and } y = 1$

Example 11.3

Solve the simultaneous equations:

$2x = 1 - 5y$

$3x + 2y = 7$

Solution

$2x = 1 - 5y \Rightarrow 2x + 5y = 1$

Bring both variables to the LHS of the equals sign.

$2x + 5y \; = 1$

$3x + 2y \; = 7$

$[2x + 5y \; = 1] \, (\times 2)$

$[3x + 2y \; = 7] \, (\times 5)$

To eliminate the variable y in this example, we must multiply **all** parts of each equation by a number that will make both coefficients the same.

$4x + 10y = 2$

$15x + 10y = 35$

$-4x - 10y = -2$

$15x + 10y = 35$

Now subtract the two equations by changing the signs on **all** parts of either one of the equations.

$11x = 33$

$\Rightarrow x = \dfrac{33}{11}$

$\Rightarrow x = 3$

$2x = 1 - 5y$

Substitute $x = 3$

$2(3) = 1 - 5y$

$\Rightarrow 6 = 1 - 5y$

$\Rightarrow 6 - 1 = -5y$

$\Rightarrow 5 = -5y$

$\dfrac{5}{-5} = y$

$\Rightarrow y = -1$

Pick either of the two original equations.

Exercise 11.1

Solve the following simultaneous equations.

1. $x - y = 4$
   $x + y = 8$
2. $x + y = 5$
   $x - y = 9$
3. $x + y = 4$
   $x - y = 2$
4. $x + y = 24$
   $x - y = 10$
5. $x + 3y = 13$
   $x - 3y = -11$
6. $x + 5y = 18$
   $2x - 5y = -9$
7. $9x + 6y = 15$
   $x + 6y = 7$
8. $x + y = 3$
   $2x + y = 5$
9. $4x + y = 14$
   $4x - 3y = 22$
10. $3x - 2y = 6$
    $2x - y = 5$
11. $x - y = 3$
    $x + 2y = 9$
12. $x + 2y = 9$
    $x - 2y = 5$
13. $x + y = 8$
    $x - y = 2$
14. $x + 2y = 10$
    $5x + 2y = 26$

15. $2x - y = 10$
    $x + 3y = 5$
16. $4x + 5y = 9$
    $3x - y = 2$
17. $4x - 3y = 14$
    $2x - 3y = 4$
18. $2x + 3y = 13$
    $3x + 2y = 12$
19. $3x + 5y = 31$
    $2x + 3y = 19$
20. $3x + 4y = 17$
    $x + 4y = 11$
21. $2x - y = 12$
    $2x + 3y = 4$
22. $3x + 4y = 18$
    $4x - 3y = -1$
23. $4x - y = 5$
    $2x + y = -2$
24. $4x - 3y = 15$
    $2x + 3y = 3$
25. $y = x + 1$
    $x + y = 5$
26. $13x + 5y = 31$
    $x + 3y = 5$
27. $2x - 3y = 6$
    $4x + 2y = -4$
28. $6x + 5y = 12$
    $3x - 2y = 6$

29. $y = 3x$
    $x - y = 8$
30. $x = 2y$
    $x - y = 6$
31. $y = 3x$
    $x + y = 20$
32. $4x = 8y$
    $2x + 2y = 12$
33. $4x + 6y = 12$
    $2x - 3y = 6$
34. $2x + 5y = 10$
    $3x - 3y = -6$
35. $2x + 3y = 12$
    $4y = 10 - 2x$
36. $6 - 5y = 2x$
    $3x = 2 - 4y$
37. $2x = 6 - 4y$
    $4x = -3y - 3$
38. $5x = 75 - 4y$
    $4y = 54 - 2x$
39. $3x + 5y = 21$
    $5x - 3y = 1$
40. $7x + 2y = 11$
    $3x + 5y = 13$

Solving quadratic equations with two terms

REMEMBER

- Solving equations means finding values for x that make the mathematical statement true.
- If A × B = 0, then either A = 0 or B = 0 or A and B are both 0.

To solve quadratic equations:

1. Move all terms to the left-hand side so that the equation equals 0.
2. Factorise the equation on the left-hand side.
3. Set each factor equal to 0.
4. Solve the linear equations from step 3.

Example 11.4

Solve each of the following.

(a) $(x - 1)(x + 7) = 0$ (b) $x(x + 5) = 0$ (c) $x^2 + 4x$ (d) $x^2 - 25 = 0$

Solution

(a) $(x - 1)(x + 7) = 0$ ⟵ This is already factorised (step 2).

     either $x - 1 = 0$ or $x + 7 = 0$

     $\Rightarrow x = 1$ or $x = -7$ ⟵ Quadratics will generally have two values for x.

(b) $x(x + 5) = 0$

     either $x = 0$ or $x + 5 = 0$

     $\Rightarrow x = 0$ or $x = -5$

(c) $x^2 + 4x = 0$

     $\Rightarrow x(x + 4) = 0$ ⟵ Factorise the left-hand side (step 1).

     either $x = 0$ or $x + 4 = 0$

     $\Rightarrow x = 0$ or $x = -4$

(d) $x^2 - 25 = 0$ ⟵ Difference of two squares.

     $\Rightarrow x^2 - 5^2 = 0$ ⟵ Factorise.

     $\Rightarrow (x - 5)(x + 5) = 0$

     either $x - 5 = 0$ or $x + 5 = 0$

     $\Rightarrow x = 5$ or $x = -5$

Exercise 11.2

Solve each of the following.

1. $(x - 2)(x + 3) = 0$

2. $(x + 4)(x - 10) = 0$

3. $(y - 2)(y + 1) = 0$

4. $(y + 4)(y + 1) = 0$

5. $(y + 4)(y - 4) = 0$

6. $(3 - p)(p + 2) = 0$

7. $(m - 1)(m + 5) = 0$

8. $(8 - a)(a + 2) = 0$

9. $b(b + 8) = 0$

10. $c(1 - c) = 0$

11. $4w(w + 2) = 0$

12. $(z - 1)z = 0$

13. $(4 - x)(x + 4) = 0$

14. $(a + 6)(a + 11) = 0$

15. $(25 - e)(5 + e) = 0$

16. $(f - 1)(f + 1) = 0$

17. $x^2 + 5x = 0$

18. $p^2 - 9x = 0$

19. $m^2 - 3m = 0$

20. $6q - q^2 = 0$

21. $a^2 + a = 0$

22. $b^2 - 7b = 0$

23. $18c - 6c^2 = 0$

24. $15y^2 + 25y = 0$

25. $4d - 12d^2 = 0$

26. $3c^2 + 16c = 0$

27. $x^2 - 4 = 0$

28. $y^2 - 9 = 0$

29. $b^2 - 25 = 0$

30. $a^2 - 1 = 0$

31. $121 - c^2 = 0$

32. $9x^2 - 9 = 0$

33. $4p^2 - 64 = 0$

34. $p^2 - 16 = 0$

35. $36 - x^2 = 0$

Solving quadratic equations with three terms

Example 11.5

Solve each of the following.

(a) $x^2 + 5x + 6 = 0$ (b) $y^2 - 9x + 18 = 0$ (c) $p^2 + 10p = 24$

Solution

(a) $x^2 + 5x + 6 = 0$ Factorise – write out all factors of 6.

      1×6 -1×-6 One set of factors will add up to give the

      2×3 -2×-3 middle number 5, i.e. 2 + 3.

$\Rightarrow x^2 + 2x + 3x + 6 = 0$ Break the middle term into two factors.

$\Rightarrow x(x + 2) + 3(x + 2) = 0$ Factorise by grouping.

$\Rightarrow (x + 2)(x + 3) = 0$

either $x + 2 = 0$ or $x + 3 = 0$

$\Rightarrow x = -2$ or $x = -3$

(b) $y^2 - 9y + 18 = 0$ Write out all factors of 18.

      18×1 -18×-1

      9×2 -9×-2 Look for factors that add up to give –9,

      6×3 -6×-3 i.e. $-6 + -3 = -9$.

$\Rightarrow y^2 - 6y - 3y + 18 = 0$

$\Rightarrow y(y - 6) - 3(y - 6) = 0$ Remember, the minus sign outside the

$\Rightarrow (y - 6)(y - 3) = 0$ bracket will change the sign of the

either $y - 6 = 0$ or $y - 3 = 0$ number inside the bracket.

$\Rightarrow y = 6$ or $y = 3$

                               Move over to LHS.

(c) $a^2 + 10a = 24$

$\Rightarrow a^2 + 10a - 24 = 0$ Write out all factors of –24.

$\Rightarrow a^2 - 2a + 12a - 24 = 0$ -1×24 -2×12 -3×8 -4×6

$\Rightarrow a(a - 2) + 12(a - 2) = 0$ 1×-24 2×-12 3×-8 4×-6

$\Rightarrow (a - 2)(a + 12) = 0$

either $(a - 2) = 0$ or $(a + 12) = 0$

$\Rightarrow a = 2$ or $a = -12$

Exercise 11.3

Solve the following equations.

1. $x^2 + 3x + 2 = 0$
2. $x^2 + 9x + 8 = 0$
3. $x^2 + 8x + 12 = 0$
4. $x^2 + 7x + 10 = 0$
5. $y^2 + 6y + 9 = 0$
6. $y^2 + 5y + 4 = 0$
7. $y^2 + 20y + 36 = 0$
8. $p^2 + 19p + 70 = 0$
9. $p^2 - 4p + 4 = 0$
10. $p^2 - 12p + 27 = 0$
11. $a^2 - 15a + 56 = 0$
12. $a^2 - 13a + 22 = 0$
13. $a^2 - 13a + 36 = 0$
14. $p^2 - p - 6 = 0$
15. $p^2 - 2p - 48 = 0$
16. $p^2 - p - 30 = 0$
17. $p^2 - 6p - 7 = 0$
18. $p^2 - 5p - 14 = 0$
19. $p^2 - 5p = 50$
20. $p^2 - 5p = 6$
21. $a^2 + a - 12 = 0$
22. $a^2 + a - 2 = 0$
23. $a^2 + 3a - 18 = 0$
24. $a^2 + 3a = 54$
25. $a^2 + 5a = 14$
26. $a^2 + 5a = 24$
27. $a^2 + 6a = 16$
28. $a^2 + 8a = 105$
29. $a^2 + 10a - 24 = 0$
30. $a^2 + 10a = 39$
31. $2x^2 - 3x - 10 = 10 - 2x + x^2$
32. $x^2 + x - 5 = 3 - x$
33. $y^2 - 2y - 4 = 10 + 3y$
34. $a^2 + 1 = 6 - 4a$
35. $2a^2 - 4a = 24 - 2a + a^2$

Exercise 11.4   (Chapter summary)

1. Solve the following simultaneous equations.

   (a) $x + y = 20$
   $x - y = 4$

   (b) $x - y = 7$
   $x + y = 11$

   (c) $5x - y = 8$
   $3x + y = 16$

   (d) $4x - 3y = 14$
   $2x - 3y = 4$

   (e) $3x + 2y = 20$
   $3x + 4y = 34$

   (f) $3x + 5y = 26$
   $2x + 3y = 16$

(g) $3x + 2y = 13$
$2x + 3y = 7$
(h) $7x - 4y = 8$
$3x - 5y = -13$
(i) $3x + 2y = 21$
$2x - y = 7$

(j) $6x + 5y = 12$
$3x - 2y = 6$
(k) $8x = y$
$x - y = 49$
(l) $6x = y$
$x = 25 + y$

2. Solve the following quadratic equations.
   (a) $(x - 4)(2 + x) = 0$
   (b) $(x + 5)(x - 5) = 0$
   (c) $(x + 7)(x - 1) = 0$
   (d) $(x + 2)(x + 2) = 0$
   (e) $x(x + 3) = 0$
   (f) $x(5 - x) = 0$
   (g) $x(x + 1) = 0$
   (h) $5x + x^2 = 0$
   (i) $x^2 + 2x = 0$
   (j) $x^2 - 6x = 0$
   (k) $x^2 - 49 = 0$
   (l) $x^2 - 121 = 0$

3. Solve the following quadratic equations.
   (a) $x^2 + 2x + 1 = 0$
   (b) $x^2 - 2x + 1 = 0$
   (c) $x^2 - 10x + 25 = 0$
   (d) $x^2 + 8x + 16 = 0$
   (e) $x^2 - 11x + 18 = 0$
   (f) $x^2 - 8x + 16 = 0$
   (g) $x^2 + 14x + 49 = 0$
   (h) $x^2 - 3x + 2 = 0$
   (i) $x^2 - 14x + 24 = 0$
   (j) $x^2 + 5x - 36 = 0$
   (k) $x^2 + 9x + 20 = 0$
   (l) $x^2 + 13x - 30 = 0$

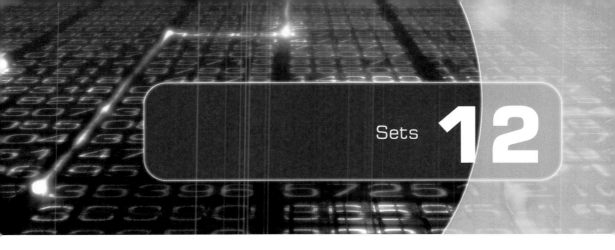

Sets **12**

In this chapter, you will learn about:

+ Terminology of sets.
+ Working with two sets.
+ Working with three sets.
+ Problem solving using two sets.
+ Problem solving using three sets.

Terminology of sets

A set is a collection of clearly defined objects. The objects in a set are called the elements, or members.

Sir, is the group of good basketball players in this class a set ?

For example, the collection of teachers over the age of 30 is a set. It would be clear whether or not a teacher was in the set or not. However, the collection of good-looking teachers would not be a set, since different people would have different ideas of who is good looking, so it would not be clear who was in the set and who was not.

NOTE: A set can be written as a rule or by listing the elements. For example, A = {a, b, c, d} is the list of elements in set A. This set could also be written as the rule A = {the first four letters of the alphabet}.

Term	Pronounced	Means	Example
{ }	Chain brackets	Elements in a set are written between chain brackets, each element written once only.	A = {The whole numbers less than 10} The elements can also be listed A = {0, 1, 2, 3, 4, 5, 6, 7, 8, 9} B = {1, 3, 5, 7, 9, 11, 13, 15, 17, 19} Can you think of a rule for set B? C = {the factors of 9} Can you list the elements of set C? D = {2, 4, 6, 8, 10}
$\in$	Is an element of	The object is in the set.	$7 \in A$
$\notin$	Is **not** an element of	The object is **not** in the set.	$12 \notin A$
$A \cap B$	A intersection B	The objects are in both A and B.	$A \cap B = \{1, 3, 5, 7, 9\}$
$A \cup B$	A union B	The objects are in set A or set B. This means joining two sets together.	$A \cup B = \{0, 1, 2, 3, 4, 5, 6, 7, 8, 9,$ $10, 11, 13, 15, 17, 19\}$
$\varnothing$ or { }	The null set	Any set that has **no** elements.	The set of teachers under the age of 15
$C \subset A$	C is a subset of A	**All** the elements of set C are also in set A.	Is D a subset of A? Explain your answer. NOTE: 1. Every set is a subset of itself. 2. The null set is a subset of every set.
$D \not\subset C$	Set D is NOT a subset of set C	**All** the elements of set D are **not** in set C.	Is A a subset of C? Explain your answer.
#A	Hash A (or the cardinal number/order of set A)	The number of elements that are in set A.	#A = 10 What is #C? What is #D?
A \ B	A less B	The elements of A that are not in B.	$A \setminus B = \{0, 2, 4, 6, 8\}$ What are the elements of B \ A? This is also called 'set difference'.

Example 12.1

A = {the first 4 months of the year}, B = {the letters of the word science},
C = {a, b, c, d, e}. List the elements of the following sets.
(a) A   (b) B   (c) B ∩ C   (d) A ∩ B   (e) B ∪ C   (f) B \ C   (g) C \ B   (h) A ∪ B
(i) Is C ⊂ B? Explain your answer.
(j) d ∈ B, true or false?   (k) a ∉ C, true or false?   (l) What is #B?
(m) What is #C?   (n) What is #B − #A?   (o) What is #(B ∩ C)?

Solution

(a) A = {January, February, March, April}
(b) B = {s, c, i, e, n} ⟵———————— An element is never repeated when listed.
(c) B ∩ C = {c, e}
(d) A ∩ B = { } or ∅ ⟵——— There are no elements in A that are also in B.
(e) B ∪ C = {a, b, c, d, e, n, s, i} ⟵——— The elements left in C after taking away those appearing in B.
(f) C \ B = {a, b, d} ⟵———
(g) B \ C = {s, i, n} ⟵——— The order of elements in a set does not matter. B \ C could have been written as {i, n, s}.
(h) A ∪ B = {January, February, March, April, s, c, i, e, n}
(i) C ⊂ B: False, since all of the elements of C are not in B.
(j) d ∈ B: False, since d is **not** an element of B.
(k) a ∉ C: False, since a **is** an element of C.
(l) #B = 5
(m) #C = 5
(n) #B − #A = 5 − 4 = 1
(o) #(B ∩ C) = 2 ⟵——— This means 'how many elements are in the set B ∩ C?' See part (c).

Exercise 12.1   (This exercise is based on ∈, ∉, ∩, ∪ and ∅)

1. Think of a rule for each of the following sets.
   (a) A = {May, June, July}
   (b) B = {5, 10, 15, 20, 25, 30}
   (c) C = {a, e, i, o, u}
   (d) D = {Ulster, Munster, Leinster, Connacht}
   (e) E = {1, 2, 3, 4, 5}

2. A = {the even numbers between 10 and 20}, B = {11, 13, 15, 17, 19},
   C = {the multiples of 3 between 10 and 20}.
   (a) List the elements of set A.
   (b) Can you think of a rule for set B?
   (c) List the elements of set C.
   (d) List the elements of A ∩ C.
   (e) List the elements of B ∩ C.

3. List the elements of the following sets.
   (a) A = {the vowels of the English alphabet}
   (b) B = {the first seven letters of the English alphabet}
   (c) C = {the factors of 20}
   (d) D = {the prime numbers between 10 and 30}

4. List the elements of the following sets.
   (a) E = {the days of the week}
   (b) F = {the first three months of the year}
   (c) G = {the months which have more than 30 days}
   (d) H = {the numbers between 1 and 40 that can be divided by 6}

5. Write out the rule for the following sets.
   (a) A = {October, November, December}
   (b) B = {20, 22, 24, 26, 28, 30}
   (c) C = {2, 3, 5, 7, 11, 13, 17, 19}
   (d) D = {Ulster, Munster, Leinster, Connacht}

6. State whether each of the following are true or false.
   (a) Monday ∈ {days of the week}
   (b) 5 ∈ {factors of 12}
   (c) e ∈ {the vowels in the English alphabet}
   (d) {3, 4, 5, 6} ∩ {2, 3, 9} = {3, 2}
   (e) 3 ∈ the factors of 9
   (f) May ∈ {the months of the year with
       exactly 30 days}

7. State whether each of the following are true or false.
   (a) April ∈ {days of the week}
   (b) 3 ∈ {the even numbers between 1 and 10}
   (c) g ∈ {the consonants in the English alphabet}
   (d) {2, 7, 8, 9, 10} ∪ {3, 1, 2} = {1, 2, 3, 10, 7, 9, 8}
   (e) 7 ∉ the factors of 9
   (f) 30 ∈ {the multiples of 6}

8. E = {10, 11, 12, 13, 14}, F = {2, 3, 4, 8}. Insert ∈ or ∉ in each of the following.

   (a) 2 __ E   (c) b__ E   (e) 11__ E   (g) $\frac{1}{2}$ of 26 __ E
   (b) 2 __ F   (d) f __ F   (f) 2^3 __ F

9. J = {3, 5, 7, 9, 10, 16}, K = {f, g, h, m}. Insert ∈ or ∉ in each of the following.
   (a) 4 __ J   (e) the fifth letter of the English alphabet __ K
   (b) f __ K   (f) 4^2 __ J
   (c) a __ J   (g) Ø __ K
   (d) 9 __ J

10. A = {the months of the year ending with the letter Y},
    B = {the months of the year}, C = {the first six months of the year},
    D = {the last four months of the year}.
    (a) List the elements of each of the sets A, B, C, D.
    (b) List the elements of (i) A ∪ B   (ii) A ∩ B   (iii) A ∩ C   (iv) A ∪ C.

11. E = {1, 2, 3, 4, 5, 9, 10}, F = {2, 4, 5, 7, 13}, G = {7, 8, 9, 14}. List the elements of the following.
    (a) E ∩ F   (d) E ∪ G
    (b) E ∪ F   (e) F ∩ G
    (c) E ∩ G   (f) F ∪ G

12. J = {the letters of the word ELEMENT}, K = {a, e, i, o, u},
    L = {a, b, c, d, e, f, g}. List the elements of the following.
    (a) J ∩ K   (c) K ∩ L   (e) L \ K   (g) J ∪ K
    (b) J ∪ L   (d) K ∪ L   (f) J ∩ L

13. P = {factors of 24}, Q = {1, 3, 4, 5}, R = {the even numbers between 1 and 11}. List the elements of the following.

    (a) P   (e) Q ∩ R

    (b) R   (f) Q ∪ R

    (c) P ∩ Q   (g) P ∩ R

    (d) P ∪ Q   (h) P ∪ R

14. Give an example of a set that would be a null set.

Term	Pronounced	Means	Example
$x\|x$	The set of all values of x where …	There is a rule next to this which will tell us what elements are in the set.	A = $\{x\|x$ is a month with five letters$\}$. This is an example of a formal, mathematical rule for a set. Can you list the elements of the set?
U	The universal set	The set containing all the elements used in the entire question.	In questions 1 to 6 of exercise 12.2, the universal set is U = {2, 3, 4, 5, 6, 7, 9, 12}.
Venn diagram	Venn	The sets in a question are represented by intersecting circles. Universal set is represented as a rectangle.	U = {1, 2, 3, 4, 8, 9, 10} A = {8, 9, 10}, B = {1, 3, 9}
A′	A complement	Every element in the question except those inside set A. A' is all the elements outside set A.	In the example above, A′ = {1, 2, 3, 4} What is B′? What is (A ∪ B)′? What is (A ∩ B)′?

NOTE: Two sets are equal if they contain exactly the same elements. The order of the elements is not important.

For example, C = {the consonants of the word country}, D = {y, n, c, r, t}, E = {n, r, t, c, y}. In this case, all three sets are equal (C = D = E), since they all contain exactly the same elements

NOTE: Subset. Cork ⊂ Ireland.

Exercise 12.2 (This exercise is based on ∈, ∉, ∩, ∪, Ø, ⊂, ⊄, #, \)

For questions 1 to 6, X = {2, 5, 6}, Y = {3, 4, 5, 6, 7, 12}, Z = {2, 5, 7, 9}, W = {4, 7, 3}, T = {6, 2, 5}.

1. Is Z ⊂ Y? Give a reason for your answer.
2. Is W ⊂ Y? Give a reason for your answer.
3. List the elements of (a) X ∩ Y   (b) Y ∪ Z   (c) Z \ W   (d) Y \ X.
4. What is (a) #X   (b) #Y   (c) #Z   (d) #W   (e) #(X ∩ Y)   (f) #Z \ W?
5. Write down two sets that are equal.
6. Write down four subsets of W.

For questions 7 to 10, A = {g, h, j, k, m}, B = {a, b, c, d}, C = {d, e, f, k, t, y}, D = {m, h, g}, E = {b}, F = {a, e, i, o, u}, G = {h, g, m}, H = {all the consonants of the English alphabet}.

7. List the elements of the following sets.
   (a) A ∩ D   (b) A ∪ D   (c) C ∩ D   (d) C ∪ F   (e) A \ D   (f) D \ A
   (g) C \ F   (h) F \ C
8. Write down the two sets that are equal.
9. Insert either ⊂ or ⊄ in each of the following.
   (a) A __ H   (b) A __ B   (c) E __ B   (d) B __ E   (e) D __ G
   (f) D __ H   (g) Ø __ C
10. Write down (a) #A   (b) #E   (c) #H   (d) #(A ∩ G)   (e) #(C ∪ F)
    (f) # A \ D   (g) #H \ A.

For questions 11 to 14, J = {1, 2, 3, 4, 5, 6, 7, 8, 9}, K = {5, 9}, L = {4, 6, 8, 10}, M = {9, 5}, N = {8, 9, 10, 11, 12}, O = {3}, P = {8, 10}, H = {all the even numbers between 1 and 21}.

11. List the elements of the following sets.

    (a) J ∩ N   (b) J ∪ K   (c) L ∩ M   (d) O ∪ P   (e) N \ P   (f) J \ K

    (g) L \ J   (h) J \ O

12. Write down the two sets that are equal.

13. Insert either ⊂ or ⊄ in each of the following.

    (a) J __ K   (b) K __ J   (c) K __ M   (d) L __ H   (e) O __ H

    (f) P __ H   (g) Ø __ J

14. Write down (a) #J   (b) #K   (c) #O   (d) #(J ∩ N)   (e) #(J ∪ K)

    (f) # N \ P   (g) # J \ O.

Working with two sets

Example 12.2

U = {a, b, c, d, e, f, g, h, o, u}, A = {a, d, f, g, o, u}, B = {b, c, d, f}.

(a) Represent U, A and B using a Venn diagram.

(b) List the elements of the following. (i) A′   (ii) A ∩ B   (iii) A \ B   (iv) B \ A
     (v) A ∪ B   (vi) (A ∪ B)′.

(c) What is (i) #A   (ii) #B   (iii) #B \ A   (iv) #U \ (A ∪ B)?

Solution

(a)

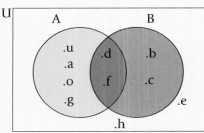

(b) (i) A′ = {b, c, e, h}   (iii) A \ B = {a, g, o, u}   (v) A ∪ B = {a, b, c, d, f, g, o, u}

(ii) A ∩ B = {d, f}   (iv) B \ A = {b, c}   (vi) (A ∪ B)′ = {e, h}

(c) (i) #A = 6   (iii) #B \ A = 2

(ii) #B = 4   (iv) #U \ (A ∪ B) = 2

1. A = {4, 5, 6, 7}, B = {3, 6, 9}.
   (a) Represent A and B on a Venn diagram.
   (b) List the elements of (i) A \ B   (ii) A ∩ B   (iii) A ∪ B.

2. C = {e, f, g, h, k}, D = {a, b, f, g}.
   (a) Represent C and D on a Venn diagram.
   (b) List the elements of (i) C \ D   (ii) C ∩ D   (iii) C ∪ D.

3. U = {1, 2, 3, 4, 5, 6}, E = {6, 1}, F = {1, 2, 5}.
   (a) Represent U, E and F using a Venn diagram.
   (b) List the elements of (i) E ∩ F   (ii) E ∪ F   (iii) E′   (iv) F′   (v) (E ∩ F)′.

4. U = {a, b, c, d, e, f}, G = {a, b, c, f}, H = {a, d}.
(a) Represent U, G and H on a Venn diagram.
(b) List the elements of (i) G ∩ H   (ii) G ∪ H   (iii) G′   (iv) H′   (v) (G ∪ H)′.

5. U = {1, 2, 3, 4, 5, 6, 9, 12, 18}, J = {x|x is a factor of 18},
K = {1, 2, 3, 4, 5, 6}.
(a) Represent U, J and K using a Venn diagram.
(b) List the elements of (i) J   (ii) J′   (iii) J ∩ K   (iv) (J ∩ K)′.

6. Using the Venn diagram below, answer the following questions.

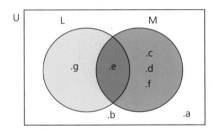

(a) List the elements of (i) L   (ii) M   (iii) L ∩ M   (iv) L ∪ M   (v) L′.
(b) What is (i) #L   (ii) #M \ L   (iii) #M′?

7. Using the Venn diagram below, answer the following questions.

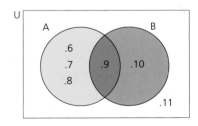

(a) List the elements of (i) A   (ii) B   (iii) A ∩ B   (iv) A ∪ B   (v) B′.
(b) What is (i) #B   (ii) #A \ B   (iii) #A′?

8. Using the diagram below, state whether the following are true or false.

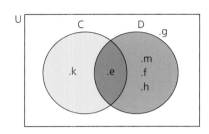

(a) k ∈ D   (d) e ∈ (C ∩ D)   (g) {m, f, k} ⊂ D   (j) #U \ C = 3.
(b) k ∈ U   (e) #C = 1   (h) U \ D = {k, g}
(c) f ∈ D   (f) #(C ∪ D) = 6   (i) C = {k}

9. U = {Derry, Donegal, Dublin, Antrim, Armagh, Cork, Down, Fermanagh, Tyrone, Laois, Monaghan, Leitrim, Cavan}, E = {x|x is a county in Ulster}, F = {Donegal, Antrim, Tyrone, Laois, Dublin, Cork}.
   (a) Represent this information on a Venn diagram.
   (b) List the following sets: (i) E   (ii) E ∩ F   (iii) E'   (iv) (E ∪ F)'.

10. U = {France, Brazil, Germany, Peru, Italy, USA, Japan, India}, G = {France, Peru, USA, India}, H = {Brazil, Italy, Japan}.
   (a) Represent this information on a Venn diagram.
   (b) List the following sets: (i) G \ H   (ii) G ∩ H   (iii) G'   (iv) (G ∪ H)'.

11. U = {1, 2, 3, 4, 5, 6, 9, 12, 15, 18}, A = {the first five multiples of 3}, B = {the factors of 18}.
   (a) List the elements of (i) A   (ii) B.
   (b) Represent these sets on a Venn diagram.
   (c) List the elements of (i) A ∪ B   (ii) B'   (iii) B \ A.

Working with three sets

Example 12.3

$U = \{1, 2, 3, 4, 5, 6, 7, 8, 9, 10, 11, 12, 13\}$, $A = \{1, 3, 6, 10, 12\}$, $B = \{3, 4, 9, 11, 12\}$, $C = \{1, 3, 5, 6, 7, 11, 13\}$.

(a) Represent these sets on a Venn diagram.

(b) List the elements of the following.

(i) A'	(iv) $B \setminus (A \cup C)$	(vii) $U \setminus (A \cup C)$
(ii) $A \cap B \cap C$	(v) $B \cup C$	(viii) $B \cap C$
(iii) $A \setminus B$	(vi) $(A \cup B)'$	(ix) $(B \cap C) \setminus A$

(c) What is (i) $\#C \setminus B$ (ii) $\#C \setminus (A \cup B)$ (iii) $\#U \setminus (A \cup B)$?

Solution

(a)

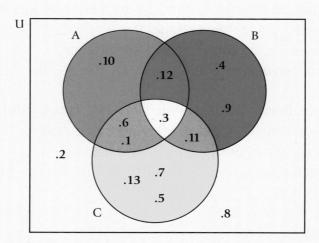

(b) (i) $A' = \{4, 9, 11, 5, 7, 13, 2, 8\}$
 (ii) $A \cap B \cap C = \{3\}$
 (iii) $A \setminus B = \{1, 6, 10\}$
 (iv) $B \setminus (A \cup C) = \{4, 9\}$
 (v) $B \cup C = \{1, 6, 3, 12, 11, 4, 9, 5, 13, 7\}$

(vi) $(A \cup B)' = \{5, 13, 7, 2, 8\}$
(vii) $U \setminus (A \cup C) = \{4, 9, 2, 8\}$
(viii) $B \cap C = \{3, 11\}$
(ix) $(B \cap C) \setminus A = \{11\}$

(c) (i) $\#C \setminus B = 5$
 (ii) $\#C \setminus (A \cup B) = 3$
 (iii) $\#U \setminus (A \cup B) = 5$

Exercise 12.4

1. Using the Venn diagram below, answer the questions that follow.

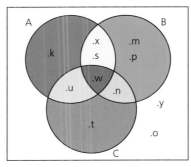

(a) List the elements of the following.

(i) A　　　　　　　(iv) A \ C　　　　(vii) (B ∪ C)′　　　　(x) (A ∪ B) \ C

(ii) C　　　　　　　(v) C \ (A ∪ B)　　(viii) U \ (A ∪ B)

(iii) A ∩ B ∩ C　　(vi) B ∪ C　　　　(ix) A ∩ B

(b) What is (i) #A \ B　(ii) #C \ (A ∪ B)　(iii) #U \ (B ∪ C)?

2. U = {4, 5, 6, 7, 8, 9, 10, 11, 12, 13, 14, 15}, X = {4, 8, 9, 12, 14, 15}, Y = {4, 7, 9, 11, 15}, Z = {6, 9, 11, 12, 13, 14}.

(a) Represent this information on a Venn diagram.

(b) List the following sets.

(i) X ∩ Y　　　　　　(iii) X ∪ Y　　　　　(v) X \ Y　　　　　(vii) X \ (Y\Z)

(ii) (X ∩ Y) \ Z　　(iv) (Y ∪ Z)′　　　(vi) X \ (Y ∪ Z)　(viii) X′ ∩ Y′

3. Using the Venn diagram below, answer the questions that follow.

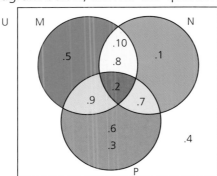

(a) List the elements of the following.

(i) M   (iv) N \ P   (vii) (M ∪ N)′   (x) (M ∩ P) \ N

(ii) N   (v) M \ (N ∪ P)   (viii) U \ (M ∪ P)

(iii) M ∩ N ∩ P   (vi) M ∪ P   (ix) M ∩ P

(b) What is (i) #P \ N   (ii) #N \ (M ∪ P)   (iii) #U \ (M ∪ N)?

4. U = {a, b, c, d, e, f, g, m}, D = {b, e, f}, E = {c, e, f, g}, F = {e, m}.

(a) Represent this information on a Venn diagram.

(b) List the following sets.

(i) D ∩ E   (iii) D ∪ F   (v) U \ E   (vii) D \ (E \ F)

(ii) (D ∩ E) \ F   (iv) (D ∪ E ∪ F)′   (vi) E \ (D ∪ F)

(c) What is (i) #(D ∪ E)   (ii) #D \ F?

5. Draw out the Venn diagram below five times and shade in each of the following areas.

(a) (B ∩ C) \ A   (b) C \ (A ∪ B)   (c) (A ∪ C)′   (d) A ∩ C   (e) (C \ A) \ B

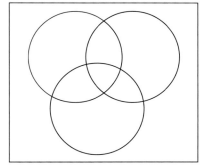

6. U = {7, 8, 9, 10, 11, 12, 13, 14, 15, 16}, X = {8, 12, 14, 15},
Y = {7, 11, 12, 14}, Z = {9, 11, 12, 15, 16}.

(a) Represent this information on a Venn diagram.

(b) List the following sets.

(i) Y ∩ Z   (iii) X ∪ Y   (v) X \ Y   (vii) (X \ Y) \ Z

(ii) (X ∩ Y) \ Z   (iv) (Y ∪ Z)′   (vi) X \ (Y ∪ Z)   (viii) X′ ∪ Y′

(c) What is (i) #(X ∪ Y)   (ii) #(X ∪ Y ∪ Z)′   (iii) #Z \ (X ∪ Y)?

7. U = {a, b, c, d, k, e, f, g, h}, M = {a, b, c, d, f, h}, N = {a, b, c, e, g},
P = {a, c, d, e, h}.

(a) Represent this information on a Venn diagram.

(b) List the following sets. (i) M ∩ N   (ii) N ∩ P   (iii) P′   (iv) (M ∩ P) \ N

Problem solving using two sets

Example 12.4

A class was asked how many of them had holidayed in Spain and Portugal. The results are shown in the Venn diagram.

How many students: (a) visited Spain (b) visited Portugal (c) visited Spain and Portugal (d) visited Spain or Portugal (e) visited Spain only (f) visited neither of these two countries (g) were in the class?

Solution

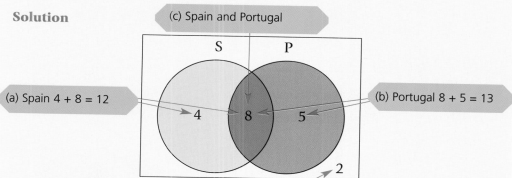

(c) Spain and Portugal

(a) Spain 4 + 8 = 12

(b) Portugal 8 + 5 = 13

(d) Spain or Portugal 4 + 8 + 5 = 17
(e) Spain only 4
(f) Neither of the two countries 2
(g) In the class 4 + 8 + 5 + 2 = 19

Example 12.5

23 students were asked if they played soccer or Gaelic football. 13 said they played soccer and 15 said they played Gaelic football. Eight said they played *both* Gaelic football and soccer. Three said they played neither of these two sports.

Represent the information on a Venn diagram and answer the following questions.
(a) How many students play soccer only?
(b) How many students play football only?
(c) How many play football or soccer?

Solution

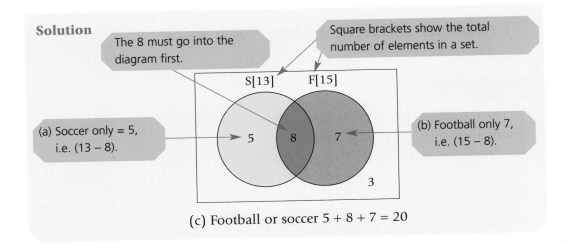

The 8 must go into the diagram first.

Square brackets show the total number of elements in a set.

S[13]   F[15]

(a) Soccer only = 5, i.e. (13 − 8).

5   8   7

3

(b) Football only 7, i.e. (15 − 8).

(c) Football or soccer 5 + 8 + 7 = 20

Exercise 12.5

1. A number of pupils were asked if they played tennis or golf. The results are shown in the Venn diagram. Answer the questions below.

   How many pupils:

   (a) played tennis?

   (b) played golf?

   (c) played both tennis and golf?

   (d) played golf but not tennis?

   (e) played neither of these two sports?

   (f) played tennis or golf?

   (g) were surveyed?

   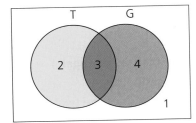

   T   G

   2   3   4

   1

2. A group of pupils was asked if they played the guitar or piano. The results are shown in the Venn diagram. Answer the questions that follow.

   How many pupils:

   (a) were in the group?

   (b) played the piano?

   (c) played both guitar and piano?

   (d) played neither of these two instruments?

   (e) played the guitar or the piano?

   (f) complete the following sentence: 'Two pupils played the...'

   G   P

   2   3   1

   7

3. In a group of 16 pupils, five said they liked studying art, six liked music and two liked both subjects. Seven said they liked neither art nor music. Represent this information on a Venn diagram and write down how many pupils (a) liked art only (b) liked art or music.

4. A survey was carried out in a supermarket. 150 of those surveyed had bought cheese, 140 had bought yoghurt and 100 had bought both cheese and yoghurt. 30 people bought neither cheese nor yoghurt. Represent this information on a Venn diagram and write down how many: (a) were in the survey (b) bought yoghurt but not cheese.

5. A group of 11 teachers was asked whether they liked apples or bananas. Four said they liked apples, six liked bananas and one liked apples and bananas. Represent this information on a Venn diagram and say how many teachers: (a) liked bananas but not apples (b) neither of these two fruits.

6. 24 students were asked if they had ever visited France or Italy. 17 said they had been to France, 14 had been to Italy and 13 had been to both France and Italy. Represent this information on a Venn diagram and say how many students: (a) had been to France or Italy (b) had visited neither of these two countries.

7. A group of 38 people was asked whether they had a brother or sister in the UK or the US or both. 18 had a brother or sister in the UK, 15 had a brother or sister in the US and 15 did not have a brother or sister in either country. Represent this information on a Venn diagram and say how many people: (a) had a brother or sister in the US only (b) had a brother or sister in either the UK or the US.

8. A group of 40 people was surveyed as to which of two sports, rugby or soccer, they like to watch. 30 like to watch soccer, 25 like to watch rugby and 18 like to watch both sports. Represent this information on

a Venn diagram and say how many people don't like to watch either of these two sports.

9. A class of 20 pupils was given the option of doing history or geography or both. 14 chose history, 13 chose geography and 11 chose both history and geography. Four chose neither of these two subjects. Represent this information on a Venn diagram and say how many pupils were doing history or geography.

10. In a survey of 100 people, 70 said they liked tea, 50 said they liked coffee and 40 said they liked both tea and coffee.
(a) Represent this on a Venn diagram.
(b) How many people liked neither tea nor coffee?

11. In a class of 27 pupils, 22 play tennis, 13 play hockey and eight play both tennis and hockey. Represent this on a Venn diagram and say how many play neither of these two sports.

12. In a group of 20 people, seven play basketball but don't play football. Nine play football but not basketball and one doesn't play either of these two sports. Represent this on a Venn diagram and say how many pupils play both basketball and football.

13. #U = 22, #A = 13, #B = 8, #(A ∩ B) = 2
(a) Represent this on a Venn diagram.
(b) What is #(A ∪ B)'?

14. #U = 190, #(C \ D) = 80, #(D \ C) = 50, #(C ∪ D)' = 40.
(a) Represent this information on a Venn diagram.
(b) Find #(C ∩ D).

15. #A = 15, #(A ∪ B) = 21, #(A ∩ B) = 8. Find #B.

Problem solving using three sets

Example 12.6

26 pupils were surveyed on whether they studied music (M), art (A) or chemistry (C). The results were as follows: 14 studied music, 12 studied art, 10 studied chemistry, five studied music and art, four studied art and chemistry, seven studied music and chemistry and three pupils studied all these subjects.

Represent this information on a Venn diagram and find how many pupils:

(a) study art only

(b) study chemistry and art but not music

(c) only study one subject

(d) study at least two subjects

(e) study none of these three subjects.

Solution

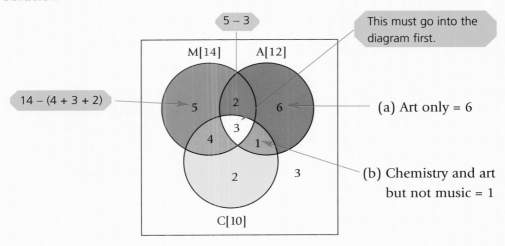

5 − 3

This must go into the diagram first.

M[14]   A[12]

14 − (4 + 3 + 2)

(a) Art only = 6

(b) Chemistry and art but not music = 1

C[10]

(c) Only one subject: 5 + 6 + 2 = 13

(d) At least two subjects: 4 + 2 + 1 + 3 = 10

(e) None of the three subjects = 3

Exercise 12.6

1. The Venn diagram represents a sports survey into soccer (SO), basketball (B) and swimming (SW). How many people:

   (a) were in the survey?

   (b) play soccer?

   (c) swim?

   (d) play soccer and basketball?

   (e) swim and play basketball?

   (f) play soccer only?

   (g) do at least two of the three sports?

   (h) play soccer or basketball?

   (i) swim or play soccer?

   (j) play exactly two of the sports?

   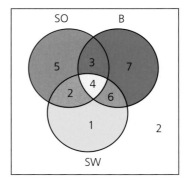

2. The Venn diagram shows the results of a survey on the number of people who like chicken (C), fish (F) or beef (B). How many people:

   (a) like all three foods?

   (b) like beef only?

   (c) like beef and chicken?

   (d) like chicken and beef?

   (e) like chicken and beef but not fish?

   (f) like exactly two of the foods?

   (g) like only one of the foods?

   (h) do not like beef?

   (i) do not like chicken or fish?

   (j) like beef or fish?

   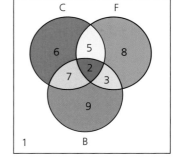

3. 41 students were surveyed on whether they had ever holidayed in France (F), Germany (G) or Sweden (S). 18 had holidayed in France, 14 in Germany and 16 in Sweden. Eight had holidayed in France and Germany, nine in Germany and Sweden and 11 in France and Sweden. Five people had visited all three countries. Represent this information on a Venn diagram and write down how many students:

   (a) holidayed in none of these three countries

   (b) visited Sweden only

   (c) visited France or Sweden.

4. 29 students were asked if they had ever visited a museum (M), art gallery (AG) or been to the pictures (P). 12 had visited a museum, 12 had been to an art gallery, 24 had been to the pictures, seven had been to a museum and an art gallery, nine had visited an art gallery and been to the pictures, eight had been to a museum and gone to the pictures and five students had been to all three places.

   Represent this on a Venn diagram and find out how many students:
   (a) had visited none of the three places
   (b) had been to a museum or art gallery
   (c) had not been to the pictures.

5. $\#U = 31$, $\#A = 20$, $\#B = 16$, $\#C = 14$, $\#(A \cap B) = 13$, $\#(B \cap C) = 8$, $\#(A \cap C) = 9$, $\#(A \cap B \cap C) = 6$. Show this on a Venn diagram and find:
   (a) $\#(A \setminus B)$
   (b) $\#(A \cup B)$
   (c) $\#(A \cup B)'$
   (d) $\#(A \cup B \cup C)'$

6. $\#U = 30$, $\#D = 14$, $\#E = 14$, $\#F = 9$, $\#(D \cap E) = 7$, $\#(E \cap F) = 5$, $\#(D \cap F) = 6$, $\#(D \cap E \cap F) = 4$. Represent this on a Venn diagram and find:
   (a) $\#(A \cup E \cup F)'$
   (b) $\#E \setminus F$
   (c) $\#F \setminus (D \cup E)$

7. 60 Leaving Cert students were asked where they had applied to go to college: Dublin, Galway or Cork. 34 had applied to Dublin, 32 had applied to Galway and 37 to Cork. 23 had applied to colleges in both Dublin and Galway. 21 applied to colleges in Galway and Cork. 22 had applied to colleges in both Cork and Dublin. 15 had applied to colleges in all three cities.

   Represent this on a Venn diagram and find how many students:
   (a) applied to none of the three cities
   (b) applied to Cork only
   (c) applied to just one of the three cities

(d) applied to Dublin or Galway

(e) applied to exactly two of the cities.

8. On an exam paper, questions 1, 2 and 3 were optional. 21 pupils in a particular class attempted question 1 (Q1), 13 pupils attempted question 2 (Q2) and 15 attempted question 3 (Q3). 10 pupils attempted question 1 and question 2, five attempted question 2 and question 3 and nine attempted question 1 and question 3. Three pupils attempted all three questions and four pupils did not attempt any of the first three questions.

Show this information on a Venn diagram and find out how many pupils:

(a) were in the class

(b) attempted question 1 only

(c) attempted just one of the three questions

(d) what percentage of pupils attempted question 3 only?

Exercise 12.7   (Chapter summary)

1. Say, giving a reason, which of the following are sets.
   (a) The collection of intelligent pupils.
   (b) The collection of pupils who have been on a visit to London.
   (c) The last 13 letters of the alphabet.
   (d) The collection of good songs released this year.

2. A = {3, 6, 9, 12}, B = {2, 5, 9, 7, 1}. Insert one of the following symbols into each question below: $\in$, $\notin$, $\subset$, $\cap$, $\cup$.
   (a) 12 _____A
   (b) 12 ___B
   (c) 2 ___ B
   (d) A ___B = 9
   (e) A ___ B = {3, 6, 9, 12, 2, 5, 7, 1}
   (f) {3, 6, 9} ___ A
   (g) {2, 7} ___ B

3. List the elements of the following:
   (a) A
   (d) A ∪ B
   (b) A ∩ B
   (e) B \ A
   (c) A'

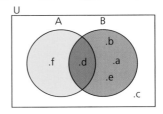

4. U = {6, 8, 10, 12, 14, 16, 18, 20}, A = {8, 12}, B = {12, 14, 16, 18, 20}
   Represent this on a Venn diagram and list the following sets:
   (a) A ∩ B   (b) B'   (c) (A ∪ B)'   (d) A \ B

5. Using the diagram, list the elements of:
   (a) P
   (e) (P ∪ Q ∪ R)'
   (b) Q ∩ R
   (f) P \ Q
   (c) P ∪ Q
   (g) (P \ Q) \ R
   (d) (P ∪ Q)'

   Find:
   (h) #P
   (i) #(P ∩ Q ∩ R)
   (j) (P ∪ R)

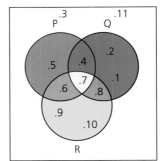

6. U = {3, 4, 5, 6, 7, 8, 9, 10, 11, 12}
   C = {4, 6, 8, 10, 12}
   D = {5, 7, 6, 8, 10, 11}
   E = {3, 4, 5, 6, 8, 10}

   (a) Represent this on a Venn diagram.
   (b) List the following.
       (i) C ∪ D   (iii) E \ C   (v) C ∩ E
       (ii) (C ∪ D)'   (iv) (E \ C) \ D   (vi) (C ∩ E)'
   (c) What is:
       (i) #C?   (iii) #(C ∩ D)?
       (ii) #(C ∪ D)?   (iv) #(C ∩ D ∩ E)?

7. A group of people was asked whether they liked athletics (A) or soccer (S). The results are shown on the Venn diagram. Answer the following questions.

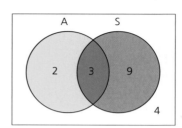

(a) How many people were surveyed?

(b) How many liked soccer only?

(c) How many liked athletics or soccer?

(d) How many liked soccer?

(e) How many liked one sport only?

8. In an interview for hotel work, applicants were asked whether they had any experience working in a kitchen (K) or serving at tables (S). Eight people said they had experience in a kitchen, 11 had experience serving tables and six people had experience of both. One person had no experience of either kitchen or serving tables. Show this information on a Venn diagram and find how many people had experience of serving tables only.

9. A group of pupils was asked whether they watched documentaries (D), films (F) or soaps (S). 17 said they watched documentaries, 22 watched films and 23 watched soaps. 12 said they watched documentaries and films, 11 watched films and soaps and 10 watched documentaries and soaps. Seven watched all three types of programme.

(a) Represent this on a Venn diagram.

(b) How many watched films and soaps but not documentaries?

(c) How many people were in the group?

(d) Finish the following sentence: 'Three people watched...'

10. The diagram represents a survey of 147 people. Find the value of x.

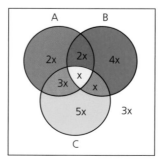

CHAPTER SUMMARY

In this chapter, you will learn about:
+ Bar charts.
+ Trend graphs.
+ Pie charts.
+ Mean and mode.

Bar charts

The three ways that we will organise and display data in this chapter will be bar charts, trend graphs and pie charts.

When information is first gathered, it is often disorganised and in no particular order. Information like this is called data. For example, the number of goals scored in 10 soccer matches might be given as 4, 2, 3, 0, 1, 3, 1, 5, 1, 1. Data like this is not of much use. We need to organise the data to make sense of it. Organised data is called information.

In a bar chart, all the bars are of equal width. The height represents the quantity.

Example 13.1

In a class of 24 pupils, the number of pupils who have chosen five different subject options is represented by the bar chart below.

(a) How many of these pupils do the following?

    (i) Art

    (ii) Music

    (iii) Geography

    (iv) Physics

    (v) Woodwork

(b) What fraction of the class studies geography? Write this fraction in its simplest form.

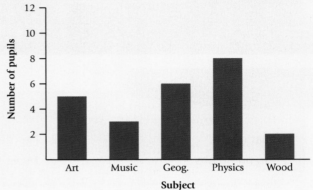

Solution

(a) The number of pupils is given by the height of each box.

    (i) Art = 5 pupils

    (ii) Music = 3 pupils

    (iii) Geography = 6 pupils

    (iv) Physics = 8 pupils

    (v) Woodwork = 2 pupils

$$\text{Fraction} = \frac{\text{geography pupils}}{\text{total pupils}}$$

(b) Fraction who studies geography = $\frac{6}{24}$ = $\frac{1}{4}$ in its simplest form.

Example 13.2

The highest daily temperature in a holiday resort was recorded in degrees centigrade for one week. The data is shown in the table below.

(a) Represent this on a bar chart.

(b) What was the average daily temperature?

Day	Mon	Tue	Wed	Thu	Fri	Sat	Sun
Temperature	34	36	43	38	32	43	40

Solution

(a)

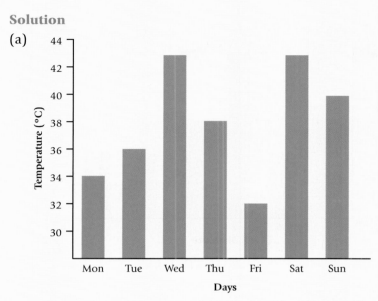

(b) $\text{average} = \dfrac{\text{total}}{\text{number of days}} = \dfrac{34+36+43+38+32+43+40}{7} = \dfrac{266}{7} = 38\,°C$

Exercise 13.1

1. The bar chart shows the highest monthly temperature in a resort over a seven-month period.

   (a) What was the temperature in (i) May (ii) September?

   (b) Which was (i) the warmest month (ii) the coldest month?

   (c) What was the average of the highest temperatures over the seven months?

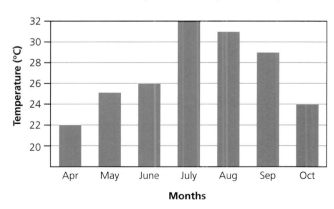

2. The bar chart shows how many pupils in a class wear certain shoe sizes.

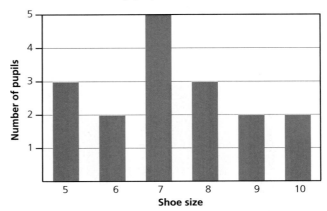

(a) How many wear (i) size 5 shoes (ii) size 8 shoes?
(b) Which shoe size is worn by more pupils than any other?
(c) How many pupils wear shoe sizes greater than 7?
(d) How many wear shoe sizes smaller than size 7?
(e) How many pupils are in the class?

3. The bar chart shows the average daily number of hours of sunshine in a resort in each of seven months.

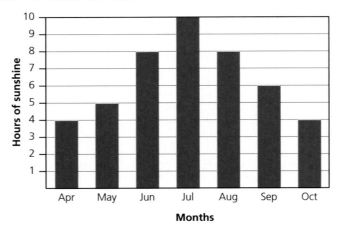

(a) Which months have more than an average of seven hours of sun per day?
(b) Which is the sunniest month?

(c) What is the difference in temperature between the sunniest month and the least sunny month?

(d) Which months have three or more hours' sunshine less than July?

4. The bar chart shows the population figures in millions for five EU countries.

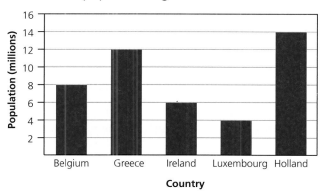

(a) Which country has the largest population?

(b) What is the total population of the five countries?

(c) What is the difference in population between the largest and the smallest countries?

(d) What is the average population of the five countries?

(e) What percentage of the total population lives in Ireland? (Answer to the nearest whole number.)

5. The table below gives the total monthly rainfall in cm (to the nearest cm) for a six-month period.

July	August	September	October	November	December
3	6	7	19	15	10

(a) Draw a bar chart to illustrate this data.

(b) What is the difference between the wettest month and the driest?

(c) What is the total rainfall in cm for the six months?

(d) What percentage of the total rainfall fell in August?

(e) What months had more than the average rainfall?

6. The table shows the percentage of the workforce (to the nearest whole number) engaged in agriculture for six EU countries.

Spain	Holland	Ireland	France	Italy	Germany
9	4	12	6	7	4

(a) Draw a bar chart to represent this information.

(b) Which two countries have the lowest percentage of the workforce engaged in agriculture?

(c) Calculate the average percentage of the workforce engaged in agriculture in the six countries.

(d) Which countries have a lower than average percentage engaged in agriculture?

7. A number of students was asked what their favourite game was. Their answers are shown in the table below.

Game	Soccer	Basketball	Tennis	Badminton	Hurling
Number of students	30	25	13	27	5

(a) Draw a bar chart to illustrate this information.

(b) How many students were surveyed?

(c) How many students listed either soccer or tennis as their favourite game?

(d) What percentage of the students said hurling was their favourite sport?

8. The table below shows how a family spends their weekly income, in euros.

Food	Mortgage	Transport	Fuel	Savings	Other
120	130	20	30	40	80

(a) Represent this information on a bar chart.

(b) Calculate the total weekly expenditure.

(c) What fraction of income is spent on food?

(d) What percentage is saved (to the nearest whole number)?

9. The table represents the subject choices of a group of students.

Subject	Art	Music	Chemistry	Geography	French
Number of pupils	9	17	20	9	10

(a) Draw a bar chart to illustrate this information.

(b) How many pupils are in the group?

(c) What is the most popular subject?

10. A record was kept of each item sold by an electrical outlet during a week. The information is shown in the table below.

Item	TV	DVD recorder	Digital camera	Camcorder	Computer
Number of units sold	4	13	8	7	3

(a) Represent this data on a bar chart.

(b) What percentage of the total units sold was camcorders?

(c) If the profit on each DVD recorder is €60, how much profit was made on the sale of DVD recorders that week?

11. Marks gained by pupils in a test are shown in the table below.

Mark	0	1	2	3	4	5
Number of pupils	3	7	12	15	11	12

(a) Show this data on a bar chart.

(b) How many pupils sat the test?

(c) If the pass mark was 2, how many pupils passed the test?

12. A number of pupils was asked to pick their favourite sport. The results are shown in the table below.

Sport	Soccer	Football	Hurling	Hockey	Rugby
Number of pupils	8	14	12	7	9

(a) Show this information on a bar chart.

(b) How many pupils were in the survey?

(c) What percentage of pupils picked either soccer or hurling?

Trend graphs

Data collected over a period of time is often best shown on a trend graph. Trend graphs are widely used for forecasting, as they can help to predict future trends.

Example 13.3

The table shows the temperature (in degrees Centigrade) measured every two hours, over a 12-hour period.

Time	8 a.m.	10 a.m.	12 p.m.	2 p.m.	4 p.m.	6 p.m.	8 p.m.
Temperature (°C)	5	6	9	10	8	4	2

(a) Represent this on a trend graph.
(b) Estimate between what times the temperature was above 8°C.
(c) Estimate the temperature at 5:00 p.m.

Solution

(a)

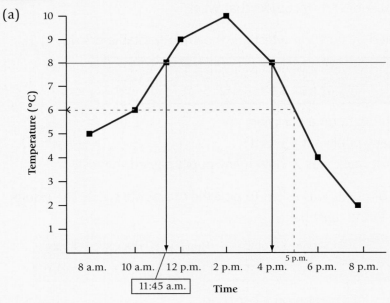

(b) Temperature above 8°C between 11:45 a.m. and 4:00 p.m.

(c) At 5:00 p.m., the temperature was approximately 6°C.

Exercise 13.2

1. The following trend graph shows the monthly rainfall in cm (to the nearest cm) over a six-month period.

   (a) Which month had the highest rainfall?

   (b) What was the total rainfall?

   (c) What percentage of the rainfall fell in the first three months?

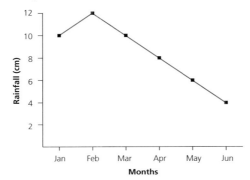

2. The following trend graph shows the amount taken by a shop for each day of the week.

   (a) Which day had the highest sales?

   (b) What is the total value of the sales for the week?

   (c) What was the total value of the sales for Saturday and Sunday?

   (d) What percentage of the sales was made on Saturday and Sunday? (Answer to the nearest whole number.)

   (e) If you were manager of the shop, which day would you advise choosing as the regular half-day for this shop?

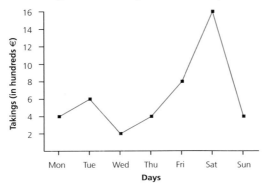

3. The trend graph represents the number of cars sold during the first six months of the year.

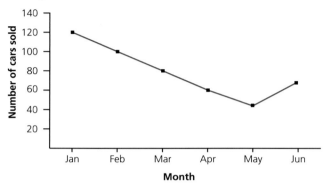

Month

(a) Complete the following table.

Month	Jan	Feb	Mar	Apr	May	Jun
Number sold						

(b) Find the total number of cars sold during the first six months.

(c) Which month had the lowest sales?

(d) What percentage of the total number of sales was in the first three months?

(e) During which months were the sales over 80?

4. The audience for a television soap is recorded in the table.

Day	Mon	Tue	Wed	Thu	Fri
Audience (in millions)	1.2	1.6	2.3	1.2	1.7

(a) Represent this data using a trend graph.

(b) Calculate the total audience for the five days.

(c) What percentage watches the Tuesday night show?

(d) There is an omnibus edition of the show on a Sunday. If the total number watching the soap, including the omnibus edition on Sunday, is 9.2 million people, how many watch the omnibus edition?

5. The table gives the height of a child in cm at different ages.

Age	11	12	13	14	15	16
Height (cm)	135	150	155	161	163	164

(a) Show this information on a trend graph.

(b) What was the height gain over the five years?

(c) During which year did this child grow most?

(d) During which year did this child grow least?

6. The weight of a baby (in kg) was recorded at the end of each week for the first six weeks from birth and the information is recorded in the table.

Week	1	2	3	4	5	6
Weight (kg)	4.2	4.1	4.0	4.3	4.5	4.8

(a) Show this information on a trend graph.

(b) During how many weeks did the baby actually lose some weight?

(c) What was the weight gain during week 4? Answer in grams.

(d) What was the increase in weight over the six weeks? Answer in grams.

7. The annual premium (in euro) on an insurance policy for a house for a five-year period is given in the table.

Year	1	2	3	4	5
Premium	150	180	220	220	210

(a) Illustrate this information on a trend graph.

(b) In which year did the premium rise most?

(c) By how much did the premium rise between year 1 and year 5?

(d) Based on this trend graph, predict whether the premium will rise or fall for year 6.

8. The table shows successive two-monthly electricity bills (in euro) for a household over the course of a year.

Period	Jan/Feb	Mar/Apr	May/Jun	Jul/Aug	Sep/Oct	Nov/Dec
Bill (€)	210	170	155	125	135	205

(a) Represent this information on a trend graph.

(b) Which bill was the highest?

(c) Calculate the total cost of electricity for the whole year.

(d) Calculate the average two-monthly bill, to the nearest euro.

Pie charts

A pie chart is a circle divided into sections, called sectors, where each sector represents the size of each share.

Example 13.4

The following pie chart shows how a weekly income of €720 is spent.
(a) Calculate the size of the angle for the heat and light sector.
(b) Calculate the amount of money spent on each sector.

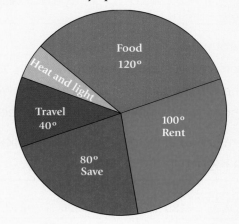

Solution

(a) Angle for heat and light = 360° − (the total of other sectors)

$$= 360° − [120° + 40° + 80° + 100°]$$
$$= 360° − 340°$$
$$= 20°$$

(b) Money spent on each sector = $\frac{\text{angle of sector}}{360}$ × total money

Food = $\frac{120}{360}$ × 720 = €240

Travel = $\frac{40}{360}$ × 720 = €80

Heat and light = $\frac{20}{360}$ × 720 = €40

Savings = $\frac{80}{360}$ × 720 = €160

Rent = $\frac{100}{360}$ × 720 = €200

NOTE: You can check your answers quickly by adding the money for each sector. Do they add to the total €720?

Example 13.5

The table shows which type of fuel is used by a number of houses.

Type of fuel	Oil	Electricity	Solid fuel	Gas
Number of houses	50	20	10	40

(a) How many houses were in the study?

(b) Represent this data using a pie chart

Solution

(a) 50 + 20 + 10 + 40 = 120 houses in total

(b) angle = $\dfrac{\text{type of fuel}}{\text{total houses}} \times 360°$

$$\text{oil} = \frac{50}{120} \times 360 = 150°$$

$$\text{electricity} = \frac{20}{120} \times 360 = 60°$$

$$\text{solid fuel} = \frac{10}{120} \times 360 = 30°$$

$$\text{gas} = \frac{40}{120} \times 360 = 120°$$

NOTE: You can check these angles quickly by adding them. They should add up to 360°. Do they?

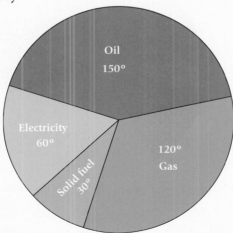

Exercise 13.3

1. The pie chart illustrates the number of pupils who achieved grades A, B, C, D and E, respectively, in a test. A total of 120 pupils sat the test.

   (a) What is the size of the angle representing grade E?

   (b) Complete the table by calculating how many pupils achieved each grade.

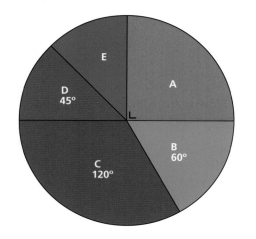

Grade	A	B	C	D	E
No. of students					

2. The pie chart represents a survey of 60 children who were asked to identify their favourite breakfast.

   (a) Calculate the size of the angle representing porridge.

   (b) Calculate how many children chose each of the four types of breakfast.

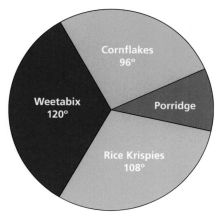

3. The pie chart represents the preferred choice of holiday destination of 1440 people.

   (a) What is the size of the angle for France?

(b) Calculate how many people are represented by each sector of the pie chart.

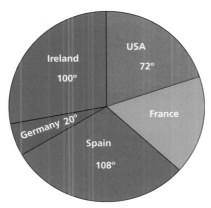

4. 40 students were asked to choose one of four subjects, French, music, art or biology. The results are illustrated on the pie chart.
(a) Find the size of the angle represented by music.
(b) Calculate how many pupils chose each subject.

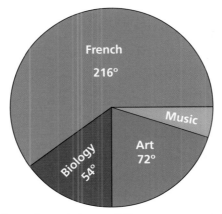

5. A shop recorded the sales of three different computer games. The results are shown in the table.

Game	A	B	C
Sales	50	42	28

(a) How many games were sold altogether?
(b) Represent the sales on a pie chart.
(c) What percentage of sales for the week were of game A? (Give your answer to the nearest whole number.)

6. A number of students were asked to choose their favourite fruit from apple, orange or banana. The results are shown in the table.

Fruit	Apple	Orange	Banana
Number of students	16	10	14

(a) How many students were surveyed?

(b) Illustrate this information using a pie chart.

(c) What percentage of the students chose orange as their favourite fruit?

7. The votes received by five candidates in an election (John, David, Mary, Eileen and Joseph) are shown in the table.

Candidate	John	David	Mary	Eileen	Joseph
Number of votes	160	200	800	400	240

(a) How many people voted in total?

(b) Represent this information on a pie chart.

(c) What fraction, in its simplest form, of the total vote did Mary get?

8. A class of 18 pupils was surveyed as to how they travel to school. The results are shown in the table.

Travelled to school	By bus	By bike	By car	By train
Number of pupils	8	5	4	x

(a) Find x, the number of pupils in the class who came to school by train.

(b) Represent this information using a pie chart.

(c) What percentage of the class travelled to school by car? (Give your answer to the nearest whole number.)

9. 80 pupils were asked to choose their favourite sport. The results are shown in the table.

Sport	Tennis	Golf	Soccer	Hurling	Football
Number of pupils	8	10	20	12	x

(a) Calculate x, the number of pupils who chose football.

(b) Illustrate this information on a pie chart.

(c) Calculate the percentage of pupils who chose golf as their favourite sport.

10. The results of a survey into where a number of people worked are given in the table.

Worked in	Hospital	Farm	Hotel	Office	Retail
Number of people	10	15	16	7	12

(a) How many people were surveyed?

(b) Represent this information on a pie chart.

(c) Find the fraction, in its simplest term, of people who worked on a farm.

11. The table shows how the 24 hours of a day are spent by a certain student.

Activity	School	Homework	Sleep	Leisure
Number of hours	7	2	8	x

(a) Calculate x, the number of hours spent at leisure.

(b) Use a pie chart to illustrate this information

(c) Calculate the percentage of the day which was spent doing homework. (Give your answer correct to one decimal place.)

12. A number of students were asked which grade they achieved in a maths exam. The grades were as follows:

A A A C
B B A D
E A B C

(a) Complete the following table.

Grade	A	B	C	D	E
Number of pupils					

(b) Present this information using a pie chart.

(c) What percentage of the students scored a grade C or D?

13. A number of students were asked about which type of TV programme they preferred. The results were as follows.

Type of programme	Comedy	Horror	Science fiction	Soap
Number of students	12	8	13	7

(a) How many students took part in the survey?

(b) Illustrate this information using a pie chart.

(c) Calculate the percentage of students who preferred horror programmes.

14. The table below shows where 720 people went on holidays.

Country	USA	Spain	England	Ireland	France
Number of people	100	60	80	x	300

(a) Find x, the number of people who holidayed in Ireland.

(b) Use a pie chart to represent this information.

(c) List the countries visited by over 20% of the people surveyed.

15. The table shows how many students got grades A, B, C, D and E in an exam.

Grade	A	B	C	D	E
Number of students	7	15	20	12	6

(a) How many students sat this test?

(b) Illustrate this information on a pie chart.

(c) How many students got a grade D or better?

(d) What percentage of students got grade E?

(e) If a C or better is an honours grade, what percentage (to one decimal place) of the students got an honour?

Mean and mode

Mean

Mean is another word for average. The mean is found by dividing the total of the values by the number of values.

Example 13.6

(a) Find the mean of the following test scores: 25, 32, 45, 58.
(b) If the mean of seven numbers is 9, find the total of the seven numbers.
(c) The mean of 2, x, 6, 5 and 10 is 6. Calculate x.

Solution

(a) $\text{mean} = \dfrac{\text{total}}{\text{no. of values}} = \dfrac{25 + 32 + 45 + 58}{4} = \dfrac{160}{4} = 40$

(b) The total of the values is before we divide by the number of values. Therefore, to find the total, multiply the mean by the number of values.

$\text{mean} = \dfrac{\text{total}}{\text{no. of values}}$

$\Rightarrow \text{total} = \text{mean} \times \text{no. of values}$

$= 9 \times 7$

$= 63 \text{ total}$

(c)

There are 5 numbers in the list.
Total = 5 × the mean
$= 5 \times 6$

$5 \times 6 = 30 \text{ Total}$

The numbers must add to give this total.

$\text{total} = 2 + x + 6 + 5 + 10 = 30$

$23 + x = 30$

$x = 30 - 23$

$x = 7$

NOTE: Sometimes the data is put into a table, called a **frequency distribution table**.

Example 13.7

The number of goals scored in 20 soccer matches is as follows.

0	3	1	0	4
1	0	1	4	2
1	0	1	1	0
2	1	4	3	1

(a) Complete the following frequency distribution table.

Number of goals	0	1	2	3	4
Number of matches					

(b) Calculate the mean number of goals per match.

Solution

(a)

Number of goals	0	1	2	3	4
Number of matches	5	8	2	2	3

This means there are five zeros in the list.

(b) Total number of goals

$$\text{mean} = \frac{5 \times 0 + 8 \times 1 + 2 \times 2 + 2 \times 3 + 3 \times 4}{5 + 8 + 2 + 2 + 3}$$

Total number of matches $= \dfrac{0 + 8 + 4 + 6 + 12}{20}$

The mean may be a decimal or a fraction.

$\dfrac{30}{20} = 1.5$ goals per match

Mode

The **mode** is the value that recurs most often or frequently.

Example 13.8

Find the mode of the following array of numbers: 8, 2, 5, 8, 5, 9, 3, 7, 5, 6.

Solution

The mode is 5, since it appears most often.

Example 13.9

Find the modal number of goals scored in Example 13.7.

Solution

Number of goals	0	1	2	3	4
Number of matches	5	8	2	2	3

The modal number of goals scored is 1, since it occurs most often (eight times).

Exercise 13.4

1. Find the mean and mode of the following collections of numbers.
   (a) 4, 7, 3, 2, 5, 3
   (b) 1, 2, 0, 2, 1, 0, 3, 1, 3, 4
   (c) 2, 6, 3, 2, 7, 9, 6
   (d) 2, 5, 7, 9, 5, 8, 5, 3, 1
   (e) 3, 2, 6, 4, 2, 8, 7, 2, 2
   (f) 1, 3, 6, 3, 1, 11, 8, 11, 8, 17, 8

2. Find the mean and mode of the following collections of numbers.
   (a) 3, 6, 9, 2, 4, 3, 8
   (b) 5, 5, 5, 6, 7, 7, 8, 5, 6
   (c) $1\frac{2}{3}$, $2\frac{5}{6}$, 3, 2, 3

   (d) $1\frac{1}{2}$, $3\frac{1}{2}$, $1\frac{1}{2}$, 3, $1\frac{1}{2}$

   (e) $1\frac{1}{4}$, $1\frac{2}{5}$, 5, $2\frac{3}{4}$, $4\frac{3}{5}$, $1\frac{1}{4}$, $4\frac{3}{4}$

3. The prices of six different textbooks were
   €18.50, €16, €20, €25, €24.50, €30.
   Calculate the mean price per book.
   (Round off to the nearest cent.)

4. A student achieved the following marks in five different maths tests:
   55, 60, 70, 80, 45. Calculate the mean mark for the five tests.

5. Six gas bills were recorded as €121.50, €130.40, €95.20, €80.30, €60.30 and €70.30. Calculate the mean gas bill.

6. (a) If the mean of seven numbers is 8, what is the total of the seven numbers?
   (b) If the mean of the seven numbers from (a) together with an eighth number is 9, what is the value of the extra number?

7. If the mean of nine numbers is 12, calculate the total of the nine numbers.

8. If the mean of 3, 5, x and 9 is 6, calculate the value of x.

9. If the mean of 2, 5, 6, x and 9 is 5, calculate the value of x.

10. If the mean of 3, 5, x, x, x and 4 is 5, calculate the value of x.

11. The marks out of 10 achieved by 12 pupils were recorded as follows.

2	4	8	4
8	10	4	2
8	4	6	6

(a) Complete the frequency distribution table.

Mark	2	4	6	8	10
Frequency					

(b) Write the modal mark.
(c) Calculate the mean mark per pupil.

12. The number of goals scored by 20 soccer teams involved in 10 matches was recorded as follows.

0	1	2	3	3
2	0	3	4	0
3	4	0	3	1
2	3	1	0	2

(a) Draw a frequency distribution table for this data.
(b) What is the modal number of goals scored?
(c) Calculate the mean number of goals scored per team.
(d) How many of the games could have ended in a draw?
(e) What is the least number of games which were definitely not drawn?
(f) What is the mean number of goals per match?

13. A survey was taken on the amount of money a number of pupils spent on a one-day school trip. The results are shown in the following frequency distribution table.

Money spent (in €)	0	10	20	30	40
Number of pupils	4	5	8	10	3

   (a)   How many pupils were in the group?

   (b)   What is the modal amount of money spent?

   (c)   Calculate the mean amount spent per pupil.

   (d)   How many pupils spent more than €10?

14. On leaving a supermarket, 30 people were asked how much they had spent. The results were then rounded off to the nearest €10, as follows.

Money spent (in €)	10	20	30	40
Number of people	2	x	12	10

   (a)   Find the value of x.

   (b)   What was the modal amount of money spent?

   (c)   Calculate the mean amount of money spent per person.

15. 15 pupils were asked to give their age. The results are shown in the frequency distribution table.

Age	10	11	12	13	14
Number of pupils	1	0	3	x	6

   (a)   Calculate the value of x.

   (b)   Write the mode.

   (c)   Calculate the mean age per pupil.

   (d)   How many pupils were younger than the mean?

Example 13.10

The mean of the following frequency distribution table is 2. Calculate the value of x.

Number	1	2	3	4
Frequency	x	6	3	1

$$\text{mean} = \frac{x.1 + 6.2 + 3.3 + 1.4}{x + 6 + 3 + 1}$$

$$= \frac{x + 12 + 9 + 4}{x + 10}$$ ← Remember, 10 (a constant) cannot be added to x (a variable).

$$= \frac{x + 25}{x + 10} = 2$$ ← This is the mean, which we are told is equal to 2.

$$\Rightarrow (x + 10)\frac{(x+25)}{(x+10)} = 2(x + 10)$$ ← Multiply both sides by x + 10.

These will cancel.

$$\Rightarrow x + 25 = 2x + 20$$

$$x - 2x = 20 - 25$$

$$-x = -5$$

$$x = 5$$

Exercise 13.5

1. The mean of the following frequency distribution is 3. Calculate the value of x.

Number	1	2	3	4
Frequency	2	3	8	x

2. The mean of the following frequency distribution table is 2. Find the value of x.

Mark	0	1	2	3	4
Frequency	3	7	7	3	x

3. The mean of the following frequency distribution table is 5. Calculate the value of x.

Mark	2	4	6	8
Frequency	4	5	x	3

4. The mean of the following frequency distribution table is 9. Calculate the value of x.

Number	4	6	8	10	12
Frequency	2	6	x	7	9

5. The mean of the following frequency distribution table is $5\frac{1}{2}$. Calculate the value of x.

Number	3	5	7	9
Frequency	5	7	6	x

Exercise 13.6   (Chapter summary)

1. The table below gives details of the number of pairs of shoes sold by a small shop over a period of six days.

Day	Mon	Tue	Wed	Thurs	Fri	Sat
Number of shoes sold	10	15	15	30	10	40

(a) Represent this table using a bar chart.
(b) Represent the table using a trend graph.
(c) What was the total number of shoes sold during the six days?
(d) Calculate the average (mean) number of pairs sold per day.

(e) On which days was the sales figure below the average figure?
(f) If the shop opened on Sunday and the average number of pairs sold for the entire week was 21, calculate how many pairs of shoes were sold on the Sunday.

2. The rainfall (in mm) was recorded for six consecutive months. The results are shown in the following table.

Month	January	February	March	April	May	June
Rainfall (mm)	46	30	24	10	5	5

(a) Illustrate this data using a bar chart.

(b) llustrate this data using a pie chart.

(c) Calculate the average rainfall for the six months.

(d) What percentage of the rainfall was in the wettest month? (Give your answer correct to one decimal place.)

3. Find the mean and mode of the following. (a) 2, 5, 7, 3, 8, 6, 3

   (b) 4, 8, 4, 7, 9, 4, 8, 4   (c) 5, 3, 2, –4, 10, 2

   (d) 6, $2\frac{1}{4}$, $5\frac{4}{7}$, 6, $4\frac{3}{4}$, 1, $2\frac{3}{7}$

4. The table below gives details of the ages of 30 pupils in a club.

Age	8	9	10	11	12
Number of pupils	3	4	7	9	7

(a) What is the modal age?

(b) Calculate the mean per pupil correct to two decimal places.

(c) If the mean age of the pupils is rounded off to the nearest whole number, how many pupils are below the mean age?

5. The marks for a test, marked out of 5, for a class of 20 pupils are recorded in the frequency distribution table below.

Mark	1	2	3	4	5
Number of pupils	2	4	5	x	3

(a)   Find the value of x, i.e. how many pupils scored 4 marks.

(b)   Write down the modal mark.

(c)   Calculate the mean mark per pupil.

(d)   How many pupils achieved more than the mean mark?

6. The mean of the frequency distribution table is 3. Calculate the value of x.

Number	1	2	3	4
Frequency	x	2	4	6

Perimeter, Area and Volume — 14

The **perimeter** of a figure is the total distance around its outer edges. It is found by adding together the lengths of all the sides. Perimeter is usually measured in length units such as cm, m, km.

The **area** of a figure is the amount of space its flat surface takes up. Area is usually measured in units such as square centimetres (cm²), square metres (m²), square kilometres (km²), ares or hectares.

NOTE: Centimetres added to centimetres gives centimetres, e.g. 15 cm + 3 cm = 18 cm. Centimetres multiplied by centimetres gives cm², e.g. 15 cm × 3 cm = 45 cm².

An aerial view of a field

Example 14.1

Find (a) the perimeter (b) the area of the following rectangle.

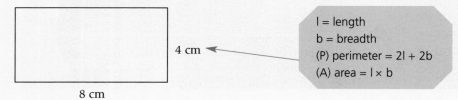

4 cm

l = length
b = breadth
(P) perimeter = 2l + 2b
(A) area = l × b

8 cm

Solution

(a) perimeter = 2 × 8 + 2 × 4

   = 16 + 8 = 24 cm

(b) A = l × b

   A = 8 × 4 = 32 cm^2

Example 14.2

Find (a) the perimeter (b) the area of the following square.

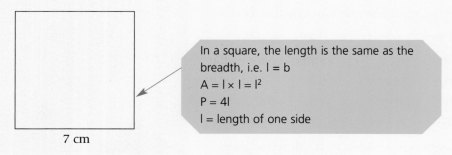

In a square, the length is the same as the breadth, i.e. l = b
A = l × l = l^2
P = 4l
l = length of one side

7 cm

Solution

(a) P = 4 × 7 = 28 cm

(b) A = 7 × 7 = 49 cm^2

Example 14.3

Find (a) the perimeter (b) the area of the following figure (measurements are in cm).

Solution

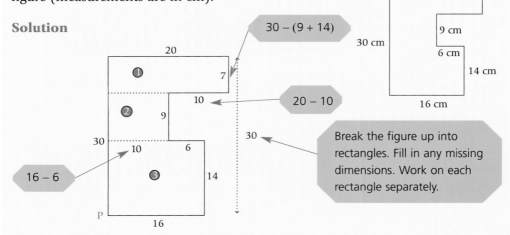

Starting at point P and moving around the diagram.

(a) perimeter = 30 + 20 + 7 + 10 + 9 + 6 + 14 + 16 = 112 cm

(b) area

Rectangle 1

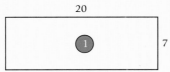

$A = 20 \times 7 = 140$ cm^2

Rectangle 2

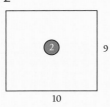

$A = 10 \times 9 = 90$ cm^2

Rectangle 3

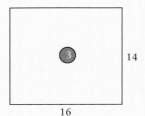

$A = 16 \times 14 = 224$ cm^2

Total area = 454 cm^2

237

Example 14.4

Find the area of each of the following triangles.

Solution

(a)

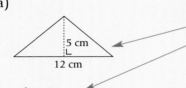

Area of triangle = $\frac{1}{2}$base × perpendicular height.
$A_\triangle = \frac{1}{2}b \times \perp h$

$A = \frac{1}{2} \times 12 \times 5 = 30$ cm^2

(b)

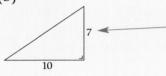

In this case, the perpendicular height is also one side of the triangle.

$A = \frac{1}{2} \times 10 \times 7 = 35$ cm^2

(c)

In this case, the perpendicular height falls outside the triangle.

$A = \frac{1}{2} \times 6 \times 4 = 12$ cm^2

Exercise 14.1

1. Find (a) the perimeter (b) the area of the following rectangles.

	Length (l)	Breadth (b)	Perimeter (P)	Area (A)
(a)	6 cm	5 cm		
(b)	10 cm	7 cm		
(c)	4 cm	12 cm		
(d)	13 cm	6 cm		
(e)	14 cm	8 cm		
(f)	12.5 cm	5.5 cm		

2. Find (a) the perimeter (b) the area of the following squares.

	Length (l)	Perimeter (P)	Area (A)
(a)	5 cm		
(b)	9 cm		
(c)	4 cm		
(d)	11 cm		
(e)	14 cm		
(f)	12.5 cm		

3. Find (a) the perimeter (b) the area of the following figures. All dimensions are in cm.

(a)

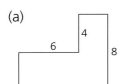

(b)

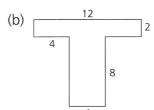

(c)

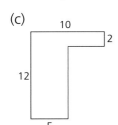

(d)

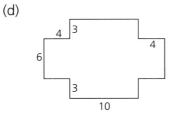

4. Find the area of the following triangles.

(a)

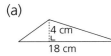

(b)

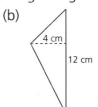

(c)

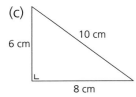

(d)

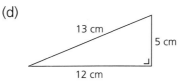

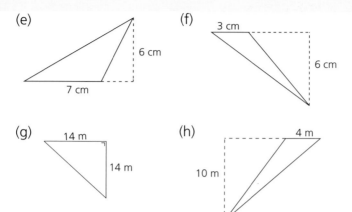

(e) 6 cm / 7 cm

(f) 3 cm / 6 cm

(g) 14 m / 14 m

(h) 4 m / 10 m

5. Find the area of the following shapes by dividing the given figure into a rectangle or triangle.

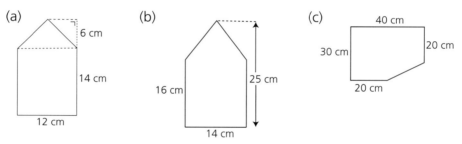

(a) 6 cm / 14 cm / 12 cm

(b) 16 cm / 25 cm / 14 cm

(c) 40 cm / 30 cm / 20 cm / 20 cm

Hint: For (a), (b) and (c), rectangle – triangle

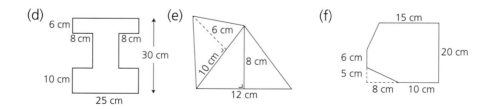

(d) 6 cm / 8 cm / 8 cm / 30 cm / 10 cm / 25 cm

(e) 6 cm / 10 cm / 8 cm / 12 cm

(f) 15 cm / 20 cm / 6 cm / 5 cm / 8 cm / 10 cm

Area of parallelograms

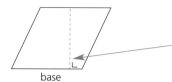

base

Perpendicular height

Area = base × perpendicular height

In a parallelogram, opposite sides are of equal length.

Example 14.5

Find the area of the following parallelogram.

Solution

$A = b \times \perp h$

$A = (15)(12)$

$A = 180 \text{ cm}^2$

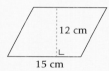

12 cm

15 cm

Example 14.6

If the area of the parallelogram below is 48 cm², find the length of the side x.

Solution

48 is substituted in for A.

$A = b \times \perp h$

$48 = (x)(8)$ Multiply both sides by 2.

$48 = 8x$

$\frac{48}{8} = x$

$x = 6 \text{ cm}$

8 cm

x

Exercise 14.2

1. Calculate the perimeter of each of the following parallelograms

(a)

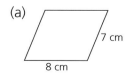

7 cm

8 cm

(b)

8 cm

3 cm

(c)

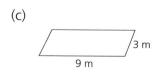

3 m

9 m

(d)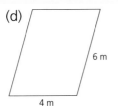
6 m
4 m

(e)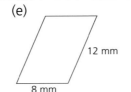
12 mm
8 mm

(f)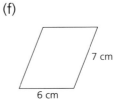
7 cm
6 cm

2. Calculate the area of the following parallelograms.

(a)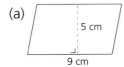
5 cm
9 cm

(b)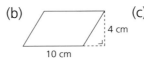
4 cm
10 cm

(c)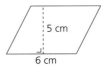
5 cm
6 cm

(d)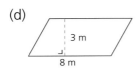
3 m
8 m

(e)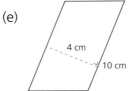
4 cm
10 cm

(f)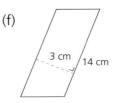
3 cm
14 cm

3. In each of the following parallelograms, calculate the length of x.

(a)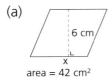
6 cm
x
area = 42 cm²

(b)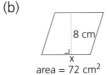
8 cm
x
area = 72 cm²

(c)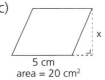
x
5 cm
area = 20 cm²

(d)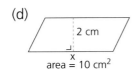
2 cm
x
area = 10 cm²

(e)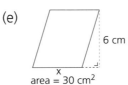
6 cm
x
area = 30 cm²

(f)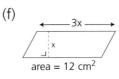
3x
x
area = 12 cm²

4. In each of the following parallelograms, calculate the length of x.

(a)
7
x
area = 56 cm²

(b)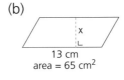
x
13 cm
area = 65 cm²

(c)
x
x
area = 16 cm²

(d)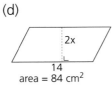
2x
14
area = 84 cm²

(e)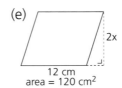
2x
12 cm
area = 120 cm²

(f)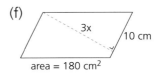
3x
10 cm
area = 180 cm²

Given the perimeter (or area), find a missing length

Example 14.7

The area of a rectangle is 56 cm². The length of one side is 14 cm. Calculate the breadth of the rectangle.

Solution

$A = l \times b$

$56 = 14 \times x$

$56 = 14x$

$x = 4$ cm

> Divide both sides by 14.

> Represent the information in the question on a diagram. Fill in as many measurements as possible.

Example 14.8

The perimeter of a rectangle is 38 cm. The length of one side is 12 cm. Calculate the length of the other side.

Solution

Perimeter = 38

$12 + 12 + x + x = 38$

$24 + 2x = 38$

$2x = 38 - 24$

$2x = 14$

$x = 7$

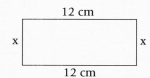

Example 14.9

The area of the triangle shown is 40 cm². Calculate the length of side x.

Solution

$A = \frac{1}{2} b \times \perp h$

$40 = \frac{1}{2} \cdot x \cdot 10$

$80 = 10x$

$x = 8$ cm

> 40 is substituted in for the area.

> Multiply both sides by 2.

243

Exercise 14.3

1. The area of a rectangle is 32 cm². The length of one side is 4 cm. Calculate the breadth of the rectangle.

2. The area of a rectangle is 45 cm². The breadth of the rectangle is 9 cm. Calculate the length of the other side.

3. The area of a square is 81 cm². Find the length of one side of the square.

4. The area of a square is 49 cm². Find the length of one side of the square.

5. The perimeter of a rectangle is 34 cm. The length of one side is 12 cm. Calculate the length of the other side.

6. The perimeter of a rectangle is 26 cm. The length of one side is 10 cm. Calculate the length of the other side.

7. The perimeter of a square is 20 cm. Find the length of the side of the square.

8. The perimeter of a square is 48 cm. Find the length of the side of the square.

9. A square has an area of 64 cm². Calculate (a) the length of the side of the square (b) the perimeter of the square.

10. The area of the triangle is 27 cm². Calculate the length of side x.

11. A triangle has a base of 6 cm. If it has an area of 30 cm², calculate its perpendicular height.

12. If the area of the triangle opposite is 15 cm², calculate the distance, b.

13. A triangle has a base of 5 cm. If it has an area of 20 cm², calculate its perpendicular height.

14. The area of the triangle opposite is 15 cm². Calculate the length of side y.

15. The triangle opposite has an area of 42 cm². Calculate the length of the side x.

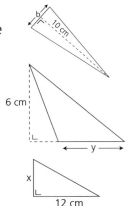

Area and circumference of a circle

A circle may also be called a disc.

The perimeter of a circle is the distance around the outside of the circle. This perimeter is called the circumference, or length. The area of a circle is the space enclosed by the circle.

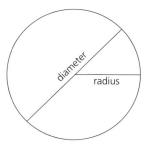

diameter = 2 × radius

circumference (C) = $2\pi r$

area (A) = πr^2

An exact value for π does not exist. However, approximations may be used. The usual approximations are $\frac{22}{7}$ or 3.14 (or the value on a calculator). In most questions you will be told which value to use.

Example 14.10

Calculate (a) the circumference (b) the area of a circle of radius 9 cm.
Take $\pi = 3.14$.

Solution

(a) r = 9 cm

    C = $2\pi r$

    C = 2 × 3.14 × 9

    C = 56.52 cm

(b) A = πr^2

    A = $(3.14)(9)^2 = 3.14 \times 9 \times 9$

    A = 254.34 cm^2

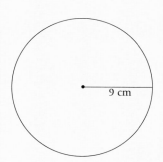

9 cm

Example 14.11

The length of a circle is 88 cm. Calculate the length of the radius. Use $\pi = \frac{22}{7}$.

Solution

C = $2\pi r$

$88 = 2\left(\frac{22}{7}\right)r$ 88 is substituted in place of C.

$88 = \frac{44}{7}r$

$616 = 44r$ Multiply both sides by 7.

$\frac{616}{44} = r$

r = 14 cm

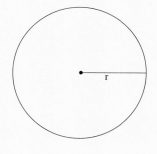

r

Sector of a circle = part of a circle.

Area of sector = $\pi r^2 \times \dfrac{\text{angle}}{360°}$

Arc length = $2\pi r \times \dfrac{\text{angle}}{360°}$

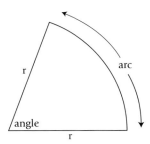

Example 14.12

In the diagram below, calculate (a) the area of the sector (b) the length of the arc ab. Use $\pi = 3.14$.

Solution

(a) Arc of sector = $\pi r^2 \times \dfrac{\text{angle}}{360°}$

$A = 3.14 \times 9^2 \times \dfrac{80°}{360}$

$A = 56.52 \text{ cm}^2$

(b) Arc length = $2\pi r \times \dfrac{\text{angle}}{360°}$

Arc ab = $2 \times 3.14 \times 9 \times \dfrac{80°}{360}$

Arc ab = 12.56 cm

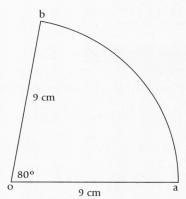

Example 14.13

Calculate, in terms of π (a) the area (b) the length of the circle with a radius of 16 cm.

> The phrase 'in terms of π' means you do not substitute in an approximation for π. You leave the symbol π in throughout the question.

Solution

(a) $A = \pi r^2$

$A = \pi \times 16^2$

$A = 256\pi \text{ cm}^2$

(b) $C = 2\pi r$

$C = 2\pi \times 16$

$C = 32\pi \text{ cm}$

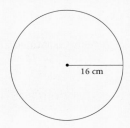

Exercise 14.4

1. Taking $\pi = 3.14$, calculate (a) the circumference (b) the area of the following circles: (i) radius = 20 cm   (ii) radius = 4 cm   (iii) radius = 10 mm (iv) radius = 8 m.

2. Taking $\pi = \frac{22}{7}$, calculate (a) the circumference (b) the area of the following circles: (i) radius = 7 cm   (ii) radius = 28 cm   (iii) radius = 2.1 cm (iv) radius = 12 m.

3. If the diameter of a circle is 26 cm, calculate
   (a) the radius   (b) the circumference   (c) the area.

4. If the diameter of a circle is 60 m, calculate (a) the radius   (b) the circumference   (c) the area.

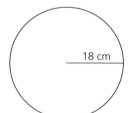

26

5. In each of the following parts, calculate the following:
   (a) the diameter (b) the circumference (c) divide the circumference by the diameter:

   (i) circle of radius 10 cm (ii) circle of radius 25 cm (iii) circle of radius 5 mm (iv) circle of radius 9 m (v) circle of radius 20.5 cm (vii) circle of radius 8.4 cm. (viii) What do you notice?

Questions 6 to 13 are in terms of π.

6. Calculate, in terms of π (a) the length (b) the area of a circle with a radius of 18 cm.

7. Calculate, in terms of π (a) the length (b) the area of a circle with a radius of 35 cm.

8. Calculate, in terms of π (a) the length (b) the area of a circle with a radius of 10.5 cm.

9. Calculate the radius of a circle whose circumference is 34π cm.

10. Calculate the radius of a circle whose circumference is 100π cm.

11. If the length of a circle is 32π cm, calculate its diameter.

12. If the area of a 49π cm², calculate its radius.

13. If the area of a 484π cm², calculate its radius.

In questions 14 to 18, use $\pi = \frac{22}{7}$.

14. The length (circumference) of a circle is 440 cm. Calculate the length of its radius.

15. The length of a circle is 352 cm. Calculate its (a) radius (b) area.

16. The circumference of a circle is 396 cm. Calculate its (a) radius (b) diameter.

17. The area of a circle is 616 cm². Calculate its radius.

18. The area of a circle is $1134\frac{4}{7}$ cm². Calculate its radius.

In questions 19 to 23, use π = 3.14.

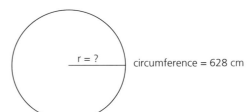

19. The length of a circle is 628 cm. Calculate its radius.

20. The length of a circle is 18.84 cm. Calculate its diameter.

21. The area of a circle is 1256 cm². Calculate its radius.

22. The area of a circle is 379.94 cm². Calculate its radius.

23. Calculate the diameter to the nearest cm of a circle whose area is 706.5 cm².

24. In each of the following sectors, calculate the (a) area (b) arc length ab (c) perimeter. Give answers correct to one decimal place.

(a)
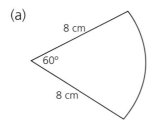

(b)
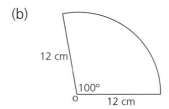

(c)
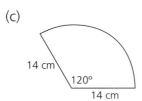

(d)
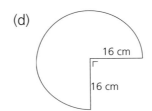

Combined shapes

Example 14.14

(a) Calculate the area of the shaded region shown below.

(b) If a piece of string was used to form the two circles, how long should it be?
(Take π = 3.14; all dimensions in centimetres.)

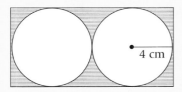

4 cm

Solution

NOTE: The method used here is shaded region = outer − inner.

The outer and inner will change in each question. In this case, the outer is the rectangle and the inner is the two circles.

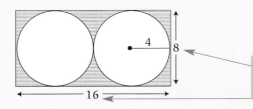

4

8

16

You should fill in as many dimensions as possible in the diagram, using the information given in the question.

(a) Outer: Rectangle area = l × b = 16 × 8 = 128 cm²

Inner: Area of one circle = πr^2 = 3.14 × 4² = 50.24 cm²

Two circles = 2 × 50.24 = 100.48 cm²

shaded = outer − inner

128 − 100.48 = 27.52 cm² = shaded region

(b) The length of the string would be twice the circumference of one of the circles.

C = $2\pi r$ = 2 × 3.14 × 4 = 25.12 cm

Both circles = 2 × 25.12 = 50.24 cm = length of string

Exercise 14.5

Unless otherwise specified, take π = 3.14 and all dimensions in centimetres.

1. (a) Calculate the area of the shaded region.
   (b) If a piece of string was used to form the two circles, how long would it be? Take $\pi = \frac{22}{7}$.

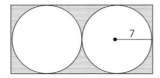

2. (a) Calculate the area of the shaded region.
   (b) If a piece of string was used to form the three circles, how long would it be?

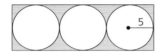

3. Find (a) the area (b) the total perimeter of the semi-circle shown.

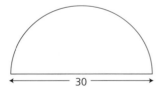

4. Calculate (a) the total area (b) the total perimeter of the figure opposite. Take $\pi = \frac{22}{7}$.

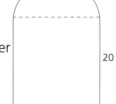

5. Calculate the area of the shaded region below.

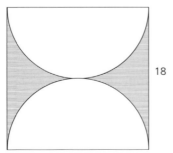

6. Calculate the area of the shaded region below.

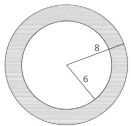

7. Calculate the area of the figure shown below.

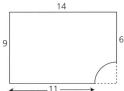

8. Calculate (a) the area (b) the perimeter of the shape shown below.

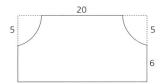

9. Calculate the area of the shape shown below.

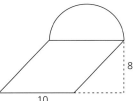

10. Calculate the area of the figure shown.

11. A running track is in the shape of a rectangle with semi-circular ends, as shown.

   (a) Write down the radius of the semi-circular ends.

   (b) Calculate the area of the two semi-circular ends (take $\pi = \frac{22}{7}$).

   (c) Calculate the total length of the running track.

   (d) How many laps would an athlete have to complete in a race which is set at 5.64 km?

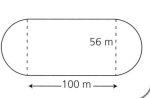

Volume and surface area of cubes and cuboids

The surface area of a solid is the total area of all its surfaces. It is measured in square units such as square metres or square centimetres.

The volume of a solid is the amount of three-dimensional space it occupies. Volume is measured in cubic units, usually cubic centimetres (cm^3) or litres.

NOTE 1:
- Centimetres added to centimetres gives centimetres, e.g. 15 cm + 3 cm = 18 cm.
- Centimetres multiplied by centimetres gives cm^2, e.g. 15 cm × 3 cm = 45 cm^2.
- Centimetres multiplied by centimetres multiplied by centimetres gives cm^3, e.g. 15 cm × 3 cm × 2 cm = 90 cm^3.

NOTE 2:
The cubic unit you want to end up with will determine the units that all measurements should be converted to at the beginning of a question, i.e. if you want to end up with m^3, then all dimensions must be in m before doing any calculations. Similarly, if you want cm^3 at the end, then all measurements must be in cm at the beginning.

NOTE 3:
Capacity is the volume of a liquid or gas and is measured in litres (1 litre = 1000 ml). The black arrow shows the conversion from litres to cm^3 and the red arrow shows the conversion from cm^3 to litres.

× by 1000

1 litre = 1000 cm^3 = 1000 ml

÷ by 1000

Example 14.15

Find (a) the volume (b) the surface area of a cube with sides of 4 cm.

Solution

(a) $V = l \times l \times l = 4 \times 4 \times 4 = 64$ cm^3

(b) Area of front = $l \times l = 4 \times 4 = 16$ cm^2

All sides = $6 \times 16 = 96$ cm^2

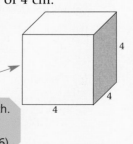

A cube has all sides the same length.
$V = l \times l \times l = l^3$
Area = $6 \times l \times l$ (area of one side × 6)

Example 14.16

A rectangular tank of internal dimensions length 1.2 m, breadth 40 cm and height 60 cm is completely filled with water.

(a) Find the capacity of the tank in litres.

(b) If the water flowed in at a rate of 12 litres per minute, how long would it take to fill the tank?

> This is an example of a cuboid.
> Volume of cuboid = l × b × h
> Surface area = 2l × b + 2b × h + 2l × h

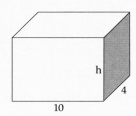

120 cm

60

40

Solution

(a) NOTE: The 1.2 m must be converted to cm.

$V = l \times b \times h = 120 \times 60 \times 40 = 288\,000 \text{ cm}^3$

$288\,000 \div 1000 = 288 \text{ litres}$

(b) $\text{time} = \dfrac{\text{volume of tank}}{\text{number of litres per minute}} = \dfrac{288}{12} = 24 \text{ minutes}$

Example 14.17

A rectangular box (cuboid) has dimensions of length 10 cm and breadth 4 cm. If the volume of the box is 280 cm³, find the height of the box.

Solution

$V = l \times b \times h$

$280 = 10 \times 4 \times h$ > The 280 is substituted in for the volume.

$280 = 40h$ > Divide both sides by 40.

$h = 7 \text{ cm}$

h

10

4

Exercise 14.6

1. Convert the following volumes to litres. (a) 7000 cm³ (b) 6800 cm³ (c) 400 cm³ (d) 29 200 cm³ (e) 6492 cm³ (f) 9500 ml

2. Convert the following litres to cm³. (a) 4 litres (b) 25 litres (c) 3.25 litres (d) 0.6 litres (e) 0.853 litres (f) 3600 litres

3. Calculate the volume of each of the following rectangular boxes. (a) length 20 cm, breadth 12 cm, height 8 cm (b) length 40 cm,

breadth 14 cm, height 18 cm (c) length 80 cm, breadth 1.5 m, height 90 cm (d) length 2 m, breadth 500 cm, height 70 cm

4. Calculate the surface area of each of the following rectangular boxes.
   (a) length 10 cm, breadth 7 cm, height 6 cm
   (b) length 30 cm, breadth 12 cm, height 9 cm
   (c) length 2.1 m, breadth 1.5 m, height 90 cm
   (d) length 1.4 m, breadth 50 cm, height 80 cm

5. Calculate (a) the volume (b) the surface area of each of the following cubes. (a) side length 20 cm (b) side length 17 cm (c) side length 12.5 cm (d) side length 6 m

6. A room is 4 m long, 2 m wide and 2 m high.
   Find (a) the area of the four walls (b) the floor area (c) the number of tins of paint required to paint the walls only, if each tin covers an area of 5 m². (Hint: If you get a decimal, you need to round it up to the nearest whole number, e.g. an answer of 6.3 would mean you need to buy seven tins).

7. A room is 3 m long and 2 m wide.
   (a) Calculate the area of the floor.
   (b) If carpet costs €20 per m², how much will it cost to carpet the room?

8. A rectangular tank of internal dimensions length 1.5 m, breadth 50 cm and height 60 cm is completely filled with water.
   (a) Find the capacity of the tank in litres.
   (b) If the water flowed in at a rate of 9 litres per minute, how long would it take to fill the tank?

9. How many cubes of side 3 cm will fit exactly into a rectangular box of dimensions 45 cm by 63 cm by 1.08 m?

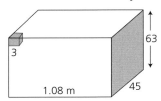

10. Find the height of a rectangular box whose volume is 36 cm³, with length 3 cm and breadth 2 cm.

11. Find the breadth of a cuboid which has a volume of 30 cm³, a length of 3 cm and a height of 4 cm.

12. A rectangular tank has a capacity of 40 litres. The length of the tank is 80 cm and the height is 25 cm. Calculate the breadth.

13. A rectangular fish tank contains 600 litres of water. If the length of the tank is 2 m and the width is 60 cm, calculate the depth of water in the tank (h).

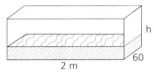

14. How many cubes of side 7 cm will fit exactly into a rectangular box of dimensions 28 cm by 63 cm by 2.1 m?

15. The surface area of a cube is 150 cm². Calculate the length of its side.

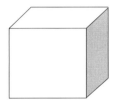

(Hint: Find the area of just one of the sides.)

16. The surface area of a cube is 294 cm². Calculate the length of its side.

17. The surface area of a cube is 864 cm². Calculate the length of its side.

18. Find the height of the rectangular block below if its volume is 1600 cm³. How many cubes, each of side 2 cm, can be cut from the block?

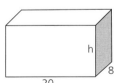

Cylinders

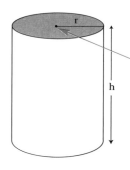

The top and the bottom of a cylinder are circles.

If the curved surface area (CSA) of a cylinder is flattened out, it is in the shape of a rectangle.

$2\pi r$

area $= 2\pi rh$ h

Volume (V) $= \pi r^2 h$

Curved surface area (CSA) $= 2\pi rh$

Total surface area (TSA) $= 2\pi rh + 2\pi r^2$

Example 14.18

Find (a) the volume (b) the total surface area of a closed cylindrical can of radius 14 cm and height 30 cm. Take $\pi = \frac{22}{7}$.

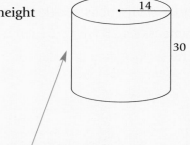

Solution

(a) $V = \pi r^2 h$

$V = \frac{22}{7} \times 14^2 \times 30 = 18\ 480 \text{ cm}^3$

(b) TSA $= 2\pi rh + 2\pi r^2$

$= 2 \times \frac{22}{7} \times 14 \times 30 + 2 \times \frac{22}{7} \times 14^2$

$= 2640 + 1232$

$= 3872 \text{ cm}^2$

Draw out a diagram of the information in the question and fill in the measurements.

Example 14.19

A cylinder has a volume of 31 878 cm³. If the cylinder has a height of 23 cm, calculate the length of its radius. Take $\pi = \frac{22}{7}$.

Solution

Identify formula.

$V = \pi r^2 h$

31 878 is substituted in for volume.

$31\,878 = \frac{22}{7} \times r^2 \times 23$

Multiply both sides by 7.

$7 \times 31\,878 = \cancel{7} \times \frac{22}{\cancel{7}} \times r^2 \times 23$

$223\,146 = 506r^2$

506 is 22 × 23. Now divide both sides by 506.

$441 = r^2$

$r = 21$ cm

Get the square root.

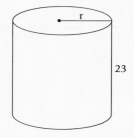

Example 14.20

The curved surface area of a cylinder is 528π cm². If the radius is 12 cm, calculate the height of the cylinder.

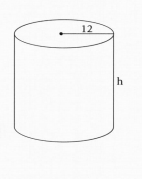

Solution

Identify the correct formula.

$CSA = 2\pi rh$

The CSA is in terms of π.

$528\pi = 2 \times \pi \ 12h$

$528 = 24h$

Now divide both sides by π.

$h = \dfrac{528}{24}$

$2 \times 12 = 24$

$h = 22$ cm

Example 14.21

A hollow metal pipe has an external diameter of 18 cm and an internal diameter of 14 cm and is 40 cm long. Calculate the volume of iron in the pipe.

Solution

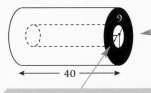

Draw out a diagram of the information in the question and fill in as many dimensions as possible.

Remember, radius is half the diameter.

volume of metal = (outer − inner) × length of pipe

The outer circle minus the inner circle gives the area of the metal in the base. This area multiplied by the length of the pipe gives the volume of metal.

outer = $\pi r^2 = 3.14 \times 9^2 = 254.34$ cm²

inner = $\pi r^2 = 3.14 \times 7^2 = 153.86$ cm²

area of base = 100.48 cm²

$100.48 \times 40 = 4019.2$ cm³ = volume of metal in pipe

Exercise 14.7

Unless otherwise specified, take $\pi = 3.14$.

1. Find the volume of a cylinder with a radius of 6 cm and a height of 13 cm.

2. Find the curved surface area of a cylinder with a radius of 9 cm and a height of 16 cm.

3. Find the area of the top of the cylinder in question 1.

4. Find (a) the volume (b) the total surface area of a closed cylindrical can with a radius of 21 cm and height of 50 cm. Take $\pi = \frac{22}{7}$.

5. Find (a) the volume (b) the total surface area of a closed cylindrical can with a radius of 3.5 cm and height of 20 cm. Take $\pi = \frac{22}{7}$.

6. Find (a) the volume (b) the total surface area of a cylindrical can, which is open at the top and closed at the bottom, with a radius of 35 cm and height of 70 cm. Take $\pi = \frac{22}{7}$.

7. Find (a) the volume (b) the total surface area of a closed cylindrical can with a radius of 16 cm and height of 60 cm.

8. Find (a) the volume (b) the total surface area of a closed cylindrical can with a radius of 9 cm and height of 30 cm.

9. Find (a) the volume (b) the total surface area of a cylindrical can, which is open at the top and closed at the bottom, with a radius of 15 cm and height of 100 cm.

10. Calculate the volume of a cylinder with a diameter of 50 cm and height of 35 cm.

11. Calculate the curved surface area of a cylinder with a diameter of 60 cm and height of 40 cm.

12. Calculate the volume of a cylinder with a diameter of 15 cm and height of 20 cm.

13. Calculate, in terms of π, the volume of a cylinder with a radius of 16 cm and height of 18 cm.

14. Calculate, in terms of π, the volume of a cylinder with a diameter of 20 cm and height of 23 cm.

15. Calculate, in terms of π, the curved surface area of a cylinder with a radius of 20 cm and height of 40 cm.

16. Calculate, in terms of π, the total surface area of a cylinder with a radius of 14 cm and height of 20 cm.

17. A hollow metal pipe has an external diameter of 14 cm, an internal diameter of 10 cm and is 40 cm long. Calculate the volume of iron in the pipe.

18. The volume of a cylinder with a height of 5 cm is 770 cm³. Calculate the radius. Take $\pi = \frac{22}{7}$.

19. The volume of a cylinder with a radius of 5 cm is 440 cm³. Calculate the height of the cylinder. Take $\pi = \frac{22}{7}$.

20. The volume of a cylinder with a height of 17 cm is 10 472 cm³. Calculate the radius. Take $\pi = \frac{22}{7}$.

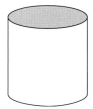

21. The volume of a cylinder with a radius of 8 cm is 4019.2 cm³. Calculate the height of the cylinder to the nearest centimetre.

22. The volume of a cylinder with a height of 24 cm is 7536 cm³. Calculate the radius to the nearest centimetre.

23. The curved surface area of a cylinder is 140π cm². If the radius is 5 cm, calculate the height of the cylinder.

24. The curved surface area of a cylinder with a radius of 7 cm is 220 cm². Calculate the height of the cylinder. Take $\pi = \frac{22}{7}$.

25. The curved surface area of a cylinder with a radius of 7.5 cm is 942 cm². Calculate the height of the cylinder to the nearest centimetre.

26. The cylinder shown has a height of 2.2 m and a radius of 1.2 m. Calculate:
(a) the volume of the tank in cm³ (b) the capacity of the tank in litres, rounded off to the nearest litre (c) the cost in euro of filling the tank with oil if oil costs 85c per litre.

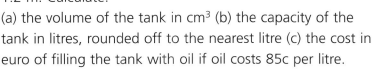

||| Spheres

A football and a golf ball are examples of spheres.

(Volume) $V = \frac{4}{3}\pi r^3$

(Curved surface area) $CSA = 4\pi r^2$

Half a sphere is called a hemisphere.

(Volume) $V = \frac{2}{3}\pi r^3$

(Curved surface area) $CSA = 2\pi r^2$

Example 14.22

A solid sphere has a radius of 12 cm. Calculate its (a) volume (b) curved surface area.

Solution

(a) $V = \frac{4}{3}\pi r^3$

$V = \frac{4}{3} \times 3.14 \times 12^3$ Identify the correct formula.

$V = 7234.56 \text{ cm}^3$

   Volume is in cubic units.

(b) $CSA = 4\pi r^2$

$CSA = 4 \times 3.14 \times 12^2$

$= 1808.64 \text{ cm}^2$ Area is in square units.

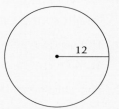

Example 14.23

A solid sphere has a volume of $\frac{34\,496}{3}$ cm³. Find the radius of the sphere.
Use $\pi = \frac{22}{7}$.

Solution

$V = \frac{4}{3}\pi r^3$ Identify correct formula.

$\frac{34\,496}{3} = \frac{4}{3}\left(\frac{22}{7}\right)r^3$ Substitute in the relevant numbers. Multiply the two fractions on the RHS.

$\overset{7}{\cancel{21}}\left(\frac{34\,496}{\cancel{3}}\right) = \left(\frac{88}{21}r^3\right)\cancel{21}$ Multiply both sides by 21.

$241\,472 = 88r^3$

$\frac{241\,472}{88} = r^3$

$2744 = r^3$

$r = \sqrt[3]{2744}$ Get the cube root of 2744.

$r = 14 \text{ cm}$

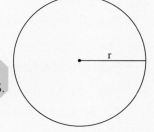

Example 14.24

A solid sphere has a curved surface area of 154 cm². Find the radius of the sphere. Use $\pi = \frac{22}{7}$.

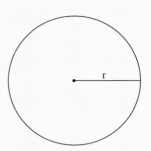

Solution

Identify the correct formula.

$CSA = 4\pi r^2$

$154 = 4\left(\frac{22}{7}\right)r^2$

Multiply both sides by 7.

$154 = \frac{88}{7}r^2$

Divide both sides by 88.

$1078 = 88r^2$

$12.25 = r^2$ ◄ Get the square root of 12.25.

$r = 3.5$ cm

Exercise 14.8

Unless otherwise specified, take $\pi = 3.14$. Where decimals arise, give your answer correct to one decimal place.

1. Calculate the volume of a sphere with a radius of 4 cm.

2. Calculate the curved surface area of a sphere with a radius of 7 cm.

   r = 4 cm

3. Calculate (a) the volume (b) the curved surface area of a sphere with a radius of 6 cm.

4. Calculate, in terms of π, (a) the volume (b) the curved surface area of a sphere with a radius of 6 cm.

5. A sphere has a radius of 9 cm. Calculate (a) its volume (b) its curved surface area.

6. Find (a) the volume (b) the curved surface area of a sphere with a diameter of 16 cm.

7. Calculate, in terms of π, (a) the volume (b) the curved surface area of a sphere with a radius of 4.5 cm.

8. Calculate, in terms of π, (a) the volume (b) the curved surface area of a sphere with a radius of 3 cm.

9. Calculate (a) the volume (b) the curved surface area of a sphere with a radius of 14 cm. Use $\pi = \frac{22}{7}$.

10. Calculate (a) the volume (b) the curved surface area of a sphere with a radius of 3.5 cm. Use $\pi = \frac{22}{7}$.

11. A sphere has a volume of 3052.08 cm³. Find the radius of the sphere to the nearest whole number.

$V =$ 3052.08 cm³

$r = ?$

12. A sphere has a volume of 972π cm³. Find the radius of the sphere to the nearest whole number.

13. A solid sphere has a volume of 288π cm³. Find the radius of the sphere to the nearest whole number.

14. Calculate the radius of a sphere which has a surface area of 314 cm².

$SA =$ 314 cm²

$r = ?$

15. Calculate the radius of a sphere which has a surface area of 324π cm².

16. A solid sphere has a volume of 33.5 cm³. Find the radius of the sphere to the nearest whole number. Use $\pi = \frac{22}{7}$.

17. Find the radius of a sphere which has a volume of $\frac{256}{3}\pi$ cm³.

18. A solid sphere has a curved surface area of 9856 cm². Find the radius of the sphere.

19. Calculate the radius of a sphere which has a surface area of 676π cm².

20. Find the radius of a sphere which has a surface area of 64π cm³.

21. A cylinder has a height of 3 cm and a radius of 4 cm. A sphere has a radius of 3.5 cm. Find which has the greater volume.

22. Two identical spheres have a combined volume of 616 cm³. Calculate the radius of each of the spheres.

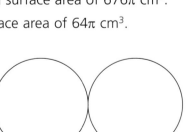

Recasting and displaced liquid

Recasting

Recasting is where a particular object is reformed in a different shape. The important point to remember is that the volume *remains the same* even though the shape has changed. For example, a metal sphere could be melted down and then reformed into a cylinder. However, the volume of the new cylinder formed is the same as the volume of the original sphere before it was melted down, assuming no material was lost in the process.

Similarly, if, for example, a sphere were to be melted down and formed into a number of smaller spheres, then the combined volume of the smaller spheres would be the same as the original sphere.

Volume of displaced liquid = volume of solid

Displaced liquid

When a solid object is fully immersed in a liquid, this moves (displaces) the level of liquid in the container. The volume of this displaced liquid is the same as the volume of the solid object immersed in the liquid.

NOTE: In both these types of questions, it is often easier to leave the calculations in terms of π, as the πs normally cancel when solving the question.

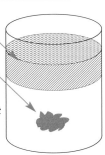

Example 14.25

A sphere with a radius of 6 cm is placed in a cylinder with a radius of 10 cm, as shown in the diagram. Calculate (a) the volume of the sphere in terms of π (b) the increase in depth of water in the cylinder when the sphere is fully immersed in the water.

Solution

(a) V sphere $= \frac{4}{3}\pi r^3$

$= \frac{4}{3} \times \pi \times 6^3$

$= 288\pi \text{ cm}^3$

(b) 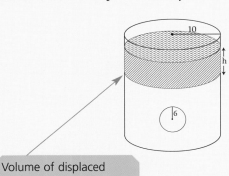 V cylinder $= \pi r^2 h$

$288\pi = \pi 10^2 h$ (divide across by π)

$288 = 100h$

$2.88 \text{ cm} = h$

Volume of displaced liquid = volume of sphere

Example 14.26

A solid sphere with a radius of 6 cm is melted down and recast as a solid cylinder. If the height of the cylinder is 32 cm, calculate the radius of the cylinder.

Solution

The volume of the sphere here is the same as the volume of the cylinder.

V sphere = V cylinder

$$\tfrac{4}{3}\pi r^3 = \pi R^2 h$$

The small r is the radius of the sphere. The capital R is the radius of the cylinder.

$$\tfrac{4}{3}\pi 6^3 = \pi R^2 32$$

$$\tfrac{4}{3}(216) = R^2 32$$

Divide both sides by π.

$$4(72) = 32R^2$$

$$\tfrac{288}{32} = R^2$$

$$R^2 = 9$$

$$R = \sqrt{9}$$

$$R = 3 \text{ cm}$$

Exercise 14.9

1. A sphere with a radius of 3 cm is placed in a cylinder with a radius of 4 cm. Calculate (a) the volume of the sphere in terms of π (b) the increase in the depth of water in the cylinder when the sphere is fully immersed in the water.

2. A solid sphere with a radius of 3 cm is melted down and recast as a solid cylinder. If the height of the cylinder is 4 cm, calculate the radius of the cylinder.

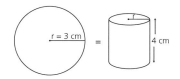

3. A solid cylinder with a radius of 4 cm and height of $5\frac{1}{3}$ cm is melted down and recast into a sphere. Calculate the radius of the sphere.

4. When a solid sphere with a radius of 3 cm is immersed in a cylinder of water, the level of water goes up by 1.44 cm. Calculate the radius of the cylinder.

5. A container is in the shape of a sphere with a radius of 3 cm. Two fills of the container are removed from a cylinder of oil with a radius of 6 cm. By how much will the level of oil fall in the cylinder?

6. A solid sphere of wax with a diameter of 18 cm is melted down and formed into a cylindrical candle with a radius of 7 cm. Calculate the height of the candle, correct to two decimal places.

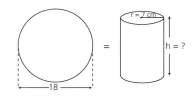

7. A sphere with a volume of $85\frac{1}{3}\pi$ cm^3 is recast as a cylinder with a height of $\frac{4}{3}$ cm. Find the radius of the cylinder.

8. A sphere with a volume of 490π cm^3 is immersed in a cylinder containing water. If the water level in the cylinder rises by 10 cm, calculate the radius of the cylinder.

9. A sphere has a volume of 363π cm^3. Two of these spheres are placed in a cylinder containing water. If the radius of the cylinder is 11 cm, calculate the rise in the level of water after the spheres are placed in it.

10. A stone is immersed in a cylinder containing water. The radius of the cylinder is 12 cm. When the stone is placed in the cylinder, the water level rises by 4 cm. Calculate the volume of the stone in terms of π.

For questions 11 to 14, substitute the given value for π.

11. A stone is immersed in a cylinder with a radius of 5 cm. The cylinder contains a certain amount of water. If the level of water increases by 3 cm when the stone is placed in the cylinder, calculate the volume of the stone. Use $\pi = \frac{22}{7}$.

12. A stone is immersed in a cylinder with a radius of 10 cm. The cylinder contains a certain amount of water. If the level of water increases by 8 cm when the stone is placed in the cylinder, calculate the volume of the stone. Use $\pi = 3.14$.

13. Juice is stored in a cylindrical container with a diameter of 14 cm. If 462 cm³ of juice is poured out, calculate the drop in the level in the cylinder. Use $\pi = \frac{22}{7}$.

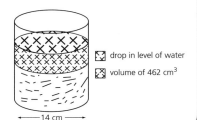

Combined shapes

Example 14.27

A cylinder is used to package three tennis balls, as shown in the diagram. The radius of a tennis ball is 5 cm. Use $\pi = 3.14$.

(a) Calculate the radius and height of the cylinder.

(b) If the cylinder was cut from cardboard, what area of cardboard is used?

(c) Calculate the volume of the cylinder.

(d) Calculate the volume of one of the tennis balls correct to one decimal place.

(e) Calculate the volume of empty space, to the nearest cm³, not taken up by the tennis balls in the cylinder.

Solution

(a) Radius of cylinder = radius of sphere

Radius of cylinder = 5 cm

Height of cylinder = 3 × diameter of 1 tennis ball

$$= 3 \times 10 \text{ cm}$$

$$= 30 \text{ cm}$$

(b) Area of cardboard = TSA = $2\pi rh + 2\pi r^2$

$$= 2(3.14)(5)(30) + 2(3.14)5^2$$

$$= 942 + 157 = 1099 \text{ cm}^2 = \text{area of cardboard used}$$

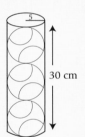

(c) V cylinder = $\pi r^2 h = (3.14)(5^2)(30) = 2355 \text{ cm}^3$

(d) V tennis ball = $\frac{4}{3}\pi r^3 = \frac{4}{3}(3.14)5^3 = 523.3 \text{ cm}^3$

(e) empty space = outer − inner

In this case, the outer is the volume of the cylinder. The inner is the volume of the three tennis balls.

empty space = ⬚ − (⊝+⊝+⊝)

empty space = 2355 − (3 × 523.3)

$$= 2355 - 1570$$

$$= 785 \text{ cm}^3 \text{ of empty space}$$

Exercise 14.10

Use $\pi = \frac{22}{7}$. Where answers involve decimals, round off to one decimal place.

1. Two tennis balls fit exactly into a cylindrical container, as shown. The diameter of each tennis ball is 8 cm.
   Calculate (a) the radius and height of the cylinder
   (b) the volume of the cylinder
   (c) the volume of one tennis ball
   (d) the volume of empty space in the cylinder not occupied by the tennis balls.

2. A cylinder is used to package five tennis balls, as shown.
   The radius of a tennis ball is 4 cm.
   Calculate (a) the radius and height of the cylinder
   (b) if the cylinder were cut from cardboard, the area
      of cardboard used
   (c) the volume of the cylinder
   (d) the volume of one tennis ball
   (e) the volume of empty space not taken up by tennis balls in the cylinder.

3. A football is packaged in a rectangular cardboard box, as shown. The radius of the football is 18 cm.
   Calculate (a) the dimensions of the box
   (b) the area of cardboard used to make the box
   (c) the volume of the football
   (d) the volume of empty space in the box not taken up by the football.

4. A cylindrical tin of paint fits exactly into a square rectangular box of base 20 cm and height 30 cm, as shown.
   Calculate (a) the volume of the box in cm³
   (b) the volume of the cylinder in cm³
   (c) the volume of free space in the box.

30 cm

20 cm

20 cm

5. Two cylindrical jars of mayonnaise fit exactly into a rectangular box, as shown. The box is 18 cm long, 9 cm wide and 15 cm high.
   Calculate (a) the radius of each jar
   (b) the volume of each jar
   (c) the volume of the box
   (d) the volume of empty space not taken up by the two jars.

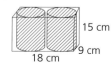

15 cm

9 cm

18 cm

Exercise 14.11   (Chapter summary)

Unless otherwise specified, take π = 3.14.

1. Copy out the table below and fill in each item from List A into its correct place in the table.

   l = length, b = breadth, h = height (perpendicular), r = radius

Name	Formula
(a) Area of rectangle =	
(b) Volume of sphere =	
(c) Area of circle =	
(d) Curved surface area of cylinder =	
(e) Area of parallelogram =	
(f) Volume of rectangular box =	
(g) Surface area of sphere =	
(h) Volume of cylinder =	
(i) Area of rectangle =	
(j) Total surface area of cylinder =	
(k) Area of triangle =	
(l) Total surface area of rectangular box =	
(m) Circumference of circle =	

List A: $2\pi rh$, $\frac{1}{2}bh$, $\frac{4}{3}\pi r^3$, lb, πr^2h, lbh, πr^2, $2lb + 2lh + 2bh$, $4\pi r^2$, bh, πr^2h, $2\pi r$, $2\pi r^2 + 2\pi rh$

2. Calculate the area of the following figures.

(a)

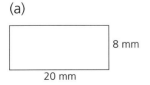

8 mm

20 mm

(b)

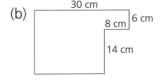

30 cm

8 cm 6 cm

14 cm

(c)

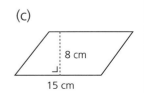

8 cm

15 cm

(d)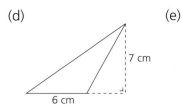
7 cm
6 cm

(e)
16
12
π = 3.14

(f)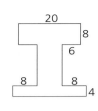
20
8
6
8
8
4

3. Find the perimeter of the following figures.

(a)
8 cm
14 cm

(b)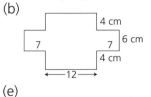
4 cm
7
7
6 cm
4 cm
12

(c)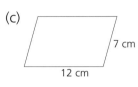
7 cm
12 cm

(d)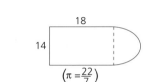
18
14
$\left(\pi = \frac{22}{7}\right)$

(e)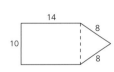
14
10
8
8

(f)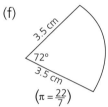
3.5 cm
72°
3.5 cm
$\left(\pi = \frac{22}{7}\right)$

4. A cylinder is used to package five tennis balls, as shown in the diagram. The radius of a tennis ball is 4 cm.
   (a) Calculate the radius and height of the cylinder.
   (b) If the cylinder was cut from cardboard, what area of cardboard is used?
   (c) Calculate the volume of the cylinder.
   (d) Calculate the volume of one tennis ball.
   (e) Calculate the volume of empty space not taken up by the tennis balls in the cylinder. Give your answer correct to one decimal place.

5. A contractor must calculate the volume of cement required to build the set of steps shown.
   (a) Calculate the area of the shaded region in square metres (m²). (Hint: Divide the shaded region into three rectangles.)
   (b) Use the answer to (a) to calculate the volume of the steps in cubic metres (m³).
   (c) If concrete costs €40 per cubic metre, find the cost of the concrete.

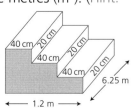
40 cm
20 cm
40 cm
20 cm
40 cm
20 cm
6.25 m
1.2 m

6. The four sides of a rectangular chimney are to be painted. The height of the chimney is 4 m, its width is 1 m and its length is 1.2 m.
   (a) Calculate the area to be painted in m².
   (b) If a tin of paint covers 3 m², how many tins will need to be bought? (Remember, if only part of a tin is required, it will be necessary to buy the full tin.)
   (c) If each tin costs €43.50, find the cost of the paint.

7. A football is packaged in a rectangular cardboard box, as shown in the diagram. The radius of the football is 18 cm. Calculate (a) the dimensions of the box (b) the area of cardboard used to make the box (c) the volume of the football (d) the volume of empty space in the box not taken up by the football.

8. A company makes hollow metal pipes with an external diameter of 18 cm and an internal diameter of 14 cm, as shown. The length of the pipe is 1.7 m.
   (a) Calculate the area of the base of the pipe (shaded in the diagram).
   (b) Find the volume of metal required for one pipe in cm³.
   (c) Find the volume of metal needed to make 20 identical pipes.
   (d) If the metal cost 45c per cm³, calculate how much the company would pay for the metal.

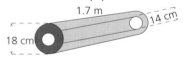

9. A company makes cylindrical jars to be filled with mayonnaise. Market research has informed the company that the most popular size of jar currently on the market is 1100 cm³. If the height of the jars is to be 14 cm, calculate the radius the company will have to make the jars so as to accommodate this volume. Use $\pi = \frac{22}{7}$.

10. Oil is stored in a rectangular tank.
    (a) Calculate, in litres, the capacity of the tank if the length is 2.5 m, the width is 1.5 m and the height is 2 m.

(b) Find the cost of filling the tank if oil costs 70c per litre. (c) If VAT is charged at a rate of 21% on top of this bill, calculate the total cost of the oil.

11. A rectangular box is used to package four golf balls with a radius of 2 cm, as shown. Calculate (a) the dimensions of the smallest box into which they would fit (b) the volume of this box (c) the volume of one of the golf balls, correct to two decimal places (d) the volume of the four golf balls together (e) the volume of empty space not occupied by the golf balls.

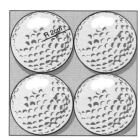

12. Oil is stored in a cylindrical tank.
    (a) Calculate, in litres, the capacity of the tank if the internal diameter is 1.6 m and the height is 2 m.
    (b) Find the cost of filling the tank if oil costs 68c per litre.
    (c) If VAT is charged at a rate of 21% on top of this bill, calculate the total cost of the oil.

13. An oil delivery tanker holds 144.6 m³ of oil when full. It is delivering to a housing estate in which the houses all have spherical domestic tanks.
    (a) If the radius of the domestic tank is 1.2 m, calculate the volume of oil required to completely fill the tank in m³, correct to two decimal places.
    (b) How many houses would the delivery tanker be able to stop at if each house required a full tank?

14. A metal gate requires circles with a diameter of 20 cm to be made from flat metal.
    (a) What length will be required to make one such circle?
    (b) If a piece of metal of 6.5 m is used to make the circles, how many full lengths could be made?
    (c) What length would be left unused?

Geometry 1 **15**

CHAPTER SUMMARY

In this chapter, you will learn about:

✦ Points and lines.
✦ Angles.
✦ Corresponding and alternate angles.
✦ Properties of triangles.

✦ Types of triangles.
✦ Quadrilaterals.
✦ Circles.

▌▌▌Points and lines

Point

A point is denoted by a small (lower-case) letter, such as a, b, x. A capital letter such as L or M is used to denote a line.

Line

A line extends indefinitely in both directions. The line below is called L. It can also be denoted by using two points anywhere on the line, e.g. the line below could be denoted by ab, bc or ac.

Line segment

The word 'segment' means 'part'. Therefore, a line segment is part of a line. It does not continue indefinitely, but rather has a starting point and end point. Square brackets, like these [ ], are used to denote a line segment. The line segment below is [cd].

The **length of a line segment** is written using parallel lines. The length of the line segment [cd] is written as |cd|, e.g. |cd| = 3 cm.

Parallel lines

Two (or more) lines which never meet are said to be **parallel lines**. The lines J, K and M below are parallel, shown as J || K || M. Arrows may be drawn on lines to indicate that they are parallel, as in the diagram. Two vertical lines, like these ||, are used to denote parallel lines.

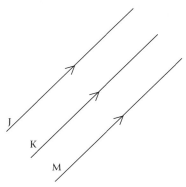

Collinear lines

Points which are on the same line are said to be **collinear**. In the diagram, the points e, f, g and h are all collinear.

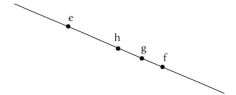

Point of intersection

The point where two lines meet is called the **point of intersection**. The set symbol ∩ is used to denote the intersection of two lines.

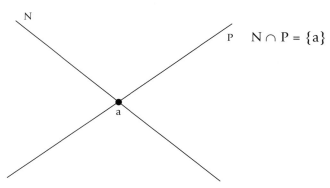

N ∩ P = {a}

Parallel lines do not have a point of intersection.

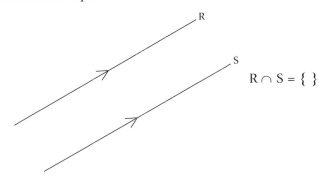

$$R \cap S = \{\ \}$$

Perpendicular lines

Two lines are perpendicular if the angle between them is 90°. The symbol ⊥ is used to denote perpendicular lines.

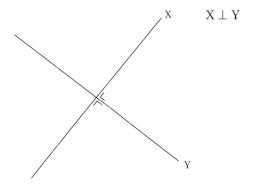

X ⊥ Y

Angles

An **angle** is a measure of the amount of turning required to move a line from one position to another. An angle may be named using one of three methods: (a) three letters; in this case, the letter in the centre indicates where the angle is located (b) a number (c) a capital letter.

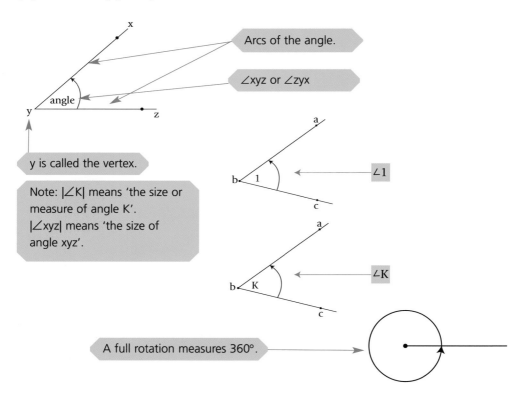

Arcs of the angle.

∠xyz or ∠zyx

y is called the vertex.

Note: |∠K| means 'the size or measure of angle K'.
|∠xyz| means 'the size of angle xyz'.

∠1

∠K

A full rotation measures 360°.

Types of angles

Type	Diagram	Explanation
Acute		Any angle between 0° and 90°.
Right angle		Any angle of exactly 90°.
Straight angle		An angle of exactly 180°.
Reflex angle		Any angle between 180° and 360°.
Full circle (complete revolution or rotation)		A complete turn 360° $\|\angle M\| + \|\angle N\| + \|\angle P\| + \|\angle R\| + \|\angle T\| = 360°$.
Angles in a straight line		Angles in a straight line add to 180° $\|\angle B\| + \|\angle A\| = 180°$ $\|\angle C\| + \|\angle D\| + \|\angle E\| = 180°$
Vertically opposite angles		Vertically opposite angles appear where two lines meet. G is opposite to J. F is opposite to H. $\|\angle F\| = \|\angle H\|$ $\|\angle G\| = \|\angle J\|$

277

Example 15.1

Calculate the size of the angles A, B, C, D, E, F and X.

(a)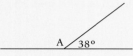

(b)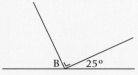

(c)

(d)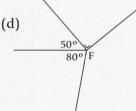

(e)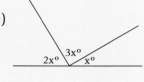

Solution

(a) A = 180° − 38°

   A = 142°

(b) B + 90° + 25° = 180°

   ⇒ B = 180 − (90 + 25)

   ⇒ B = 180 − 115

   ⇒ B = 65°

(c) ∠ D is vertically opposite to the 68°

   ⇒ |∠ D| = 68°

   C + 68° = 180°

   ⇒ C = 180 − 68

   ⇒ C = 112°

   ⇒ E = 112° (vertically opposite to C)

(d) 50 + 80 + 90 + F = 360° (full rotation)

   220° + F = 360

   ⇒ F = 360 − 220

   ⇒ F = 140°

(e) The angles 2x, 3x and x are in a straight line and therefore must add up to 180°.

   2x° + 3x° + x° = 180° (x can be written as 1x)

   6x = 180

   $x = \dfrac{180}{6}$

   x = 30°

Exercise 15.1

1. Use your protractor to measure the size of the angles A and B. In each case write down the size of angles A and B. Find the value of $|\angle A| + |\angle B|$.

(a)

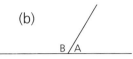

(b)

(c)

(d)

2. In each case (i) use your protractor to measure the size of the angles C, D and E (ii) find the sum of the three angles $|\angle C| + |\angle D| + |\angle E|$.

(a)

(b)

(c)

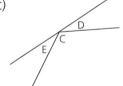

(d)

In questions 3 to 5, calculate the measure of the angles shown by letters.

3. (a)

135° F

(b)

G 30°

(c)

H 18°

(d)

148°
J

(e)

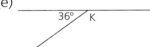

36° K

(f)

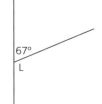

67°
L

4. (a)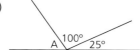

(b)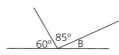

(c)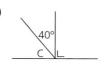

(d)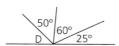

(e)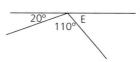

(f)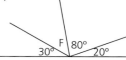

5. (a)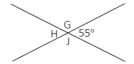

(b)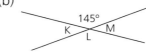

(c)

(d)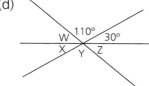

(e)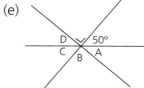

6. Calculate the value of x in each of the following.

(a)

(b)

(c)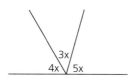

(d)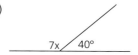

7. Calculate the value of x and any unknown angle in each of the following.

(a)

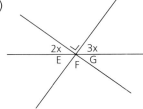

(b)

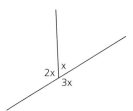

(c)

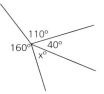

(d)

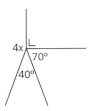

8. Calculate the value of x in each of the following.

(a)

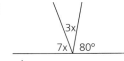

(b)

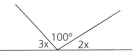

(c)

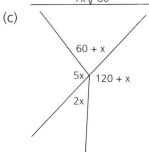

(d)

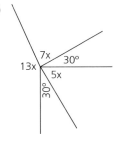

9. Calculate the value of x in each of the following.

(a)

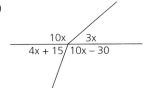

(b)

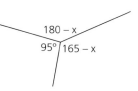

(c)

(d)

Corresponding and alternate angles

Corresponding and alternate angles appear when a line crosses two or more parallel lines.

Corresponding angles

Corresponding angles are the same size. In the diagram below, the angles A and E are an example of a pair of corresponding angles. Angles K and H are another example. Can you find more?

NOTE: A method used sometimes to identify a pair of corresponding angles is to slide a particular angle up or down and see if you can pick out which angle it will fall onto when moved. In the diagram, if you slide angle K over to the left, along the line, it would fall exactly on top of the angle H (or C). Therefore, angle K is corresponding to angle H (and C).

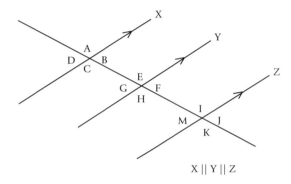

X || Y || Z

Alternate angles

The angles on opposite sides of the cutting line and between the parallel lines (the blue line in the diagram) are called alternate angles. They occur in pairs and are the same size.

In the diagram above, angle B is alternate to angle G. Can you find more?

NOTE: A method often used to identify pairs of alternate angles is to look for a Z shape. The alternate pairs occur in the inside of this shape, as shown.

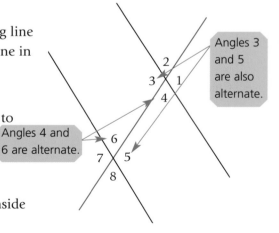

Angles 3 and 5 are also alternate.

Angles 4 and 6 are alternate.

Example 15.2

(a) Calculate the size of the angles A, B, C, D, E, F, G.

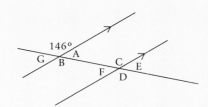

(b) Complete the following table.

Angle		Angle
A	is corresponding to	
B	is corresponding to	
A	is alternate to	
B	is alternate to	
G	is corresponding to	

Solution

(a) A = 180° − 146°

    A = 34°

    B = 146° (vertically opposite
       to angle 146°)

    G = A = 34°

    C = 146° (alternate to B)

    D = 146° (corresponding to B)

    E = 34°

    F = 34°

(b) Table completed

Angle		Angle
A	is corresponding to	E
B	is corresponding to	D
A	is alternate to	F
B	is alternate to	C
G	is corresponding to	F

Exercise 15.2

1. Complete the table using the diagram.

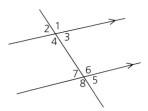

Angle		Angle
1	is corresponding to	
7	is corresponding to	
4	is alternate to	
3	is corresponding to	
7	is alternate to	

2. Calculate the value of the angle represented by each letter.

(a)

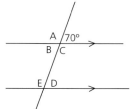

(b)

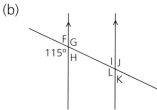

(c)

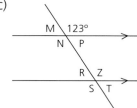

(d)

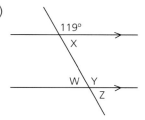

3. Calculate the value of the angle represented by each letter.

(a)

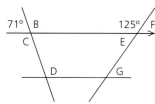

(b)

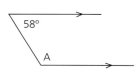

4. Calculate the value of the angle represented by each letter.

(a)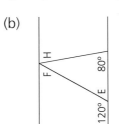

(b) (c)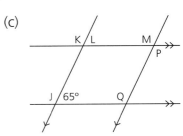

(d)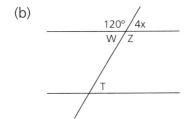

5. Calculate the value of x and the measure of each angle marked with a letter.

(a)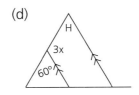

(b)

(c)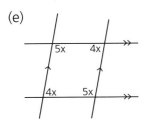

(d)

(e)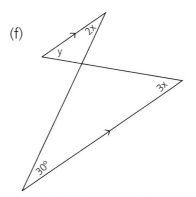

(f)

Properties of triangles

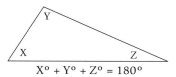

1. The three angles of a triangle add up to 180°.

$X° + Y° + Z° = 180°$

Example 15.3

Find $|\angle A|$.

Solution

$A + 100 + 50 = 180$

$\Rightarrow A = 180 - (100 + 50)$

$\Rightarrow A = 30°$

2. The exterior angle of a triangle is equal to the sum of the two interior opposite angles.

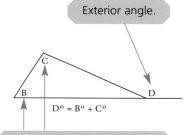

Exterior angle.

$D° = B° + C°$

Two interior opposite angles.

Example 15.4

Find $|\angle E|$.

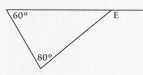

Solution

$E = 60 + 80$

$E = 140°$

Types of triangles

Isosceles triangle

Two equal sides
⇒ Two equal angles
The two equal angles are opposite the two equal sides.

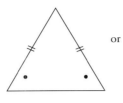 or

The reverse of this is also true:

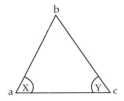

If $|\angle X| = |\angle Y|$, then the triangle abc is isosceles and $|ab| = |bc|$.

Example 15.5

Calculate (a) $|\angle A|$ (b) $|\angle B|$.

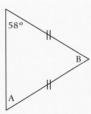

Solution

(a) $|\angle A| = 58°$ (two angles opposite equal sides is an isosceles triangle)

(b) $58° + A + B = 180°$

$58 + 58 + B = 180$ (since $|\angle B| = 58°$)

$\Rightarrow B = 180 - (58 + 58)$

$\Rightarrow |\angle B| = 180 - 116 = 64°$

Example 15.6

Find (a) $|\angle C|$ (b) $|\angle D|$.

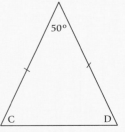

Solution

Angle C = angle D since they are the two angles opposite the two equal sides in an isosceles triangle.

(a) C + D + 50 = 180°

    C + D = 180 – 50 = 130°

    $|\angle C| = 130 \div 2 = 65°$

(b) $|\angle D| = 65°$

Equilateral triangle

Three equal sides.

⇒ Three equal angles.

⇒ Each angle = 60°.

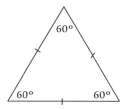

Example 15.7

Find the size of angles E, F and G if the triangle is equilateral.

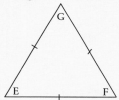

Solution

This is an equilateral triangle, so all angles are equal.

$180 \div 3 = 60° = |\angle E| = |\angle F| = |\angle G|$

Scalene triangle

Three unequal sides.

⇒ Three unequal angles.

Exercise 15.3

1. Find the size of the unknown angles in each of the following.

(a)

(b)
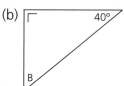

(c)
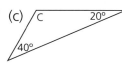

(d)
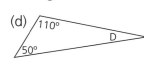

2. Find the size of the unknown angles in each of the following.

(a)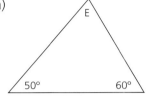

(b)

(c)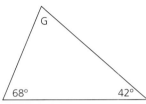

(d)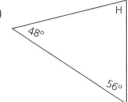

3. In each of the following, calculate the size of angle x.

(a)

(b)

(c)

4. In each of the following, calculate the size of angle x.

(a)

(b)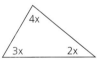

(c)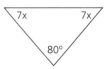

5. Find the size of the unknown angles in each of the following.

(a)   (b) 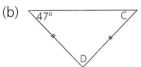 (c)   (d)

6. Find the size of the each of the unknown angles in each of the following.

(a) 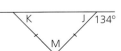 (b) 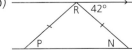 (c)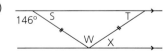

7. Find the size of each of the unknown angles in each of the following.

(a) 70° A B

(b) 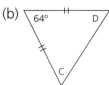 64° D C

(c)  E F 24°

(d) 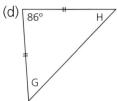 86° H G

8. Find the size of each of the unknown angles in each of the following.

(a) 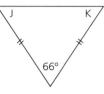 J K 66°

(b)  38° M P

(c) 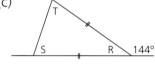 T S R 144°

9. (a) Calculate $|\angle abc|$. (b) Calculate $|\angle acb|$.

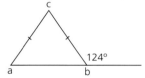 c 124° a b

10. (a) Calculate $|\angle def|$. (b) Calculate $|\angle fde|$.

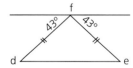 f 43° 43° d e

11. (a) Calculate $|\angle mhg|$. (b) Calculate $|\angle mhk|$. (c) Calculate $|\angle hkm|$.

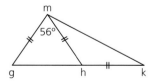 m 56° g h k

12. (a) Calculate $|\angle rqp|$. (b) Calculate $|\angle rqs|$. (c) Calculate $|\angle rsq|$.

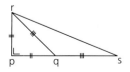 r p q s

Quadrilaterals

A quadrilateral is any closed four-sided figure. The sum of the angles in any quadrilateral is 360°, since it can be divided into two triangles by drawing one diagonal, as shown in the diagram.

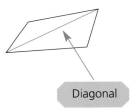

Diagonal

Types of quadrilateral

Type	Diagram	Description
Parallelogram		Opposite sides are parallel, e.g. ab||dc. Opposite sides are equal, e.g. |ad| = |bc|.
		Opposite angles are equal.
		Diagonals bisect each other, e.g. |ho| = |of|.
Rhombus		All sides are equal.
		Opposite sides are parallel. Opposite sides are equal.

Type	Diagram	Description
Rhombus		Diagonals bisect each other.
		Diagonals intersect at right angles, e.g. $|\angle kom| = 90°$.
Rectangle		Opposite sides are parallel. All angles are 90° right angles.
		Opposite sides are equal.
		Diagonals bisect each other and are equal.
Square		Opposite sides are parallel. All angles are right angles. All sides are equal.
		Diagonals bisect each other and are at right angles.

Example 15.8

Calculate the size of the unknown angles in each of the following.

(a)

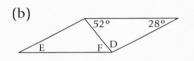

Solution

(a) A = 68° opposite angles in a parallelogram

Angle C = Angle B

68° + A + B + C = 360°

B + C = 360 − (2 × 68) = 360 − 136 = 224°

224 ÷ 2 = 112° = B = C

(b)

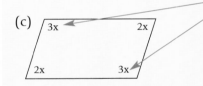

(b) 52° = F alternate

E = 28° opposite angles in a parallelogram

D = 180 − (28 + 52)

⇒ D = 180 − 80 = 100°

(c) 3x + 3x + 2x + 2x = 360°

Opposite angles in a parallelogram are equal.

(c)

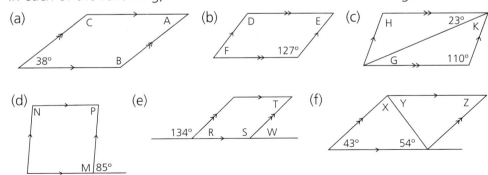

Angles in any quadrilateral add up to 360°.

10x = 360°

x = 36°

Exercise 15.4

1. In each of the following, calculate the size of the unknown angles.

(a)

(b)

(c)

(d)

(e)

(f)

2. Calculate the size of angle x in each of the following.

(a)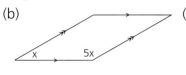

(b)

(c)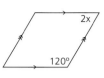

(d)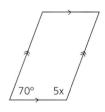

(e)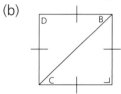

(f)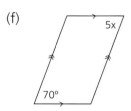

3. Calculate the size of the unknown angles in each of the following.

(a)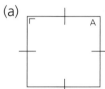

(b)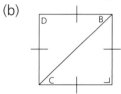

(c)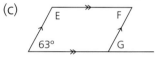

(d)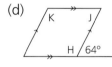

(e)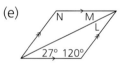

(f)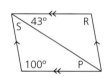

4. Find (a) |∠dcb| (b) |dc| (c) |da| (d) perimeter of rectangle.

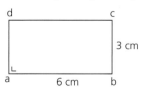

5. If |ho| = 3 cm, calculate (a) |of| (b) |eo| (c) |eg|.

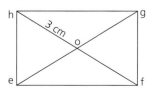

6. If |nk| = 10 cm, calculate (a) |no| (b) |jm| (c) |om| (d) |nk| + |jm|.

7. Calculate (a) |∠adb| (b) |∠dcb| (c) |∠dbc| (d) |∠dcb| (e) |∠adc|.

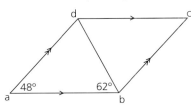

8. Calculate (a) |∠eof| (b) |∠hgf| (c) |∠gho| (d) |∠ofg| (e) |∠ehg|.

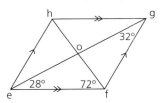

9. jklm is a rhombus. Find (a) |∠mlo| (b) |∠klj| (c) |∠mlk|
   (d) |∠mkj| (e) |∠jok|.

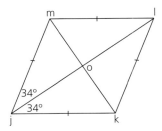

   Name a line segment equal in length to each of the following:
   (f) |jm| (g) |mo|.

Circles

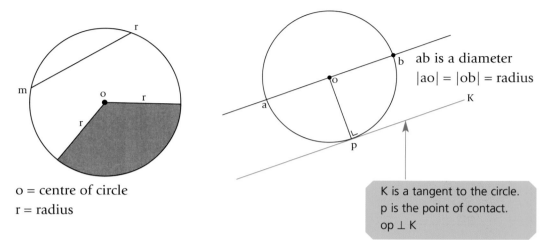

o = centre of circle
r = radius

ab is a diameter
|ao| = |ob| = radius

K is a tangent to the circle.
p is the point of contact.
op ⊥ K

Properties of circles

Fact	Diagram	Explanation
The angle in a semi-circle is always 90°.		The angle at c and also the angle at d are each 90°. [ab] must be a diameter in this situation.
The sum of the opposite angles in a cyclic quadrilateral is 180°.		A cyclic quadrilateral is any four-sided figure which has all four vertices on the circumference of a circle. In this case: $E° + G° = 180°$ $F° + H° = 180°$

Example 15.9

Calculate (a) $|\angle bco|$ (b) $|\angle bca|$ (c) $|\angle cab|$ (d) $|\angle coa|$.

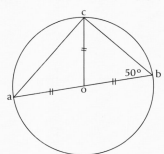

Solution

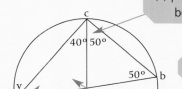

(a) $|\angle bco| = 50°$ The triangles boc and aoc are isosceles.

(b) $|\angle bca| = 90°$ (angle in a semi-circle)

(c) $|\angle cab| = 40°$ since the triangle aoc is isosceles

(d) $|\angle coa| = 180 - (40 + 40)$
$= 180 - 80$
$= 100°$

Example 15.10

Calculate (a) $|\angle X|$ (b) $|\angle Y|$.

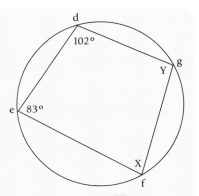

Solution
The figure (quadrilateral) efgh is a cyclic quadrilateral.

(a) $X + 102° = 180°$ (since $102°$ is opposite to the angle X)
$\Rightarrow X = 180 - 102°$
$\Rightarrow X = 78°$

(b) $Y + 83° = 180°$ (since $83°$ is opposite to angle Y)
$Y = 180° - 83°$
$Y = 97°$

Exercise 15.5

1. In each of the following circles, calculate the size of the unknown angles. [ab] is a diameter of the circle.

(a)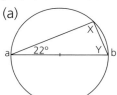

(b)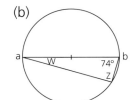

(c)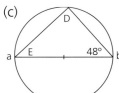

(d)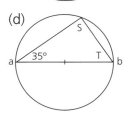

(e)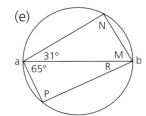

(f)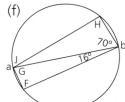

2. In each of the following circles, calculate the size of the unknown angles. [ab] is a diameter.

(a)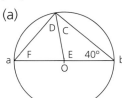

(b)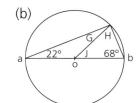

(c)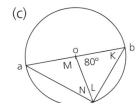

(d)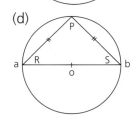

(e)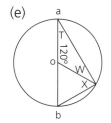

(f)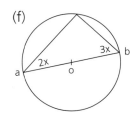

3. Calculate the size of the unknown angles in each of the following.

(a)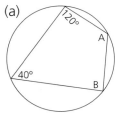

(b)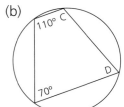

(c)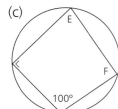

(d)
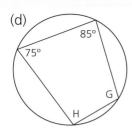

(e)
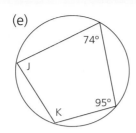

(f)
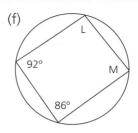

4. In each of the following, calculate the value of x. [ab] is a diameter.

(a)
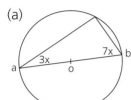

(b)
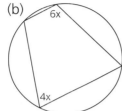

(c)
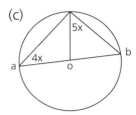

(d)
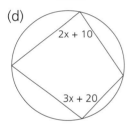

(e)
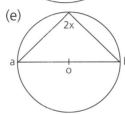

(f)
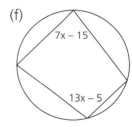

5. In each of the following, calculate the size of angles X, Y and Z. T is a tangent line.

(a)
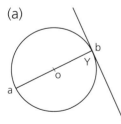

(b)
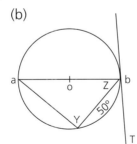

(c)
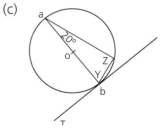

(d)
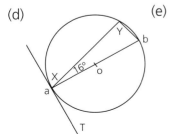

(e)
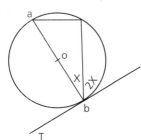

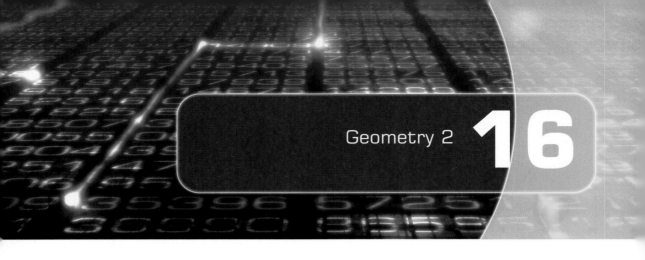

Geometry 2 **16**

In this chapter, you will learn about:

+ Drawing parallel lines.
+ Translations.

+ Central symmetry.
+ Axial symmetry.

In this chapter we study changes in the position of a shape or figure. When a figure moves from one place to another, it is called a **transformation.** Transformations are also called mappings. The original figure is mapped (moved) to a new position.

The transformations studied in this chapter are translations, central symmetry and axial symmetry.

Drawing parallel lines

You will need a set square, ruler and pencil.
To draw a line parallel to K and passing through point a:

1. Place a set square so any one edge is along line K.
2. Place a ruler along a different edge of the set square, as shown.
3. Keeping the ruler fixed, move the set square along the ruler until the same edge passes through point a. Draw the parallel line (shown as a dotted line in the diagram).

▌▌▌Translations

A translation moves all of the shape (figure) in the same direction for the same distance. The new position of the figure is called the image. A translation may be denoted by an arrow above two letters, e.g. $\overrightarrow{ab}$.

Example 16.1

Draw the image of the triangle abc under the translation $\overrightarrow{xy}$.

Solution

c^1 means the image of c, similarly for a^1 and b^1.
To find c^1, draw a line parallel to xy and passing through point c.
Mark a point c^1 so that $|cc^1| = |xy|$.
Can you pick out two more translations that are exactly the same?
The triangle $a^1b^1c^1$ is the image of the triangle abc under the translation $\overrightarrow{xy}$.

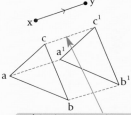

cc^1 is the same distance and in the same direction as $\overrightarrow{xy}$.

Note: The phrase 'in the same direction' is another way of saying parallel. However, the translation $\overrightarrow{xy}$ is not equal to the translation $\overrightarrow{yx}$.

The translation $\overrightarrow{xy}$ is going upwards, whereas the translation $\overrightarrow{yx}$ is going downwards.

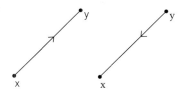

Example 16.2

abde is a rectangle. abcd is a parallelogram.
(a) Name one other translation equal to each of the following translations: (i) $\overrightarrow{ae}$ (ii) $\overrightarrow{ad}$ (iii) $\overrightarrow{db}$.
(b) Under the translation $\overrightarrow{dc}$, write down the image of the following: (i) a (ii) [ae] (iii) Δade.

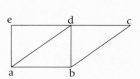

Solution

(a)   (i) $\overrightarrow{ae} = \overrightarrow{bd}$ (same distance and in the same direction)
      (ii) $\overrightarrow{ad} = \overrightarrow{bc}$
      (iii) $\overrightarrow{db} = \overrightarrow{ea}$

301

(b) 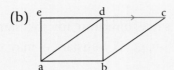 When working with translations, it is often helpful to colour the given translation in a different colour, i.e. red in the diagram on the left. Now move the given points in the same direction as $\overrightarrow{dc}$.

(i) a → b. (a is moved onto b OR b is the image of a.)

(ii) a → b, e → d ⇒ [ae] → [bd]. (Line segment [bd] is the image of [ae].)

(iii) a → b, d → c, e → d ⇒ Δade → Δbcd. (The triangle bcd is the image of the triangle ade.)

Exercise 16.1

1. Copy the diagram and draw the image of [xy] under the translation $\overrightarrow{ab}$.

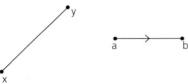

2. Copy the diagram and draw the image of Δcde under the translation $\overrightarrow{fg}$.

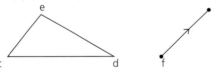

3. Copy the diagram and draw the image of Δhij under the translation $\overrightarrow{ji}$.

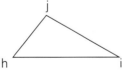

4. Copy the diagram and draw the image of the square abcd under the translation $\overrightarrow{bc}$.

5. abcd and befc are identical rectangles.

   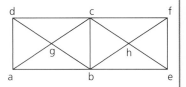

   (a) Name two other translations equal to each
   of the following translations:
   (i) $\overrightarrow{ad}$ (ii) $\overrightarrow{da}$ (iii) $\overrightarrow{dc}$ (iv) $\overrightarrow{dg}$.

   (b) Name one translation equal to $\overrightarrow{db}$.

6. Copy out the diagram above and shade the translation $\overrightarrow{be}$ in red. Write down the image of each of the following under the translation $\overrightarrow{be}$:

   (a) a (b) c (c) [ad] (d) [dc] (e) Δacd (f) [dg] (g) Δcgb.

7. abde and bcde are parallelograms.

   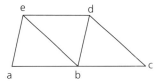

   (a) Copy out the diagram above and colour the translation $\overrightarrow{cb}$ in red.

   (b) Name two other translations equal to $\overrightarrow{cb}$.

   (c) Write down the image of each of the following under the translation $\overrightarrow{cb}$: (i) b (ii) [bd] (iii) Δbcd.

   (d) Name one translation equal to (i) $\overrightarrow{ea}$ (ii) $\overrightarrow{be}$ (iii) $\overrightarrow{ed}$.

8. abcd and cefg are identical parallelograms.

   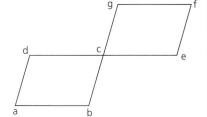

   (a) Write down the image of the following under the translation $\overrightarrow{cf}$:
   (i) a (ii) d (iii) b (iv) [bc] (v) parallelogram abcd.

   (b) Name two translations equal to
   (i) $\overrightarrow{ce}$ (ii) $\overrightarrow{gc}$ (iii) $\overrightarrow{be}$.

9. Copy the rectangle efgh and draw the image of it under translation $\overrightarrow{hf}$.

10. jklm is a parallelogram. State whether each of the following is true or false and give a reason for your answer.

(a) $\overrightarrow{jk} = \overrightarrow{kl}$ (b) $\overrightarrow{ml} = \overrightarrow{kj}$ (c) $\overrightarrow{mo} = \overrightarrow{ko}$ (d) $\overrightarrow{jo} = \overrightarrow{ol}$ (e) $\overrightarrow{jl} = 2\overrightarrow{jo}$ (twice the translation $\overrightarrow{jo}$)

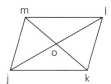

11. abef and bcde are two identical squares.

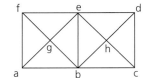

(a) Name two translations equal to (i) $\overrightarrow{ab}$ (ii) $\overrightarrow{be}$ (iii) $\overrightarrow{ga}$ (iv) $\overrightarrow{bh}$ (v) $\overrightarrow{gh}$.

(b) Name the image of the following under $\overrightarrow{bc}$:
   (i) f (ii) [ab] (iii) [ag] (iv) Δegb.

(c) In each case, write down a translation which will:
   (i) map e → c (ii) map [ge] → [bh] (iii) map Δbde → Δafe.

12. abcd, cefg and hije are identical rectangles.

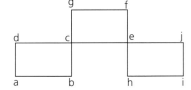

(a) Name three translations equal to
   (i) $\overrightarrow{gf}$ (ii) $\overrightarrow{fe}$ (iii) $\overrightarrow{ge}$.

(b) In each of the following, name a
   translation which will: (i) map d → a
   (ii) map [cb] → [eh]   (iii) map [db] → [ch]
   (iv) map Δceg → Δabd (v) map ▢abcd → ▢hije.

(c) Copy out the diagram and draw the image of ▢cefg under the translation $\overrightarrow{ab}$.

(d) If |dj| = 15 cm and |bg| = 8 cm, calculate the area of ▢abcd.

(e) Name one translation that is the same as the translation $3\overrightarrow{ab}$.

Central symmetry

Central symmetry is reflection through a point. The diagram shows reflection in the point a.

Central symmetry in the point a is written as S_a.

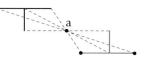

Example 16.3

Draw the image of the triangle abc under S_b (central symmetry) in the point b.

Solution

b is the midpoint of the line segment [aa¹].

a^1 is the image of a.

c^1 is the image of c.

b is the image of b, since this is the point used for the central symmetry.

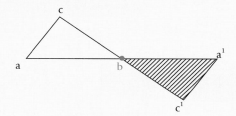

Example 16.4

xyzw is a parallelogram. Write down the image of the following under S_o, central symmetry in the point o:

(a) w   (b) [wx]   (c) o   (d) Δxoy.

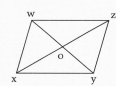

Solution

Highlight the point o in red. Everything will go through this red point and on the same distance on the other side.

(a) w → y

(b) w → y, x → z

   ⇒ [wx] → [yz]

(c) o → o (since it is the point being used for the central symmetry)

(d) x → z, o → o, y → w

   ⇒ Δxoy → Δzow

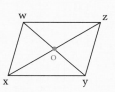

Example 16.5

In each of the following, indicate whether or not a point could be used for central symmetry so that the object would be symmetrical about that point.

(a)   (b)   (c)   (d)

Solution

(a)

(b) Y

(c)

This point is called the centre of symmetry.

This shape does not have a centre of symmetry.

The centre of symmetry here is where the diagonals meet.

(d) B ← This figure does not have a centre of symmetry.

Exercise 16.2

1. In each of the following, copy the diagram and draw the image under S_b.

(a) 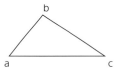　　(b) 　　(c)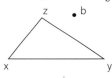

(d) 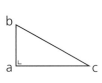　　(e) 　　(f)

2. In each of the following, copy the diagram and draw the image under S_c.

(a) 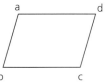　　(b) 　　(c)

(d) 　　(e) 　　(f)

3. In the parallelogram shown, use S_o, central symmetry in the point o, to find the image of the following:
(a) c (b) [dc] (c) o (d) [ao] (e) Δcob (f) ▱ abcd.

4. In the diagram shown, use S_b to find the image of the following: (a) g (b) f (c) b (d) [cb] (e) Δbef. (Note: abcd and befg are identical rectangles.)

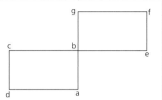

5. The rectangle xyzw is divided into four identical rectangles. Find the image of each of the following under S_a: (a) s (b) z (c) y (d) a (e) [wr] (f) Δaxm (g) ▭tarw (h) ▭xmat (i) ▭xyzw (j) Δxyz.

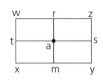

6. The square abcd is divided into four identical squares, as shown. Using central symmetry for each of the following, identify the point under which:
(a) b would be the image of d
(b) b would be the image of c
(c) b would be the image of a
(d) c would be the image of d
(e) ▭efid would be the image of ▭gfhb.

7. (a) Copy the diagram shown and draw the image of Δabc under S_b.
(b) Now draw the image of this new triangle under S_a.

8. Draw the image of the dustbin shown under S_b.

9. In each of the following, state whether the shape has a centre of symmetry, and if so, indicate where it is.

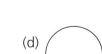

(a) (b) (c) (d)

(e) (f) (g)

Axial symmetry

Symmetrical shapes: Some shapes can be folded along a line so that one half of the figure folds exactly on top of the other half. Such shapes are said to be symmetrical. The shapes below are symmetrical and can be folded along the dotted lines.

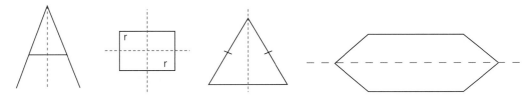

Axial symmetry: This means reflection in a line. It is like reflection in a mirror. The original shape and the image shape are exactly the same distance away from the reflection line or mirror line. Some examples are shown below.

Example 16.6

$a^1b^1c^1$ is the image of the original triangle abc under S_L, axial symmetry in the line L.

Note 1: The image 'flips over' the mirror line.

Note 2: The distance from a to the line L is the same as the distance from a^1 to the line L. Similarly for the other points (vertices) of the triangles.

Note 3: S_L means axial symmetry. The L is a capital letter for a line.

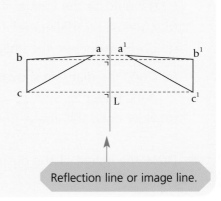

Reflection line or image line.

Example 16.7

$a^1 b^1 c^1 d^1$ is the image of the square abcd under S_T, axial symmetry in the line T. Note that d is the image of d under S_T since it lies on the line T.

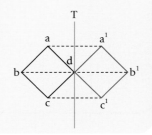

Example 16.8

abcd and befc are two identical rectangles.
Under S$_{cb}$, axial symmetry in the line cb, find the image
of: (a) d (b) b (c) [ab] (d) Δaod.

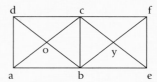

Solution

Copy the diagram and draw a line along the axial
symmetry line (cb), as shown by the red line. This red
line is the mirror line (reflection line).
(a) d → f
(b) b → b (since it is on the mirror line)
(c) Δaod (coloured black here):

    a → e   original → image
    o → g ⇒ Δaod → Δegf (shown as a dotted triangle here)
    d → f

Exercise 16.3

1. Copy each of the following and draw (using a different colour) any lines of
   symmetry each figure may have (some have no axes (lines) of symmetry).

    Square   Sector

(a)   (b)   (c)   (d)

(e)   (f)   (g)   (h)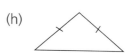

2. Copy each of the diagrams and draw the image of the original shape
   under S$_A$, axial symmetry in the line A.

(a)   (b)   (c)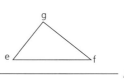

(d) 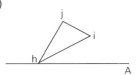   (e)   (f)

3. Copy each of the following figures and draw the image under S_B, axial symmetry in the line B.

(a)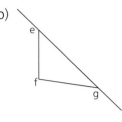

(b)

(c)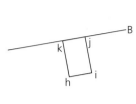

(d)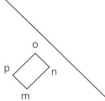

(e)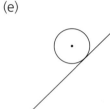

(f)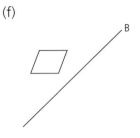

4. Using S_{bc}, axial symmetry in the line bc, write down the image of the following: (a) y (b) b (c) [xy] (d) Δxbc (e) Δbwt.

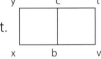

5. (a) The large rectangle bdfh is divided into four identical rectangles. Name the image of each of the following under S_{cg}.
   (i) a (ii) [bc] (iii) [ah] (iv) [gi] (v) Δcie (vi) □ cdei
   (b) What is the image of each of the following under S_{ae}?
   (i) g (ii) f (iii) [bc] (iv) [ci] (v) Δcie (vi) □ cdei

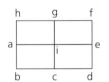

6. In the diagram, [db] and [ac] are both diameters of the circle.
   (a) Write down the image of the following under S_{db}.
   (i) a (ii) d (iii) [db] (iv) semi-circle dab (v) sector boc
   (b) Write down the image of the following under S_{ac}.
   (i) a (ii) d (iii) [db] (iv) semi-circle dab (v) sector boc

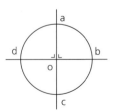

7. xyzw is a rhombus.
   (a) Under S_{xz}, write down the image of each of
   (i) w (ii) o (iii) [xy] (iv) Δyoz (v) Δxyz.
   (b) Under S_{wy}, write down the image of
   (i) x (ii) o (iii) [yz] (iv) Δyoz (v) Δxwz.

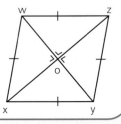

Exercise 16.4 (Chapter summary)

1. cdef and dghe are two identical rectangles.

   (a) Under the translation $\overrightarrow{he}$, write down the image of (i) d (ii) [hg] (iii) [dk] (iv) Δekh (v) Δdgh.

   (b) Under S_k, write down the image of (i) d (ii) [hg] (iii) [dk] (iv) Δekh (v) Δdgh.

   (c) Under S_{ed}, axial symmetry in the line ed, write down the image of (i) d (ii) [hg] (iii) [dk] (iv) Δekh (v) Δdgh.

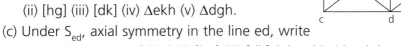

2. The large rectangle mnop is divided into four identical rectangles using the following transformations: S_r, S_{ts}, S_{wx}, $\overrightarrow{pt}$, $\overrightarrow{pm}$, $\overrightarrow{tr}$.

   Copy out the table below and write in a correct transformation in each case (the first is done for you).

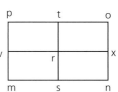

	Transformation
(a) x is mapped onto r	$\overrightarrow{tp}$
(b) o is mapped onto n	
(c) [ox] is mapped onto [pw]	
(d) [ms] is mapped onto [sn]	
(e) o is mapped onto m	
(f) ▭ wrtp is mapped onto ▭ wrsm	
(g) Δrtx is mapped onto Δrtw	
(h) [pw] is mapped onto [nx]	
(i) Δrtx is mapped onto Δsrm	
(j) Δmsr is mapped onto Δotr	

3. For each of the following transformations, copy the diagram on the right and draw the image of ▭ abdc under (a) $\overrightarrow{ab}$ (b) S_b (c) S_{ad} (d) $\overrightarrow{da}$.

4. (a) For each of the following, name a transformation which would map the following: (i) h → i (ii) [he] → [gf] (iii) [he] → [ij] (iv) Δfmi → Δgij (v) ▭ gijk → ▭ gimf.

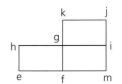

(b) Write down three translations equal to $\vec{ji}$.

(c) Write down two transformations which would map
[he] → [im].

5. nopq is a parallelogram.

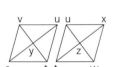

(a) Copy the diagram and shade the triangle Δpro in
black. Then shade the image of Δpro under S_r in red.

(b) Name one other translation equal to each of the
following:

(i) $\vec{op}$ (ii) $\vec{qp}$ (iii) $\vec{nr}$ (iv) $\vec{or}$.

(c) Draw the image of ▱ nopq under $\vec{qn}$.

6. stuv is a rhombus. twxu is an identical rhombus.

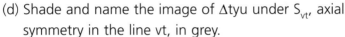

(a) Copy the diagram and shade Δtyu in black.

(b) Shade and name the image of Δtyu under $\vec{st}$ in red.

(c) Shade and name the image of Δtyu under Sy in blue.

(d) Shade and name the image of Δtyu under S_{vt}, axial
symmetry in the line vt, in grey.

(e) Name two translations equal to (i) $\vec{vu}$ (ii) $\vec{vs}$ (iii) $\vec{sy}$ (iv) $\vec{ux}$.

7. [ac] and [bd] are diameters of a circle with centre o.

(a) Copy the diagram and shade the triangle aod in black.

(b) Shade in red and name the image of Δaod under S_o,
central symmetry in the point o.

(c) Under S_o, what is the image of each of (i) b (ii) o
(iii) Δdoc (iv) [dc]?

(d) Name one translation equal to (i) $\vec{ad}$ (ii) $\vec{ab}$ (iii) $\vec{ao}$ (iv) $\vec{ob}$.

(e) What type of triangle is aob? Explain your answer.

8. [ef] is the diameter of a circle with centre h. g is any point
on the circle.

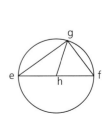

(a) Copy the diagram.

(b) Name an isosceles triangle in the diagram.

(c) Write down the angle in the diagram of measure 90°.

(d) Draw the image of Δhfg under S_h, central symmetry in the point h.

9. [xk] is the diameter of a circle with centre m.
   (a) Identify three line segments which are of equal length.

   (b) Copy the diagram and draw the image of $\triangle$xjk under S_m, central symmetry in m.
   (c) If $|\angle xjm| = 25°$, find (i) $|\angle mxj|$ (ii) $|\angle jmk|$ (iii) $|\angle mkj|$.

10. abcd is a square. The midpoints of the sides are f, g, h and k, as shown.
    (a) Copy the diagram and shade in the triangle dko in black.
    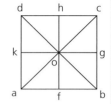
    (b) Shade in red and name the image of $\triangle$dko under S_o, central symmetry in o.
    (c) Shade in blue and name the image of $\triangle$dko under S_{kg}, axial symmetry in the line hg.
    (d) Shade in green and name the image of $\triangle$dko under $\overrightarrow{kf}$.
    (e) For each of the following, write down a transformation which would map: (i) [cg] $\to$ [ak] (ii) [cg] $\to$ [dk] (iii) [cg] $\to$ [gb] (iv) $\triangle$hoc $\to$ $\triangle$fob (v) $\square$fbgo $\to$ $\square$fako.

11. Copy the diagram. Using the information below, name each of the vertices of the parallelogram correctly and the point of intersection of the diagonals: (a) $\overrightarrow{de} = \overrightarrow{ac}$
    (b) c is the image of d under S_b (c) $\overrightarrow{ab} = \overrightarrow{be}$.
    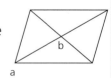

12. The diagram is of a circle with two intersecting diameters, as shown. Using the information below, name each of the vertices of the rectangle and also the centre of the circle:
    (a) $\overrightarrow{fx} = \overrightarrow{jk}$ (b) $\triangle$ hgx is mapped onto $\triangle$ fgj under central symmetry in the centre of the circle (c) $\overrightarrow{hx} = \overrightarrow{jf}$ (d) $\overrightarrow{xg} = \overrightarrow{gj}$.

13. (a) Draw the rectangle.
    (b) Label the vertices and the point where the diagonals intersect. (Do not use consecutive letters. Use random letters.)

    (c) Make up clues similar to the clues in questions 11 and 12 and see if a classmate can correctly identify all the points.

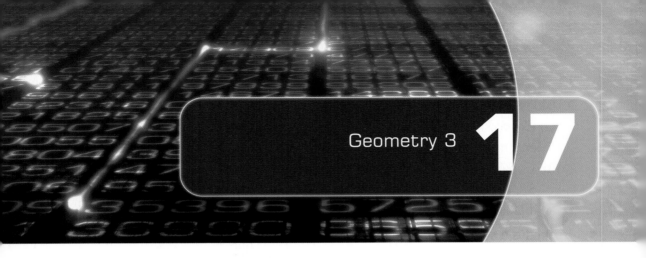

Geometry 3 **17**

In this chapter, you will learn about:
+ Pythagoras' Theorem and right-angled triangles.
+ Constructions: bisectors, triangles.
+ Dividing a line segment into three equal parts.
+ Congruent triangles.

Pythagoras' Theorem and right-angled triangles

Pythagoras was a Greek mathematician who lived around 500 BC. Although he devoted his entire life to the study of mathematics and philosophy, he is best known for his theorem on right-angled triangles. In actual fact, the theorem was known to other cultures long before it was popularised by Pythagoras, but history attributes the discovery to him. Pythagoras' Theorem is important in architecture, trigonometry and maritime navigation. It is one of the most useful and widely known theorems.

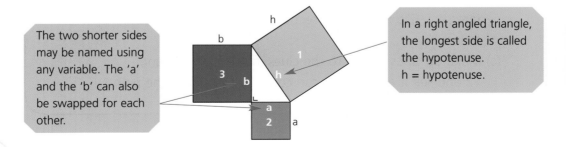

The two shorter sides may be named using any variable. The 'a' and the 'b' can also be swapped for each other.

In a right angled triangle, the longest side is called the hypotenuse.
h = hypotenuse.

Pythagoras' Theorem states that in any right-angled triangle, the square on the hypotenuse is equal to the sum of the squares on the other two sides.

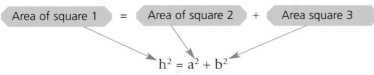

$$h^2 = a^2 + b^2$$

Note 1: The opposite (called converse) of this is also true, i.e. in any triangle, if $h^2 = a^2 + b^2$, then this triangle must be right-angled.

Note 2: Pythagoras' Theorem is used to find the missing side in a right-angled triangle, provided we know the lengths of the two other sides.

Note 3: In a right-angled triangle, the hypotenuse is always the longest side.

Example 17.1

In each of the following, calculate the length of the unknown side.

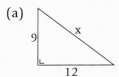

Solution

(a)

(b)

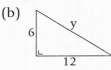

(c)

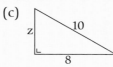

(d)

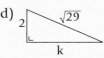

Note: $\left(\sqrt{29}\right)^2 = \sqrt{29}$

(a)

$h^2 = a^2 + b^2$
$x^2 = 9^2 + 12^2$
$x^2 = 81 + 144$
$x^2 = 225$
$x = \sqrt{225}$
$x = 15$

(b)

$h^2 = a^2 + b^2$
$y^2 = 6^2 + 12^2$
$y^2 = 36 + 144$
$y^2 = 180$
$y = \sqrt{180}$
[Leave your answer in this form, called surd form, unless you are told otherwise.]

(c)

$h^2 = a^2 + b^2$
$10^2 = z^2 + 8^2$
$100 = z^2 + 64$
$100 - 64 = z^2$
$36 = z^2$
$\sqrt{36} = z$
$z = 6$

(d)

$h^2 = a^2 + b^2$
$\left(\sqrt{29}\right)^2 = 2^2 + k^2$
$29 = 4 + k^2$
$29 - 4 = k^2$
$25 = k^2$
$\sqrt{25} = k$
$k = 5$

Example 17.2

In each of the following, investigate if the triangle is right-angled.

(a)

18 | 30
24

(b)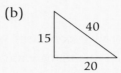

15 | 40
20

Solution

(a)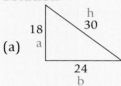

h
18 | 30
a
24
b

h² = a² + b²

$h^2 = a^2 + b^2$

$30^2 = 18^2 + 24^2$

$900 = 324 + 576$

$900 = 900$ TRUE

⇒ It **is** a right-angled triangle.

(b)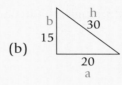

b
15 | 30
20
a

h
h² = a² + b²

$h^2 = a^2 + b^2$

$30^2 = 20^2 + 15^2$

$900 = 400 + 225$

$900 = 625$ FALSE

⇒ It is **not** a right-angled triangle.

The square on the hypotenuse is equal to the sum of the squares on the other two sides.

Exercise 17.1

1. In each of the following right-angled triangles, use Pythagoras' Theorem to find the length of the hypotenuse.

(a)

3
4

(b)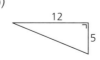

12
5

(c)

12
16

(d)

40
9

2. In each of the following, use Pythagoras' Theorem to find the length of the side x.

(a) 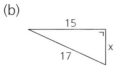 (b) 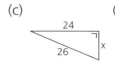 (c) (d)

3. Use Pythagoras' Theorem to find the length of the third side of each of the following right-angled triangles.

(a)   (b)   (c) (d)

4. In each of the following, use Pythagoras' Theorem to find the length of the third side of the triangle. (Remember, $\left(\sqrt{7}\right)^2 = 7$.)

(a) 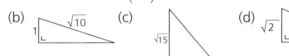 (b) (c)   (d)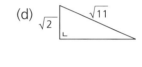

(e) 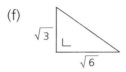 (f)   (g)   (h)

5. In each of the following, investigate whether or not the triangle is right-angled.

(a)   (b) (c) 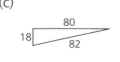 (d)

(e)   (f)   (g)

6. For each of the following right-angled triangles, use your ruler to measure the distances x, y and h. Then test these sides on Pythagoras' Theorem.

(a)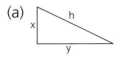

(b)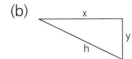

(c)

7. A rectangle has sides measuring 6 cm and 10 cm. Calculate the length of the diagonal of the rectangle.

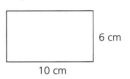

8. A rectangle has a diagonal length of 25 cm and one side of length 20 cm. Calculate the length of the other side of the rectangle.

9. A square has diagonal length $\sqrt{72}$. Calculate the length of the side of the square (x).

10. A square has diagonal length $\sqrt{162}$. Calculate the length of the side of the square (y).

11. A pole 3 m high is held in place by a support wire. The wire is secured to the ground at a distance of 6 m from the base of the pole. Calculate the length of wire needed correct to two decimal places.

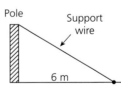

12. Lengths of wood are being prepared for a roof. The house is 10 m wide and the house must have a height of 2 m from the ceiling to the apex of the roof, as shown in the diagram. Calculate |ab|, the length of each piece of wood required, to two decimal places.

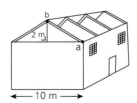

13. In the semi-circle shown, centre o, |bc| = 6 cm,
radius = 5 cm. Find (a) |ab| (b) |ac|.

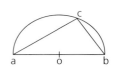

14. The diagram shows a circle where [de] is a
diameter, m, centre of circle. If |df| = 15 cm and
|ef| = 36 cm, calculate the radius of the circle.

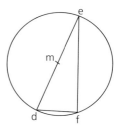

15. [gj] is a diameter of the circle with centre c.
If |ch| = 6 cm and |jh| = 8 cm, calculate |gh|.

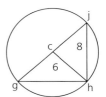

16. Four identical right-angled triangles are used to
form the figure shown. Calculate the area of the
shaded square.

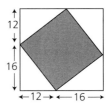

Constructions: bisectors, triangles

Parallel lines

To construct a line B parallel to a given line (line A):

1. Set up a ruler and set square 1, as shown in the diagram.
2. Move the set square over to where you wish the line to appear (set square 2 in the diagram).
3. Draw the line B, as shown.

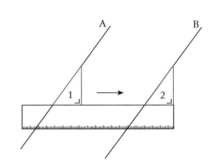

Perpendicular lines

To construct a line D perpendicular to a given line (line C):

1. Place a ruler along line C.
2. Place the set square 1 along the ruler.
3. Move the set square 1 along the ruler until you reach the point where you would like the perpendicular line. (point 'x')
4. Draw the line D, as shown.

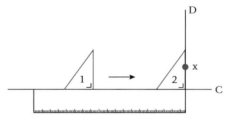

Bisecting angles

To bisect an angle using a ruler and compass only:

1. Draw any acute angle, as shown.

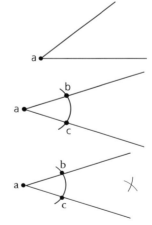

2. Set your compass to some small distance, e.g. 2 cm.

3. Place the point of the compass at point a and drawn an arc as shown (arc bc).

4. Then set your compass to a higher length, e.g. 3 cm.

5. Place the point of the compass at b and draw an arc.

6. Then place the sharp point of the compass at c and draw an arc to cut through the last arc.

7. We will call the point where these arcs meet d.

8. Join d to a.

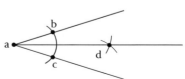

NOTE: Using your protractor, measure $|\angle bad|$. Then measure $|\angle cad|$. If your drawing is accurate, these two angles will be the same.

||| Construction 2

| Perpendicular bisector of a line segment

To construct the perpendicular bisector of a line segment using a ruler and compass only:

1. Draw a line segment on your page of any length.
2. Label this line segment [ab].
3. Place the point of the compass at a and move the pencil out until it is nearly at b, as shown in the diagram.

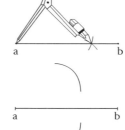

4. Draw two arcs, as shown.

5. Now place the point of the compass at b, without letting the setting change.

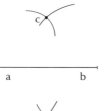

6. Draw the arcs again above and below the line segment.

7. Label the intersection of these arcs c and d.

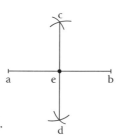

8. Join c to d. ([cd] is the perpendicular bisector.)

9. Using your ruler, measure |ae|. Then measure |eb|.

10. If your drawing is accurate, |ae| will equal |eb|.

Construction 3

Constructing triangles

Make a rough sketch of each triangle before starting the construction.

1. Given all three sides

Example 17.3

Construct Δabc where |ab| = 8 cm, |bc| = 6 cm and |ac| = 5 cm.

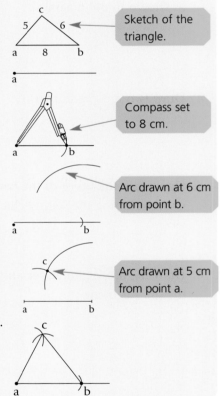

Sketch of the triangle.

Solution

1. Draw a horizontal line and label it as shown.

2. Set your compass to 8 cm and place the point of the compass at a. Draw an arc as shown. Label the point b as shown.

   Compass set to 8 cm.

3. Set your compass to 6 cm, place the point of the compass at b and draw an arc as shown. The point c will lie on this arc.

   Arc drawn at 6 cm from point b.

4. Set your compass to 5 cm, place the point of the compass at a and draw an arc as shown to cut the last arc.

   Arc drawn at 5 cm from point a.

5. Label the point of intersection of the arcs c.

6. Joint a to c and c to b.

NOTE: The arcs are called construction lines.

2. Given one side and two angles

Example 17.4

Construct Δdef where |de| = 7 cm, |∠def| = 50° and |∠dfe| = 60°.

Solution

In this case, we need |∠fde| to construct the Δ.

|∠fde| + 60° + 50° = 180°

|∠fde| = 180 − 110 = 70°

sketch:

1. Draw a horizontal line and label it as shown.

2. Set your compass to 7 cm and place the point of the compass at d. Draw an arc and label the point e as shown.

3. Place the centre of your protractor at e. Find 0° on the left-hand side of the protractor and count up to 50°.

4. Make a dot at 50° and draw a line as shown.

5. Place the centre of your protractor at d. Find 0° on the right-hand side of the protractor and count up to 70°.

6. Make a dot at 70° and draw a line as shown. The intersection of these lines is point f.

7. Join f to d and f to e.

NOTE: Using your protractor, measure |∠dfe|. If your construction is accurate, |∠dfe| will be 60°.

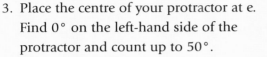

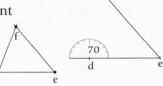

3. Given two sides and one angle

Example 17.5

Construct Δghi where |gh| = 6.5 cm, |gi| = 5 cm and |∠igh| = 40°.

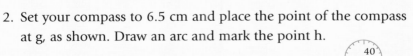

sketch

Solution

1. Draw a horizontal line and label it as shown.

2. Set your compass to 6.5 cm and place the point of the compass at g, as shown. Draw an arc and mark the point h.

3. Place the centre of your protractor at g. Find 0° on the right-hand side of the protractor and count up to 40°.

4. Make a dot at 40° and draw a line.

323

5. Set your compass to 5 cm. Place the point of the compass at g and draw an arc. The intersection of this arc and the line is i.

6. Join i to g and i to h.

Exercise 17.2

1. Draw each of the following angles. Construct the bisector of each angle, showing all construction lines clearly.

(a)   (b)   (c)

  60°    45°   70°

(d)   (e)

  55°    80°

2. Draw each of the following line segments, then construct the perpendicular bisector of each line segment, showing all construction lines. (a) |ab| = 9 cm (b) |cd| = 10 cm   (c) |ef| = 5 cm   (d) |gh| = 7.5 cm   (e) |jk| = 6.5 cm

3. Construct each of the following triangles, showing all construction lines clearly.

(a)   (b)   (c)

  6 cm 7 cm 10 cm   60° 70° 4.5 cm   100° 30° 8.5 cm

(d)   (e)   (f)

  4 cm 45° 9 cm   10 cm L 6 cm   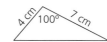 4 cm 100° 7 cm

4. Construct each of the following triangles, showing all construction lines clearly.

(a)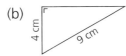

(b)

(c)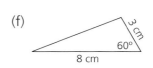

(d)

(e)

(f)

For questions 5 to 13, draw a sketch before attempting the construction.

5. Construct Δabc, where |ab| = 4 cm, |bc| = 3 cm and |ac| = 2 cm.

6. Construct Δdef, where |de| = 7.5 cm, |∠def| = 75° and |∠edf| = 40°.

7. Construct Δghk, where |gh| = 3 cm, |gk| = 2 cm and |∠kgh| = 45°.

8. Construct Δjkl, where |jk| = 5.5 cm, |∠jkl| = 30° and |∠jlk| = 70°.

9. Construct Δmno, where |mn| = 7 cm, |on| = 5 cm and |∠nom| = 90°.

10. (a) Construct Δpqr, where |pq| = 13 cm, |rq| = 12 cm and |pr| = 5 cm.
    (b) Construct Δstu, where |st| = 13 cm, |tu| = 12 cm and |∠tus| = 90°.
    (c) What do you notice about the triangles in (a) and (b)?

11. Construct an equilateral triangle of side 5 cm.

12. (a) Construct Δabc, where |ab| = 7 cm, |bc| = 7 cm and |∠abc| = 40°.
    (b) What do you call this type of triangle?
    (c) Using your protractor, measure |∠bac| and |∠acb|. What do you notice?

13. (a) Construct a circle of radius 4 cm, centre o, as shown.
    (b) Choose any two points on the circle. Label these points c and d.
    (c) Join c to o, c to d and o to d.
    (d) What kind of triangle is this? How can you be sure?

325

Construction 4

Divide a line segment [ab] into three equal parts

1. Draw a line segment [ab] of any length. Draw a line x at an acute angle, as shown in the diagram.

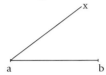

2. Set your compass to a short distance. Place the point of the compass at a and mark off point p, as shown.

3. Place the point of the compass at p, without changing the setting, and mark off point q, as shown.

4. Place the compass at point q and mark off point r, as shown.

5. Using a ruler, join r to b.

6. Using a ruler and set square, draw line segments [qd] and [pc] parallel to [rb].

7. Using your ruler, measure [ac], [cd] and [db]. If your construction is accurate, these three distances will be equal.

Exercise 17.3

1. (a) Construct line segment [ab] so that |ab| = 6 cm.
   (b) Divide this line segment into three equal parts, showing all construction lines clearly.
   (c) Using your ruler, measure the three segments created on [ab]. If your construction is accurate, each segment will be 2 cm long.

2. (a) Construct each of the following line segments.
   (i) |ab| = 7 cm　(ii) |cd| = 9 cm　(iii) |ef| = 8 cm　(iv) |gh| = 6.5 cm
   (b) In each case, divide the line segment into three equal parts, showing all construction lines clearly.

3. (a) Construct each of the following line segments.
   (i) |xj| = 5 cm　(ii) |kl| = 4.5 cm　(iii) |mn| = 3.5 cm
   (b) In each case, divide the line segment into three equal parts, showing all construction lines clearly.
   (c) Using your compass, set the compass to the length of one of the line segments, as shown in the diagram (for example, ix). Then move the compass to point x and check |xy|. Similarly, |yj| can be checked using the compass. If your construction is accurate, all three parts should be equal.

4. (a) Construct line segment [ab] so that |ab| = 7.5 cm.
   (b) Divide [ab] into three equal parts and label as shown below.
   (c) Using a ruler, measure the following distances.
   (i) |ac|　(ii) |pc|　(iii) |ad|　(iv) |qd|　(v) |ab|　(vi) |rb|
   (d) Calculate the following. What do you notice?
   (i) $\dfrac{|ac|}{|pc|}$　(ii) $\dfrac{|ad|}{|qd|}$　(iii) $\dfrac{|ab|}{|rb|}$

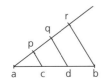

Congruent triangles

Two shapes are said to be congruent if they are identical in every way. One shape could be cut out and would fit exactly on top of the other. For example, in the diagrams, rectangle 1 is congruent to rectangle 2 and shape 3 is congruent to shape 4.

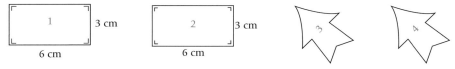

The symbol for congruence is ≡.

We say rectangle 1 ≡ rectangle 2. Also, shape 3 ≡ shape 4.

If two shapes are not congruent, we use the symbol ≢.

Example 17.6

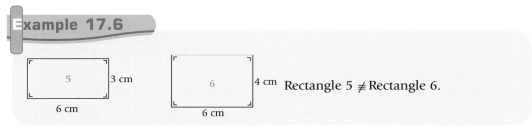

Rectangle 5 ≢ Rectangle 6.

NOTE: When dealing with triangles, there are four tests that tell us whether two triangles are congruent or not. If two triangles pass any **one** of the tests, then they are congruent (identical).

Test 1 SSS

This means that all three sides in one triangle are equal in measure to all three sides in the other triangle.

Example 17.7

NOTE: Sides marked in the same way are equal in length.

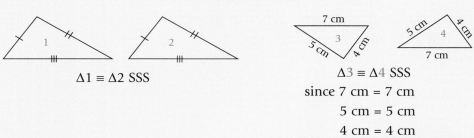

Δ1 ≡ Δ2 SSS

Δ3 ≡ Δ4 SSS

since 7 cm = 7 cm

5 cm = 5 cm

4 cm = 4 cm

NOTE: The triangle does not need to be in the same position.

Test 2 SAS

This means that two sides and the included angle in one triangle are equal to two sides and the included angle in the other triangle.

Example 17.8

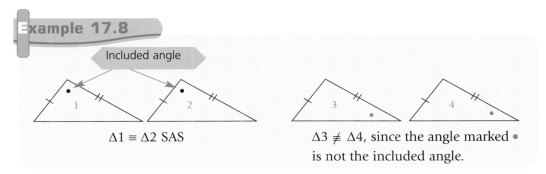

Included angle

Δ1 ≡ Δ2 SAS

Δ3 ≢ Δ4, since the angle marked • is not the included angle.

Test 3 ASA

This means that two angles and one side in one triangle are equal to two angles and one side in the other triangle.

Example 17.9

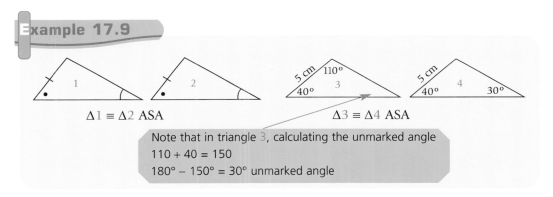

Δ1 ≡ Δ2 ASA

Δ3 ≡ Δ4 ASA

Note that in triangle 3, calculating the unmarked angle
110 + 40 = 150
180° − 150° = 30° unmarked angle

Test 4 RHS

This test only applies to right-angled triangles. It means that the right-angle (R), hypotenuse (H) and any other side (S) in one triangle must be equal to the right angle, hypotenuse and side in the other triangle.

Example 17.10

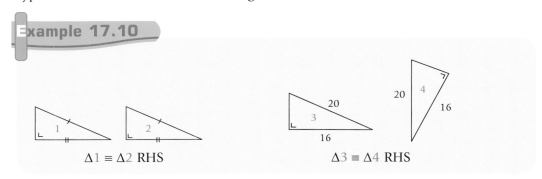

Δ1 ≡ Δ2 RHS

Δ3 ≡ Δ4 RHS

329

Exercise 17.4

In questions 1 to 4, the triangles are constructed accurately and a ruler and protractor can be used.

1. Using test 1 SSS, investigate whether or not each of the following pairs of triangles are congruent.

   (a)  (b)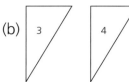

   (c)  (d)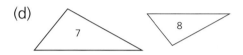

2. Using test 2 SAS, investigate whether or not each of the following pairs of triangles are congruent.

   (a)  (b)

   (c)  (d)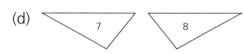

3. Using test 3 ASA, investigate whether or not each of the following pairs of triangles are congruent.

   (a)  (b)

   (c)  (d)

4. Using test 4 RHS, investigate whether or not each of the following pairs of triangles are congruent.

(a)

(b)

(c)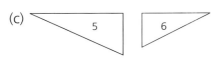

(d)

5. Using the four tests for congruence, investigate whether or not the following pairs of triangles are congruent. If the triangles are congruent, state which test indicates this and list the measurements that are equal. If the triangles are not congruent, give a reason why.

(a)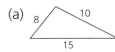

(b)

(c)

(d)

(e)

(f)

(g)

(h)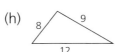

(i)

(j)

(k)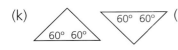

(l)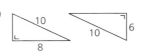

6. Explain, giving reasons, why Δ1 ≡ Δ2 on the diagram shown.

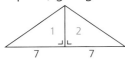

7. abcd is a parallelogram. Using one of the four tests for congruence, explain, giving reasons, why △abd ≡ △cbd. (**Note:** ∠1 and ∠2 are marked to aid you.)

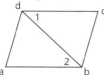

8. The diagram shows a circle with centre o, with [db] and [ac] as diameters. Explain why △aob ≡ △cod.

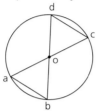

9. If |∠x| = |∠y|, explain, giving reasons, why △adb ≡ △cdb.

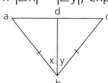

10. The diagram shows a circle with centre b, where |∠abc| = |∠dbc|. Explain, giving reasons, why △bca ≡ △bcd.

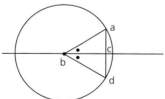

Exercise 17.5 (Chapter summary)

1. In each of the following triangles, calculate the length of the unknown side.

(a) 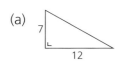 (b) (c)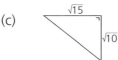

(d) 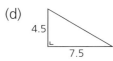 (e) (f)

2. Use Pythagoras' Theorem to identify which of the following triangles are right-angled.

(a)  (b) 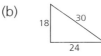 (c)

(d)  (e) (f)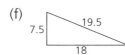

3. A ladder 3 m long exactly reaches the top of a wall 2.5 m high. Calculate the distance, d, which the base of the ladder is away from the base of the wall. Give your answer correct to two decimal places.

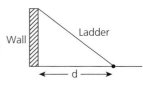

4. Draw each of the following angles. Construct the bisector of each angle, showing all construction lines clearly.

(a) 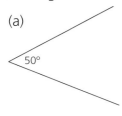 (b) (c)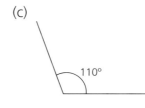

5. (a) Construct the following line segments to the measurements given.
(b) Construct the perpendicular bisector of each segment.

(i)  (ii)  (iii) a 9.5 cm b

6. Construct each of the following triangles.

   (a) Triangle abc, where |ab| = 6 cm, |bc| = 4.5 cm and |ac| = 3 cm.

   (b) Triangle def, where |de| = 5 cm, |fe| = 4 cm and |∠def| = 35°.

   (c) Triangle ghk, where |gk| = 5.5 cm, |∠kgh| = 50° and |∠gkh| = 60°.

   (d) Triangle mno, where |mn| = 4 cm, |∠omn| = 90° and |on| = 5 cm.
       Using a ruler, measure the length of line segment [om].

7. Construct each of the following line segments to the measurements given and divide each into three parts, showing all construction lines clearly.

   (a) ├──────┤ (b) ├──────┤ (c) ├──────┤
       a 7 cm b   c 8.5 cm d   e 6.8 cm f

8. Using the four tests for congruence, explain whether or not the following pairs of triangles are congruent.

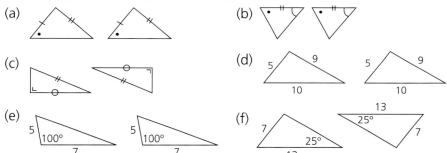

(a)   (b)

(c)   (d)

(e)   (f)

9. (a) abc is an isosceles triangle where |ab| = |bc|.
      |∠adb| = 90°. Draw a sketch of this diagram and fill in the information given above. Using the test RHS, explain in detail why Δabd ≡ Δcdb.

   (b) If |∠bce| = 122°, find: (i) |∠dcb| (ii) |∠dbc|
       (iii) |∠bad| (iv) |∠abc|.

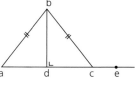

10. The diagram shows a circle with centre o. Using one of the four tests for congruence, explain, giving reasons, why Δabo ≡Δcbo.

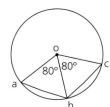

11. Carry out the following tests.

    (a) Think of a number between 1 and 25. We will call this number P.
       (**Note:** Any number will do, but keep it relatively low for your own convenience. However, P must be an integer.)

    (b) Think of another number, less than P, between 1 and 25. We will call this number Q.

    (c) If $x = 2pq$, calculate the value of x.

    (d) If $y = p^2 - q^2$, calculate the value of y.

    (e) If $h = p^2 + q^2$, calculate the value of h.

    (f) Substitute the values found for x, y and h into $h^2 = x^2 + y^2$.
       What do you find? What have you created?

In this chapter, you will learn about:
+ Co-ordinate geometry.
+ Transformations.
+ Length of a line segment.
+ Midpoint of a line segment.
+ Slope of a line.
+ Equation of a line.
+ Intersection of a line with the x-axis and with the y-axis.

Co-ordinate geometry

René Descartes was a Frenchman who lived in the 1600s. Descartes spent a considerable amount of his life in bed as a result of illness. While in bed, he noticed a fly crawling across the ceiling. As he watched the fly he wondered how he could describe the fly's position to someone else. Finally he realised that he could describe the position of the fly by its distance from each of the two perpendicular walls. He had invented the co-ordinate plane, which is also known as the Cartesian plane, after Descartes.

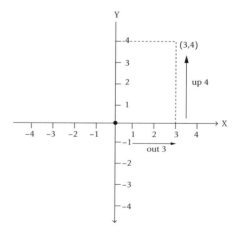

Any point on the Cartesian plane can be identified by an ordered pair, e.g. (3, 4). The first number in the pair represents the position on the x-axis and the second number represents the position on the y-axis. The x-axis is the horizontal axis and the y-axis is the vertical axis.

Example 18.1

List the co-ordinates of the points marked on the diagram.

Solution

A = (8, 5) ← Out 8, up 5

B = (5, 3) ← Out 5, up 3

C = (2, 7)

D = (−1, 7)

E = (−4, 4)

F = (−6, 6)

G = (−5, −2)

H = (−7, −4)

I = (−3, −6)

J = (3, −7)

K = (1, −1)

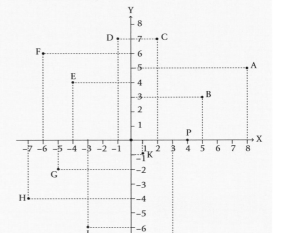

Example 18.2

Use the Cartesian plane to uncover the following phrase.

(3, 3)(6, 6)(4, 4)(−6, −4)

(4, −3)(−3, −4)(−2, 5)

(4, 4)(5, −5)(−2, 1)(−2, 5)

Solution

(3, 3)	(6, 6)	(4, 4)	(−6,−4)
W	A	L	K

(4, −3)	(−3, −4)	(−2, 5)
T	H	E

(4, 4)	(5, −5)	(−2, 1)	(−2, 5)
L	I	N	E

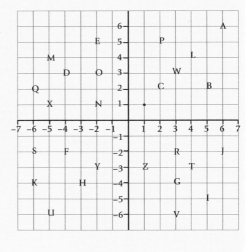

Example 18.3

Plot the following points.

(a) (4, −1)

(b) (3, 5)

(c) (−7, 1)

(d) (−4, −1)

(e) (6, −2)

(f) (−3, 4)

Solution

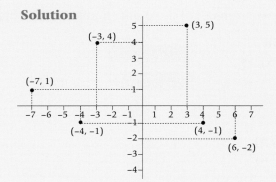

Exercise 18.1

1. Write down the co-ordinates of the points a, b, c, d, e, f, g, h, i, j, k, marked on the diagram.

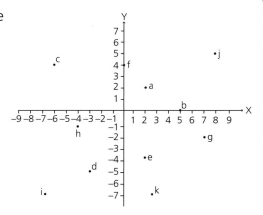

2. Write down the co-ordinates of the points a, b, c, d, e, f, g, h, i, j, k, l, m in the following diagram.

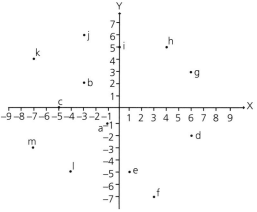

3. Write down the co-ordinates of the points marked l, m, n, o, p, q, r, s, t, u, v, w, x, y, z in the diagram below.

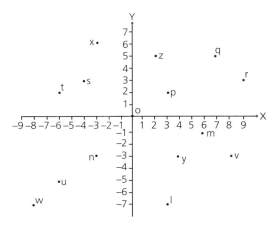

4. Use the Cartesian grid below to uncover the following movie titles.
   (a) (3, −4) (4, 4) (6, 6) (−4, 3) (5, −5) (6, 6) (4, −3) (−2, 3) (3, −2)
   (b) (6, 6) (4, 4) (5, −5) (−2, 5) (−2, 1)
       (6, 6) (−5, −6) (4, −3) (−2, 3) (2, 5) (−6, −2) (−2, −3)
   (c) (2, 5) (−5, −6) (4, 4) (2, 5)
       (−4, −2) (5, −5) (2, 2) (4, −3) (5, −5) (−2, 3) (−2, 1)
   (d) (−6, −2) (2, 2) (−3, −4) (5, −5) (−2, 1) (−4, 3) (4, 4), (−2, 5) (3, −2) (−6, −2)
       (4, 4) (5, −5) (−6, −2) (4, −3)
   (e) (4, −3) (5, −5) (4, −3) (6, 6) (−2, 1) (5, −5) (2, 2)
   (f) (−4, −2) (−2, 3) (3, −2) (−2, 5) (−6, −2) (4, −3)
       (3, −4) (−5, −6) (−5, 4) (2, 5)

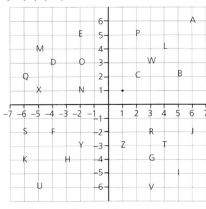

5. Use the co-ordinate plane below to uncover the following TV programmes.
   (a) (–5, 4) (–4, –5) (–7, –4) (–4, –5) (5, –5) (–3, –2) (2, 5) (–6, –2) (–4, –5)
   (5, –5)
   (6, –1) (2, 5) (–7, –4) (–5, –4) (–5, –4) (2, 5)
   (b) (–5, –4) (–3, –2) (6, –1) (2, 5) (–5, –4) (5, –4) (4, –3) (–5, –4) (–7, –4) (6, –1)
   (c) (–2, 5) (–7, –4) (–6, –2) (2, –4)
   (–5, –4) (2, 5) (–6, –2) (2, –4) (–5, –4)
   (d) (–6, 1) (5, 4) (–5, –4) (6, –1) (2, 5) (–6, –2) (–4, –5), (5, –5) (6, –1)
   (–3, –2) (5, –5) (4, –3)
   (–3, –2) (5, –5) (6, –1) (2, –2) (–5, –4) (–7, –4) (6, –1)
   (e) (3, 3) (–6, –2) (6, 3)
   (3, 3) (–7, –4) (–4, –5) (2, 5) (–3, 2) (–5, –4) (–7, –4)

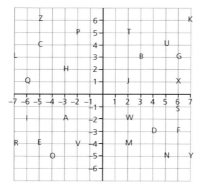

6. Use the co-ordinate plane to uncover the following phrases.
   (a) (–5, –2) (6, 2) (6, 2)
   (4, –5) (7, 4) (1, –3)
   (7, 4) (–3, –3) (–2, –5)
   (–5, –2) (–3, –3) (–3, 3)
   (7, 4) (–3, –3) (–2, –5)
   (4, –5) (7, 4) (1, –3)
   (–5, –2) (6, 2) (6, 2)
   (b) (2, 5) (3, 2) (–2, –5)
   (7, 4) (–4, 4) (–2, –5) (1, –3) (–5, –2)
   (–5, –2) (4, 5) (–3, –3) (2, 5)
   (7, 4) (–2, 5) (–2, –5) (1, –3)

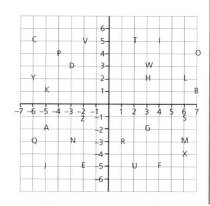

(2, 5) (4, 5) (6, 2) (6, 2)

(2, 5) (3, 2) (–2, –5)

(4, –5) (–5, –2) (2, 5)

(6, 2) (–5, –2) (–3, 3) (–6, 2)

(6, –1) (4, 5) (–3, –3) (3, –2) (6, –1)

(c) (7, 4) (–3, –3) (–2, –5)

(6, –1) (6, –3) (–5, –2) (6, 2) (6, 2)

(6,–1) (2, 5) (–2, –5) (–4, 4)

(4, –5) (7, 4) (1, –3)

(6, –3) (–5, –2) (–3, –3)

(7, 4) (3, –3) (–2, –5)

(3, –2) (4, 5) (–5, –2) (–3, –3) (2, 5)

(6, 2) (–2, –5) (–5, –2) (–4, 4)

(4, –5) (7, 4) (1, 3)

(6, –3) (5, –2) (–3, 3) (–5, 1) (4, 5) (–3, –3) (–3, 3)

7. Draw a Cartesian plane (x-axis and y-axis) and plot the following points.
   a(–3, 2), b(–1, 1), c(4, –4), d(0, 4), e(4, 0), f(–5, 0), g(0, 0), h(–3, –5),
   i(1, –5), j(–4, 2)

8. Plot the following points on a co-ordinate plane.
   a(5, 5), b(–7, 1), c(6, –4), d(1, –1), e(0, 3), f(–1, 7), g(0, –6), h(–3, –3),
   i(–6, 0), j(–3, 0)

▮▮▮ Transformations

▮ Translations

• A **translation** moves a point or object a certain distance in a certain direction.

Example 18.4

Find the image of the point (2, 1) under the translation b (1, 3) → c (5, 4).

Solution

$(1, 3) \xrightarrow[\text{y changes by +1}]{\text{x changes by +4}} (5, 4)$

$\Rightarrow (2, 1) \rightarrow (2 + 4, 1 + 1)$

$= (6, 2)$

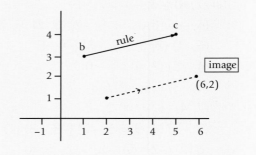

Always draw the diagram when trying to find the image of any point or object under a transformation.

Example 18.5

Find the image of the triangle a (1, 1), b (4, 2), c (2, 3) under the translation (4, −1) → (1, −3).

Solution

$(4, -1) \rightarrow (1, -3)$

$x \Rightarrow 1 - 4 = -3$ ⟵ x changes by −3.

$y \Rightarrow -3 - -1 = -3 + 1 = -2$ ⟵ y changes by −2.

$(1, 1) \rightarrow (1 - 3, 1 - 2) = (-2, -1)$

$(4, 2) \rightarrow (4 - 3, 2 - 2) = (1, 0)$

$(2, 3) \rightarrow (2 - 3, 3 - 2) = (-1, 1)$.

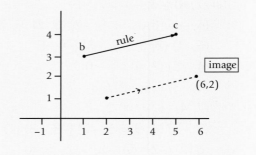

Central symmetry in the origin

When finding the image of a point under a central symmetry in the origin, the signs of both co-ordinates change.

Example 18.6

Find the image of $(4, 3)$ and $(-3, 5)$ under a central symmetry in the origin, S_o.

S = symmetry, o = small o in the origin.

Solution

$(-3, 5) \rightarrow (3, -5)$

$(4, 3) \rightarrow (-4, -3)$

Change the sign of both co-ordinates.

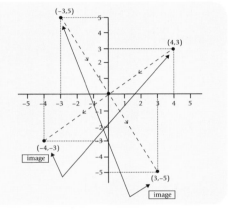

Axial symmetry in the x-axis

Axial symmetry is symmetry through a line. Any point reflected through the x-axis will change the sign of the y co-ordinate.

Example 18.7

Find the image of the points $(4, 5)$ and $(-4, -2)$ under an axial symmetry in the x-axis, S_x.

Solution

$(4, 5) \rightarrow (4, -5)$

$(-4, -2) \rightarrow (-4, 2)$

S = symmetry, x = x-axis.

Change the sign on the y co-ordinate.

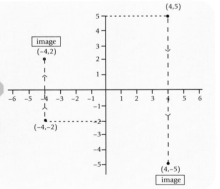

Axial symmetry in the y-axis

Any point reflected through the y-axis will change the sign of the x co-ordinate.

Example 18.8

Find the image of the points $(-4, 2)$ and $(5, -3)$ under an axial symmetry in the y-axis, S_y.

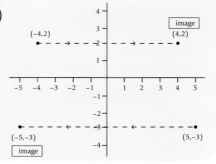

Solution

S = symmetry, y = y-axis.

$(-4, 2) \rightarrow (4, 2)$

$(5, -3) \rightarrow (-5, -3)$

Change the sign on the x co-ordinate.

Exercise 18.2

1. Find the image of the following points under the translation $(1, 1) \rightarrow (3, 4)$.

   (a) $(3, 5)$ (b) $(0, 0)$ (c) $(-1, 4)$ (d) $(-3, -4)$ (e) $(2, -6)$

   (f) $(0, 2)$ (g) $(4, -5)$ (h) $(2, 0)$ (i) $(1, 1)$ (j) $(-5, -4)$

2. Find the image of the following points under the translation $(4, 5) \rightarrow (1, 2)$.

   (a) $(3, 4)$ (b) $(0, 0)$ (c) $(-4, -1)$ (d) $(4, 0)$ (e) $(3, -5)$

   (f) $(-3, 0)$ (g) $(-4, -2)$ (h) $(1, -5)$ (i) $(1, -1)$ (j) $(2, 6)$

3. Find the image of the following points under the translation $(-4, 1) \rightarrow (2, -3)$.

   (a) $(-3, -2)$ (b) $(5, -4)$ (c) $(0, 0)$ (d) $(6, -8)$ (e) $(1, 4)$

   (f) $(1, 0)$ (g) $(-5, 4)$ (h) $(-3, -5)$ (i) $(0, 1)$ (j) $(1, 7)$

4. Find the image of the following points under the translation $(4, 2) \rightarrow (-2, 0)$.

   (a) $(-4, 1)$ (b) $(-3, 6)$ (c) $(4, 0)$ (d) $(-5, -5)$ (e) $(3, 5)$

   (f) $(0, 1)$ (g) $(0, 0)$ (h) $(6, -4)$ (i) $(1, 1)$ (j) $(1, 6)$

5. Find the image of the following points under central symmetry in the origin S_o.
   (a) (−2, −6) (b) (1, −5) (c) (0, 0) (d) (2, 2) (e) (4, 4)
   (f) (−4, −2) (g) (4, −7) (h) (3, −2) (i) (0, 5) (j) (5, 1)

6. Find the image of each of the following points under a central symmetry in the origin, S_o.
   (a) (4, 5) (b) (−3, 4) (c) (−4, −7) (d) (5, −1)
   (e) (7, 1) (f) (0, −4) (g) (−4, 0) (h) (0, 0)

7. Find the image of each of the following points under an axial symmetry in the x-axis, S_x.
   (a) (2, 3) (b) (3, −2) (c) (4, 6) (d) (−6, 1)
   (e) (−3, −2) (f) (0, 4) (g) (0, −5) (h) (3, 0)

8. Find the image of each of the following points under an axial symmetry in the y-axis, S_y.
   (a) (3, 2) (b) (4, −1) (c) (−5, −1) (d) (7, −4)
   (e) (−6, −3) (f) (−5, 1) (g) (2, 0) (h) (0, −3)

9. Find the image of the triangle a (1, 2), b (5, 0), c (3, 4) under the following.
   (a) The translation (4, 2) → (−1, −3).
   (b) A central symmetry in the origin, S_o.
   (c) An axial symmetry in the x-axis, S_x.
   (d) An axial symmetry in the y-axis, S_y.

10. Find the image of the triangle a (3, 2), b (−1, 1), c (0, 5) under the following.
    (a) A central symmetry in the origin.
    (b) An axial symmetry in the x-axis followed by an axial symmetry in the y-axis (i.e. put the △abc through the x-axis first, then put this image through the y-axis). Do you notice anything about your answers to parts (a) and (b) ?

11. Find the image of the square a (1, 2), b (1, 5), c (5, 5), d (5, 2) under the following.

(a) The translation (1, 1) → (−3, −5) .

(b) Under a central symmetry in the origin, S_o.

(c) Under an axial symmetry in the x-axis, S_x.

12.

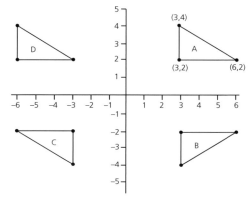

(a) Name the transformation that maps:

(i) triangle A to triangle B

(ii) triangle A to triangle C

(iii) triangle B to triangle C.

(b) Name three translations that map triangle A to D.

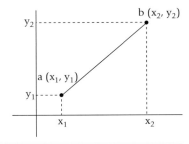

▌▌▌Length of a line segment

Distance or length formula:

$$|ab| = \sqrt{(x_2 - x_1)^2 + (y_2 - y_1)^2}$$

Example 18.9

Find the length of the line segment |cd| given c (−4, 1) and d (8, 6).

Solution

(−4, 1) (8, 6)

$x_1\ y_1$ $x_2\ y_2$

$x_1 = -4$

$y_1 = 1$

$x_2 = 8$

$y_2 = 6$

$$|cd| = \sqrt{(8 - -4) + (6 - 1)^2}$$

$$= \sqrt{(8 + 4)^2 + (5)^2} = \sqrt{12^2 + 5^2}$$

$$= \sqrt{144 + 25} = \sqrt{169} = 13$$

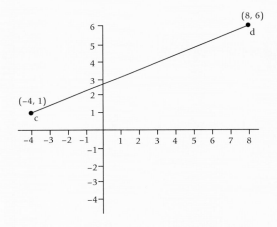

Example 18.10

Prove by finding the lengths of the sides that the triangle a (4, 1), b (7, 0), c (4, −1) is isosceles.

REMEMBER

An isosceles triangle has two equal sides.

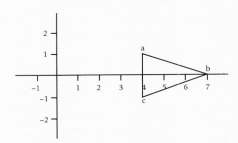

By drawing the diagram, you will be able to see the two sides you should find the length of. If you do not draw the diagram, then you will have to find the length of all three sides.

|ab|: a = (4, 1), b = (7, 0)

|cb|: c = (4, −1), b = (7, 0)

Solution

$x_1 = 4$

$y_1 = 1$

$x_2 = 7$

$y_2 = 0$

$$|ab| = \sqrt{(7-4)^2 + (0-1)^2}$$
$$= \sqrt{3^2 + (-1)^2}$$
$$= \sqrt{9+1} = \sqrt{10}$$

$$|cb| = \sqrt{(7-4)^2 + (0--1)^2}$$
$$|cb| = \sqrt{3^2 + 1^2}$$
$$|cb| = \sqrt{9+1} = \sqrt{10}$$

Both sides are the same length, i.e. $|ab| = |cb|$, therefore $\triangle abc$ is isosceles.

Exercise 18.3

1. Find $|ab|$ in each of the following line segments.

   (a) a = (3, 2), b = (1, 1)   (f) a = (0, 4), b = (4, 0)

   (b) a = (4, 1), b = (1, 4)   (g) a = (3, 4), b = (0, 0)

   (c) a = (4, 1), b = (3, 5)   (h) a = (0, 3), b = (4, 0)

   (d) a = (1, 3), b = (6, 12)   (i) a = (2, 2), b = (6, 6)

   (e) a = (5, 5), b = (8, 9)   (j) a = (3, 6), b = (3, 10)

2. Find $|cd|$ in each of the following line segments.

   (a) c = (1, 1), d = (−3, 5)   (f) c = (0, −4), d = (−3, 0)

   (b) c = (−6, −1), d = (−2, −2)   (g) c = (0, 0), d = (−4, −3)

   (c) c = (−4, 3), d = (3, −4)   (h) c = (−2, 6), d = (−4, 3)

   (d) c = (−4, 4), d = (4, −4)   (i) c = (5, −2), d = (3, −3)

   (e) c = (2, 0), d = (0, −6)   (j) c = (−2, −5), d = (−4, 1)

3. Investigate whether or not the following triangles are isosceles.

   (a) a(−6, 2), b(−4, 5), c(−2, 2)   (d) a(1, 4), b(−4, 1), c(4, 4)

   (b) a(−3, 0), b(3, 0), c(0, −3)   (e) a(1, 5), b(3, 2), c(−2, 3)

   (c) a(5, 7), b(1, 3), c(3, 1)

4. a(5, 7), b(1, 3), c(3, 1)

   (a) Find $|ab|$, $|bc|$ and $|ac|$.

   (b) Using Pythagoras' Theorem ($h^2 = x^2 + y^2$), investigate whether or not the triangle abc is right angled. $\left(\text{Hint}: \left(\sqrt{8}\right)^2 = 8.\right)$

5. d(−1, 3), e(3, 6), f(−3, −2)
   (a) Find |de|, |ef| and |df|.
   (b) Using Pythagoras' Theorem, investigate whether or not the triangle def is right angled.

6. (a) Calculate the lengths of the sides of the right-angled triangle a(−5, 1), b(−3, −2), c(−5, −2).
   (b) Find the area of the triangle abc.

7. (a) Find the length of the sides of the right-angled triangle a(0, 4), b(0, 0), c(3, 0).
   (b) Find the area of the triangle abc.

8. A square has vertices a(−5, −2), b(−2, −2), c(−2, 1), d(−5, 1). Find the length of the:
   (a) side of the square
   (b) diagonals of the square.

9. a(−5, −3), b(−3, 1), c(6, 1), d(4 −3) are the vertices of a parallelogram.
   (a) Find the length of the sides of the parallelogram.
   (b) Find the length of the diagonals.

10. a(4, 0), b(2, −4), c(−2, −2), d(0, 2) are the vertices of a parallelogram.
    (a) Find the length of the sides of the parallelogram.
    (b) Find the length of the diagonals.
    (c) Are the diagonals equal in length?
    (d) Can this be described as any other type of quadrilateral?

11. Use the distance formula to show that the points a(−3, −5), b(1, −1), c(4, 2) are all on a straight line. (Hint: Check if |ac| = |ab| + |bc|.)

12. Use the distance formula to investigate if the points a(−2, 4), b(3, −2), c(5, −4) are all on the same line.

13. Use the distance formula to investigate if the points a(6, 1), b(2, 3), c(−3, 5) are all on the same line.

Midpoint of a line segment

Midpoint formula:

$$\left(\frac{x_1+x_2}{2}, \frac{y_1+y_2}{2}\right)$$

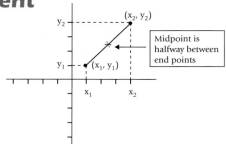

Midpoint is halfway between end points

Example 18.11

Find the midpoint of a (4, 5), b (−2, 3).

Solution

$x_1 = 4$
$y_1 = 5$
$x_2 = -2$
$y_2 = 3$

$$\text{Midpoint} = \left(\frac{4 + -2}{2}\right), \left(\frac{5+3}{2}\right)$$

$$= \left(\frac{2}{2}, \frac{8}{2}\right)$$

$$= (1, 4)$$

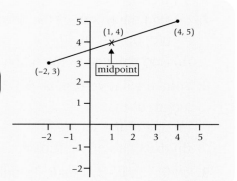

Example 18.12

(1, 3) is the midpoint of [ab]. If a is the point (5, 2), find the point b.

Solution

x co-ordinates are equal.

Let b = (x, y).

$x_1 = 5$

$$\left(\frac{5+x}{2}, \frac{2+y}{2}\right) = (1, 3)$$

y co-ordinates are equal.

$y_1 = 2$

$$\Rightarrow \frac{5+x}{2} = 1$$

$x_2 = x$
$y_2 = y$

$\Rightarrow 5 + x = 2$

$x = 2 - 5$

$x = -3$

AND

$$\frac{2+y}{2} = 3$$

$2 + y = 6$

$y = 6 - 2$

$y = 4$

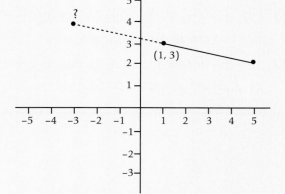

Point b = (−3, 4)

Exercise 18.4

1. Find the midpoint of the line segment [ab] in each of the following.
   (a) a = (4, 2), b = (2, 6)
   (b) a = (1, 3), b = (3, 1)
   (c) a = (2, 2), b = (0, 2)
   (d) a = (4, 3), b = (2, 3)
   (e) a = (1, 5), b = (3, 3)
   (f) a = (4, 5), b = (5, 2)
   (g) a = (3, 1), b = (4, 5)
   (h) a = (1, 4), b = (3, 2)
   (i) a = (5, 5), b = (1, 6)
   (j) a = (2, 3), b = (4, 1)

2. Find the midpoint of the line segment [cd] in each of the following.
   (a) c = (1, −2), d = (3, −4)
   (b) c = (3, 4), d = (1, −5)
   (c) c = (−2, −4), d = (−6, −8)
   (d) c = (0, 4), d = (−4, 2)
   (e) c = (−2, 2), d = (−3, 5)
   (f) c = (−5, −1), d = (−1, −3)
   (g) c = (−4, −6), d = (−1, 1)
   (h) c = (6, 4), d = (−4, −2)
   (i) c = (3, 7), d = (−1, 1)
   (j) c = (−8, 3), d = (−2, 3)

3. The points a (4, 2) and b (−6, 8) are the end points of the diameter of a circle. Find the centre of the circle.

4. The points d (−3, −5) and e (−2, −1) are the end points of the diameter of a circle.
   (a) Find the centre of the circle.
   (b) Use the distance formula to find the radius of the circle.

5. The points a (–5, 1), b (–2, 3), c (3, –1), d (0, –3) form a parallelogram.
   (a) Find the midpoint of the diagonal [ac].
   (b) Find the midpoint of the diagonal [bd].
   (c) Explain why both answers are the same.

6. The points a (4, –1), b (1, –3), c (–2, –1), d (1, 1) form a parallelogram.
   Find the midpoint of both diagonals.

7. The point c (1, 1) is the midpoint of [ab]. If point a is (7, 5), find
   point b.

8. The point m (–2, 1) is the midpoint of the line segment [hk]. If the
   co-ordinates of the point h are (4 –3), find the co-ordinates of the
   point k.

9. abcd are the vertices of a parallelogram and m (–3, –3) is the midpoint of
   the diagonals. If a = (–3, –6) and b = (5, –3), find the co-ordinates of the
   other vertices, c and d.

10. abcd are the vertices of a parallelogram and m (0, 1) is the midpoint of the
    diagonals. If a = (1, 4) and b = (3, 1), find the co-ordinates of the other
    vertices, c and d.

11. a (4, –2) is one end of the diameter of a circle. If (–1, 3) is the centre
    of the circle, find the co-ordinates of the other end point of the diameter.

12. a (–5, 3) is one end of the diameter of a circle. If (1, –2) is the centre of
    the circle, find the co-ordinates of the other end of the diameter.

Slope of a line

The slope of a line (sometimes called the gradient) is a measure of the steepness of the line as you move from left to right.

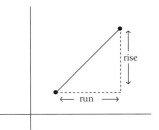

$$\text{slope} = \frac{\text{change in vertical height}}{\text{change in horizontal length}} = \frac{\text{rise}}{\text{run}}$$

Example 18.13

The diagram shows the line segment [ab].
Find the: (a) rise (b) run (c) slope.

Solution

(a) Rise = 5 − 1 = 4

(b) Run = 3 − 1 = 2

(c) Slope = $\frac{4}{2}$ = 2

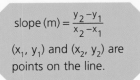

Note this slope is positive, i.e. as we move from left to right, the line slopes up.

Formula for calculating slope with two points on the line:

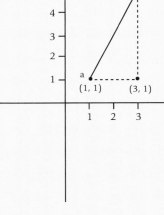

$$\text{slope } (m) = \frac{y_2 - y_1}{x_2 - x_1}$$

(x_1, y_1) and (x_2, y_2) are points on the line.

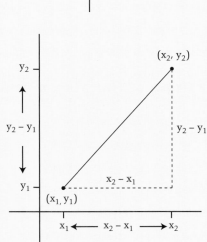

Example 18.14

Find the slope of the line containing the points $(3, -1)$ and $(1, 4)$.

Solution

$x_1 = 1$ $m = \dfrac{-1 - 4}{3 - 1}$

$y_1 = 4$ $m = \dfrac{-5}{2}$

$x_2 = 3$

$y_2 = -1$

Note the slope is negative, i.e. as we move from left to right, the line slopes down.

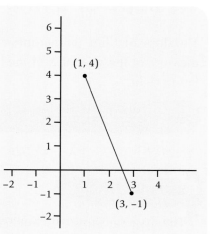

Positive and negative slopes

Positive slope

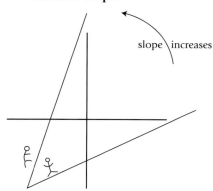

slope increases

Negative slope

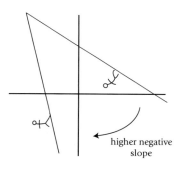

higher negative slope

Slope of horizontal and vertical lines

$$\text{slope} = \frac{y_2 - y_1}{x_2 - x_1}$$

$x_1 = 1$ $\text{slope} = \dfrac{2 - 2}{4 - 1}$

$y_1 = 2$ $\text{slope} = \dfrac{0}{3}$

$x_2 = 4$ $\text{slope} = 0$

$y_2 = 2$

Horizontal lines

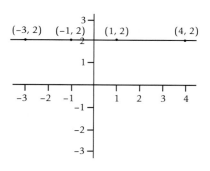

NOTE: The slope of all horizontal lines will be 0, as $y_2 = y_1$ on all horizontal lines.

$$\text{slope} = \frac{y_2 - y_1}{x_2 - x_1}$$

$x_1 = 2$
$y_1 = 3$
$x_2 = 2$
$y_2 = 1$

$$\text{slope} = \frac{1 - 3}{2 - 2} = \frac{-2}{0}$$

Vertical lines

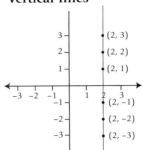

NOTE: We cannot divide by 0. In mathematics, division by 0 is undefined. Therefore, vertical lines have no slope, i.e. their slope does not exist.

The slopes of parallel lines are equal.

L||M
$\Rightarrow$ slope L = slope M

Parallel lines

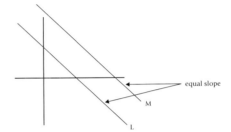

Example 18.15

Show that the line through the points a $(1, -3)$ and b $(4, -1)$ is parallel to the line through the points h $(-4, -1)$ and k $(-1, 1)$.

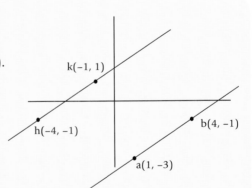

Solution

Slope ab:

$x_1 = 1$ $\text{slope} = \frac{y_2 - y_1}{x_2 - x_1}$

$y_1 = -3$ $\text{slope} = \frac{-1 - -3}{4 - 1}$

$x_2 = 4$ $\text{slope} = \frac{-1 + 3}{4 - 1}$

$y_2 = -1$ $\text{slope} = \frac{2}{3}$

Slope hk:

$x_1 = -4$ $\text{slope} = \frac{y_2 - y_1}{x_2 - x_1}$

$y_1 = -1$ $\text{slope} = \frac{1 - -1}{-1 - -4}$

$x_2 = -1$ $\text{slope} = \frac{1 + 1}{-1 + 4}$

$y_2 = 1$ $\text{slope} = \frac{2}{3}$

Slopes are equal, so the lines are parallel.

$\therefore$ ab||hk.

355

Example 18.16

Show that the point (4, −1) is on the line 2x + 3y = 5.

Solution

2(4) + 3(−1) = 8 − 3 = 5

∴ (4, −1) is on the line.

Substitute the x co-ordinate for x. Substitute the y co-ordinate for y. If left-hand side = right-hand side, then the point is on the line.

Exercise 18.5

1. Find the slope of the line passing through the given points.
   - (a) (2, 4), (3, 3)
   - (b) (0, 0), (1, 3)
   - (c) (2, 2), (5, 5)
   - (d) (1, 0), (4, 2)
   - (e) (1, 3), (3, 1)
   - (f) (2, 4), (2, 1)
   - (g) (5, 4), (0, 1)
   - (h) (3, 5), (4, 5)

2. Find the slope of the line containing the following points.
   - (a) (−3, 1), (4, −2)
   - (b) (−7, −1), (−1, −2)
   - (c) (−4, −1), (0, −3)
   - (d) (0, 0), (−3, −3)
   - (e) (−5, −2), (1, 3)
   - (f) (0, 1), (0, −4)
   - (g) (3, −6), (6, −3)
   - (h) (−5, −2), (3, −2)

3. Find the slope of the line passing through the given points. (Use a calculator to help you.)
   - (a) $\left(1, -\frac{1}{2}\right)$, (3, 1)
   - (b) $\left(\frac{1}{4}, 0\right)$, (4, −1)
   - (c) (1, 1), $\left(\frac{2}{3}, -3\right)$
   - (d) (2, −1), $\left(0, -\frac{1}{4}\right)$
   - (e) (6, −3), $\left(\frac{1}{3}, -\frac{1}{6}\right)$
   - (f) $\left(\frac{2}{3}, \frac{1}{4}\right)$, $\left(-\frac{1}{3}, -\frac{3}{4}\right)$
   - (g) $\left(4, \frac{2}{5}\right)$, $\left(\frac{2}{5}, -4\right)$
   - (h) (3, 4), $\left(\frac{-1}{3}, -\frac{1}{4}\right)$

4. Show that the line through the points a (1, −4) and b (−3, 2) is parallel to the line through the points h (−1, 11) and k (3, 5). What type of shape is abhk?

5. Show that the line through the points a (2, 1) and b (3, 4) is parallel to the line through c (−1, 6) and d (−2, 3).

6. If a = (3, −2), b = (5, 2), c = (1, 1) and d = (−1, −3), show that the points abcd form a parallelogram.

7. If a = (−1, 4), b = (2, 3), c = (3, 2) and d = (0, 3), show that abcd are the vertices of a parallelogram.

8. If a = (2, 3), b = (−2, 1), c = (3, −2) and d = (−1, −4), investigate whether or not ab||cd.

9. If p = (3, −1), q = (5, 1), z = (7, −4) and w = (4, −6), investigate whether or not pq||zw.

10. Investigate whether or not a (3, −1), b (−2, −4), c (−3, 0) and d (2, 3) are the vertices of a parallelogram.

In questions 11 to 21, show that the given point is on the line L.

11. (2, 1); L: x + y = 3

12. (3, 4); L: 3x + y = 13

13. (4, 2); L: 2x + 3y = 14

14. (−5, 1); L: 2x + y = −9

15. (−2, −4); L: 3x − 2y = 2

16. (−4, 0); L: 3x + 5y = −12

17. (−1, −6); L: x − 3y = 17

18. (−5, −2); L: −2x + 3y = 4

19. (−2, 4); L: −2x + 4y = 20

20. (−3, 2); L: 5x + 8y = 1

21. (1, −4); L: 6x − 4y = 22

For questions 22 to 28, the given point is on the line K. Find the value of t.

22. (2, t); K: 3x − y = 2

23. (0, t); K: 3x + y = 2

24. (t, 5); K: 3x − y = 1

25. (t, −1); K: x + y = 3

26. (t, −4); K: 3x + y = 8

27. (t, 2); K: 5x + y = 12

28. (5, t); K: 3x − 2y = 17

29. The point (c, 1) is on the line 4x − 2y = 6. Find the value of c.

30. The point (2, d) is on the line 3x + 2y = 8. Find the value of d.

31. The point (e, 2) is on the line 3x + 2y = 4. Find the value of e.

Equation of a line

The formula for the equation of a line is: $y - y_1 = m(x - x_1)$.

(Any point (x, y) on the line satisfies the equation.)

m = slope of a line and (x_1, y_1) is a point on the line.

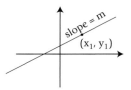

Example 18.17

Find the equation of the line through the point $(2, 4)$ with a slope of 3.

Solution

$x_1 = 2$ $y - y_1 = m(x - x_1)$

$y_1 = 4$ $y - 4 = 3(x - 2)$ ← Substitute values for x_1, y_1 and m (the slope).

$m = 3$ $y - 4 = 3x - 6$

                 $0 = 3x - y - 2$

Example 18.18

Find the equation of the line through the points $(3, -1)$ and $(2, -4)$.

Solution

$x_1 = 3$ $\text{slope} = \dfrac{y_2 - y_1}{x_2 - x_1}$ ← If you are given two points, then you must find the slope first before you proceed to find the equation.

$y_1 = -1$ $\text{slope} = \dfrac{-4 - -1}{2 - 3}$

$x_2 = 2$ $\text{slope} = \dfrac{-4 + 1}{2 - 3}$

$y_2 = -4$ $\text{slope} = \dfrac{-3}{-1}$ ← Remember, a minus divided by a minus is a plus.

                 $\text{slope} = 3$

$x_1 = 3$ $y - y_1 = m(x - x_1)$

$y_1 = -1$ $y - -1 = 3(x - 3)$

$m = 3$ $y + 1 = 3x - 9$

                 $-3x + y = -9 - 1$ ← Equation of the line through the given points.

                 $-3x + y = -10$

Exercise 18.6

For questions 1 to 10, find the equation of the line through the point a and with the slope m.

1. a(4, −2); m = 2

2. a(7, 1); m = −1

3. a(−1, −3); m = 4

4. a(2, 1); $m = \frac{1}{2}$

5. a(−3, −4); $m = \frac{3}{4}$

6. a(5, 2); $m = -\frac{2}{5}$

7. a(−1, −4); $m = -\frac{2}{3}$

8. a(4, 2); m = 0

9. a(−1, 0); $m = -\frac{3}{7}$

10. a(0, 0); m = −1

For questions 11 to 16, find the equation of the line through the given points.

11. (4, 2), (1, 1)

12. (6, 2), (−3, 4)

13. (−3, −2), (1, 4)

14. (−4, −2), (−3, 0)

15. (−1, 0), (0, 1)

16. (−3, 4), (7, 1)

17. Find the equation of the line through the points (4, 5) and (4, −1). What type of line is this?

18. Find the equation of the line through the points (−1, −3) and (4, −3). What type of line is this?

19. Find the equation of the line through the points (−4, −4) and (5, 5).

Intersection of a line with the x-axis and with the y-axis

x-axis

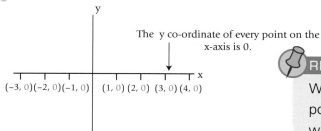

The y co-ordinate of every point on the x-axis is 0.

REMEMBER

When we want to find the point of intersection of a line with the x-axis, we let y = 0.

Example 18.19

Find the point of intersection of the line 3x + 4y = 12 and the x-axis.

Solution

y = 0 ◄──── Any point on the x-axis has a y co-ordinate of 0.

$\Rightarrow 3x + 4y = 12$

$\Rightarrow 3x + 4(0) = 12$

$\Rightarrow 3x + 0 = 12$

$\Rightarrow 3x = 12$

$\Rightarrow x = \dfrac{12}{3}$

$\Rightarrow x = 4$

$(4, 0)$ ◄──── Point of intersection of line and x-axis or point at which the line cuts the x-axis.

y-axis

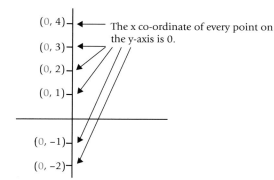

The x co-ordinate of every point on the y-axis is 0.

REMEMBER

When we want to find the point of intersection of a line and the y-axis, we let x = 0.

Example 18.20

Find the point of intersection of the line $2x - 5y = 10$ and the y-axis.

Solution

$x = 0$ ← Any point of the y-axis has an x co-ordinate of 0.

$2x - 5y = 10$

$\Rightarrow 2(0) - 5y = 10$

$-5y = 10$

$\Rightarrow y = \frac{10}{-5} \Rightarrow y = -2$ $\quad \therefore (0, -2)$ ← Point of intersection of $2x - 5y = 10$ with the y-axis.

Exercise 18.7

For questions 1 to 6, find the point of intersection of the line L and the x-axis.

1. L: $2x + 4y = 8$
2. L: $x + y = 8$
3. L: $2x - y = 6$
4. L: $3x - y = 9$
5. L: $2x + 3y = -6$
6. L: $5x + 3y = 15$

For questions 7 to 16, find the point of intersection of the line K and the y-axis.

7. K: $2x + 4y = 12$
8. K: $x - 2y = 6$
9. K: $3x - 4y = 12$
10. K: $5x - y = 10$
11. K: $x + 4y = -8$

12. K: $-3x - 6y = -12$
13. K: $-2x + y = 3$
14. K: $-5x - 6y = 30$
15. K: $2x - 10y = 20$
16. K: $x - 3y = 18$

17. Find the points on the line $3x + 4y = 24$ where it cuts the x-axis and where it cuts the y-axis.
18. Find the points on the line $x - y = 4$ where it cuts the x-axis and where it cuts the y-axis.
19. Find the points on the line $6x - 3y = 24$ where it cuts the x-axis and where it cuts the y-axis.

Exercise 18.8   (Chapter summary)

1. (a) Plot the points a (1, −3) and b (4, 5).
   (b) Find |ab|.
   (c) Find the midpoint of [ab].
   (d) Find the equation of the line ab.

2. (a) Plot the points h (2, 1), k (4, 6), z (3, 4) and w (1, −1).
   (b) Find the midpoint of hz.
   (c) Find the midpoint of kw.
   (d) Find the slope of hk.
   (e) Find the slope of zw.
   (f) What can you say about the quadrilateral hkzw?

3. (a) Plot the points a (−1, 4), b (3, −2), c (1, −8) and d (−3, −2).
   (b) Find the slope of ab.
   (c) Find the slope of cd.
   (d) Find the equation of ab.
   (e) Find the equation of dc.
   (f) Find |ab|.
   (g) Find |cd|.

4. a = (1, 4), b = (3, 2)
   (a) Find |ab|.
   (b) Find the slope of ab.
   (c) Find the equation of the line ab.
   (d) Calculate the co-ordinates of the point where the line cuts the x-axis.

5. a (−1, 2) and b (3, 6) are two points.
   (a) Find q, the midpoint of ab.
   (b) Verify that |aq| = |qb|.
   (c) Find the slope of ab.
   (d) Find the equation of ab.
   (e) Find the co-ordinates of the points where the line ab cuts the x-axis
       and the y-axis.

6. L is the line $3x + 4y = 12$, c = (3, 8) and d = (7, 5).
   (a) L cuts the x-axis at a. Find the co-ordinates of a.
   (b) L cuts the y-axis at b. Find the co-ordinates of b.
   (c) Find |ab|.
   (d) Find |cd|.
   (e) Find |bc|.
   (f) Find |ad|.
   (g) Find p, the midpoint of [ca].
   (h) Find q, the midpoint of [bd].
   (i) Show that bc||ad and ab||ad.
   (j) What type of quadrilateral is abcd?

7. a (1, 1), b (3, 2) and c (2, 4) are the vertices of a triangle.
   (a) Find the lengths of the three sides of the triangle.
   (b) Find the image of the triangle under a central symmetry in the origin, S_o.
   (c) Verify that the lengths of the three sides of the image triangle are the same as the lengths of the sides of the triangle abc.
   (d) Plot a, b and c on a diagram.
   (e) Plot the image of $\triangle$abc on the same diagram.
   (f) What do you notice about the image?

8. a (−1, 5), b (4, 2) and c (1, 3) are the vertices of a triangle.
   (a) Find the image of $\triangle$abc under the translations (−4, 2) → (−1, −1).
   (b) Plot both triangles on the same diagram.
   (c) Find the slopes of the sides of $\triangle$abc.
   (d) Find the slopes of the sides of the image of $\triangle$abc.
   (e) Find the equation of the line ab.

9. L is the line $4x − y + 13 = 0$.
   (a) The line cuts the y-axis at the point a. Calculate the co-ordinates of point a.
   (b) The point b (3t, −t) is on the line L. Calculate the value of t.
   (c) Use your results for (a) and (b) to draw the line.

(d) Find $|ab|$.

(e) Find the equation of the image of the line L under an axial symmetry in the x-axis.

(f) Show the image on your diagram.

10. M is the line $3x + 2y = 12$.

    (a) Find the points of intersection of the line with the x-axis and with the y-axis.

    (b) The point $(2, p)$ is on the line M. Find the value of p.

    (c) Draw the graph of the line M.

    (d) Find the equation of the image of M under an axial symmetry in the y-axis.

    (e) Show the graph of this on your diagram.

CHAPTER SUMMARY

In this chapter, you will learn about:

+ Domain and range.
+ Arrow diagrams.
+ Relations and notation format.
+ Functions.
+ Flow diagrams (inputs/outputs).

+ Graphing straight lines.
+ Using your graph to answer questions.
+ Graphing quadratic functions.
+ Using quadratic graphs.
+ Practical examples.

▮▮▮Domain and range

The set of first elements of each couple is called the domain.

The set of second elements in each couple is called the range.

R = {(1, 4), (2, 6), (3, 8), (4, 10)}

In the above example,

domain = {1, 2, 3, 4}
range = {4, 6, 8, 10}

Example 19.1

The function f = {(3, 3), (4, 2), (5, 1), (6, 0), (7, −1)}. Write down:
(a) the domain of f
(b) the range of f.

Solution

(a) Domain = {3, 4, 5, 6, 7}
(b) Range = {3, 2, 1, 0, −1}

Arrow diagrams

Arrow diagrams of couples

If f is the function {(3, 4), (5, 6), (7, 8), (9, 10)}, then the arrow diagram will look like this:

Example 19.2

Draw the arrow diagram for the relation
f = {(1, 4), (2, 8), (3, 16), (4, 32)} from the set
P = {1, 2, 3, 4} into the set Q = {4, 5, 8, 16, 20, 32}.

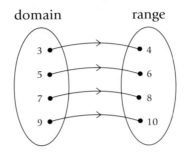

Arrow diagrams on a set

Example 19.3

A = {1, 2, 3, 4, 5, 6, 9, 16, 25, 36}. Draw the arrow
diagram of the relation 'is a square root of'
on the set A.

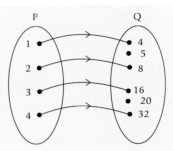

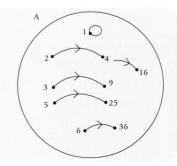

Exercise 19.1

1. Write out the domain and range of each of the following functions.
   (a) f = {1, 1), (2, 2), (3, 3), (4, 4), (5, 5)}
   (b) h = {1, −1), (2, −2), (3, −3), (4, −4), (5, −5)}
   (c) g = {1, a), (2, b), (3, c), (4, d)}

2. From each of the following arrow diagrams, write down the domain and the range.
   (a)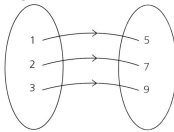

   (b)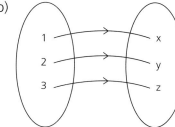

   (c)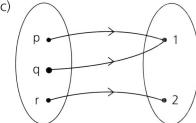

   (d)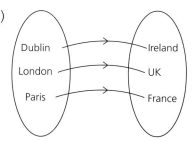

3. Draw the arrow diagram for each of the following relations between two sets.
   (a) f = {(2, 1), (−3, 3), (4, 1), (5, 3)}
   (b) g = {(3, 2), (2, 3), (−1, 2), (4, 3)}
   (c) h = {(1, 1), (−1, −1), (2, 2), (−2, −2), (3, 5)}

4. Draw the arrow diagram of the relation 'is a factor of' from the set x = {2, 3, 7} onto the set y = {4, 6, 7, 9, 10}. List all the couples of the relation.

5. Draw the arrow diagram of the relation 'is the square root of' from the set X = {1, 2, 7, 3, 5, 6} into the set Y = {1, 4, 9, 25, 36}. List the set of couples of the relation.

6. Draw the arrow diagram of the relation 'is the square root of' from the set X = {16, 25, 36, 49, 64, 81} into the set Y = {9, 7, 5, 4, 6, 1, 8}. List the set of couples that form the relation.

7. Draw the arrow diagram of the relation 'is three more than' from the set X = {3, 5, 7, 9, 15, 20} into the set Y = {1, 2, 3, 4, 0, 6, 17}. List the set of couples of the relation.

8. List the couples in each of the following relations.

(a)   (b)   (c)   (d)

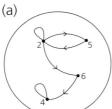 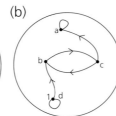 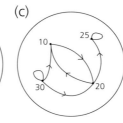 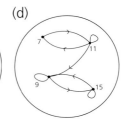

9. Draw an arrow diagram of the relation 'is less than' on the set A = {1, 2, 3, 4}. List all the couples in the relation.

10. Draw an arrow diagram of the relation 'is two less than' on the set B = {2, 4, 6, 8}. List all the couples in the relation.

11. Draw an arrow diagram of the relation 'is a factor of' on the set C = {3, 4, 6, 12, 9}. List the set of couples in the relation.

12. Draw an arrow diagram of the relation 'is 5 less than' on the set D = {1, 2, 5, 7, 10}. List the set of couples in the relation.

13. Draw an arrow diagram of the relation 'is four more than' on the set E = {1, 2, 7, 5, 11, 3}. List the set of couples in the relation.

Relations and notation format

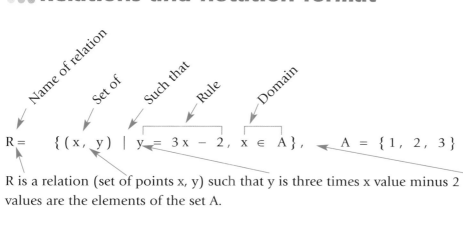

$$R = \{(x, y) \mid y = 3x - 2, x \in A\}, \quad A = \{1, 2, 3\}$$

R is a relation (set of points x, y) such that y is three times x value minus 2 and the x values are the elements of the set A.

Example 19.4

Write out the set of couples of the relation $R = \{(x, y) \mid y = 2x - 4, x \in A\}$ where $A = \{0, 2, 4\}$.

Solution

$x \in A \Rightarrow x = 0 \Rightarrow y = 2(0) - 4 = -4 \Rightarrow y = -4 \rightarrow (0, -4)$

$\qquad \Rightarrow x = 2 \Rightarrow y = 2(2) - 4 = 0 \Rightarrow y = 0 \rightarrow (2, 0)$

$\qquad \Rightarrow x = 4 \Rightarrow y = 2(4) - 4 = 4 \Rightarrow y = 4 \rightarrow (4, 4)$

$R = \{(0, -4), (2, 0), (4, 4)\}$

Exercise 19.2

For questions 1 to 5, write out the set of couples in the relation.

1. $R = \{(x, y) \mid y = 2x + 1, x \in A\}$ where $A = \{0, 1, 2, 3\}$.

2. $R = \{x, y) \mid y = x + 2, x \in B\}$ where $B = \{3, 4, 5\}$.

3. $R = \{(x, y) \mid y = x - 3, x \in C\}$ where $C = \{0, 1, 2\}$.

4. $R = \{(x, y) \mid y = 3x - 4, x \in D\}$ where $D = \{-2, -1, 0, 1\}$.

5. $R = \{(x, y) \mid y = 4x - 5, x \in E\}$ where $E = \{-5, -4, -3, -2\}$.

6. (a) Write out the set of couples in the relation
   $R = \{(x, y) \mid y = 5 - x, x \in F\}$ where $F = \{-3, -2, -1, 0, 1, 2\}$.
   (b) Draw the arrow diagram of the relation from set F into the set
   $Q = \{2, 3, 4, 5, 6, 7, 8, 9\}$.

7. (a) Write out the set of couples in the relation
   $R = \{(x, y) \mid y = 3 - 2x, x \in G\}$ where $G = \{-4, -3, -2, -1, 0, 1, 2\}$.
   (b) Draw the arrow diagram on G to represent the relation.

8. (a) Write out the set of couples in the relation
   $R = \{(x, y) \mid y = \frac{1}{2}x, x \in H\}$ where $H = \{2, 4, 6, 8, 10\}$.
   (b) Represent the relation R on an arrow diagram from the set H into K
   where $K = \{0, 1, 2, 3, 4\}$.

9. (a) Write out the set of couples in the relation
   $R = \{(x, y) \mid y = x^2 + 2, x \in I\}$ where $I = \{2, 3, 4, 5\}$.
   (b) Represent the relation R on an arrow diagram from I to M
   where $M = \{4, 6, 11, 18, 20\}$.

10. (a) Write out the set of couples in the relation
    $R = \{(x, y) \mid y = 2x^2 - 4, x \in J\}$ where $J = \{1, 2, 3, 4, 5\}$.
    (b) Represent the relation R on an arrow diagram from J to P
    where $P = \{2, 4, 10, 14, 28, 46, 50\}$.

Functions

REMEMBER

A function is a relation where any element of the domain is not repeated in another couple.

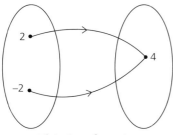

This is a function
$\{(2, 4), (-2, 4)\}$

Elements of the domain are not repeated.

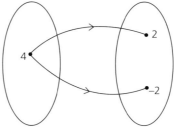

This is not a function
$\{(4, 2), (4, -2)\}$

An element of the domain is repeated in both couples $\Rightarrow$ not a function.

Example 19.5

$R = \{(1, -2), (2, 0), (3, 2), (4, 4), (5, 6)\}$
Represent the relation (R) on an arrow diagram and state whether or not R is a function. Give a reason for your answer.

Solution

R is a function because no element of the domain is repeated in another couple, i.e. only one arrow starts from each element of the domain.

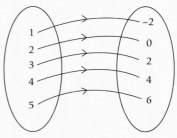

Example 19.6

$R = \{(x, y) \mid y = 3x - 6, x \in M\}$ where $M = \{-1, 0, 1, 2, 3\}$.

Draw the arrow diagram of the relation R from set M into a set P and state whether or not R is a function.

Solution

$y = 3(-1) - 6 = -9$

$y = 3(0) - 6 = -6$

$y = 3(1) - 6 = -3$

$y = 3(2) - 6 = 0$

$y = 3(3) - 6 = 3$

Yes, R is a function as no element of the domain is repeated.

Exercise 19.3

1. State, giving a reason, whether or not each of the following is a function.

(a)

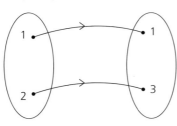

(b)

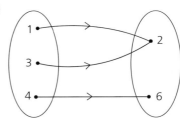

(c)

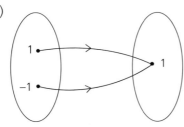

(d)

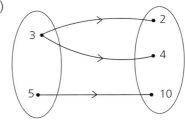

(e)

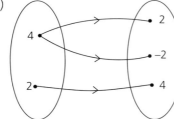

(f)

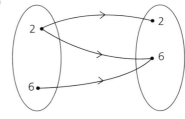

2. State, giving reasons, whether or not each of the following is a function.

(a)　　　　　　　　(b)　　　　　　　　(c)

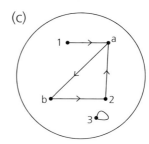

3. $f = \{(x, y) \mid y = 3x, x \in A\}$ where $A = \{1, 2, 3\}$.
　(a) Write out the set of couples of f.
　(b) State whether or not f is a function and give a reason for your answer.

4. $f = \{(x, y) \mid y = x^2, x \in B\}$ where $B = \{-2, -1, 0, 1, 2\}$.
　(a) Write out the set of couples of f.
　(b) State whether or not f is a function and give a reason for your answer.

5. $f = \{(x, y) \mid y = x^2 + 2, x \in C\}$ where $C = \{-3, -2, -1, 0\}$.
　(a) Write out the set of couples of the relation f.
　(b) State whether or not the relation f is a function and give a reason for
　　your answer.

6. $f = \{(x, y) \mid y = 3 - x^2, x \in E\}$ where $E = \{-4, -3, -2, -1, 0, 1, 2\}$.
　(a) Write out the set of couples of the relation f.
　(b) State whether or not the relation f is a function and give a reason for
　　your answer.

7. $f = \{(x, y) \mid y = 2x, x \in L\}$ where $L = \{1, 2, 3, 4\}$.
　(a) Represent the relation f on an arrow diagram between two sets.
　(b) State whether or not f is a function and give a reason for your answer.

8. $f = \{(x, y) \mid y = 4, x \in M\}$ where $M = \{0, 1, 2, 3\}$.
　(a) Represent the relation f on an arrow diagram between two sets.
　(b) State whether or not f is a function and give a reason for your answer.

9. $f = \{(x, y) \mid y = 3 - x^2, x \in P\}$ where $P = \{-3, -2, -1, 0, 1, 2, 3\}$.
　(a) Represent the relation f on an arrow diagram between two sets.
　(b) State whether or not f is a function and give a reason for your answer.

373

Flow diagrams (inputs/outputs)

REMEMBER

The function $y = x + 6$ may also be written as

$$f(x) = x + 6$$

$$\text{or } f{:}x \rightarrow x + 6$$

The flow diagram for $x + 6$ would look like

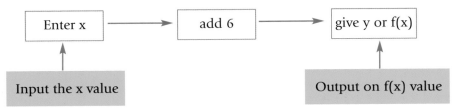

| Enter x | → | add 6 | → | give y or f(x) |

Input the x value

Output on f(x) value

Example 19.7

If $f(x) = 2x - 3$, find the value of each of the following.

(a) $f(0)$ (b) $f(4)$ (c) $f(-1)$ (d) $f(0.5)$ (e) $f(0) + f(4)$

Solution

$f(x) = 2x - 3$

(a) $f(0) = 2(0) - 3 = 0 - 3 = -3$ (replacing x with 0)

(b) $f(4) = 2(4) - 3 = 8 - 3 = 5$

(c) $f(-1) = 2(-1) - 3 = -2 - 3 = -5$

(d) $f(0.5) = 2(0.5) - 3 = 1 - 3 = -2$

(e) $f(0) + f(4) = -3 + 5 = 2$ ←   From (a) and (b).

Example 19.8

If $f(x) = x^2 + 2x - 6$, find the value of the following.

(a) $f(2)$ (b) $f(-1)$ (c) $f(0)$ (d) $f(-3)$

Solution

(a) $f(2) = 2^2 + 2(2) - 6 = 4 + 4 - 6 = 2$

(b) $f(-1) = (-1)^2 + 2(-1) - 6 = 1 - 2 - 6 = -7$

(c) $f(0) = (0)^2 + 2(0) - 6 = 0 + 0 - 6 = -6$

(d) $f(-3) = (-3)^2 + 2(-3) - 6 = 9 - 6 - 6 = -3$

Exercise 19.4

1. If $f(x) = x + 6$, find:
   (a) $f(1)$ (b) $f(2)$ (c) $f(-1)$ (d) $f(-5)$

2. If $f(x) = 2x + 3$, find:
   (a) $f(0)$ (b) $f(-1)$ (c) $f(4)$ (d) $f(3)$

3. If $f(x) = x - 5$, find:
   (a) $f(1)$ (b) $f(2)$ (c) $f(-3)$ (d) $f(5)$

4. If $f(x) = 6x - 2$, find:
   (a) $f(2)$ (b) $f(1)$ (c) $f(-3)$ (d) $f(0)$

5. If $f(x) = 3 - x$, find:
   (a) $f(4)$ (b) $f(2)$ (c) $f(-4)$ (d) $f(-3)$

6. If $f(x) = 5 - 2x$, find:
   (a) $f(1)$ (b) $f(-1)$ (c) $f(0)$ (d) $f(-4)$

7. If $f(x) = x^2$, find:
   (a) $f(2)$ (b) $f(3)$ (c) $f(-1)$ (d) $f(0)$

8. If $f(x) = x^2 + 2x$, find:
   (a) $f(3)$ (b) $f(-3)$ (c) $f(0)$ (d) $f(-1)$

9. If $f(x) = x^2 + 3x + 6$, find:
   (a) $f(4)$ (b) $f(-2)$ (c) $f(0)$ (d) $f(3)$

10. If $f(x) = 2x^2 + 4$, find:
    (a) $f(2)$ (b) $f(4)$ (c) $f(-2)$ (d) $f(0)$

11. If $f(x) = 3x^2 - 8$, find:
    (a) $f(3)$ (b) $f(-1)$ (c) $f(-2)$ (d) $f(0)$

12. If $f(x) = 6 + 2x - x^2$, find:
    (a) $f(-1)$ (b) $f(0)$ (c) $f(-3)$ (d) $f(4)$

▌▌▌Graphing straight lines

Straight line graphs are functions where the highest power of the variable x is 1.

REMEMBER

Functions can be written in several ways:

$f(x) = 2x + 5$
$f:x \rightarrow 2x + 5$
$y = 2x + 5$

When plotted on co-ordinated axes, this function will be a straight line.

Example 19.9

If x = {−3, −2, −1, 0, 1, 2, 3}, graph the line y = 2x − 4.

x	−3	−2	−1	0	1	2	3
2x	−6	−4	−2	0	2	4	6
−4	−4	−4	−4	−4	−4	−4	−4
y = 2x − 4	−10	−8	−6	−4	−2	0	2

giving the points (−3,−10), (−2,−8), (−1,−6), (0,−4), (1,−2), (2,0), (3,2)

Plotting these points and joining them results in the following diagram.

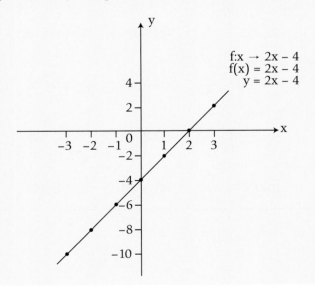

Calculators with natural display:

Input graph

Change mode to table, i.e. Mode 3 for a Casio calculator.

f(x) = appears on display.

Enter

2 | Alpha | x | − | 4 | =

Start? will appear on display.

Enter −3 | =

End? will appear on display.

Enter 3 | =

Step? appears. Enter =

You should use a calculator to check your answers.

Example 19.10

Graph the function f(x) = 4x − 8 in the domain −1 ≤ x ≤ 4.

x =	−1	0	1	2	3	4
4x	−4	0	4	8	12	16
− 8	−8	−8	−8	−8	−8	−8
y = 4x − 8	−12	−8	−4	0	4	8

giving the points (−1, −12), (0, −8), (1, −4), (2, 0), (3, 4), (4, 8).

Plotting these points and joining them results in the following diagram.

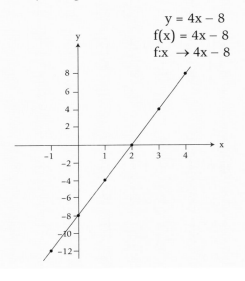

y = 4x − 8
f(x) = 4x − 8
f:x → 4x − 8

377

Exercise 19.5

1. Complete the table given and hence draw the graph of the function
   y = x + 2 for x ∈ {1, 2, 3, 4}.

x =	1	2	3	4
y =	3			

2. Complete the table given and hence draw the graph of the function
   y = 3x − 2 for x ∈ {−1, 0, 1, 2, 3}.

x =	−1	0	1	2	3
y =	−5			4	

3. Complete the table given and hence draw the graph of the function
   y = 2x + 2 for x ∈ {−3, −2, −1, 0, 1, 2}.

x =	−3	−2	−1	0	1	2
y =	−4		0			

4. Complete the table given and hence draw the graph of the function
   y = 3x − 4.

x =	−2	−1	0	1	2	3	4
y =		−7			2		

5. Complete the table given and hence draw the graph of the function
   y = 8 − 3x.

x =	−4	−3	−2	−1	0	1	2	3	4
y =		17		11					

6. Complete the table given and hence draw the graph of the function
   y = 5x − 10.

x =	1	2	3	4	5
y =	−5		5		

Using your graph to answer questions

Example 19.11

Graph the function $f(x) = 2x - 3$ in the domain $-2 \le x \le 3$, $x \in R$.
Use your graph to find the following.
(a) The value of $f(x)$ when $x = 2.5$.
(b) The point where the line cuts the x-axis.
(c) The point where the line cuts the y-axis.
(d) The value of x when $f(x) = 0$.

Solution

$y = 2x - 3$

x	−2	−1	0	1	2	3
2x	−4	−2	0	2	4	6
−3	−3	−3	−3	−3	−3	−3
y = 2x − 3	−7	−5	−3	−1	1	3

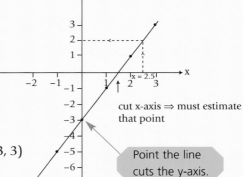

cut x-axis ⇒ must estimate that point

Point the line cuts the y-axis.

$\Rightarrow (-2, -7), (-1, -5), (0, -3), (1, -1), (2, 1), (3, 3)$

(a) $f(x) = y$: $x = 2.5 \Rightarrow y = 2$
(b) Cuts the x-axis at $(1.5, 0)$.
(c) Cuts the y-axis at $(0, -3)$.
(d) $f(x) = 0 \Rightarrow y = 0$
As $y = 0$ all along the x-axis, this asks
for the value of x where the line cuts the x-axis $\Rightarrow x = 1.5$.

Example 19.12

(a) On the same axes and scales, graph, in the domain $-4 \le x \le 2$, the
functions $f(x) = 2x - 4$ and $g(x) = 2 - 2x$.
(b) Use your graph to estimate the point of intersection of the graphs of $f(x)$ and $g(x)$.

f(x):

x =	−4	−3	−2	−1	0	1	2
y =	−12	−10	−8	−6	−4	−2	0

g(x):

x =	−4	−3	−2	−1	0	1	2
y =	10	8	6	4	2	0	−2

379

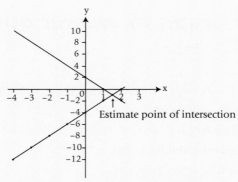

Point of intersection = $(1\frac{1}{2}, -1)$

NOTE: We could have found the point of intersection by solving the simultaneous
equations

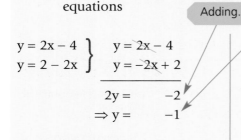

Adding.

Substitute back into either
of the two equations.

$y = 2x - 4$
$\left. \begin{array}{l} y = 2x - 4 \\ y = 2 - 2x \end{array} \right\}$ $\begin{array}{l} y = 2x - 4 \\ y = -2x + 2 \end{array}$

$2y = \quad -2$
$\Rightarrow y = \quad -1$

$y = 2x - 4$
$\Rightarrow -1 = 2x - 4 \Rightarrow 2x = -1 + 4$
$\Rightarrow 2x = 3$
$\Rightarrow x = \frac{3}{2} = 1\frac{1}{2}$

Point of intersection $= \left(1\frac{1}{2}, -1\right)$

Exercise 19.6

1. Draw the graph of the function f:x → x + 4, x ∈ R in the domain −2 ≤ x ≤ 4,
   x ∈ R. Use your graph to estimate:
   (a) the value of y when x = 2.5
   (b) the solution of f(x) = 0.

2. Graph the function f(x) = 3 − x, x ∈ R in the domain −2 ≤ x ≤ 4, x ∈ R.
   Use your graph to estimate:
   (a) the value of x when f(x) = 0
   (b) the value of y when x = −1.5.

3. Graph the function y = 3x − 2, x ∈ R in the domain −3 ≤ x ≤ 5, x ∈ R.
   Use your graph to estimate:
   (a) the value of y when x = −2.5
   (b) the point where the line cuts the x-axis.

4. Graph the function f(x) = 6x − 10, x ∈ R in the domain 0 ≤ x ≤ 3, x ∈ R.
   Use your graph to estimate:
   (a) the value of y when x = $\frac{1}{2}$
   (b) the solution of the equation f(x) = 0.

5. Graph the function f(x) = 3x + 4, x ∈ R in the domain − 4 ≤ x ≤ 1, x ∈ R.
   Use your graph to estimate:
   (a) the value of y when x = $-2\frac{1}{2}$
   (b) the solution to the equation 3x + 4 = 0.

6. (a) On the same axes and same scales, draw the graph of f(x) = 3x and
       g(x) = 8 − x in the domain −2 ≤ x ≤ 4, x ∈ R.
   (b) Use your graph to estimate the point of intersection of both lines.

7. (a) On the same axes and same scales, draw graphs of f(x) = 19 − x and
       g(x) = x + 7 in the domain 3 ≤ x ≤ 8, x ∈ R.
   (b) Use your graph to find the point of intersection of both lines.

8. (a) On the same axes and same scales, draw the graphs of f(x) = x − 1 and
       g(x) = 3 − x in the domain −1 ≤ x ≤ 5, x ∈ R.
   (b) Use your graph to estimate the point of intersection of both lines.

9. (a) On the same axes and same scales, draw the graphs of y = 6 − x and
       y = x − 4 in the domain 2 ≤ x ≤ 7, x ∈ R.
   (b) Use your graph to estimate the point of intersection of both lines.
   (c) Solve the simultaneous equations and compare your answer to your
       estimate from the graph.

10. (a) On the same axes and the same scales, draw the graph of y = 5 − x and
       y = x − 3 in the domain 2 ≤ x ≤ 7, x ∈ R.
   (b) Use your graph to estimate the point of intersection of both lines.
   (c) Solve the simultaneous equations and compare your answers.

11. (a) On the same axes and the same scales, draw the graphs f:x → 3x − 3 and
       g:x → x + 3 in the domain −2 ≤ x ≤ 4, x ∈ R.
   (b) Use your graph to find the point of intersection of both lines.
   (c) Solve the simultaneous equations and compare both your answers.

Graphing quadratic functions

REMEMBER

Quadratic functions are algebraic expressions where the highest power of the variable is 2, i.e. any expression with an x^2.

Example 19.13

Graph the function $f:x \to x^2 + 2x - 6$, $x \in R$ in the domain $-3 \le x \le 3$, $x \in R$.

Solution

x	−3	−2	−1	0	1	2	3
x^2	9	4	1	0	1	4	9
2x	−6	−4	−2	0	2	4	6
−6	−6	−6	−6	−6	−6	−6	−6
y	−3	−6	−7	−6	−3	2	9

(flowchart: x → Square x → Multiply x by 2 → Subtract 6 → y)

giving the points $(-3, 3)$, $(-2, -6)$, $(-1, -7)$, $(0, -6)$, $(1, -3)$, $(2, 2)$, $(3, 9)$

Plotting these points and joining them with a smooth curve gives this.

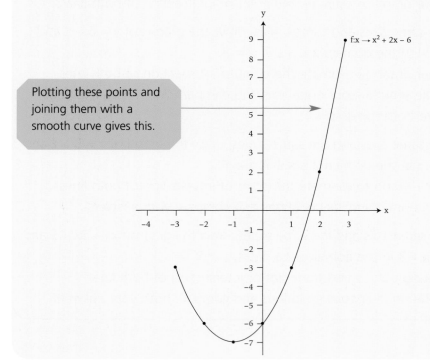

Example 19.14

Graph the function $f:x \rightarrow 6 - x - x^2$ in the domain $-4 \leq x \leq 3$, $x \in R$.

Solution

x
↓
Minus (x to be squared)
↓
Multiply x by −1
↓
Plus 6
↓
y

x	−4	−3	−2	−1	0	1	2	3
$-x^2$	−16	−9	−4	−1	0	−1	−4	−9
$-x$	4	3	2	1	0	−1	−2	−3
$+6$	6	6	6	6	6	6	6	6
y	−6	0	4	6	6	4	0	−6

−x means −1x, i.e. multiply the x values by −1.

giving the points $(-4, -6)$, $(-3, 0)$, $(-2, 4)$, $(-1, 6)$, $(0, 6)$, $(1, 4)$, $(2, 0)$, $(3, -6)$

Check the y values on your calculator before you draw the graph.

Step 1: Change the mode to table, i.e. mode 3 for Casio calculators.

Step 2: Enter the function,

i.e. $\boxed{-}$ $\boxed{\text{Alpha}}$ $\boxed{x}$ $\boxed{x^2}$ $\boxed{-}$

$\boxed{\text{Alpha}}$ $\boxed{x}$ $\boxed{+}$ $\boxed{6}$ $\boxed{=}$

Step 3: Enter the domain,

i.e. Start ? $\boxed{-}$ $\boxed{4}$ $\boxed{=}$

End ? $\boxed{3}$ $\boxed{=}$

Step ? $\boxed{1}$ $\boxed{=}$

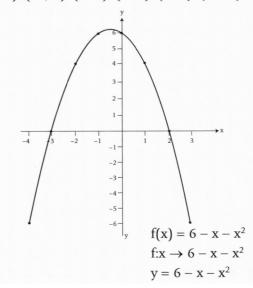

$f(x) = 6 - x - x^2$
$f:x \rightarrow 6 - x - x^2$
$y = 6 - x - x^2$

Exercise 19.7

For questions 1 to 20, graph the function f(x) in the given domain.

1. $f(x) = x^2 - 3x - 4$; domain $-3 \leq x \leq 4$, $x \in R$.

2. $f(x) = x^2 - x - 6$; domain $-4 \leq x \leq 5$, $x \in R$.

3. $f(x) = x^2 + x - 6$; domain $-5 \leq x \leq 3$, $x \in R$.

4. $f(x) = x^2 + 4x - 5$; domain $-6 \le x \le 2$, $x \in R$.

5. $f(x) = x^2 + 8x + 12$; domain $-7 \le x \le 0$, $x \in R$.

6. $f(x) = x^2 - 9$; domain $-4 \le x \le 4$, $x \in R$.

7. $f(x) = x^2 + 2x$; domain $-3 \le x \le 3$, $x \in R$.

8. $f(x) = x^2 - 3x$; domain $-2 \le x \le 5$, $x \in R$.

9. $f(x) = -x^2 + x + 6$; domain $-3 \le x \le 4$, $x \in R$.

10. $f(x) = -x^2 - 3x + 4$; domain $-5 \le x \le 2$, $x \in R$.

11. $f(x) = -x^2 - 6x + 8$; domain $-6 \le x \le 1$, $x \in R$.

12. $f(x) = -x^2 - x + 6$; domain $-4 \le x \le 3$, $x \in R$.

13. $f(x) = -x^2 - 2x + 8$; domain $-5 \le x \le 3$, $x \in R$.

14. $f(x) = 2x^2 + 6x + 4$; domain $-4 \le x \le 2$, $x \in R$.

15. $f(x) = 6x^2 + 18x + 12$; domain $-4 \le x \le 1$, $x \in R$.

16. $f(x) = 2x^2 + 8x + 6$; domain $-5 \le x \le 2$, $x \in R$.

17. $f(x) = 2x^2 - 2x - 4$; domain $-4 \le x \le 4$, $x \in R$.

18. $f(x) = 3x^2 - 12$; domain $-4 \le x \le 4$, $x \le R$.

19. $f(x) = 2x^2 + 2x - 12$; domain $-4 \le x \le 4$, $x \in R$.

20. $f(x) = -2x^2 - 5x + 3$; domain $-4 \le x \le 2$, $x \in R$.

Using quadratic graphs

REMEMBER

Equations of the form $x^2 + 5x + 4 = 0$ have two solutions, i.e. two values for x. These are the points where the graph cuts the x-axis.

Example 19.15

Graph the function $f(x) = x^2 + 5x + 4$ in the domain $-5 \leq x \leq 1$, $x \in$ R. Use your graph to estimate:

(a) the solutions of the equation $f(x) = 0$ (b) the minimum value of $f(x)$
(c) the value of $f(0.5)$ (d) the axis of symmetry of the graph.

Solution

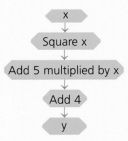

x	−5	−4	−3	−2	−1	0
x^2	25	16	9	4	1	0
5x	−25	−20	−15	−10	−5	0
4	4	4	4	4	4	4
y	4	0	−2	−2	0	4

Check your answers using your calculator.

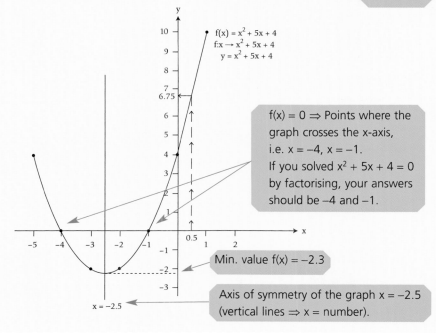

$f(x) = 0 \Rightarrow$ Points where the graph crosses the x-axis, i.e. $x = -4$, $x = -1$.
If you solved $x^2 + 5x + 4 = 0$ by factorising, your answers should be −4 and −1.

Min. value $f(x) = -2.3$

Axis of symmetry of the graph $x = -2.5$ (vertical lines $\Rightarrow$ x = number).

385

(a) Estimate solution for f(x) = 0

From the graph, these are the points where the graph cuts the x-axis

⇒ x = −4 or x = −1

(b) The minimum value of f(x)

This is the lowest value of y on the graph, i.e. the point where the graph turns

⇒ Minimum value = −2.3

(c) The value of f(0.5)

The x value is 0.5. We must find the y value. Start at 0.5 on the x-axis, go up until you hit the graph, then draw a horizontal line and read the y value, i.e. f(0.5) = 6.75.

(d) The axis of symmetry will always be a vertical line. Remember, vertical lines have the form x = some number. The number is the point where the line cuts the x-axis. In this case, the axis of symmetry is x = −2.5.

Example 19.16

Graph the function f:x → $-x^2 + 2x + 3$ in the domain $-2 \leq x \leq 4$, x ∈ R. Use your graph to estimate the following:

(a) the value of f(3.5)

(b) the maximum value of the graph

(c) the solution of $-x^2 + 2x + 3 = 0$

(d) what is the axis of symmetry of the graph?

Solution

x	−2	−1	0	1	2	3	4
$-x^2$	−4	−1	0	−1	−4	−9	−16
2x	−4	−2	0	2	4	6	8
3	3	3	3	3	3	3	3
y	−5	0	3	4	3	0	−5

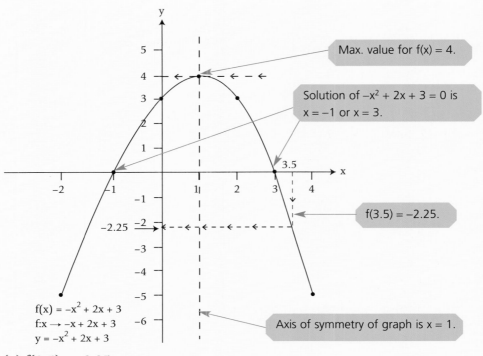

$f(x) = -x^2 + 2x + 3$
$f:x \rightarrow -x + 2x + 3$
$y = -x^2 + 2x + 3$

Max. value for f(x) = 4.

Solution of $-x^2 + 2x + 3 = 0$ is x = −1 or x = 3.

f(3.5) = −2.25.

Axis of symmetry of graph is x = 1.

(a) $f(3.5) = -2.25$.
(b) Maximum value of $f(x) = 4$.
(c) $-x^2 + 2x + 3 = 0$ when x = −1 or x = 3.
(d) Axis of symmetry of the graph is x = 1.

Exercise 19.8

1. Draw the graph of $f:x \rightarrow x^2 + 2x - 3$ in the domain $-4 \le x \le 2$, $x \in$ R. Use your graph to estimate the following.
   (a) The minimum value of f(x).
   (b) The value of f(−1.5).
   (c) The axis of symmetry of the graph.
   (d) The solution to the equation $x^2 + 2x - 3 = 0$.

2. Draw the graph of $f:x \rightarrow x^2 - 7x + 6$ in the domain $0 \le x \le 7$, $x \in$ R. Use your graph to estimate the following.
   (a) The minimum value of f(x).
   (b) The value of f(2.5).

(c) The solution to the equation f(x) = 0.

(d) Find the axis of symmetry of the graph.

3. Draw the graph of $f(x) = x^2 + x - 6$ in the domain $-5 \leq x \leq 4$, $x \in$ R. Use your graph to estimate the following.

(a) The solutions to the equation $x^2 + x = 6$.

(b) The minimum value of f(x).

(c) The value of f(2.5).

4. Draw the graph of $f:x \rightarrow x^2 - 2x - 3$ in the domain $-3 \leq x \leq 5$, $x \in$ R. Use your graph to estimate the following.

(a) The value of f(−0.5).

(b) The minimum value of $x^2 - 2x - 3$.

(c) The solutions of the equation $x^2 - 2x - 3 = 0$.

5. Draw the graph of $f:x \rightarrow x^2 - x - 6$ in the domain $-4 \leq x \leq 4$, $x \in$ R. Use your graph to estimate the following.

(a) The value of f(−1.25).

(b) The minimum value of f(x).

(c) The solutions to the equation f(x) = 0.

6. Draw the graph of $f:x \rightarrow -x^2 + x + 2$ in the domain $-2 \leq x \leq 3$, $x \in$ R. Use your graph to estimate the following.

(a) The value of f(−1.5).

(b) The maximum value of the graph.

(c) The solutions to the equation $-x^2 + x + 2 = 0$.

7. Draw the graph of $f(x) = -x^2 + x + 6$ in the domain $-3 \leq x \leq 4$, $x \in$ R. Use your graph to estimate the following.

(a) The maximum value of f(x).

(b) The value of $f\left(2\frac{1}{4}\right)$.

(c) The solutions of the equation $-x^2 + x + 6 = 0$.

8. Draw the graph of $f(x) = 6x^2 - 6$ in the domain $-3 \leq x \leq 3$, $x \in$ R. Use your graph to estimate the following.

(a) The value of f(1.5).

(b) The solutions to the equation f(x) = 0.

(c) The minimum value of f(x).

9. Draw the graph of f:x → $5x^2 + 12x - 9$ in the domain $-4 \le x \le 2$, x ∈ R.
   Use your graph to estimate the following.
   (a) The value of f(−3.5).
   (b) The solutions to the equation $5x^2 + 12x - 9 = 0$.
   (c) The minimum value of f(x).

10. Draw the graph of f:x → $25 - x^2$ in the domain $-6 \le x \le 6$, x ∈ R. Use
    your graph to estimate the following.
    (a) The value of $f\left(\frac{23}{6}\right)$.
    (b) The solutions to the equation f(x) = 0.
    (c) The maximum value of $25 - x^2$.
    (d) The axis of symmetry of the graph.

11. Draw the graph of f(x) = $12 - 3x^2$ in the domain $-3 \le x \le 3$, x ∈ R. Use
    your graph to estimate the following.
    (a) The maximum value of f(x).
    (b) The value of $f\left(2\frac{1}{3}\right)$.
    (c) The solutions to the equation $12 - 3x^2 = 0$.
    (d) The axis of symmetry of the graph.

12. Draw the graph of f(x) = $4x^2 - 11x - 3$ in the domain $-3 \le x \le 5$, x ∈ R.
    Use your graph to estimate the following.
    (a) The minimum value of $4x^2 - 11x - 3$.
    (b) The value of f(3.5).
    (c) The solutions to the equation f(x) = 0.

13. Draw the graph of f(x) = $7x - 5x^2$ in the domain $-2 \le x \le 3$, x ∈ R. Use
    your graph to estimate the following.
    (a) The value of $f\left(2\frac{1}{4}\right)$.
    (b) The maximum value of $7x - 5x^2$.
    (c) The solutions to the equation $7x - 5x^2 = 0$.

14. Draw the graph of f:x → $4 - 3x - x^2$ in the domain $-5 \le x \le 2$, x ∈ R. Use
    your graph to estimate the following.
    (a) The maximum value of $4 - 3x - x^2$.
    (b) The value of $f\left(\frac{1}{2}\right)$.
    (c) The solutions to the equation $-x^2 - 3x + 4 = 0$.
    (d) The axis of symmetry of the graph.

Practical examples

REMEMBER

With all practical questions on graphs, relabel both axes with the correct units.

Example 19.17

The graph shows the relationship between the number of electrical units used and the cost of the electricity bill. The x-axis shows the number of units in 100s, i.e. 1 on the x-axis represents 100 units, 2 is 200 units, etc. The y-axis shows the cost in €10 intervals, i.e. 1 represents €10.

Use the graph to find the following.
(a) The standing charge, i.e. the charge every month even if no units of electricity are used.
(b) The electricity bill if 350 units of electricity are used.
(c) The number of units used if the bill was €30.

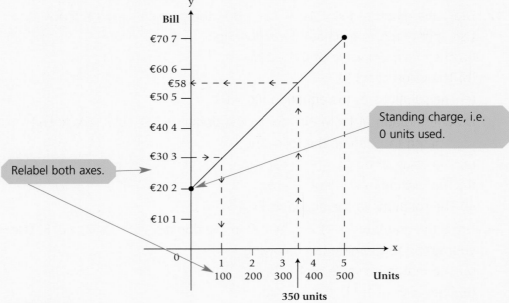

Solution
(a) Standing charge = €20
(b) Bill with 350 units = €58
(c) Bill of €30 means that 100 units of electricity were used

Example 19.18

The graph $f(x) = 8x - x^2$ represents the path travelled by a football from the time the goalkeeper kicks it out until it hits the pitch again.

The x-axis measures the time in seconds that the ball is in the air and the y-axis measures the height in metres the ball is above the ground.

Draw the graph of the flight of the ball. Use your graph to estimate the following.
(a) The maximum height of the ball.
(b) The length of time the ball takes to reach the maximum height.
(c) The length of time the ball is in the air.

Solution

x	0	1	2	3	4	5	6	7	8
$-x^2$	0	−1	−4	−9	−16	−25	−36	−49	−64
$8x$	0	8	16	24	32	40	48	56	64
y	0	7	12	15	16	15	12	7	0

x
↓
−1 multiplied by x^2
↓
Plus 8 multiplied by x
↓
y

Use your calculator to check this.

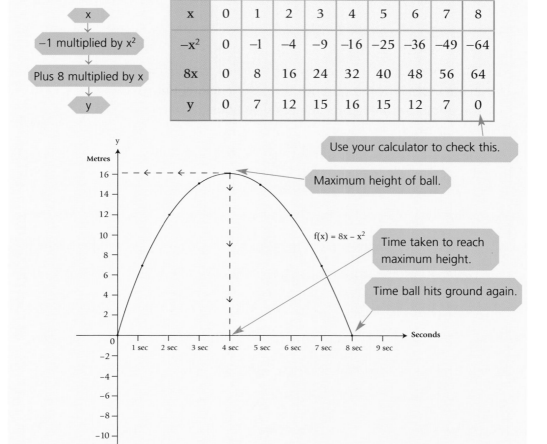

Maximum height of ball.

$f(x) = 8x - x^2$

Time taken to reach maximum height.

Time ball hits ground again.

(a) Maximum height of ball = 16 m
(b) The ball will take four seconds to reach the maximum height.
(c) The ball will be in the air for eight seconds.

391

Exercise 19.9

1. The graph shows the distance a
   cyclist travels in a five-hour journey.
   From the graph, estimate the
   following.
   (a) The distance travelled after two
   hours.
   (b) The time it takes to
   travel 50 km.
   (c) The total distance travelled
   in five hours.
   (d) The average speed of the
   cyclist. (Remember, speed =
   distance ÷ time).

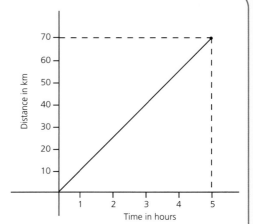

2. The function y = 100x represents the time travelled in hours and the
   y-axis represents the distance travelled in kilometres. Draw the graph of
   the distance travelled for the first five hours. Use your graph to estimate
   the following.
   (a) The distance travelled after $3\frac{1}{2}$ hours.
   (b) The time it takes to travel 150 km.
   (c) The total distance travelled after five hours.
   (d) The average speed of the car.

3. The average weight of a baby measured every two weeks for the first
   12 weeks of life is given by the equation 3y = x + 10.5.
   The x-axis represents the age of the baby in weeks and the y-axis
   represents the weight of the baby during the first 12 weeks of life. Use
   your graph to estimate the following.
   (a) The average weight of a baby at birth.
   (b) The average weight of a baby six weeks old.
   (c) The age of a baby weighing 4.5 kg.
   (d) The weight of a 12-week-old baby.

4. Telephone charges are given by the function $y = 0.2x + 22$. The x-axis represents the number of units used in 100s up to 600 and the y-axis is the cost in euro. Draw a graph representing the telephone billing. From your graph, estimate the following.

(a) The line rental (standing order charge is 0 units used).

(b) The bill if the customer uses 350 units.

(c) How many units were used if the bill was €45.

(d) The cost of 230 units without line rental.

5. An insurance company uses the following function in determining the cost of life insurance for its clients: $y = 2x + 50$.

The x-axis represents the age of the client in multiples of 10, i.e. 1 = 10 years, 2 = 20 years, etc., and the y-axis represents the cost of the policy in multiples of €10, i.e. 1 = €10, 2 = €20, etc.

Draw the graph of the cost function from 0 to 100 years of age. Use your graph to estimate the cost of the following.

(a) A policy for someone who is 45 years old.

(b) The administration fee attached to the policy, i.e. before the amount for the age is added, age = 0.

(c) The age of a person who is charged €100 for a policy.

6. Derry and Belfast are 120 km apart. A motorist starts from Derry and drives at a constant speed, arriving in Belfast three hours later. Another motorist leaves Belfast one hour after the first leaves Derry and drives at a constant speed towards Derry. It takes the second motorist $1\frac{1}{2}$ hours to reach Derry.

Let the x-axis represent the time in half-hour intervals and the y-axis represent the distance each car travels.

On the same axes and scales, draw the straight line graph for each motorist (second motorist starts at 120 km).

From your graph, estimate the following.

(a) The distance travelled by the both motorists when they meet.

(b) The time the second motorist has travelled when they meet on the road.

(c) The average speed of both motorists. (speed = distance ÷ time)

7. A plane left New York for Dublin. Flying at a constant speed, the plane took seven hours to cover the 3500 km journey.

One hour after the New York plane took off, an executive jet left Dublin for New York. This plane took five hours flying at a constant speed.

On the same axes and same scale, draw the straight line graph for each plane.

Let the x-axis represent the time taken for the journey and let the y-axis represent the distance travelled by each plane.

Use your graph to estimate the following.
(a) The distance travelled by the first plane when both planes meet.
(b) The time the second plane was flying before both planes meet.
(c) The average speed of both planes.

8. The graph shows the temperature recorded from 6 a.m. to 6 p.m. on a winter's day. From the graph, estimate the following.

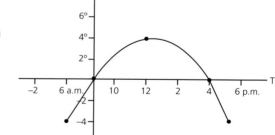

(a) The maximum temperature recorded.
(b) The time the maximum temperature was recorded.
(c) The lowest temperature recorded.
(d) The time(s) the temperature was 2°.

9. The function $f(x) = x^2 + x - 3$ traces the temperature through the night from 8 p.m. to 6 a.m. If −3 on the x-axis represents 8 p.m., −2 = 10 p.m., etc., draw the graph showing the temperature on the y-axis.
From your graph, estimate the following.
(a) The minimum temperature.
(b) The time the minimum temperature was recorded.
(c) At what times(s) the temperature was 0°.

10. The path of a missile is given by the function $f(x) = 64x - 16x^2$. If the x-axis represents the time in seconds the missile is in the air and the y-axis represents the height of the missile above the ground, draw the path of the missile. Use your graph to estimate the following.
    (a) The maximum height of the missile.
    (b) The length of time the missile was in the air.

11. The path of a high board diver is given by the function $y = x^2 - 6x + 8$. If the x-axis represents the time in seconds the diver is in motion and the y-axis represents the height above water and the depth under the water, draw the path of the diver from 0 to 4 seconds. From your graph, estimate the following.
    (a) The height of the board above the water.
    (b) The lowest depth the diver reaches.
    (c) The length of time underwater.

Exercise 19.10 (Chapter summary)

1. Draw the arrow diagram for the relation R = {(1, 4), (2, −6), (3, 8), (4, −10)}.

2. Write out the set of couples in the relation
   $R = \{(x, y) \mid = 3x - 6, x \in A\}$ where $A = \{0, 1, 2, 3, 4\}$.
   Draw the arrow diagram for the above relation. Is the relation a function?
   Give a reason for your answer.

3. If $f(x) = 2x^2 - 6$, find:
   (a) $f(a)$
   (b) $f(-1)$
   (c) $f(0)$
   (d) $f(x - 1)$

4. Draw the graph of the function
   $f: x \rightarrow 3x - 4$ in the domain $-3 \leq x \leq 3$, $x \in R$.

5. (a) On the same axes and the same scales, draw the graph of $f: x \rightarrow x + 2$
       $g: x \rightarrow 4 - x$ in the domain $-2 \leq x \leq 3$, $x \in R$.
   (b) From the graph, estimate the point of intersection of both lines.
   (c) Solve the equations simultaneously and compare both answers.

6. Graph the function $f: x \rightarrow 8x^2 - 4x$ in the domain $-2 \leq x \leq 2$, $x \in R$.

7. Graph the function $f: x \rightarrow 4 - x^2$ in the domain $-3 \leq x \leq 3$, $x \in R$. From your
   graph, estimate the following.
   (a) Solutions to the equation $4 - x^2 = 0$
   (b) The maximum value of $f(x)$
   (c) $f\left(1\frac{1}{2}\right)$

8. Draw the graph of the function $2x^2 + 2x - 12$ in the domain $-5 \leq x \leq 4$.
   Use your graph to estimate the following.
   (a) $f\left(-3\frac{1}{2}\right)$
   (b) The minimum value of the graph.
   (c) The solutions to the equation $f(x) = 0$.
   (d) The axis of symmetry of the graph.

9. The graph shows the relationship between the height of a golf ball and the time it was in the air.

   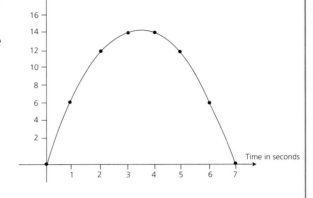

   Height in metres

   Time in seconds

   (a) From the graph, estimate the maximum height of the golf ball.

   (b) How long did it take to reach the maximum height from when the ball was hit?

   (c) What was the height of the ball after 2.5 seconds?

   (d) At what time(s) was the ball 12 m above the ground?

   (e) How long was the ball in the air?

10. The graph $f(x) = 2x^2 - 13x + 15$ represents the path travelled by a high board diver. The x-axis represents the time in seconds the diver is in motion and the y-axis represents the height in metres above the water and the depth below the water that the diver travelled. Draw the graph of the path the diver takes from 0 seconds to 5 seconds. From your graph, estimate the following.

    (a) The height the board is above the water.

    (b) The lowest depth the diver reaches.

    (c) The length of time the diver is underwater.

Trigonometry 20

Trigonometry is the study of triangles and the relationship between the lengths of the sides and the size of the angles in the triangle.

The Junior Certificate Ordinary Level syllabus deals only with right-angled triangles.

398

Labelling the sides of a right-angled triangle

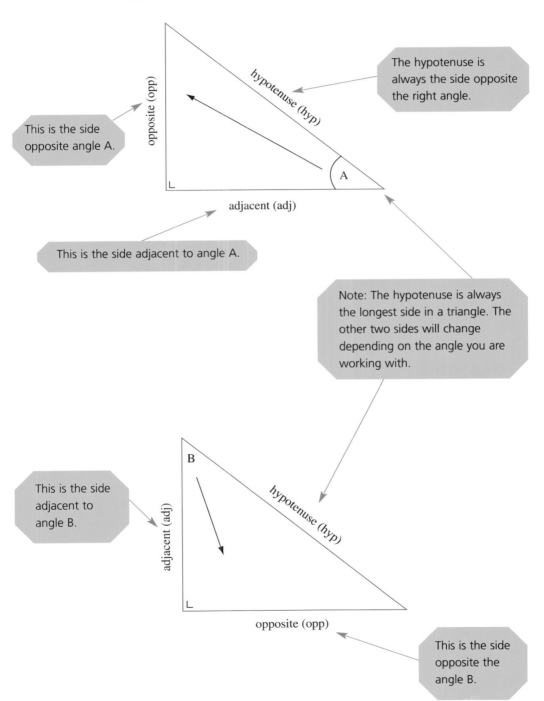

The hypotenuse is always the side opposite the right angle.

This is the side opposite angle A.

This is the side adjacent to angle A.

Note: The hypotenuse is always the longest side in a triangle. The other two sides will change depending on the angle you are working with.

This is the side adjacent to angle B.

This is the side opposite the angle B.

Trigonometric ratios

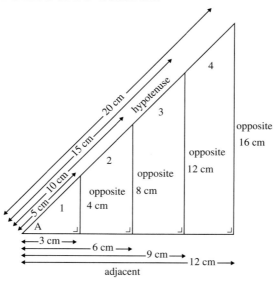

	Triangle 1	Triangle 2	Triangle 3	Triangle 4
Length of opposite side	4	8	12	16
Length of adjacent side	3	6	9	12
$\dfrac{\text{opposite}}{\text{adjacent}}$	$\dfrac{4}{3}$	$\dfrac{8}{6}=\dfrac{4}{3}$	$\dfrac{12}{9}=\dfrac{4}{3}$	$\dfrac{16}{12}=\dfrac{4}{3}$

Note that the ratio of opposite : adjacent is the same for each of the triangles.

This particular ratio is called $\tan A = \dfrac{\text{opposite}}{\text{adjacent}}$.

	Triangle 1	Triangle 2	Triangle 3	Triangle 4
Length of opposite side	4	8	12	16
Length of hypotenuse	5	10	15	20
$\dfrac{\text{opposite}}{\text{hypotenuse}}$	$\dfrac{4}{5}=\dfrac{4}{5}$	$\dfrac{8}{10}=\dfrac{4}{5}$	$\dfrac{12}{15}=\dfrac{4}{5}$	$\dfrac{16}{20}=\dfrac{4}{5}$

Again, the ratio of the opposite : hypotenuse is the same for each of the triangles.

This particular ratio is called $\sin A = \dfrac{\text{opposite}}{\text{hypotenuse}}$.

	Triangle 1	Triangle 2	Triangle 3	Triangle 4
Length of adjacent	3	6	9	12
Length of hypotenuse	5	10	15	20
$\dfrac{\text{opposite}}{\text{adjacent}}$	$\dfrac{3}{5}$	$\dfrac{6}{10} = \dfrac{3}{5}$	$\dfrac{9}{15} = \dfrac{3}{5}$	$\dfrac{12}{20} = \dfrac{3}{5}$

Yet again, the ratio of the adjacent : hypotenuse is the same for each of the triangles.

This particular ratio is called $\cos A = \dfrac{\text{adjacent}}{\text{hypotenuse}}$.

REMEMBER

$$\sin A = \frac{\text{opposite}}{\text{hypotenuse}} \qquad \cos A = \frac{\text{adjacent}}{\text{hypotenuse}} \qquad \tan A = \frac{\text{opposite}}{\text{adjacent}}$$

These ratios are very important when working with right-angled triangles. Your log tables have these ratios worked out for all angles between 0 and 90°, but most people use their calculators to work them out.

Make sure your calculator is set on Deg before you start to work.

One way of remembering the different ratios is to remember the word 'SOHCAHTOA':

SOH CAH TOA

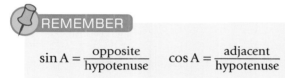

$$\sin = \frac{\text{opp}}{\text{hyp}} \qquad \cos = \frac{\text{adj}}{\text{hyp}} \qquad \tan = \frac{\text{opp}}{\text{adj}}$$

Example 20.1

Write the side that is:
(a) the hypotenuse
(b) the adjacent to angle A
(c) the opposite to angle A
(d) the adjacent to angle B
(e) the opposite to angle B.

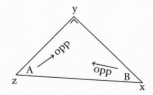

Solution

(a) hypotenuse = [xz]

(b) adjacent to angle A = [yz]

(c) opposite to angle A = [xy]

(d) adjacent to angle B = [xy]

(e) opposite to angle B = [yz]

401

Example 20.2

Using the triangle shown, write the following ratios.

(a) sin A   (d) sin B
(b) cos A   (e) cos B
(c) tan A   (f) tan B

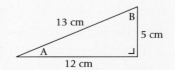

Solution

(a) $\sin A = \dfrac{\text{opp}}{\text{hyp}} = \dfrac{5}{13}$

(b) $\cos A = \dfrac{\text{adj}}{\text{hyp}} = \dfrac{12}{13}$

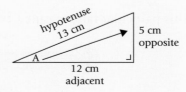

(c) $\tan A = \dfrac{\text{opp}}{\text{adj}} = \dfrac{5}{12}$

(d) $\sin B = \dfrac{\text{opp}}{\text{hyp}} = \dfrac{12}{13}$

(e) $\cos B = \dfrac{\text{adj}}{\text{hyp}} = \dfrac{5}{13}$

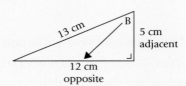

(f) $\tan B = \dfrac{\text{opp}}{\text{adj}} = \dfrac{12}{5}$

Exercise 20.1

1. In each of the following triangles, the sides are labelled a, b and c. Name
(i) the hypotenuse (ii) the opposite side to angle X (iii) the adjacent side to angle X.

(a)

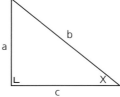

(b)

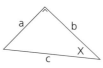

(c)

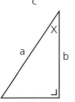

(d)

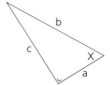

2. Write the side that is:
   (a) the hypotenuse
   (b) the side adjacent to angle E
   (c) the side opposite to angle D
   (d) the side opposite to angle E
   (e) the side adjacent to angle D.

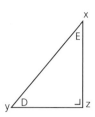

3. In each triangle shown, name the sides in relation to angle X.

(a)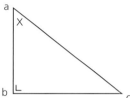
(b)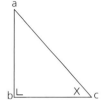
(c)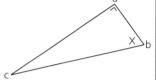

4. Use the diagram to write the following ratios.
   (a) sin A   (d) sin B
   (b) cos A   (e) cos B
   (c) tan A   (f) tan B

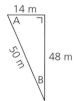

5. Use the diagram to write the following ratios.
   (a) sin A   (d) sin B
   (b) cos A   (e) cos B
   (c) tan A   (f) tan B

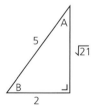

6. Use the diagram to find the following ratios.
   (a) tan B   (d) cos B
   (b) cos A   (e) sin B
   (c) sin A   (f) tan A

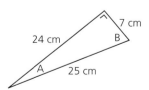

Using your calculator to find sine, cosine and tangent

Example 20.3

Use your calculator to find the following, correct to four decimal places.

(a) cos 25°   (b) sin 50°   (c) tan 34°

Solution

First, make sure your calculator is in degree mode.

(a) cos 25° = .906307787

         = .9063

Using the calculator

$\boxed{\cos}\ \boxed{25}\ \boxed{=}$

(b) sin 50° = .7660444431

         = .7660 ◄——————————— Correct to four decimal places.

Using the calculator

$\boxed{\sin}\ \boxed{50}\ \boxed{=}$

(c) tan 34° = .6745085168

         = .6745

Using the calculator

$\boxed{\tan}\ \boxed{34}\ \boxed{=}$

Example 20.4

Use your calculator to find the following angles to the nearest degree.

(a) tan θ = .47   (b) sin A = .83   (c) cos B = .64

(d) $\tan X = \frac{5}{7}$ (e) $\cos P = \frac{3}{4}$ (f) $\sin Q = \frac{1}{5}$

Solution

To find the angle on the calculator, you must use the $\boxed{\text{inv}}$, $\boxed{\text{2nd}}$ or $\boxed{\text{shift}}$ button.

(a) tan θ = .47

   ⇒ $\boxed{\text{inv}}\ \boxed{\tan}\ \boxed{.47}$ → = 25.17352452°

   ⇒ θ = 25°

(b) sin A = .83

   ⇒ $\boxed{\text{inv}}\ \boxed{\sin}\ \boxed{.83}$ = 56.098738°   To the nearest degree.

   ⇒ A = 56°

(c) cos B = .64°

$\Rightarrow$ |inv| |cos| |.64| |=| 50.2081805°

$\Rightarrow$ B = 50°

(d) $\tan X = \frac{5}{7}$

$\Rightarrow$ |inv| |tan| |□/□| |5| |↓| |7| |=| 35.53767779

$\Rightarrow$ X = 36°

(e) $\cos P = \frac{3}{4}$

$\Rightarrow$ |inv| |cos| |□/□| |3| |↓| |4| |=| 41.40962211

$\Rightarrow$ P = 41°

(f) $\sin Q = \frac{1}{5}$

$\Rightarrow$ |inv| |sin| |□/□| |1| |↓| |5| |=| 11.53695903

$\Rightarrow$ Q = 12°

Exercise 20.2

1. Use your calculator to evaluate each of the following to four decimal places.

   (a) cos 32°   (d) cos 60°   (g) cos 10°
   (b) sin 56°   (e) tan 74°   (h) sin 80°
   (c) cos 45°   (f) sin 32°

2. Use your calculator to evaluate each of the following.

   (a) cos 0°   (d) cos 90°   (g) tan 45°
   (b) sin 0°   (e) sin 90°   (h) sin 30°
   (c) tan 0°   (f) cos 60°

3. Use your calculator to check whether the following are true or false.

   (a) 2 sin 40° = sin 90°   (d) cos 70° = 2 cos 35°
   (b) 3 cos 20° = cos 60°   (e) tan 90° = 2 tan 45°
   (c) 2 sin 15° = sin 30°   (f) 3 cos 15° = cos 45°

4. Use your calculator to check whether the following are true or false.
   (a) cos 30° = sin 60°
   (b) sin 20° = cos 70°
   (c) cos 35° = sin 55°
   (d) sin 57° = cos 33°
   (e) sin 38° = cos 52°
   (f) $\tan 45° = \dfrac{\sin 45°}{\cos 45°}$
   (g) $\tan 60° = \dfrac{\sin 60°}{\cos 60°}$
   (h) $\tan 35° = \dfrac{\sin 35°}{\cos 35°}$

5. Use your calculator to find each of the following angles to the nearest degree.
   (a) cos A = .71
   (b) sin B = .47
   (c) cos C = .89
   (d) tan D = 1.42
   (e) sin E = 0.142
   (f) cos F = 0.25
   (g) tan G = 2.66
   (h) sin H = 0.34
   (i) cos I = 0.91
   (j) cos J = 0.21

6. Use your calculator to find each of the following angles to the nearest degree.
   (a) $\sin K = \dfrac{4}{9}$
   (b) $\cos L = \dfrac{1}{7}$
   (c) $\sin M = \dfrac{15}{30}$
   (d) $\sin N = \dfrac{8}{12}$
   (e) $\tan O = \dfrac{7}{2}$
   (f) $\cos P = \dfrac{3}{5}$
   (g) $\tan Q = \dfrac{12}{4}$
   (h) $\tan R = \dfrac{40}{6}$
   (i) $\sin S = \dfrac{1}{7}$
   (j) $\cos T = \dfrac{23}{33}$

7. Use your calculator to find each of the following angles.
   (a) $\cos \theta = \dfrac{1}{\sqrt{2}}$
   (b) $\sin \beta = \dfrac{\sqrt{3}}{2}$
   (c) $\sin \alpha = \dfrac{1}{\sqrt{2}}$
   (d) $\tan \delta = \sqrt{3}$
   (e) $\sin \mu = \dfrac{4}{4}$
   (f) $\tan \Omega = \dfrac{1}{\sqrt{3}}$
   (g) $\sin \delta = \dfrac{1}{2}$
   (h) $\cos \ell = \dfrac{\sqrt{3}}{2}$
   (i) $\cos n = \dfrac{0}{30}$
   (j) $\cos K = \dfrac{6}{12}$

||| Pythagoras' Theorem

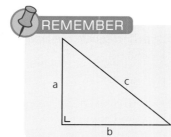

REMEMBER

Pythagoras' Theorem:
$a^2 + b^2 = c^2$

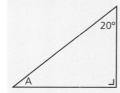

REMEMBER

Three angles in a triangle add up to 180°.
$\Rightarrow A = 180° - (90° + 20°)$
$A = 70°$

Example 20.5

In the triangles shown, find the length of the side marked x.

(a)

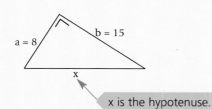

x is the hypotenuse.

(b)

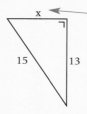

x is one of the shorter sides.

Solution

(a) $a^2 + b^2 = c^2$

$8^2 + 15^2 = x^2$

$\Rightarrow 64 + 225 = x^2$

$\Rightarrow 289 = x^2$

$\Rightarrow \sqrt{289} = x$

$17 = x$

(b) $13^2 + x^2 = 15^2$

$\Rightarrow 169 + x^2 = 225$

$\Rightarrow x^2 = 225 - 169$

$\Rightarrow x^2 = 56$

$\Rightarrow x = \sqrt{56}$

As 56 is not a perfect square, we leave the answer as $x = \sqrt{56}$.

Example 20.6

Write the measure of the missing angle in the following right-angled triangles.

(a)

(b)

(c)

Solution

(a)

$A = 180° - (60° + 90°)$

$A = 180° - 150°$

$A = 30°$

(b)

$A = 180° - (90° + 70°)$

$A = 180° - 160°$

$A = 20°$

(c)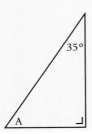

$A = 180° - (90° + 35°)$

$A = 180° - 125°$

$A = 55°$

Exercise 20.3

Find the length of the side marked x in questions 1 to 12. (You may leave your answer in surd form if x is not a perfect square.)

1.

2.

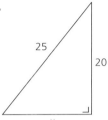

3.

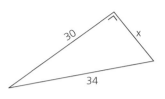

4.

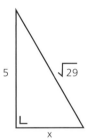

5.

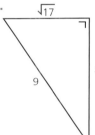

6.

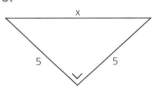

7.

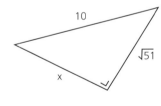

8.

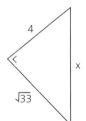

9.

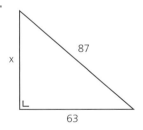

10.

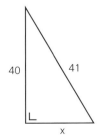

11.

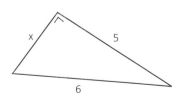

12.

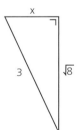

In questions 13 to 18, calculate the measure of angle A.

13.

14.

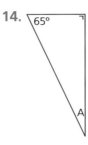

15.

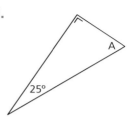

16.

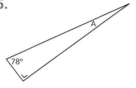

17.

18.

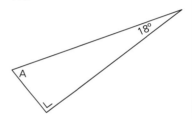

In questions 19 to 24: (a) calculate the length of the sides marked x and (b) write the values of (i) sin B (ii) cos B and (iii) tan B.

19.

20.

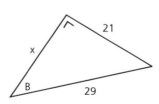

21.

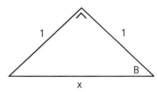

22.

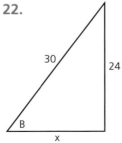

23.

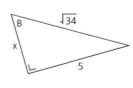

24.

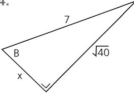

Solving right-angled triangles

Solving a right-angled triangle means finding the lengths of missing sides and the measure of missing angles.

Example 20.7

In the triangle abc, find |ac|, correct to two decimal places.

Given the hypotenuse.

Solution

The side we must find is the side adjacent to 60°.
The other side is the hypotenuse.
The ratio that uses adjacent and hypotenuse is cos.

$$\Rightarrow \cos 60° = \frac{\text{adj}}{\text{hyp}} = \frac{|ac|}{10}$$

$$0.5 = \frac{|ac|}{10}$$

ac is the adjacent side.

$$\Rightarrow |ac| = 10(0.5)$$

$$\Rightarrow |ac| = 5 \text{ cm}$$

Use your calculator to find cos 60.

Example 20.8

In the triangle xyz, find the measure of the angle |∠xzy| to the nearest degree.

Solution

Since we are given the opposite side (4 cm) and the adjacent side (3 cm), we must use the tan ratio.

We are working with this angle.

$$\tan \angle xzy = \frac{\text{opp}}{\text{adj}} = \frac{4}{3}$$

$$\tan \angle xzy = \frac{4}{3}$$

Use the calculator

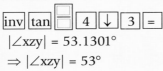

$$|\angle xzy| = 53.1301°$$

$$\Rightarrow |\angle xzy| = 53°$$

411

Example 20.9

In the triangle opq find the length |oq|, correct to two decimal places.

Solution

$$\sin 40° = \frac{15}{x}$$

$$\Rightarrow .6428 = \frac{15}{x}$$

$$\Rightarrow .6428(x) = 15$$

$$\Rightarrow x = \frac{15}{.6428}$$

$$\Rightarrow x = 23.34$$

$$\sin = \frac{\text{opposite}}{\text{hypotenuse}}$$

We are given the 40° angle, the side opposite and asked to find the hypotenuse.

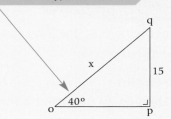

Exercise 20.4

In questions 1 to 15, calculate, correct to two decimal places, the length of the side marked x.

1.

2.

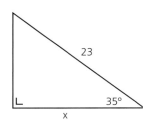

3.

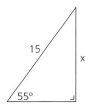

4.

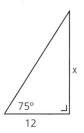

5.

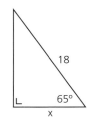

6.

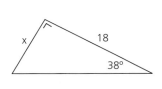

7.

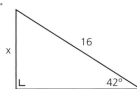

8.

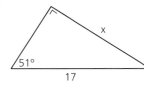

9.

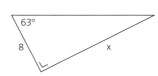

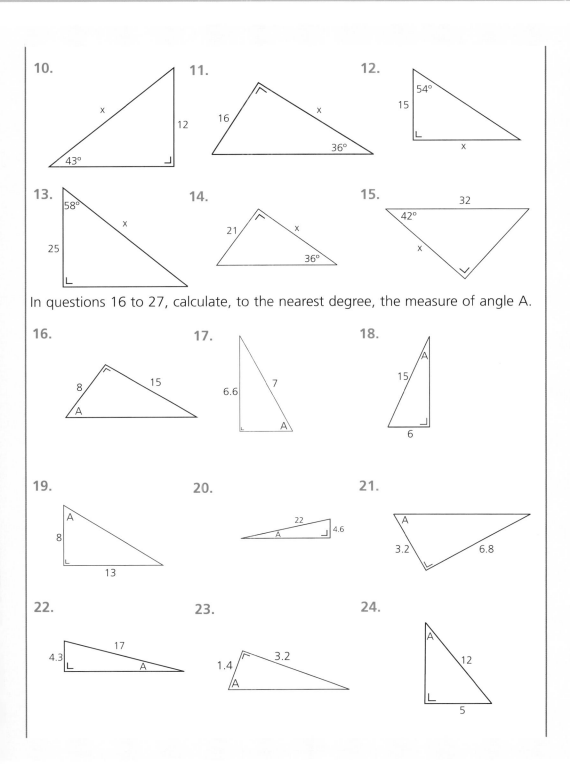

10.

x

12

43°

11.

x

16

36°

12.

54°

15

x

13.

58°

x

25

14.

21

x

36°

15.

32

42°

x

In questions 16 to 27, calculate, to the nearest degree, the measure of angle A.

16.

8

15

A

17.

6.6

7

A

18.

A

15

6

19.

A

8

13

20.

22

A

4.6

21.

A

3.2

6.8

22.

17

4.3

A

23.

1.4

3.2

A

24.

A

12

5

25.

26.

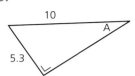

27.

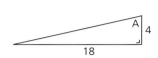

In questions 28 to 39, calculate: (a) any missing side correct to two decimal places (b) any missing angle to the nearest degree.

28.

29.

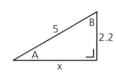

30.

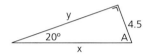

31.

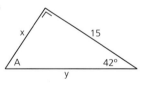

32.

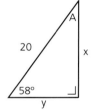

33.

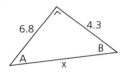

34.

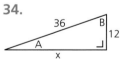

35.

36.

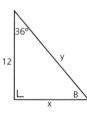

37.

38.

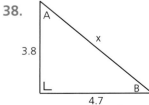

39.

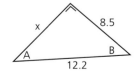

Practical applications of trigonometry

Angle of depression

The angle of depression is the angle through which someone looks down from the horizontal eye level at an object.

Angle of elevation

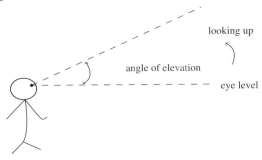

The angle of elevation is the angle with the horizontal through which someone looks up at an object

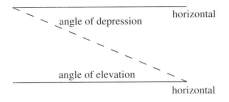

In the diagram, we see that the angles of elevation and depression are alternate angles, therefore:

angle of elevation = angle of depression

A clinometer is used to find the angle of elevation or depression.

Example 20.10

A boat sails 100 m from the base of a lighthouse. At this point, the angle of elevation of the top of the lighthouse is 25°. Calculate the height of the lighthouse correct to one decimal place.

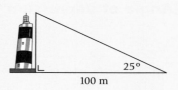

100 m

Solution

The lighthouse corresponds to the opposite side to 25°.
The 100 m corresponds to the adjacent side to 25°.

$$\tan = \frac{\text{opp}}{\text{adj}}$$

$$\Rightarrow \tan 25° = \frac{x}{100}$$ ← x represents the height of the lighthouse.

$$.4663 = \frac{x}{100}$$ ← Use your calculator to find tan 25°.

$$\Rightarrow x = 100(.4663)$$

$$x = 46.63 \text{ m}$$

$$x = 46.6 \text{ m}$$

Example 20.11

A tree casts a shadow of 10 m when the angle of elevation of the sun is 65°. Calculate the height of the tree to the nearest m.

angle of elevation

shadow

Solution

$$\tan 65° = \frac{h}{10}$$ h = height of the tree.

$$2.1445 = \frac{h}{10}$$ Use your calculator to find tan 65°.

$$h = 10(2.1445)$$

$$h = 21.445 \text{ m}$$ Find the opposite side to 65°.

$$h = 21 \text{ m}$$

h

65°

10 m

Adjacent side to 65°.

Example 20.12

From the top of a vertical cliff, the angle of depression of a yacht at anchor at sea if found to be 36°. The yacht is known to be 75 m from the base of the cliff. Calculate, to the nearest metre, the height of the cliff.

Solution

Tan uses opposite and adjacent.

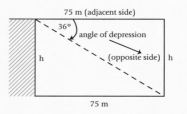

$$\tan = \frac{opp}{adj}$$

$$\tan 36° = \frac{h}{75}$$

$$0.7265 = \frac{h}{75}$$

$h = 75(.7265)$

$h = 54.4875$ m

$h = 54$ m

Exercise 20.5

1. A ladder 10 m long leans against a vertical wall. The ladder makes an angle of 60° with the ground. Calculate the height up the wall to which the ladder reaches.

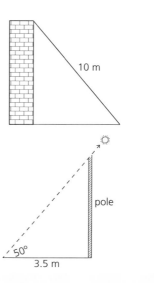

2. A vertical pole casts a shadow of 3.5 m on level ground when the angle of elevation of the sun is 50°. Calculate the height of the pole to the nearest metre.

3. A vertical pole 7 m high casts a shadow 5 m long on level ground. Calculate the angle of elevation of the sun to the nearest degree.

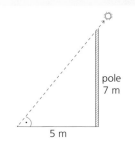

4. A flagpole casts a shadow of 12 m on level ground. If the angle of elevation of the sun is 30°, calculate the height of the flagpole.

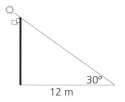

5. The angle of depression of a boat from the top of a cliff 200 m high is 25°. Calculate how far out to sea the boat is, correct to the nearest metre.

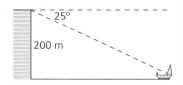

6. A space shuttle is standing vertically on the launch pad. The angle of elevation of the nose of the shuttle, from a point 50 m from the base of the launch pad, is found to be 40°. Calculate the height of the nose of the shuttle above the ground.

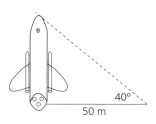

7. A plane takes off at an angle of 35° to the ground. What height is the plane vertically above ground when it has travelled 3500 m?

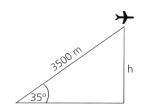

8. A kite is attached to the ground by a string 65 m long. If the kite-string makes an angle of 68° with the ground, calculate, to the nearest metre, how far the kite is above ground.

9. The angle of elevation of the top of a building from a point 20 m from the base is 75°. Find the height of the building to the nearest metre.

10. A plane takes off from a level runway, travelling at a constant speed of 100 m/s. After 15 seconds, travelling in a straight line, the plane is 150 m above the ground.
    (a) How far has the plane travelled in this time?
    (b) Calculate, to the nearest degree, the angle at which the plane left the ground.

11. From a point 50 m from the base of a chimney stack, the angle of elevation of the top of the stack is measured as 38°. Calculate, correct to one decimal place, the height of the stack.

12. A mobile phone mast has been erected on top of a building. The angles of elevation of the top of the building and of the top of the mast are measured from a point 40 m away from the bottom of the building. The angle of elevation of the top of the building is 37°. The angle of elevation of the top of the mast is 53°. Calculate, correct to two decimal places: (a) the height of the building (b) the height of the mast.

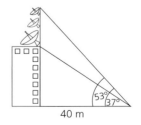

Exercise 20.6 (Chapter summary)

1. Using the angle X, name the side on the following triangles.
    (a) 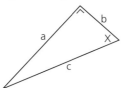 (b) 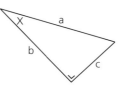 (c)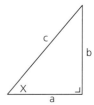

2. Use the diagram to find the following trigonometry ratios.

    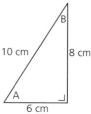

    (a) sin A
    (b) cos B
    (c) tan A
    (d) tan B

3. Evaluate each of the following correct to four decimal places.
    (a) cos 32°
    (b) tan 75°
    (c) sin 65°
    (d) 2 sin 45°
    (e) 3 sin 60° + 2 cos 40°
    (f) 6 sin 90° − 3 cos 45°
    (g) sin 90° − $\sqrt{2}$ cos 45°
    (h) $\frac{1}{\sqrt{3}}$ cos 30°
    (i) 2 sin 60°

4. Find each angle to the nearest degree.
    (a) cos A = 0.49
    (b) sin B = 0.15
    (c) tan C = 3.45
    (d) sin D = 0.56
    (e) cos E = 0.19
    (f) tan F = $\frac{1}{4}$
    (g) cos G = $\frac{13}{15}$
    (h) sin H = $\frac{5}{6}$
    (i) sin I = $\frac{4}{9}$
    (j) tan J = $21\frac{3}{4}$

5. Find the length of the hypotenuse in the following triangles.
    (a) (b) 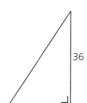 (c)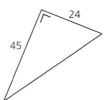

(d)

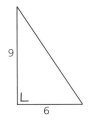

(e)

6. Find the length of the sides marked x.

(a)

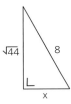

(b)

(c)

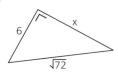

(d)

(e)

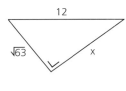

7. Calculate the length of the side marked x to the nearest whole number.

(a)

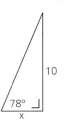

(b)

(c)

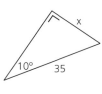

(d)

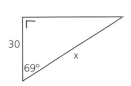

(e)

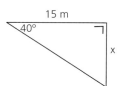

(f)

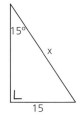

8. Calculate the measure of the angle X to the nearest degree in each of the following.

(a)

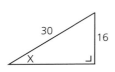

(b)

(c)

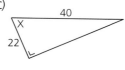

9. Find the measure of the angle X in each of the following.

(a)

(b)

(c)

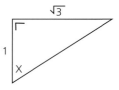

10. When the angle of elevation of the sun is 48°, find, in metres correct to one decimal place, the length of the shadow cast on level ground by a vertical pole of height 12 m.

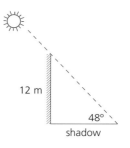

11. When the angle of elevation of the sun is 32°, a person casts a shadow of length 2.5 m. Calculate the height of the person correct to two decimal places.

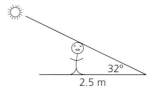

12. A boat out at sea is observed to have an angle of depression of 55° from the top of a vertical cliff 84 m high. How far, to the nearest metre, is the boat out at sea?

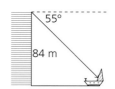

13. (a) A vertical tree casts a shadow 7.2 m long on level ground when the angle of elevation of the sun is 35°. Calculate the height of the tree.
    (b) Find, correct to one decimal place, the length of the shadow when the angle of elevation of the sun is 20°.

14. (a) From a point p, 30 m from the bottom of a building, the angle of elevation of the top of the building is found to be 40°. Calculate the height of the building.
    (b) From a point q further away from the bottom of the building, the angle of elevation of the top of the building is found to be 25°. Calculate |pq|.

⫙ Practical exercise

Take a clinometer and tape measure out to the front of your school. Pick a point 20 m back from the front of the school. From this point, find the angle of elevation of the top of the building. Now calculate the height of your school.

In this chapter, you will learn about:

+ Translating from English to mathematics.

+ Problems leading to linear equations.

+ Problems leading to simultaneous equations.

Translating from English to mathematics

The most difficult part of using algebra to solve practical problems is translating English language into mathematical statements.

The following table should help you.

Add	Subtract	Multiply	Divide	Equals
Plus	Minus/ take away	Product	Into	Same as
Sum	Difference	Times	Over	Gives
More than	Less than	Twice ($\Rightarrow \times 2$)	Half ($\Rightarrow \div 2$)	Result is
Greater than	Smaller than	Of	Quotient	Is

When translating from English to mathematics:

1. Choose letters to use as the unknowns.
2. Decide which operations, i.e. add, subtract, multiply or divide, say the same thing as the phrase.
3. Put the letters and operations together in a mathematical equation.
4. Solve the equation(s).

Example 21.1

Match the following English phrases to their mathematical equivalent by filling the appropriate letter in the box below.

(i) The sum of x and y is z.

(ii) Subtract y from x and then divide by z.

(iii) x is added to y plus z.

(iv) Twice the product of x and y divided by z.

(v) x less y is z.

(vi) z multiplied by x less y.

(vii) The difference between x and y divided by z.

(viii) x divided by the product of y and z.

(ix) x times the sum of y and z.

(x) x less z all divided by y.

(xi) Twice x plus z then divided by x is y.

(a) $x + (y + z)$

(b) $\dfrac{x - z}{y}$

(c) $\dfrac{y - x}{z}$

(d) $x(y + z)$

(e) $\dfrac{x}{y \cdot z}$

(f) $z(x - y)$

(g) $\dfrac{2xy}{z}$

(h) $x - y = z$

(i) $\dfrac{2x + z}{x} = y$

(j) $x + y = z$

(k) $\dfrac{x - y}{z}$

Solution

i	ii	iii	iv	v	vi	vii	viii	ix	x	xi
j	k	a	g	h	f	c	e	d	b	i

425

Exercise 21.1

1. Match the English phrase with the mathematical equivalent by filling the appropriate letter in the box below.

   (i) $\dfrac{pq}{2r}$ (a) Sum of p and q minus r.

   (ii) $\dfrac{p + q}{r}$ (b) The product of r and p then minus q.

   (iii) pqr   (c) Twice p minus the product of r and q.

   (iv) (p + q) – r   (d) p divided by r then minus q.

   (v) p(q + r)   (e) Product of p and q divided by twice r.

   (vi) q – (r + p)   (f) The sum of p and q is r.

   (vii) rp – q   (g) Half of p plus half of q plus half of r.

   (viii) $\dfrac{p}{r} - q$ (h) The product of p, q and r.

   (ix) 2p – rq   (i) q minus sum of r and p.

   (x) r(p + q)   (j) p is the difference between q and r then divided by 2.

   (xi) $\dfrac{r}{2} + \dfrac{p}{2} + \dfrac{q}{2}$ (k) p times the sum of q and r.

   (xii) p + q = r   (l) The sum of p and q then divide by r.

   (xiii) $p = \dfrac{q - r}{2}$ (m) r times the sum of p and q.

(i)	(ii)	(iii)	(iv)	(v)	(vi)	(vii)	(viii)	(ix)	(x)	(xi)	(xii)	(xiii)

Write the following phrases into mathematical statements.

2. Three more than a certain number x.

3. One less than a certain number x.

4. Five more than twice a certain number x.

5. Jack's age in 10 years' time if he is x years old now.

6. Mary's age six years ago if she is x years old now.

7. The number of matches in a box holding x matches if 12 are removed.

8. The amount of money left in a bank account after half of what is there, €x, has been withdrawn.

9. The perimeter of a square of side x cm.

10. The difference between 55 and a certain number x.

11. Shaun's age is four years more than twice his sister's age, who is x years old.

12. Ann's age is 10 years less than three times her son's age, who is x years old.

13. The cost of a roaming mobile phone call is four times the cost of the same phone call from a land line, which costs x cent.

14. A bar of fruit and nut chocolate has 30% less chocolate than the plain bar which has x g of chocolate.

15. Jamie's age, x, divided by 5.

16. If the length of a rectangle is twice its width, what is the length in terms of x?

17. Monica spends €14 out of €x she currently has. How much does she have left?

18. Double the lotto jackpot of €x.

19. Prize fund, €x, shared equally among nine people. Each share = ?

20. An Audi A4 is €1500 cheaper than a BMW 316i, which costs €x. Write down what the Audi costs in terms of x.

Problems leading to linear equations

Example 21.2

When 5 is added to a certain number, the result is 9.
(a) Write this information as an equation in x.
(b) Hence find the number.

Solution
(a) Step 1:   Let x = the number
    Step 2:   5 is added $\Rightarrow$ x + 5
    Step 3:   The result is (equal) $\Rightarrow$ x + 5 = 9

(b) x + 5 = 9
    x = 9 – 5
    x = 4

Example 21.3

When three times a certain number is added to 8, the result is 20. Find the number.

Solution
Step 1:   Let x = the number
Step 2:   Three times (multiply) $\Rightarrow$ 3x
Step 3:   Added to 8 (add) $\Rightarrow$ 3x + 8
Step 4:   Is 20 (equal) $\Rightarrow$ 3x + 8 = 20
Step 5:   Solve 3x + 8 = 20
          $\Rightarrow$ 3x = 20 – 8
          $\Rightarrow$ 3x = 12
          $\Rightarrow$ x = $\frac{12}{3}$
          x = 4

Example 21.4

A builder knows half the cost of the house is labour, three-tenths is material and the rest is profit. If the profit is €50 000, what was the cost of the house?

Solution

Let x = cost of house

$$\Rightarrow \frac{x}{2} + \frac{3x}{10} + \frac{50\,000}{1} = \frac{x}{1}$$

$$\Rightarrow \frac{5x+3x+500\,000 = 10x}{10}$$

$\Rightarrow 8x + 500\,000 = 10x$

$\Rightarrow 500\,000 = 10x - 8x$

$\Rightarrow 500\,000 = 2x$

$\Rightarrow \frac{500\,000}{2} = x$

$\Rightarrow 250\,000 = x$

Cost of house is €250 000.

$\frac{x}{2}$ = cost of labour.

$\frac{3}{10} \times (x) = \frac{3x}{10}$ = cost of materials.

labour + materials + profit = cost of house

Exercise 21.2

1. When 7 is added to a certain number, the result is 12.
   (a) Write this information as an equation in x, where x is the unknown number.
   (b) Hence find the number.

2. When 3 is added to a certain number, the result is 7.
   (a) Write this information as an equation in x, where x is the unknown number.
   (b) Hence find the number.

3. When 12 is added to a certain number, the result is 15.
   (a) Write this information as an equation in x, where x is the unknown number.
   (b) Hence find the number.

4. When 4 is subtracted from a certain number, the result is 2.
   (a) Write this information as an equation in x, where x is the unknown number.
   (b) Hence find the number.

5. When 10 is subtracted from a certain number, the result is 15.
   (a) Write this information as an equation in x, where x is the unknown number.
   (b) Hence find the number.

6. When 11 is subtracted from a certain number, the result is 5.
   (a) Write this information as an equation in x, where x is the unknown number.
   (b) Hence find the number.

7. When 3 is added to 5 times a certain number, the result is 23.
   (a) Write this information as an equation in x, where x is the unknown number.
   (b) Hence find the number.

8. When 5 is added to twice a certain number, the result is 17.
   (a) Write this information as an equation in x, where x is the unknown number.
   (b) Hence find the number.

9. When 10 is added to six times a certain number, the result is 22.
   (a) Write this information as an equation in x, where x is the unknown number.
   (b) Hence find the number.

10. When 8 is subtracted from twice a certain number, the result is 10.
   (a) Write this information as an equation in x, where x is the unknown number.
   (b) Hence find the number.

11. When 4 is subtracted from five times a certain number, the result is 11.
    (a) Write this information as an equation in x, where x is the unknown number.
    (b) Hence find the number.

12. When 6 is subtracted from three times a certain number, the result is 15.
    (a) Write the information as an equation in x, where x is the unknown number.
    (b) Hence find the number.

13. A jet now carries 20 tonnes less than it used to. How much weight did the plane carry before the reduction if it carries x tonnes now?

14. The sum of twice a certain number and 6 is 28. What is the number?

15. The perimeter of a square is 48 cm. What is the length of one side?

16. Mari will be four times her current age in 15 years' time. What is her age now?

17. Joe weighs 18 kg less than Tom. Their combined weight is 184 kg. What is Joe's weight?

18. If 28 is five less than seven times a number, what is the number?

19. A rectangular plot of ground is twice as long as it is wide. The perimeter is 162 m. Find the length and width of the plot.

20. Bill earns €15 000 more than Tony. Jack earns twice as much as Tony. The combined income of all three is €105 000. How much does each earn?

Problems leading to simultaneous equations

REMEMBER

Simultaneous equations are equations with two or more variables.

NOTE: Each equation can be formed by breaking the written statement into its punctuated English.

Example 21.5

The sum of two natural numbers is 10. The difference is 2. Find the numbers.

Solution

Let x = the larger number

Let y = the smaller number

$x + y = 10$ ← The sum of two natural numbers is 10.

$x - y = 2$ ← The difference is 2.

$$x + y = 10$$
$$\underline{x - y = 2}$$ ← Add both equations.
$$2x = 12$$
$$x = \frac{12}{2}$$

$x = 6$

$x + y = 10$ ← Select either of your first two equations.

$6 + y = 10$ ← Substitute your new value for x.

$y = 10 - 6$ ← Solve the equation.

$y = 4$

Example 21.6

Jim paid €12.20 for two burgers and three bags of chips. The next night he paid €13.30 for three burgers and two bags of chips.

Let €x be the cost of a burger and €y be the cost of a bag of chips.
(a) Write down two equations, each in x and y, to represent the above information.
(b) Solve these equations to find the cost of a burger and the cost of a bag of chips.

Solution

Jim paid €12.20 for two burgers and three bags of chips.

(a) $2x + 3y = 12.20$

$3x + 2y = 13.30$

The next night he paid €13.30 for three burgers and two bags of chips.

(b) $2x + 3y = 12.20$

$3x + 2y = 13.30$
_____

$2x + 3y = 12.20 \times 2$

To get the coefficients of y to be the same, we must multiply the top equation by 2 and the bottom equation by 3.

$3x + 2y = 13.30 \times 3$
_____

$4x + 6y = 24.40$

$9x + 6y = 39.90$

To eliminate the ys we must change the signs on one of the equations.

$-4x - 6y = -24.40$

$9x + 6y = 39.90$
_____

$5x \quad = 15.50$

$x \quad = \dfrac{15.50}{5}$

$x \quad = €3.10$

Cost of a burger is €3.10.

$2x + 3y = 12.20$

$2(3.10) + 3y = 12.20$

Substitute the price of the burger for x, i.e. €3.10.

$6.20 + 3y = 12.20$

$3y = 12.20 - 6.20$

$3y = 6.00$

$y = \dfrac{6.00}{3}$

$y = €2.00$

Cost of a bag of chips is €2.00.

Example 21.7

A cinema has 500 seats. On a night when all the seats are taken, the amount received from the sale of all the tickets was €1800. The price of an adult seat was €5 and a child seat was €3.

Let x be the number of adult seats and y be the number of child seats.
(a) Write down two equations in x and y to represent the above information.
(b) Solve these equations to find how many of each type of seats were sold.

Solution

(a) $x + y = 500$ ← | A cinema has 500 seats.

$5x + 3y = 1800$ ← | The amount received from the sale of all the tickets was €1800. The price of an adult seat was €5 and a child seat was €3.

(b) $x + y = 500 \times 3$
$\underline{5x + 3y = 1800}$
$3x + 3y = 1500$ ← | To get the y coefficients the same, we must multiply the top equation by 3.
$5x + 3y = 1800$

$\underline{-3x - 3y = -1500}$ ← | To eliminate the ys we must change the signs on one of the equations.
$5x + 3y = 1800$
$\overline{2x \quad\quad = 300}$

$x \quad\quad = \dfrac{300}{2}$

$x \quad\quad = 150$ ← | There were 150 adult seats sold.

$x + y = 500$
$150 + y = 500$
$y = 500 - 150$
$y = 350$ ← | There were 350 child seats sold.

Exercise 21.3

1. The sum of two natural numbers is 28. The difference is 12.
   Let x be one of the natural numbers and y be the other.
   (a) Write down two equations, each in x and y, to represent the information above.
   (b) Solve the equations to find both natural numbers.

2. The sum of two natural numbers is 45. The difference is 15.
   Let x be one of the natural numbers and y be the other.
   (a) Write down two equations, each in x and y, to represent the information above.
   (b) Solve the equations to find both natural numbers.

3. The sum of two natural numbers is 25. The difference is 3.
   Let x be one of the natural numbers and y be the other.
   (a) Write down two equations, each in x and y, to represent the information above.
   (b) Solve the equations to find both natural numbers.

4. The sum of two natural numbers is 19. The difference is 11.
   Let x be one of the natural numbers and y be the other.
   (a) Write down two equations, each in x and y, to represent the information above.
   (b) Solve the equations to find both natural numbers.

5. The sum of two natural numbers is 26. The difference is 16.
   Let x be one of the natural numbers and y be the other.
   (a) Write down two equations, each in x and y, to represent the information above.
   (b) Solve the equations to find both natural numbers.

6. The sum of two natural numbers is 21. The difference is 3.
   Let x be one of the natural numbers and y be the other.
   (a) Write down two equations, each in x and y, to represent the information above.
   (b) Solve the equations to find both natural numbers.

7. The sum of two natural numbers is 40. The difference is 8.
   Let x be one of the natural numbers and y be the other.
   (a) Write down two equations, each in x and y, to represent the information above.
   (b) Solve the equations to find both natural numbers.

8. The sum of two natural numbers is 44. The difference is 2.
   Let x be one of the natural numbers and y be the other.
   (a) Write down two equations, each in x and y, to represent the information above.
   (b) Solve the equations to find both natural numbers.

9. The sum of two natural numbers is 31. The difference is 3.
   Let x be one of the natural numbers and y be the other.
   (a) Write down two equations, each in x and y, to represent the information above.
   (b) Solve the equations to find both natural numbers.

10. The sum of two natural numbers is 63. The difference is 5.
    Let x be one of the natural numbers and y be the other.
    (a) Write down two equations, each in x and y, to represent the information above.
    (b) Solve the equations to find both natural numbers.

11. The cost of cinema tickets for two adults and three children is €19. The cost of cinema tickets for one adult and two children is €11.
    Let €x be the cost of a cinema ticket for an adult and €y be the cost of a cinema ticket for a child.
    (a) Write down two equations in x and y to represent the information above.
    (b) Solve the equations to find the cost of a cinema ticket for an adult and the cost of a cinema ticket for a child.

12. Three bars of chocolate and four bottles of water cost €5.48. Four bars of chocolate and three bottles of water cost €4.74.
    Let €x = cost of a bar of chocolate
    Let €y = cost of a bottle of water

(a) Write down two equations in x and y to represent the information above.

(b) Solve the equations to find the cost of a bar of chocolate and a bottle of water.

13. Two DVDs and five CDs cost €85.50. Five DVDs and two CDs cost €93.
Let €x = cost of a DVD
Let €y = cost of a CD
(a) Write down two equations in x and y to represent the information above.
(b) Solve the equations to find the cost of a DVD and the cost of a CD.

14. Three chairs and four stools cost €220. Five chairs and two stools cost €208.
Let €x = cost of a chair
Let €y = cost of a stool
(a) Write down two equations in x and y to represent the information above.
(b) Solve the equations to find the cost of a chair and the cost of a stool.

15. There were 2200 people in attendance at a recent FAI match. If the takings on the night were €15 000 and the cost for an adult was €10 and €5 for a child, how many adults and children were in the grounds that night?

16. The takings at a recent rugby match were €175 000. The cost of an adult ticket was €20 and a student ticket was €10. If the attendance was 12 000, how many adults and children were in attendance at the match?

17. The capacity at Croke Park is now 80 000. If the cost of an adult seat is €35 and a child's seat is €15, how many adults and children were in attendance if the gate receipts were €2 200 000?

18. A business received a bill from its accountants for €4500. An accountant is charged at €110 per hour and an audit clerk at €50 per hour. The total hours' work on the bill was 60. How many hours did each work on the firm's accounts?

19. A firm of architects charged €40 000 for designing a house. The firm charges €180 per hour for an architect and €80 per hour for draftsmen. If the total hours worked on the project were 240, how many hours did each work on the project?

20. John had two types of coins in his pocket, €1 and 50c. There were 12 coins in total which amounted to €9.50. How many of each coin did John have in his pocket?

21. Nadine had 26 coins of two different types, €1 and €2, in her purse. If the total amount in the purse was €42, how many of each type of coin did Nadine have?

22. Yvonne had saved €140 and needed to buy eight presents for her friends at Christmas. She decided she would buy either CDs or DVDs. If the cost of a CD was €15 and the cost of a DVD was €20, how many of each did she buy if she spent all her savings?

23. A factory makes chairs and tables. It can only produce 150 items per week. The cost of a chair is €40 and the cost of a table is €100. The factory can only spend €9600 per week. How many tables and chairs will the factory manufacture?

24. A grocer sold 10 apples and four oranges for €10.70 and 15 apples and three oranges for €14.40. What was the price of the apples and oranges?

25. A supermarket sells four bottles of still water and six bottles of sparkling water for €12.20 and eight bottles of still water and four bottles of sparkling for €14. What was the cost of each type of bottle of water?

26. A bar of chocolate costs 50c less than a can of cola. The total cost of four bars of chocolate and two cans of cola is €2.80. Find the cost of a can of cola and a bar of chocolate.

Exercise 21.4 (Chapter summary)

1. Match the English phrases to their mathematical equivalent by filling the appropriate letter in the box below.

   (i) The difference between x and y is 4.   (a) $xy = 4$

   (ii) Twice one number added to three times another is 4.   (b) $3x - 2y = 4$

   (iii) The sum of x and y is 4.   (c) $2x(3y) = 4$

   (iv) The product of x and y is 4.   (d) $2xy = 4$

   (v) x divided by y is 4.   (e) $2x + 3y = 4$

   (vi) Three times one number minus twice another is 4.   (f) $2x + y = 4$

   (vii) Two times x multiplied by three times y is 4.   (g) $3x + 2y = 4$

   (viii) Twice x plus y is 4.   (h) $x - y = 4$

   (ix) Twice the product of x and y is 4.   (i) $\frac{x}{y} = 4$

   (x) Three times one number plus twice another is 4.   (j) $x + y = 4$

(i)	(ii)	(iii)	(iv)	(v)	(vi)	(vii)	(viii)	(ix)	(x)

2. Solve the following equations.

   (a) $2x + 4 = 6$ (b) $5x + 3 = 13$ (c) $7x - 3 = 11$

   (d) $2x - 4 = 12$ (e) $6x - 4 = 4x + 10$ (f) $x + 2 = 10 - 3x$

   (g) $6x - 12 = 24 - 6x$ (h) $2(x + 6) = 20$ (i) $3(x - 4) = 3$

   (j) $4(2x - 6) = 5x + 18$

3. Twice a certain number added to 5 is 9.

   (a) Write this information as an equation in x, where x is the unknown number.

   (b) Hence find the number.

4. Four times a certain number added to 10 is 26.

   (a) Write this information as an equation in x, where x is the unknown number.

   (b) Hence find the number.

5. The difference between five times a certain number and 8 is 12.
   (a) Write this information as an equation in x, where x is the unknown number.
   (b) Hence find the number.

6. The difference between six times a certain number and 20 is 40.
   (a) Write this information as an equation in x, where x is the unknown number.
   (b) Hence find the number.

7. Mary has €5 more than Lorna. The total amount they have between them is €28.
   (a) Write this information as an equation in x, where x is the amount of money that Lorna has.
   (b) Solve the equation to find out how much money each one has.

8. Bertie and Tom have €66 between them. If Bertie was to give €5 to Tom, Tom would have five times as much as Bertie.
   (a) Write this information as an equation in x, where x is the amount of money that Bertie has.
   (b) Solve the equation to find out how much money each one has.

9. In a rectangle, the length is 8 cm longer than its width. The length of the perimeter is 56 cm.
   (a) Write this information as an equation in x, where x is the width of the rectangle.
   (b) Solve the equation to find the length and width of the rectangle.

10. Twelve chairs were bought for €820. Some of the chairs cost €60 and the rest cost €80 each.
    (a) Write this information as an equation in x, where x represents the number of chairs bought for €60.
    (b) Solve the equation to find how much each chair was.

11. Solve the following simultaneous equations.
    (a) $5x + y = 16$
    $x + y = 4$

    (b) $3x + y = 12$
    $2x + y = 10$

    (c) $2x - y = 12$
    $2x + 3y = 4$

    (d) $3x + 4y = 27$
    $2x + y = 13$

(e) $6x + 5y = -14$ (f) $5x + 2y = 1$ (g) $5x + 2y = 17$ (h) $2x + 3y = -11$

   $2x + 3y = -2$ $-2x + 3y = 30$ $2x - 3y = 3$ $6x - y = -3$

(i) $5x - 3y = 29$ (j) $5x - 3y = 3$

   $2x + 5y = -7$ $12x - 5y = 16$

12. The sum of two numbers is 15. The difference is 1.
    (a) Write down two equations in x and y to represent the above information.
    (b) Solve these equations to find both numbers.

13. The sum of two numbers is 31. The difference is 11.
    (a) Write down two equations in x and y to represent the above information.
    (b) Solve these equations to find both numbers.

14. One burger and two bags of chips cost €5. Three burgers and two bags of chips cost €9.
    Let €x = price of a burger
    Let €y = price of a bag of chips
    (a) Write down two equations in x and y to represent the information above.
    (b) Solve the equations to find the price of a burger and the price of a bag of chips.

15. The cost of taking eight people to the cinema was €44. Adults were charged €8 each and students €4 each.
    Let x be the number of adults and y be the number of students.

    (a) Write down two equations in x and y to represent the information above.
    (b) Solve the equations to find the number of adults and the number of students who were at the cinema.

Calculator Guide

Calculator Guide

The calculator used throughout this textbook is the Casio fx-83 ES Natural Display, which may be used in examinations set by the State Examinations Commission. The following few pages are intended as a guide to the main functions of the calculator.

Fraction button. Displays fractions and mixed numbers. Represented in this book as ⊟.

The ALPHA button. Gives access to anything in the calculator in red.

The SHIFT button. Sometimes called the second function button. Represented in this book as 2nd.

Replay button.

This button gives the value of the cube of any number.

The power or index button raises a number to a given power. Represented in this book as $x^\blacksquare$.

This gives the square root of a number. Represented in this book as $\sqrt{\blacksquare}$.

Trigonometric buttons.

This button is used to store and recall numbers in memory.

Alternates the display between fractions and decimals. Represented in this book as $S \Leftrightarrow D$.

The DEL button deletes only the last number (or function) used on the calculator.

The AC button clears the display before a new transaction.

443

The Replay Button

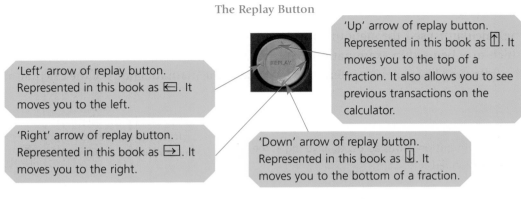

'Left' arrow of replay button. Represented in this book as ⬅. It moves you to the left.

'Up' arrow of replay button. Represented in this book as ⬆. It moves you to the top of a fraction. It also allows you to see previous transactions on the calculator.

'Right' arrow of replay button. Represented in this book as ➡. It moves you to the right.

'Down' arrow of replay button. Represented in this book as ⬇. It moves you to the bottom of a fraction.

The Second Function Button (SHIFT)

This button allows access to any function on the calculator in brown.

TASK: Evaluate $3\frac{1}{2} + 4$ on the calculator.

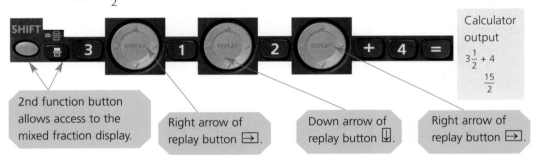

2nd function button allows access to the mixed fraction display.

Right arrow of replay button ➡.

Down arrow of replay button ⬇.

Right arrow of replay button ➡.

Calculator output

$3\frac{1}{2} + 4$

$\frac{15}{2}$

Using the Memory Function:

(a) Storing a number in memory

TASK: Store 7.3 in memory.

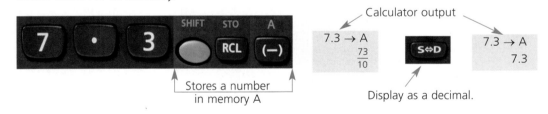

Stores a number in memory A

Calculator output

$7.3 \rightarrow A$

$\frac{73}{10}$

Display as a decimal.

$7.3 \rightarrow A$

7.3

(b) Recalling and using a number stored in memory.

TASK: Evaluate $5(7.3)^2 - 8(7.3)$ using the memory recall function on the calculator.

Recalls a number stored in memory A

$5(A)^2 - 8(A)$

$\frac{4161}{20}$

$5(A)^2 - 8(A)$

208.05

Calculator output

Calculator practice

	Calculator Display

Fractions:

1) Evaluate $\frac{1}{2} \div \frac{1}{4}$

 1 ↓ 2 → ÷ ▢ 1 ↓ 4 → =   2

2) Evaluate $\frac{2}{3} \times \frac{3}{5}$

▢ 2 ↓ 3 → × ▢ 3 ↓ 5 → = $\frac{2}{5}$

Trigonometry:

1) Set the calculator to degree Mode

2nd MODE 3

Note: The "SHIFT" button is represented as 2nd

2) Evaluate sin 60°.

Sin 60 = $\frac{\sqrt{3}}{2}$

3) Find the size of angle x if:

(a) sin x = 0.5   30

2nd Sin 0.5 =

(b) cos x = $\frac{1}{\sqrt{2}}$ 45

2nd Cos ▢ 1 ↓ √▪ 2 → =

Indices (Powers):

1) Evaluate 2^6.

2 $x^▪$ 6 → =   64

2) Simplify $81^{\frac{1}{4}}$.

81 $x^▪$ ▢ 1 ↓ 4 → =   3

Square root:

Evaluate $\sqrt{81} + \sqrt{20}$ (correct to two decimal places).

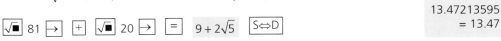   13.47213595
= 13.47

445

Scientific notation:

1) Evaluate $3.2 \times 10^4 + 1.6 \times 10^5$.

3.2 ☒ 10 $\boxed{x^{\blacksquare}}$ 4 → ⊞ 1.6 ☒ 10 $\boxed{x^{\blacksquare}}$ 5 → ☲

192 000

2) Evaluate $1.47 \times 10^6 \times 2.3 \times 10^7$.

1.47 ☒ 10 $\boxed{x^{\blacksquare}}$ 6 → ☒ 2.3 ☒ 10 $\boxed{x^{\blacksquare}}$ 7 → ☲

3.381×10^{13}

Volume

Calculate the volume of a cylinder of radius 6 cm and height 9 cm. Use $\pi = \frac{22}{7}$.
(Round off answer to two decimal places.)

Volume cylinder = $\pi r^2 h$ = $\frac{22}{7}$ 6^2 9

 22 ↓ 7 → ☒ 6 $\boxed{x^2}$ ☒ 9 ☲

Calculator output

$\frac{7128}{7}$ S⇔D   1018.29 cm³

(rounded off to two decimal places)

Clearing all settings on the calculator:

This will clear all the settings on the calculator and reset it back to the original settings.

$\boxed{2^{nd}}$ ☒9☒ ☒3☒ ☲ ☒AC☒

Answers

Chapter 1

Exercise 1.1

1. **(a)** 1, 2, 3, 6 **(b)** 1, 2, 3, 4, 6, 12 **(c)** 1, 17 **(d)** 1, 2, 3, 6, 9, 18 **(e)** 1, 2, 3, 4, 6, 8, 12, 24 **(f)** 1, 2, 3, 4, 5, 6, 10, 12, 15, 20, 30, 60 **(g)** 1, 2, 4, 7, 8, 14, 28, 56 **(h)** 1, 2, 3, 4, 5, 6, 8, 10, 12, 15, 20, 24, 30, 40, 60, 120
2. 6   3. 4   4. 5   5. 13   6. 3   7. 15   8. 2
9. **(a)** 2^3 **(b)** $2^2 \times 3$ **(c)** 2×3^2 **(d)** $3^2 \times 5$ **(e)** $2 \times 3^2 \times 5$ **(f)** $2^2 \times 5^2$ **(g)** $2^3 \times 3^2$
10. **(a)** $2^3 \times 3 \times 5$ **(b)** $2 \times 3 \times 5^2$ **(c)** $2^2 \times 7^2$ **(d)** $2^2 \times 5^3$ **(e)** $3^2 \times 5^2$ **(f)** $2^2 \times 5^4$ **(g)** $2^4 \times 5^4$

Exercise 1.2

1. **(a)** 3, 6, 9, 12, 15 **(b)** 7, 14, 21, 28, 35 **(c)** 8, 16, 24, 32, 40
2. **(a)** 20, 40, 60, 80, 100 **(b)** 19, 38, 57, 76, 95 **(c)** 17, 34, 51, 68, 85 **(d)** 24, 48, 72, 96, 120 **(e)** 31, 62, 93, 124, 155
3. **(a)** 4, 8, 12, 16, 20, 24, 28, 32 **(b)** 5, 10, 15, 20, 25, 30, 35, 40 **(c)** 20
4. 56   5. 12   6. 144   7. 60   8. 42
9. 84   10. 70

Exercise 1.3

1. **(a)** Both **(b)** Integer **(c)** Both **(d)** Neither **(e)** Both **(f)** Both
2. −3   3. −5   4. −2   5. −3   6. − 7
7. 6   8. −5   9. 2   10. 5   11. −11
12. −17   13. 0   14. 0   15. −11   16. −7
17. 5   18. −10   19. 0   20. −5
21. 6   22. −20   23. 12   24. −30
25. 12   26. −5   27. −5   28. 0   29. 0
30. 6   31. −6

Exercise 1.4

1. −2   2. 18   3. −18   4. 2   5. −5
6. 4   7. −4   8. 0   9. −12   10. −9
11. −16   12. 0   13. 3   14. −3   15. 0
16. −17   17. −25   18. −14   19. 3   20. −46
21. 46   22. −12   23. −82   24. −23   25. −49
26. −5   27. −7   28. −4   29. 3   30. 12
31. −4

32. **(a)** −€390 **(b)** −€430 **(c)** −€290 **(d)** −€175 **(e)** €0
33. **(a)** +11 **(b)** −4 **(c)** 0 **(d)** −4 **(e)** 19
34. **(a)** €410 **(b)** €120 **(c)** −€30 **(d)** −€270

Exercise 1.5

1. 12   2. 12   3. −12   4. −12   5. 2
6. 2   7. −2   8. −2   9. 32   10. −35
11. −24   12. 18   13. 28   14. −28   15. 28
16. −6   17. 6   18. −6   19. −5   20. −6
21. −3   22. −12   23. 6   24. −5   25. 20
26. 20   27. 5   28. −20   29. 5   30. −24
31. 40   32. −36   33. 60   34. −1

Exercise 1.6

1. −10   2. 21   3. −1   4. −90   5. −18
6. 72   7. 2   8. −6   9. 2   10. −5
11. 240   12. 180   13. 20   14. −63
15. −57   16. −3   17. 0   18. 128
19. −14   20. −30   21. 16

Exercise 1.7

1. **(a)** 64 **(b)** 512 **(c)** 16 **(d)** 36 **(e)** −729 **(f)** −32
2. 625   3. 0   4. 144   5. −1728
6. 25   7. 256   8. 256   9. −1331
10. 1   11. 1   12. −1

Exercise 1.8

1. 24   2. 60   3. 12   4. 384   5. 18
6. −5   7. 1   8. 18   9. 1   10. 10
11. 33   12. 160   13. 0   14. 16   15. 5
16. −2   17. 2   18. 1   19. −8   20. −2
21. 6   22. −3   23. 3

Exercise 1.9

1. 20   2. 26   3. **(a)** $2^2 \times 3^2$ **(b)** $2 \times 5 \times 7$ **(c)** $2^2 \times 17$ **(d)** $2^2 \times 5 \times 7$ **(e)** $2^2 \times 3 \times 5^2$
4. 45   5. 84   6. −9   7. −8   8. −7
9. −35   10. 35   11. 35   12. −24   13. −2
14. 5   15. **(a)** 4, 3, 2, 1, 0 **(b)** 4, 3, 2, 1, 0, −1, −2... **(c)** −3, −2, −1, 0, 1, 2...
16. 2   17. Top down: 118; 63, 55; 31, 24; 15, 17, 10; 6, 6   18. 5, 3, 4

Chapter 2

Exercise 2.1

1. **(b)** $\frac{13}{26}$ 2. **(b)** $\frac{30}{50}$ 3. **(b)** $\frac{12}{42}$ 4. **(b)** $\frac{35}{56}$

5. **(b)** $\frac{27}{81}$ 6. **(b)** $\frac{1}{3}$ 7. **(b)** $\frac{9}{45}$ 8. **(b)** $\frac{30}{36}$

9. **(b)** $\frac{18}{27}$ 10. **(b)** $\frac{3}{5}$

Exercise 2.2

1. $\frac{1}{4}$ 2. $\frac{2}{5}$ 3. $\frac{2}{3}$ 4. $\frac{3}{7}$ 5. $\frac{3}{5}$

6. $\frac{2}{3}$ 7. $\frac{2}{3}$ 8. $\frac{3}{7}$ 9. $\frac{3}{4}$ 10. $\frac{1}{8}$

11. $\frac{13}{22}$ 12. $\frac{21}{32}$ 13. $\frac{2}{3}$ 14. $\frac{1}{3}$ 15. $\frac{5}{9}$

16. $\frac{3}{8}$ 17. $\frac{1}{12}$ 18. $\frac{1}{4}$ 19. $\frac{11}{100}$ 20. $\frac{1}{4}$

Exercise 2.3

1. $\frac{17}{4}$ 2. $\frac{7}{5}$ 3. $\frac{17}{3}$ 4. $\frac{15}{4}$ 5. $\frac{23}{7}$

6. $\frac{58}{9}$ 7. $\frac{19}{8}$ 8. $\frac{82}{11}$ 9. $\frac{23}{6}$ 10. $\frac{125}{13}$

11. $\frac{29}{4}$ 12. $\frac{35}{3}$ 13. $\frac{211}{16}$ 14. $\frac{99}{8}$ 15. $\frac{141}{8}$

16. $\frac{101}{14}$ 17. $\frac{22}{7}$ 18. $\frac{147}{4}$ 19. $\frac{126}{5}$ 20. $\frac{151}{12}$

Exercise 2.4

1. $\frac{3}{10}$ 2. $\frac{4}{21}$ 3. $\frac{2}{15}$ 4. $\frac{16}{27}$ 5. $\frac{1}{5}$ 6. $\frac{12}{35}$

7. $\frac{8}{7}$ 8. 1 9. $\frac{21}{10}$ 10. $\frac{13}{10}$ 11. $\frac{28}{3}$ 12. $\frac{49}{3}$

13. $\frac{28}{5}$ 14. $\frac{18}{5}$ 15. 12 16. $\frac{9}{4}$ 17. $\frac{16}{9}$ 18. $\frac{39}{8}$

19. $\frac{189}{20}$ 20. 11 21. $\frac{22}{3}$ 22. $\frac{2}{3}$ 23. $\frac{22}{15}$ 24. $\frac{65}{16}$

25. $\frac{29}{7}$ 26. $\frac{16}{3}$ 27. $\frac{9}{4}$ 28. $\frac{11}{14}$ 29. 6 30. $\frac{8}{5}$

Exercise 2.5

1. $\frac{11}{12}$ 2. $1\frac{3}{20}$ 3. $\frac{17}{12}$ 4. $1\frac{1}{6}$ 5. $1\frac{1}{4}$ 6. $1\frac{1}{10}$

7. $1\frac{7}{24}$ 8. $3\frac{5}{6}$ 9. $7\frac{8}{15}$ 10. $2\frac{11}{12}$ 11. $2\frac{3}{4}$ 12. $5\frac{1}{3}$

13. $5\frac{11}{12}$ 14. $3\frac{19}{20}$ 15. $\frac{1}{2}$ 16. $\frac{18}{35}$ 17. $\frac{1}{6}$ 18. $\frac{4}{9}$

19. $\frac{3}{10}$ 20. $1\frac{1}{5}$ 21. $1\frac{1}{6}$ 22. $\frac{11}{12}$ 23. $1\frac{1}{6}$ 24. $\frac{1}{12}$

25. $\frac{47}{20}$ 26. $7\frac{1}{2}$ 27. $\frac{7}{12}$ 28. $\frac{11}{30}$

Exercise 2.6

1. $\frac{1}{4}$ 2. $\frac{9}{25}$ 3. $\frac{27}{64}$ 4. $\frac{1}{32}$ 5. $\frac{49}{9}$ 6. $\frac{343}{27}$

7. $\frac{1}{9}$ 8. $-\frac{1}{32}$ 9. $-\frac{343}{64}$ 10. $\frac{25}{4}$ 11. $\frac{100}{9}$ 12. $\frac{484}{25}$

Exercise 2.7

1. $\frac{17}{30}$ 2. $\frac{14}{3}$ 3. $6\frac{11}{24}$ 4. $3\frac{11}{12}$ 5. $\frac{2}{5}$ 6. $\frac{11}{5}$

7. 11 8. $\frac{5}{4}$ 9. $\frac{13}{12}$ 10. $\frac{23}{24}$ 11. $\frac{32}{15}$ 12. $\frac{13}{9}$

13. 4 14. $4\frac{1}{2}$ 15. $\frac{25}{36}$ 16. $2\frac{1}{2}$ 17. $\frac{49}{40}$ 18. $\frac{7}{5}$

Exercise 2.8

1. 0.6 2. 0.75 3. 0.125 4. 0.1
5. 1.75 6. 0.308 7. 3.25 8. 0.28
9. 0.01 10. 0.001 11. 0.013 12. 0.625
13. 1.75 14. 2.333 15. 3.8 16. 10.2
17. 8.142 18. 4.75 19. 1.714 20. 1.952
21. −1.2 22. −0.429 23. −4.167 24. −3.143
25. −2.667 26. −3.4 27. −0.1 28. −0.04
29. −2.1 30. −3.75

Exercise 2.9

1. 14; 14.94 2. 8; 8.26 3. 150; 149.55
4. 45; 26.38 5. 46; 36.37 6. 42; 35.83
7. 16; 14.65 8. 4; 4.19 9. 2; 2.19
10. 5; 4.26 11. 5; 6.50 12. 13; 12.77
13. 3; 1.93 14. 6; 5.63 15. 5; 4.77
16. 10; 10.20 17. 5; 4.79 18. 9; 14.07
19. 11; 13.47 20. 38; 37.87 21. 31; 31.00
22. 9; 8.80 23. 84; 89.55 24. 84; 89.69
25. 2; 1.10 26. 8; 7.68 27. 98; 102.51
28. 38; 35.49

Exercise 2.10

1. **(a)** $\frac{1}{3}$ **(b)** 3 **(c)** $\frac{4}{5}$ **(d)** $\frac{1}{3}$ **(e)** $\frac{1}{3}$

(f) $\frac{1}{5}$ **(g)** $\frac{2}{3}$ **(h)** $\frac{3}{5}$ **(i)** $\frac{2}{5}$ **(j)** $\frac{2}{3}$

449

2. (a) $\frac{6}{5}$ (b) $\frac{10}{3}$ (c) $\frac{15}{8}$ (d) $\frac{23}{4}$ (e) $\frac{31}{11}$

(f) $\frac{39}{8}$ (g) $\frac{101}{8}$ (h) $\frac{29}{3}$ (i) $\frac{77}{12}$ (j) $\frac{106}{13}$

3. (a) $\frac{15}{28}$ (b) 1 (c) 2 (d) $\frac{8}{35}$ (e) $\frac{5}{8}$

(f) $\frac{209}{12}$ (g) $\frac{45}{28}$ (h) $\frac{17}{6}$ (i) $\frac{9}{20}$ (j) $\frac{16}{5}$

4. (a) $\frac{3}{2}$ (b) $\frac{1}{2}$ (c) $\frac{3}{8}$ (d) $\frac{15}{8}$ (e) $\frac{8}{3}$

(f) 6 (g) $\frac{152}{63}$ (h) $\frac{202}{41}$ (i) $\frac{452}{159}$

5. (a) $\frac{17}{20}$ (b) $\frac{53}{63}$ (c) $\frac{47}{45}$ (d) $\frac{73}{52}$ (e) $\frac{257}{35}$

(f) 11 (g) $\frac{115}{24}$ (h) $\frac{326}{45}$ (i) $\frac{175}{30}$ (j) $7\frac{1}{2}$

6. (a) $\frac{43}{32}$ (b) $\frac{1}{8}$ (c) $\frac{14}{15}$ (d) $\frac{5}{6}$ (e) $\frac{9}{20}$

(f) $\frac{22}{21}$ (g) $\frac{13}{10}$ (h) $\frac{19}{5}$ (i) $\frac{51}{10}$ (j) $\frac{7}{6}$

7. (a) $\frac{9}{16}$ (b) $\frac{8}{125}$ (c) $\frac{1}{32}$ (d) $-\frac{1}{8}$ (e) $\frac{1}{64}$

(f) $\frac{1}{27}$ (g) $\frac{125}{64}$ (h) $\frac{64}{81}$ (i) $\frac{25}{16}$ (j) $\frac{4}{25}$

8. (a) $\frac{4}{3}$ (b) $\frac{11}{12}$ (c) 1 (d) $\frac{3}{4}$ (e) $\frac{133}{4}$

(f) $\frac{23}{24}$ (g) $\frac{11}{25}$ (h) $\frac{7}{3}$

9. (a) 40; 32.47 (b) 3; 3.11 (c) 105; 97.02
(d) 33; 21.16 (e) 4; 4.20 (f) 23; 24.62
(g) 16; 17.69

Chapter 3

Exercise 3.1

1. $x \div 5, + 2$ 2. $x \div 6, - 1$ 3. $x - 2, + 6$
4. $x \div 2, - 4$ 5. $x - 4, - 4$ 6. $x \div 1, - 6$
7. $x - 4, \div 3$ 8. $+ 6, \div 5$ 9. $- 2, \div - 3$
10. $- 1, \div - 2$ 11. $- 12, \div 7$

Exercise 3.2

1. $10x$ 2. $3x$ 3. $15x$ 4. $4a$ 5. $9y$
6. $6x$ 7. $13y^2$ 8. $5y^3 + 7y^3$ 9. $10xy$
10. $6y + 9$ 11. $6a + 11y + 5$ 12. $8x + 9y + 3$
13. $5x^2 + 17x$ 14. $5x^2 + 13x + 8$
15. $5a^2 + 9a + 4$ 16. $5x^3 + 8x^2 + 10x$
17. $7y^3 + 7y^2 + 9y$ 18. $9x + 7y + 4$
19. $5x^2 + 17y + 12$ 20. $3a + 4b + 4c + 8$
21. $9ab + 7a + 2b + 3$ 22. $14xy + 2y + 4$
23. $8x$ 24. $5y$ 25. $3z$ 26. 0
27. $5a$ 28. $5x$ 29. $3y^2$ 30. $4x + 2y$
31. $p^2 + 11p$ 32. $-2y - 1$
33. $7x^2 + 8x$ 34. $6a^2 + 8a$
35. $4x^2 + 7x - 4$ 36. $-2y^2 - x - 9y + 10$
37. $a^2 + 2a - 11$ 38. $-19y - 12$
39. $4x^3 - 2x^2 + 8x$ 40. $3p^3 + 9p + 4 + x$
41. $a^3 + 3a^2 - 5$ 42. $4p^3 - 2p^2 - 7p - 6$
43. $9x^2 - 3x - 11$ 44. $6xy + 7x - 15$
45. $-4ab - 10b - 8$ 46. $9xyz + 3xy - 6xz$
47. $-5x^2 + 9x + 2$ 48. $8x^3 + 6x^2 + 16x + 8$
49. $4a^3 + 9a^2 + 11a + 8$
50. $5x^3 + 10y^2 + 5x + 6$
51. $6x^3 + 7x^2 + 4x + 2$

Exercise 3.3

1. $6x + 8$ 2. $10y + 30$ 3. $12k + 24$
4. $12x - 28$ 5. $35k - 30$ 6. $-12x - 15$
7. $-8y + 12$ 8. $-18k + 12$ 9. $20x^2 + 10x + 25$
10. $2y^2 + 14y + 6$ 11. $21x + 22$
12. $17y + 19$ 13. $17k + 30$
14. $14x$ 15. $-24y + 36$
16. $27x - 9$ 17. $-7x + 8$
18. $14x^2 + 11x + 19$ 19. $24y^2 + 36y + 44$
20. $-14x^2 - 13x + 19$ 21. $-y - 1$
22. $-3x^2 + 15x + 13$ 23. $x^2 + 6x + 1$
24. $16x^2 - 16x - 16$ 25. $-2y^2 - 15y + 26$
26. $-7y^2 - 12y + 1$ 27. $-6x^2 - 5x + 29$
28. $-6x$ 29. $-6y - 21$
30. $2k - 17$ 31. $-10x^2 + 4x + 22$
32. $-12x^2 + 3x + 1$

Exercise 3.4

1. (a) x^2 (b) b^2 (c) k^3 (d) y^5 (e) $4x^2$ (f) $30y^3$
(g) $-12x^3$ (h) ab (i) $3ab^2$ (j) $-30k^2$ (k) xyz
(l) $10x^2y^2$
2. $3x^2 + 2x$ 3. $y^2 + 3y$ 4. $4k^2 + 8k$
5. $12x^2 - 8x$ 6. $12k^2 - 24k$ 7. $-4x^2 - 3x$
8. $-4y^2 + 5y$ 9. $-5k^2 + 2k$
10. $2x^3 + 2x^2 + 5x$ 11. $6y^3 + 8y^2 + 6y$
12. $2x^2 + 16x + 4$ 13. $6y^2 + 4y + 6$
14. $8k^2 + 23k + 9$ 15. $10x^2 - 4x + 16$
16. $8y^2 + 5y + 6$ 17. $6x^2 - 7x + 6$

18. $15x^2 - 6x - 6$
19. $6x^3 + 11x^2 + 12x + 10$
20. $6y^3 + 21y^2 + 15y + 12$
21. $2x^3 - 34x^2 + 18x + 6$
22. $3y^3 - 15y^2 - 2y + 14$
23. $-4x^3 + 5x^2 + 14x + 9$
24. $6x^3 - 12x^2 - 2x + 14$
25. $4y^3 + 4y^2 - 8y + 10$
26. $3y^3 - 26y^2 + 9y + 4$
27. $8x^3 + 4x^2 - 26x + 5$
28. $12x - 16$

Exercise 3.5

1. $2x^2 + 11x + 12$ 2. $8x^2 + 8x + 2$
3. $10y^2 + 21y + 18$ 4. $4k^2 + 8k + 3$
5. $8y^2 - 8y - 6$ 6. $6x^2 - 18x + 12$
7. $4y^2 - 16y - 20$ 8. $x^2 - 10x + 24$
9. $15x^2 - 11x + 2$ 10. $4x^2 - 20x + 25$
11. $y^2 + 4y + 4$ 12. $36x^2 - 36x + 9$
13. $12a^2 - 17a + 6$ 14. $10a^2 - 14a - 12$
15. $k^2 - 2k + 1$ 16. $2x^3 - 10x^2 + 10x - 2$
17. $21y^3 - 41y^2 + 16y - 10$
18. $x^3 - 4x^2 - 2x + 5$
19. $28y^3 + 13y^2 + 6y + 9$
20. $6x^3 + 20x^2 + 18x + 4$
21. $4x^3 - 9x^2 - 15x + 18$
22. $3y^3 - 4y^2 - 15y - 9xy + 12x + 20$
23. $6x^3 - 21x^2 + 11x + 10$
24. $12y^3 - 29y^2 + 23y - 6$
25. $7x^3 + 12x^2 - 11x + 2$
26. $4x^3 - 19x - 15$ 27. $x^2 + 4x + 4$
28. $4x^2 + 12x + 9$ 29. $25x^2 + 30x + 9$
30. $4y^2 - 8y + 4$ 31. $x^2 + 10x + 25$
32. $25y^2 + 20y + 4$ 33. $9x^2 - 12x + 4$
34. $9k^2 + 6k + 1$ 35. $x^2 - 8x + 16$
36. $36x^2 + 24x + 4$ 37. $16x^2 - 16x + 4$
38. $k^2 - 6k + 9$ 39. $25x^2 - 10x + 1$
40. $9m^2 - 6m + 1$

Exercise 3.6

1. 2 2. $2b$ 3. $2c$ 4. $2z$
5. $3a$ 6. $5g$ 7. $5x$ 8. $7x^2y^2z^2$
9. $\frac{1}{(a-1)}$ 10. $\frac{2}{(a+2)}$ 11. $\frac{2}{(3x+3)}$ 12. $\frac{3n}{(1-2n)}$
13. $\frac{(2-x)}{3x^2}$ 14. $3x - 2$ 15. $\frac{(4x-y)}{3}$

Exercise 3.7

1. $\frac{31}{6}$ 2. $\frac{47}{10}$ 3. $\frac{55}{12}$ 4. 7 5. $\frac{23}{6}$
6. $\frac{8}{15}$ 7. $\frac{1}{4}$ 8. $\frac{23}{3}$ 9. $\frac{17}{3}$

10. $\frac{5a+1}{6}$ 11. $\frac{5x+1}{4}$ 12. $\frac{24c-41}{21}$
13. $\frac{4j+8}{10}$ 14. $\frac{10x-11}{12}$ 15. $\frac{-7x+53}{20}$
16. $\frac{-x-21}{10}$ 17. $\frac{5x-12}{9}$ 18. $\frac{5x-11}{12}$
19. $\frac{-23m-37}{28}$ 20. $\frac{6-5x}{x^2}$ 21. $\frac{-5y}{2}$
22. $\frac{3+2y}{y^3}$ 23. $\frac{-13a}{3}$ 24. $\frac{4b-5}{4}$
25. $\frac{9c-15}{10}$

Exercise 3.8

1. (a) 6 (b) 15 (c) 14 (d) 9 (e) 9 (f) 36
   (g) 27 (h) 64 (i) 1 (j) 54
2. (a) 13 (b) 4 (c) -1 (d) -8 (e) 76 (f) 36
3. (a) 8 (b) 3 (c) 1 (d) -1 (e) 2 (f) 10 (g) 12
4. (a) 1 (b) 8 (c) -19 (d) 1 (e) 10 (f) 42
   (g) -1 (h) -6 (i) 9 (j) -1 (k) -33
5. (a) $\frac{-1}{3}$ (b) $5\frac{1}{2}$ (c) 19 (d) 2 (e) 2 (f) 2
6. (a) -15 (b) 0 (c) 20 (d) -16 (e) 4 (f) 58
   (g) 4 (h) 25 (i) 4 (j) -27
7. (a) 6 (b) 21 (c) -23 (d) -4 (e) 24 (f) 4
   (g) 75 (h) 9 (i) 4 (j) 64
8. (a) -8 (b) $\frac{-14}{5}$ (c) 5 (d) -2 (e) $\frac{-5}{3}$ (f) 4
9. (a) -1 (b) 18 (c) 20 (d) -45 (e) -15
   (f) -60 (g) 45 (h) 55 (i) 4 (j) 39
10. (a) $\frac{-1}{4}$ (b) $\frac{-1}{8}$ (c) $-\frac{1}{3}$ (d) 1 (e) $\frac{-3}{7}$ (f) 7

Exercise 3.9

1. (a) $5x^2 + 10x - 9$ (b) $9x + 7y - 1$
   (c) $6x^3 - 2x^2 + 7x - 3$ (d) $14x - 3$
   (e) $6y^2 + 8y + 8$ (f) -5
2. (a) $12x + 9$ (b) $15x^2 + 10x$ (c) $8x^2 - 16x - 4$
   (d) $20x^3 + 12x^2 - 8x$ (e) $8y^2 + 6y - 6$
   (f) $10x^3 - 4x^2 - 12x$
3. (a) $3x^2 + 11x + 10$ (b) $6y^2 + 8y - 30$
   (c) $12x^2 - 10x + 2$ (d) $6x^3 + 20x^2 + 13x - 4$
   (e) $3y^3 + 20y^2 - 8$ (f) $15x^3 - 28x^2 - 3x + 18$
4. (a) $9x^2 + 6x + 1$ (b) $25x^2 - 40x + 16$
   (c) $9y^2 - 42y + 49$ (d) $49x^2 - 56x + 16$
   (e) $4k^2 - 12k + 9$ (f) $9m^2 + 12m + 4$
5. (a) $\frac{(11x+5)}{15}$ (b) $\frac{(8y-2)}{4}$ (c) $\frac{(-2x+1)}{12}$
6. (a) -29 (b) 25 (c) -16 (d) -64 (e) 45
   (f) 0 (g) -2 (h) 7 (i) -7 (j) -6 (k) 60
   (l) 10

Chapter 4

Exercise 4.1

1. **(a)** 120 **(b)** 3000 **(c)** 53 **(d)** 1650 **(e)** 32.6
2. **(a)** 14.5 **(b)** 5000 **(c)** 2.57 **(d)** 37.6 **(e)** 0.25
   (f) 2400 **(g)** 600 **(h)** 2.34
3. **(a)** 30 **(b)** 320 **(c)** 45 000 **(d)** 230
   (e) 234 **(f)** 34 **(g)** 4500 **(h)** 404.5
4. **(a)** 3 **(b)** 8.5 **(c)** 0.156 **(d)** 3.264
   (e) 0.82 **(f)** 0.03 **(g)** 0.15 **(h)** 0.043
5. **(a)** 1006.3 **(b)** 4959.5 **(c)** 1502.74 **(d)** 6.25
6. $3\frac{3}{4}$ 7. **(a)** 5000 **(b)** 15 000
8. **(a)** €32.25 **(b)** €39 **(c)** €22.61
9. **(a)** €828 **(b)** €806 **(c)** €2507.50
10. **(a)** 10 **(b)** €31
11. **(a)** 14 lengths, 19 lengths, 23 lengths
    (b) 3 packs, 4 packs, 5 packs
    (c) €115.20, €183.60, €312.50

Exercise 4.2

1. **(a)** 5000 **(b)** 3.2 **(c)** 250 **(d)** 2.3 **(e)** 3.85
   (f) 1450 **(g)** 3120 **(h)** 40
2. **(a)** 4 **(b)** 4.3 **(c)** 35 **(d)** 0.4
   (e) 5.016 **(f)** 3.700 **(g)** 4.05 **(h)** 2.04
3. **(a)** 12.005 **(b)** 1648 **(c)** 5.95
   (d) 18.83
4. **(a)** 1950 **(b)** 0.85 **(c)** 2.512 **(d)** 1.66
5. **(a)** 28 **(b)** 21.84 **(c)** 9 **(d)** 9.09
6. 30 7. 5 8. 3 9. 5000
10. **(b)** €1.52
11. 16 kg flour, 12 kg margarine
12. 20 **13.** 40 **14.** 250 **15.** 110 kg
16. **(a)** 1.66c, 0.44c, 0.42c, .0.39c **(b)** €4.38
17. **(a)** 27c, 17c, 24c, 15c **(b)** 1.25 litres
    (d) (a) Jim **(d)** Joan, €3

Exercise 4.3

1. **(a)** 06:00 **(b)** 15:00 **(c)** 02:30
   (d) 04:50 **(e)** 15:30 **(f)** 17:50
   (g) 10:55 **(h)** 21:25 **(i)** 23:05
   (j) 10:07
2. **(a)** 7 a.m. **(b)** 9:30 a.m. **(c)** 1 p.m.
   (d) 6 p.m. **(e)** 10:30 a.m. **(f)** 7:30 p.m.
   (g) 2:55 a.m. **(h)** 3:35 p.m. **(i)** 4:55 p.m.
   (j) 8:35 a.m.
3. 12:05 **4.** 1 hour 50 minutes **5.** 20:13
6. 1 hour 33 minutes **7.** 14:10
8. 5:52 p.m. **9.** 20:12
10. **(a)** 7 hours 25 minutes **(b)** 1 hour 45 minutes
    (c) 3 hours **(d)** 09:15

11. **(a)** 5 hours 5 minutes
    (b) 5 hours 30 minutes
    (c) 3 hours 25 minutes
    (d) Armagh, Portadown
12. **(a)** 2 hours 10 minutes
    (b) 1 hour 4 minutes
    (c) 14:15
13. **(a)** 16:55 **(b)** 11:55
14. **(a)** 14 minutes **(b)** 18:20 **(c)** 5:15 p.m.
    (d) 2 hours 25 minutes
15. **(a)** 21:50 **(b)** 03:35
16. **(a)** 2 hours 5 minutes; 07:30 or 10:15
    (b) 5:45 p.m. **(c)** 7:50 p.m. **(d)** 21:15
17. **(a)** 01:45 **(b)** 22:45

Exercise 4.4

1. **(a)** 40 **(b)** 42 **(c)** 60 **(d)** 34
   (e) 24 **(f)** 24 **(g)** 36 **(h)** 48
   (a) 27 **(j)** 24
2. **(a)** 40 **(b)** 63 **(c)** 90 **(d)** 180
   (e) 28 **(f)** 81 **(g)** 18 **(h)** 2.5
   (a) 9 **(j)** 26
3. **(a)** 4 hours **(b)** 5 hours
   (c) 3 hours 36 **(d)** 5 hours 20
   minutes minutes
   (e) $3\frac{3}{4}$ hours **(f)** 3 hours 20 minutes
   (g) $1\frac{1}{2}$ hours **(h)** 25 minutes
   (i) 10 minutes 25 seconds
   (j) 20 seconds
4. 7 km **5. (a)** 4 **(b)** 14.4
6. **(a)** 9 **(b)** 32.4 **7. (a)** 10 **(b)** 36
8. 4500 km **9.** 6 minutes 40 seconds
10. **(a)** 4 km **(b)** 36 km **(c)** 20 km/h
11. **(a)** 195 km **(b)** 65 km/h **(c)** 71 km/h
12. **(a)** 13:05 **(b)** 69 km/h
13. **(a)** 44 seconds **(b)** 33 km/h
14. **(a)** $1\frac{1}{2}$ hours **(b)** 28
15. **(a)** 990 **(b)** 440 km/h **(c)** 485

Exercise 4.5

1. **(a)** 1000 **(b)** 750 **(c)** 4.5 **(d)** 1.25
   (e) 12.5 **(f)** 0.09 **(g)** 1.8 **(h)** 24.5
   (i) 1226.4 **(j)** 1660 **(k)** 1.3 **(l)** 6.76
2. **(a)** 3120 **(b)** 3.2 **(c)** 4.025 **(d)** 4035
   (e) 2.575 **(f)** 4010 **(g)** 0.336 **(h)** 3154
   (i) 5250 **(j)** 1240 **(k)** 3.595 **(l)** 1600
3. **(a)** 3.4 **(b)** 3.4 **(c)** 5.85 **(d)** 37.8 l

4. **(a)** 40   **(b)** €355
5. **(a)** 10:30   **(b)** 21:45   **(c)** 12:00
   (d) 00:04   **(e)** 19:35
6. **(a)** 1:40 p.m. **(b)** 10:12 a.m. **(c)** 8:17 p.m.
   (d) 2:25 p.m. **(e)** 9:20 a.m.
7. **(a)** 1 hour 13 minutes
   (b) 2 hours 15 minutes
   (b) $2\frac{1}{2}$ hours, $2\frac{1}{4}$ hours, $2\frac{1}{2}$ hours,
       2 hours 25 minutes, 2 hours 35 minutes
   (c) 8:50 p.m.
8. **(a)** 5 hours 50 minutes
   (b) 4 hours 15 minutes   **(c)** 08:40
   (d) 2 hours 20 minutes   **(e)** 252 km
9. **(a)** 42 **(b)** 56 **(c)** 25 **(d)** 36 **(e)** 57.6
10. **(a)** $7\frac{1}{2}$ hours **(b)** 30 minutes
    (c) 20 minutes **(d)** 2 hours 15 minutes
    (e) 3 hours 40 minutes

11. **(a)** 50 **(b)** 244 **(c)** 2.5
    (d) 297.5   **(e)** 144
12. **(a)** $7\frac{1}{2}$ minutes   **(b)** 35 seconds
    (c) 25 minutes
    (d) 2 hours 46 minutes 40 seconds
    (e) 1 hour 13 minutes 20 seconds
13. **(a)** 0.1   **(b)** 33   **(c)** 12
    (d) 4.5   **(e)** 300
14. **(a)** 40   **(b)** 80   **(c)** 25.2
    (d) 36   **(e)** 20
15. **(a)** 120   **(b)** 45 km/h   **(c)** 60
16. **(a)** 33 m **(b)** 1 hour 23 minutes 20 seconds
17. **(a)** 675   **(b)** 825   **(c)** 15:25
    (d) 16:55   **(e)** 500
18. **(a)** 5 km   **(b)** 3.6 km   **(c)** 11.5

Chapter 5

Exercise 5.1

1. 2	2. −2	3. −7	4. 3	5. −5
6. 7	7. 4	8. −9	9. 7	10. 14
11. −11	12. 2	13. 3	14. 9	15. −6
16. −6	17. −7	18. 1	19. 2	20. −2
21. 4	22. 12	23. 3	24. 2	25. −5
26. 8	27. −4	28. 4	29. −7	30. −2
31. 1	32. $\frac{-1}{2}$	33. $\frac{-6}{7}$	34. −3	35. 1

Exercise 5.2

1. 8	2. 5	3. 8	4. 1	5. 6
6. −2	7. $6\frac{1}{2}$	8. $2\frac{1}{4}$	9. −10	10. 5
11. 0	12. 3	13. $\frac{7}{3}$	14. 0	15. 4
16. 2	17. 5	18. 4	19. 1	20. 2
21. 6	22. $\frac{13}{5}$	23. 1	24. 2	25. −3
26. −2	27. 4	28. $\frac{15}{8}$	29. $\frac{-1}{2}$	30. 6

Exercise 5.3

1. 12	2. 45	3. 12	4. −8	5. −4
6. −6	7. 24	8. 10	9. 36	10. 6
11. −4	12. 4	13. 6	14. −2	15. 5
16. 3	17. $\frac{-1}{9}$	18. 5	19. 3	20. 4

21. $\frac{-33}{23}$ 22. 14   23. 19   24. 7   25. 4

26. 11   27. 12   28. 7   29. 1   30. 9

31. $\frac{7}{3}$ 32. 4   33. $8\frac{1}{2}$ 34. 10   35. 15

Exercise 5.4

7. $x \le -6$ 8. $x \ge 4$ 9. $x \ge 3$ 10. 0, 1, 2
11. $x \ge 2$ 12. $x > 4$ 13. $t \ge 3$ 14. $x \ge 3$
15. $m \ge 2$ 16. $x > 4$ 17. $x \le 0$ 18. $x \ge 2$
19. 0, 1, 2, 3   20. 0, 1, 2, 3, 4
21. 0, 1, 2, 3   22. 0, 1, 2, 3, 4, 5   23. $x \ge 4$
24. $x \le 4$ 25. $x \le 4$ 26. $x \ge -2$
27. $t < -6$ 28. $x > 2$ 29. $x \ge -2$
30. $k \le -4$ 31. $x \ge 4$ 32. $x > 3$
33. $x \ge -1\frac{3}{4}$ 34. $x > 4\frac{1}{2}$ 35. $x < -1$
36. $x > -3$ 37. $x \le -3 \Rightarrow \{\,\}$ 38. $x > -3\frac{3}{4}$
39. $m > 3$ 40. $x \le \frac{-13}{7}$ 41. $x \ge -1$

Exercise 5.5

1. 8   2. 1   3. 6   4. −4   5. $3\frac{3}{4}$ 6. 5
7. 4   8. 4   9. −4 10. 3   11. −4   12. 2
13. 3   14. $\frac{-2}{3}$ 15. 6   16. 20   17. 3   18. 3
19. −2   20. 7   24. $x < 4$ 25. $x \le 2$ 26. $x \ge -8$
27. $x > -9$ 28. $x \ge 2$ 29. $x < 9$ 30. $x \ge 3\frac{1}{2}$

Chapter 6

Exercise 6.1

1. 15%   2. 11%   3. 17%
4. (e), (j), (a), (g), (c), (h), (i), (f), (d), (b)

5. (a) $\frac{7}{10}$ (b) $\frac{3}{5}$ (c) $\frac{9}{20}$ (d) $\frac{3}{4}$ (e) $\frac{2}{5}$ (f) $\frac{11}{25}$

6. (a) $\frac{19}{20}$ (b) $\frac{31}{50}$ (c) $\frac{6}{5}$ (d) $\frac{3}{2}$ (e) $\frac{8}{5}$

7. (a) $\frac{1}{8}$ (b) $\frac{1}{3}$ (c) $\frac{5}{8}$ (d) $\frac{2}{3}$

8. (a) 2 (b) $\frac{3}{8}$ (c) $\frac{29}{500}$ (d) $\frac{73}{500}$

9. (a) 0.4 (b) 0.8 (c) 0.55 (d) 0.65 (e) 0.3
   (f) 0.28 (g) 0.67

10. (a) 0.43 (b) 1.42 (c) 1.85 (d) 1.6 (e) 2.1

11. (a) 0.375 (b) 0.026 (c) 0.248 (d) 0.125
    (e) 0.333 (f) 0.666

12. (a) 45% (b) 60% (c) $62\frac{1}{2}$% (d) 47%

    (e) 28% (f) 60% (g) 20% (h) 2%

13. (a) 25% (b) 8% (c) 80% (d) $33\frac{1}{3}$%

    (e) $22\frac{1}{2}$% (f) 80% (g) 125% (h) $137\frac{1}{2}$%

    (i) 320% (j) $87\frac{1}{2}$% (k) 24% (l) 2.4%

Exercise 6.2

1. €108	2. €150	3. €282
4. 80	5. €200	6. €48
7. €8.47	8. 33	9. €2.16
10. €85	11. €4.41	12. 30
13. 16.5	14. €422.50	15. €600
16. 126	17. €36	18. €72
19. 460	20. €367.50	21. 1000
22. €507	23. €0.70	24. 10c
25. €3.24	26. €41	

Exercise 6.3

1. 3400	2. 5000	3. 280
4. 200	5. 66	6. 35
7. 48	8. 63	9. 1300
10. 500	11. 3200	12. 1400
13. 168	14. 1500	15. 6000
16. 1500	17. 288	18. 56
19. €50	20. €180	21. €2000

Exercise 6.4

1. (a) 24 (b) 75 (c) $33\frac{1}{3}$ (d) $16\frac{2}{3}$ (e) 100
   (f) 37.5 (g) 75

2. (a) 40 (b) 47 (c) 15 (d) 27 (e) $41\frac{2}{3}$ (f) 8

3. 22   4. 15   5. 76   6. 46   7. 23
8. (a) $33\frac{1}{3}$ (b) $66\frac{2}{3}$

9. 27   10. 31   11. 20
12. (a) €144 000 (b) 72

13. $46\frac{2}{3}$ 14. 12   15. 20   16. 30

Exercise 6.5

1. 25   2. 17.5   3. 8   4. 5   5. 2   6. 16
7. (a) €50 (b) 20   8. 5   9. €1250
10. 20   11. €5.67   12. $33\frac{1}{3}$

13. (a) €27 000 (b) 6   14. €31.80
15. (a) €624 million (b) €5824 million
16. €238 000   17. €294 000
18. (a) €263 200 (b) 6
19. (a) €126 (b) 28
20. (a) €5.40 (b) €12.60   21. 50
22. €2484   23. (a) €3 (b) €17
24. €14   25. (a) €700 (b) €490
26. (a) €170 (b) 12.5   27. €500
28. (a) $3\frac{1}{3}$% (b) $16\frac{2}{3}$%

Exercise 6.6

1. (a) €2000 (b) 25   2. 18   3. 12.5
4. 26   5. (a) €450 (b) €2250   6. €5.50
7. 15%   8. (a) €27 (b) €153
9. (a) €6250   (b) €375
10. (a) €140   (b) €157.50   (c) €175
11. (a) €420   (b) 300%
12. (a) €1600   (b) €9600
13. (a) €1850   (b) €222   (c) 12%
14. 25%   15. €161   16. €8000
17. (a) €90 (b) 25%
18. €200   19. €20   20. €650

Exercise 6.7

1. €90   2. €225   3. €235
4. €160   5. €800
6. (a) 15% (b) 40% (c) $87\frac{1}{2}$%
   (d) 55% (e) 32%
7. 530   8. 150   9. 64%   10. 104
11. €14 725   12. $16\frac{2}{3}$%   13. 1960

14. 70%   15. (a) €150 (b) $37\frac{1}{2}$%

16. €10 500   17. €24

18. (a) €3000 (b) $33\frac{1}{3}$%

19. $\frac{1}{3}, \frac{1}{4}, \frac{2}{3}, \frac{1}{5}$

Chapter 7

Exercise 7.1

1. (a) €180   (b) €3180
2. (a) €200   (b) €4200
3. (a) €76   (b) €1026
4. €3120
5. €6420
6. €9540
7. (a) €250, €262.50, €275.63
   (b) €5788
8. (a) €87.13   (b) €937.13
9. (a) €665.60   (b) €4665.60
10. (a) €530.40   (b) €7030.40
11. (a) €939.58   (b) €7939.58
12. €10 450
13. (a) €900.17   (b) €4900.17
14. (a) €590.06   (b) €2590.06
15. (a) €126.10   (b) €926.10
16. (a) €705.83   (b) €5705.83
17. €1741.60
18. €2816
19. €1579.60
20. €1485.13

Exercise 7.2

1. (a) €315.04   (b) €2315.04
2. (a) €1351.80   (b) €10 351.80
3. (a) €1577.46   (b) €8977.46
4. €1212.24
5. €192.04
6. €787.28
7. €3276
8. €908.54
9. (a) €1241.76   (b) €13 241.76
10. (a) €4555.01   (b) €31 555.01
11. €5787.60
12. €7594.86
13. €1210
14. €5512.50
15. €3694.11
16. €7473.95
17. €19 366.88
18. €32 089.30
19. €2640.75
20. €3502.72

Exercise 7.3

1. €212.50
2. €38 400
3. €1800
4. €1498.50
5. €7776
6. €216
7. €16 384

8. €28 425.60
9. €1197
10. €10 153.13
11. (a) €3600   (b) 15%
12. €666.40
13. (a) €336   (b) 14%

Exercise 7.4

1. €96.80
2. (a) €252   (b) €1452
3. (a) €315
4. (a) €14.70   (b) €84.70
5. (a) €120   (b) €720
6. (a) €10   (b) €90
7. €98.60
8. (a) €6300   (b) €36 300
9. €736
10. €50
11. €42 834
12. €109
13. (a) €204   (b) €1404
14. €28.44
15. €139 80
16. (a) €192   (b) €992
17. (a) 20c   (b) €1.15   (c) €2300
18. (a) €21.78   (b) 50
19. €36
20. (a) 1438   (b) €215.70
   (c) €38.83   (d) €254.53

Exercise 7.5

1. (a) €200   (b) €42
2. (a) €29 000   (b) €6090
3. €396.69
4. (a) €110   (b) 17%
5. (a) €25   (b) €30.25
6. €710
7. (a) €6500   (b) 23%
8. (a) €420   (b) €88.20
9. €500
10. (a) €58 000   (b) €70 180
11. (a) €190   (b) €40
12. 60c
13. (a) €450   (b) 12%
14. €30 000
15. (a) 90c   (b) 21%
16. €3540
17. €500   18. €15.25

Exercise 7.6

1. (a) €1530   (b) €18 530
2. (a) €20   (b) €420

3. €164
4. (a) €217.35   (b) €1717.35
5. (a) €57.12   (b) €757.12
6. (a) €1006.52   (b) €7006.52
7. €16 581
8. (a) €11 600   (b) 8%
9. €4755.71
10. €27 000
11. €2672.74
12. €864
13. €484

14. (a) €378   (b) €2178
15. €19
16. (a) €776   (b) €271.60
    (c) €57.04   (d) €328.64
17. (a) €21 450   (b) €4505
18. (a) €1260   (b) 14%
19. (a) €80   (b) €96.80
20. (a) €785   (b) €165
21. (a) €45 000   (b) €54 450
22. €1.47

Chapter 8

Exercise 8.1

1. (a) 1 : 3   (b) 10 : 9   (c) 1 : 7   (d) 2 : 3
2. (a) 2 : 3   (b) 5 : 4   (c) 7 : 9   (d) 4 : 5
3. (a) 3 : 5   (b) 7 : 11   (c) 5 : 8   (d) 6 : 7
4. (a) 10 : 9   (b) 2 : 3   (c) 2 : 1
5. (a) 6 : 1   (b) 16 : 45   (c) 14 : 9
6. (a) 1 : 2   (b) 10 : 3   (c) 1 : 2
7. (a) 2 : 3 : 4   (b) 3 : 6 : 10
    (c) 1 : 2 : 12   (d) 4 : 10 : 15
8. (a) 4 : 7 : 11   (b) 10 : 6 : 5   (c) 4 : 5 : 9
9. (a) 4 : 7 : 12   (b) 3 : 4 : 5
10. (a) 1 : 10   (b) 1 : 6
11. (a) 6 : 1   (b) 1 : 3
12. (a) 10 : 1   (b) 20 : 1
13. (a) 1 : 3   (b) 1 : 5
14. (a) 3 : 20   (b) 1 : 15
15. (a) 1 : 7   (b) 1 : 7
16. (a) 5 : 1   (b) 4 : 1
17. (a) 2 : 3   (b) 3 : 4
18. 9 : 5   19. 3 : 1
20. 9 : 8 : 12   21. 3 : 8 : 20
22. 3 : 1 : 4 : 1 : 3   23. 4 : 3 : 5

Exercise 8.2

1. €250, €50   2. €96, €120   3. 30g, 50g
4. 15, 9   5. €150, €50   6. 15 cm, 39 cm
7. €480, €240   8. 360 g, 600 g
9. €48 000, €32 000   10. €80, €160, €240
11. 14, 7, 35   12. €112, €304, €384
13. €4000, €800, €3200   14. €20, €80, €70
15. 39, 26, 52   16. 40, 60, 60
17. €400, €200, €1000
18. €12 000, €18 000, €42 000
19. 5000, 3000, 2000
20. €5600, €4000, €2400
21. (a) €24   (b) €84
22. (a) 162 g   (b) 432 g
23. €30, €75
24. €320, €400

25. (a) €150   (b) €210
26. €480, €320
27. 120 g, 90 g, 270 g
28. €120, €60, €240
29. €150, €50, €100
30. (a) 20   (b) 14   (c) 10   (d) 24   (e) 5   (f) $8\frac{1}{3}$

Exercise 8.3

1. (a) $450   (b) €200
2. (a) €4000   (b) $7840
3. (a) 45 000   (b) €50
4. (a) 69 000   (b) €8696
5. (a) €20 000   (b) R1352
6. €85.71
7. €30
8. €180.60
9. Dublin, €43.23
10. (a) £488   (b) £188   (c) €308.20
11. $6500
12. (a) €2800   (b) €700   (c) R1960
13. Ireland, €1000
14. €1000

Exercise 8.4

1. (a) (i) €15 600   (ii) €36 400
    (b) (i) €10 700   (ii) €29 300
    (c) (i) €8000   (ii) €23 200
    (d) (i) €10 040   (ii) €25 060
2. (a) €9520   (b) €28 480
3. (a) €10 184   (b) €33 376
4. €14 700
5. €21 500
6. €24 700
7. (a) €27 140   (b) €521.92
8. €17 300   9. €19 800
10. (a) €13 680   (b) €9 680   (b) €186.15
11. (a) €34 280   (b) €659.23
12. (a) E = €35 520; J = €33 760   (b) €1760
13. (a) M = €27 080; P = €29 560
    (b) P by €2480

Exercise 8.5

1. **(a)** 3 : 13 **(b)** 10 : 9 **(c)** 4 : 3 **(d)** 3 : 5
2. **(a)** 5 : 6 **(b)** 1 : 5
3. **(a)** 3 : 1 **(b)** 8 : 15
4. **(a)** 20 : 3 **(b)** 1 : 30
5. **(a)** 4 : 75 **(b)** 7 : 25
6. €300, €200
7. €120, €60, €420
8. J = €320, E = €1120
9. **(a)** €890 **(b)** $1744.40
10. **(a)** $10 080 **(b)** €7000
11. €286   12. €215.38
13. €39 800   14. €8688
15. €18 760

Chapter 9

Exercise 9.1

1. **(a)** 81 **(b)** 225 **(c)** 16 **(d)** 512 **(e)** 1000
2. **(a)** 5^6 **(b)** 5^4 **(c)** 7^2 **(d)** 8^6 **(e)** 4^8
3. **(a)** 7^8 **(b)** 8^9 **(c)** 3^{11} **(d)** 4^{10} **(e)** 3^7
4. **(a)** 6^2 **(b)** 7^1 **(c)** 8^2 **(d)** 3^4 **(e)** 4^2
5. **(a)** 9^3 **(b)** 2^5 **(c)** 6^3 **(d)** 3^7 **(e)** 7^5
6. **(a)** 4^6 **(b)** 5^{12} **(c)** 6^8 **(d)** 5^1 **(e)** 8^2
7. **(a)** 9^6 **(b)** 3^{20} **(c)** 7^2 **(d)** 5^9 **(e)** 12^3
8. **(a)** 4 **(b)** 6 **(c)** 27 **(d)** 35 **(e)** 10
9. **(a)** 16 **(b)** 125 **(c)** 8 **(d)** 343 **(e)** 27
10. **(a)** 250 **(b)** 83 **(c)** 2 **(d)** 59 **(e)** 30
11. **(a)** $9y^2$ **(b)** $125x^3$ **(c)** $16y^4$ **(d)** $49x^2$ **(e)** $81y^4$
12. **(a)** a^7 **(b)** a^7 **(c)** a^5 **(d)** a^6

Exercise 9.2

1. **(a)** 2 **(b)** 4 **(c)** 1 **(d)** 7 **(e)** 3
2. **(a)** 1 **(b)** 4 **(c)** 5 **(d)** 4 **(e)** 5
3. **(a)** 8×10^3 **(b)** 1.9×10^4 **(c)** 2.85×10^5
4. **(a)** 4.7×10^2 **(b)** 5.62×10^2 **(c)** 7.5×10^3
5. **(a)** 4.8×10^5 **(b)** 9.03×10^2 **(c)** 7.005×10^3
6. **(a)** 3.2×10^8 **(b)** 9.2×10^7 **(c)** 9×10^9
7. **(a)** 7.62×10^{11} **(b)** 5×10^9
   (c) 5.678942×10^7
8. **(a)** 5.2×10^1 **(b)** 5.02×10^2
   (c) 5.0002×10^4
9. **(a)** 6.07×10^2 **(b)** 6.78×10^4 **(c)** 8.57×10^6
10. **(a)** 1.68×10^2 **(b)** 1.68×10^5 **(c)** 1.68×10^9
11. **(a)** 4500 **(b)** 610 **(c)** 53 000
12. **(a)** 360 000 **(b)** 22 000 **(c)** 9370
13. **(a)** 62 500 **(b)** 492 000 **(c)** 3790
14. **(a)** 283 **(b)** 430 000 **(c)** 63 900
15. 380, 420, 900, 4200, 6950, 42 000,
    1 200 000
16. 897, 1300, 6500, 8000, 12 000, 65 000,
    230 000
17. 1.77×10^3 18. 8.73×10^4
19. 5.49×10^3 20. 7.175×10^4
21. 4.1×10^3 22. 3.508×10^5
23. **(a)** 6.43×10^4 **(b)** 9.14×10^5
    (c) 5.413×10^4
24. **(a)** 6.1034×10^3 **(b)** 4.48×10^5
    (c) 4.42×10^6
25. **(a)** 9.61×10^5 **(b)** 3.19×10^5
    (c) 6.86×10^4
26. **(a)** 5.09×10^3 **(b)** 3.1×10^3
    (c) -2.05×10^4
27. **(a)** 1.2×10^8 **(b)** 1×10^8
    (c) 2.76×10^7
28. **(a)** 1×10^{11} **(b)** 6.12×10^9
    (c) 3.41536×10^7
29. **(a)** 6.58×10^8 **(b)** 1.426×10^7
    (c) 7.44×10^8
30. **(a)** 2×10^1 **(b)** 6.5×10^1 **(c)** 5×10^2
31. **(a)** 2×10^3 **(b)** 2×10^2 **(c)** 2×10^0
32. **(a)** 3×10^3 **(b)** 4×10^2 **(c)** 3×10^3
33. **(a)** 2.9×10^5 **(b)** 1.74×10^7
    (c) 1.044×10^9 **(d)** 2.5056×10^{10}
34. **(a)** 5.8×10^7 **(b)** 108 000 000
    (c) 1.5×10^8 **(d)** 228 000 000
    (e) 7.78×10^8 **(f)** 1.427×10^9
    (g) 5 900 000 000

Exercise 9.3

1. **(a)** 0.13 **(b)** 0.33 **(c)** 0.08
   (d) 0.11 **(e)** 0.07
2. **(a)** 0.17 **(b)** 0.07 **(c)** 0.40
   (d) 0.05 **(e)** 0.29
3. **(a)** $1\frac{1}{4}$ **(b)** $2\frac{2}{3}$ **(c)** 6
4. **(a)** 1.75 **(b)** 0.09. **(c)** 0.46 **(d)** 0.65 **(e)** 0.10

Exercise 9.4

1. **(a)** 18, 18.1 **(b)** 10, 9.2 **(c)** 12, 12.12
   (d) 52, 52.41 **(e)** 49, 48.61
2. **(a)** 27, 31.104 **(b)** 63, 56.952 **(c)** 3, 3.4
   (d) 5, 4.9125
3. **(a)** 9, 6.76 **(b)** 16, 14.14 **(c)** 9, 8.94
   (d) 6, 6.32
4. **(a)** 0.1, 0.11 **(b)** 0.1, 0.15 **(c)** 1, 0.92
   (d) 4, 5.76
5. **(a)** 7.11, 6.91 **(b)** 1, 1.08   **(c)** 1, 0.54
6. €100   7. €63   8. €860
9. €45, €48.54   10. €7   11. €24
12. €25   13. 300   14. €14 000

Exercise 9.5

1. **(a)** 49 **(b)** 27 **(c)** 1000 **(d)** 20.25
2. **(a)** 6^7 **(b)** 6^5 **(c)** 6^3 **(d)** 6^2
3. **(a)** 7^8 **(b)** 6^6 **(c)** 8^8 **(d)** 13^2
4. **(a)** 12 **(b)** 1 **(c)** 15 **(d)** 12
5. **(a)** 1 **(b)** 3 **(c)** 4 **(d)** 6
6. **(a)** 1.4×10^4 **(b)** 2.684×10^3
   (c) 3.9×10^1 **(d)** 4.75×10^2
7. **(a)** 280 **(b)** 320 000 **(c)** 6215 **(d)** 18
8. e, d, g, a, f, c, b
9. **(a)** 3.52×10^3 **(b)** 5.74×10^2
   (c) 1.48×10^4 **(d)** 8.14×10^3
10. **(a)** 2.76×10^6 **(b)** 1.548×10^6
    (c) 2×10^1 **(d)** 2×10^3
11. 9.14544×10^{12} km
12. Greece = 9.9×10^6; Ireland = 3.55×10^6;
    Italy = 5.7×10^7; UK = 5.6×10^7;
    Norway = 4.2×10^6; Portugal = 1.02×10^7;
    Spain = 3.8×10^7
13. **(a)** 0.05 **(b)** 0.07 **(c)** 2.67 **(d)** 0.18
14. **(a)** 60 **(b)** 40 **(c)** 8 **(d)** 4.5
15. **(a)** 5 **(b)** 7 **(c)** 9 **(d)** 10
16. **(a)** 45 **(b)** 11.75 **(c)** 1.7 **(d)** 12
17. **(a)** 42.12 **(b)** 10.94 **(c)** 1.76 **(d)** 11.01
18. €210
19. 600
20. **(a)** 400 **(b)** €280 **(c)** €275.21

Chapter 10

Exercise 10.1

1. $2(a + 4)$
2. $3(b + 3)$
3. $5(x - 5)$
4. $2(5y + 4)$
5. $6(2a + 3)$
6. $15(b + 2)$
7. $2(2x + 9)$
8. $7(4y + 7)$
9. $7(2c + 3)$
10. $9c(c + 3)$
11. $12d(d + 3)$
12. $8(x^2 - 2)$
13. $y(4y + 1)$
14. $4m(1 - 4m)$
15. $2p(12p + 5)$
16. $7m(5m + 6)$
17. $45n(n + 2)$
18. $6a(3 - 4a)$
19. $b(1 - b)$
20. $x(2y + 1)$
21. $bd(1 - 3d)$
22. $5c(3a - 2c)$
23. $7xy(1 + 2y)$
24. $10w(2w - 3xy)$
25. $7c^2d^2(c - 2d)$
26. $xy(x - y)$
27. $mn(3n - 7m)$
28. $6b(5y + 7b)$
29. $pq(20 - pq)$
30. $3pq(-2p + 3)$
31. $3a(b - 3d + 2c)$
32. $6v(-3uv + u - 2v)$
33. $y(x - 1 - xz)$
34. $a(-a - 1 + b)$
35. $2y(3y + 2 - p)$
36. $3x(3x - 4 + x^2)$
37. $2xy(x + 4 - 6y)$
38. $5ab(5a + 1 - 2ab)$
39. $pq(2p + 3q + 5)$
40. $5ab(a + 3b - 40ab)$

Exercise 10.2

1. $(2 + b)(x + y)$
2. $(x - b)(y + p)$
3. $(3a + 8)(a + b)$
4. $(x^2 + 2a)(b + 5)$
5. $(y + 2b)(y + 2)$
6. $(p - 3)(p + 2q)$
7. $(n + 3)(m + 2p)$
8. $(y + v)(y + 1)$
9. $(2a - 1)(a + 3b)$
10. $(a + 1)(b - 1)$
11. $(x + 1)(y + 1)$
12. $(3x + 2a)(x - 5)$
13. $(2p + q)(p + 2)$
14. $(x + a)(x + 1)$
15. $(7b + c)(2b + 1)$
16. $(4y + p)(y - 2)$
17. $(4a + 3b)(a + 7)$
18. $(3 + x)(m - 2n)$
19. $(2 + 4x)(a - 2) = (1 + 2x)(2a - 4)$
20. $(x - 4y)(2 + x)$
21. $(p + 1)(q + 1)$
22. $(1 - n)(m + 1)$
23. $(2p + a)(p + 3)$
24. $(a + b)(p - q)$
25. $(2c - d)(a + 3b)$
26. $(-a - m)(b + c)$
27. $(pq - 3r)(p + 2q)$
28. $(4a^2 + 4)(a + 2) = (a^2 + 1)(4a + 8)$
29. $(5xy - 18)(x^2 + 2y^2)$
30. $(k^2 + 12)(p + q)$

Exercise 10.3

1. $(x + 2)(x + 1)$
2. $(x + 2)(x + 3)$
3. $(a + 2)(a + 5)$
4. $(y + 3)(y + 7)$
5. $(b + 4)(b + 3)$
6. $(y + 4)(y + 10)$
7. $(x + 1)(x + 1)$
8. $(a + 3)(a + 5)$
9. $(y + 9)(y + 1)$
10. $(p + 7)(p + 2)$
11. $(a + 2)(a + 5)$
12. $(p + 9)(p + 5)$
13. $(q + 6)(q + 3)$
14. $(m + 7)(m + 3)$
15. $(n + 4)(n + 1)$
16. $(y + 2)(y + 7)$
17. $(b + 14)(b + 1)$
18. $(a + 3)(a + 7)$
19. $(c + 3)(c + 3)$
20. $(d + 3)(d + 14)$
21. $(x - 1)(x - 5)$
22. $(y - 3)(y - 4)$
23. $(y - 5)(y - 3)$
24. $(m - 9)(m - 2)$
25. $(p + 5)(p + 5)$
26. $(x - 10)(x - 3)$
27. $(b - 7)(b - 1)$
28. $(d - 3)(d - 9)$
29. $(c - 6)(c - 7)$
30. $(a + 2)(a - 1)$
31. $(x - 3)(x + 5)$
32. $(b - 11)(b - 3)$
33. $(a + 4)(a - 5)$
34. $(x - 6)(x - 4)$
35. $(p - 9)(p + 2)$
36. $(y + 4)(y - 10)$
37. $(c - 3)(c + 1)$
38. $(a + 3)(a - 12)$
39. $(x - 8)(x + 2)$
40. $(y - 4)(y + 4)$
41. $(x - 4)(x + 3)$
42. $(a - 2)(a + 1)$
43. $(b + 7)(b - 10)$
44. $(d + 1)(d - 5)$
45. $(y - 6)(y + 2)$
46. $(g + 2)(g - 8)$
47. $(h - 8)(h + 1)$
48. $(x - 6)(x + 1)$
49. $(y + 15)(y - 2)$
50. $(a + 9)(a - 2)$

Exercise 10.4

1. $(x + 9)(x - 9)$
2. $(a - 8)(a + 8)$
3. $(b + 10)(b - 10)$
4. $(y + 15)(y - 15)$

5. (m + 12)(m − 12)   6. (7 − p)(7 + p)
7. (14 − x)(14 + x)   8. (5 − p)(5 + p)
9. (6 − c)(6 + c)   10. (11 − d)(11 + d)
11. (5x + 9)(5x − 9)   12. (4y − 13)(4y + 13)
13. (2p − 1)(2p + 1)   14. (4v − w)(4v + w)
15. (3a − 5b)(3a + 5b)   16. (1 − x)(1 + x)
17. (1 − 7y)(1 + 7y)   18. (4k − 1)(4k + 1)
19. (20r − 1)(20r + 1)   20. (1 − 18y)(1 + 18y)

Exercise 10.5

1. 40   2. 400   3. −4000
4. 600   5. 190 000 6. −3200
7. 39.2   8. 82   9. 9.6
10. 9919   11. 320   12. 1260

Exercise 10.6

1. **(a)** 3(3x + 5) **(b)** 10(2y + 5) **(c)** 8(m + 4)
(d) 2a(a + 4) **(e)** 7b(2b − 5) **(f)** x(y − a)

(g) 9(6 − 5a^2) **(h)** 21b(b − 2) **(i)** cd(d − 1)
(j) 3(9 − 4m)
2. **(a)** (3a + 2b)(a − 5) **(b)** (b + c)(b + 1)
(c) (d + e)(d − 1) **(d)** (x − q)(y + p)
(e) (3a + 2b)(a − 5) **(f)** (x − y)(x − 2)
(g) (m + n)(m + 1) **(h)** (4x + 7)(x + y)
(i) (x + b)(p − q) **(j)** (c + 3)(d + 2g)
3. **(a)** (a + 6)(a + 7) **(b)** (b + 6)(b + 1)
(c) (c + 11)(c + 8) **(d)** (d − 2)(d − 2)
(e) (e − 5)(e − 3) **(f)** (f − 8)(f − 8)
(i) (g + 12)(g + 2) **(h)** (h + 7)(h − 1)
(a) (k + 8)(k − 4) **(j)** (m − 14)(m + 5)
4. **(a)** (x − 7)(x + 7) **(b)** (2y − 5)(2y + 5)
(c) (3a − 6b)(3a + 6b)
(d) (15m − 14n)(15m + 14n)
(e) (10p − 1)(10p + 1)
(f) (1 − 8q)(1 + 8q) **(g)** 4(x − 6y)(x + 6y)
(h) (7y − 10x)(7y + 10x)
(i) (a − 13b)(a + 13b) **(j)** (3e − 1)(3e + 1)

Chapter 11

Exercise 11.1

1. x = 6, y = 2   2. x = 7, y = −2
3. (3, 1)   4. (17, 7)   5. (1, 4)
6. (3, 3)   7. (1, 1)   8. (2, 1)
9. (4, −2)   10. (4, 3)   11. (5, 2)
12. (7, 1)   13. (5, 3)   14. (4, 3)
15. (5, 0)   16. (1, 1)   17. (5, 2)
18. (2, 3)   19. (+2, +5)   20. (3, 2)
21. (5, −2)   22. (2, 3)   23. $\left(\frac{1}{2}, −3\right)$
24. (3, −1)   25. (2, 3)   26. (2, 1)
27. (0, −2)   28. (2, 0)   29. (−4, −12)
30. (12, 6)   31. (5, 15)   32. (4, 2)
33. (3, 0)   34. (0, 2)   35. (9, −2)
36. (−2, +2)   37. (−3, 3)   38. (7, 10)
39. (2, 3)   40. (1, 2)

Exercise 11.2

1. (2, −3)   2. (−4, 10)   3. (2, −1)
4. (−4, −1)   5. (−4, +4)   6. (3, −2)
7. (1, −5)   8. (8, −2)   9. (0, −8)
10. (0, 1)   11. (0, −2)   12. (1, 0)
13. (4, −4)   14. (−6, −11)   15. (25, −5)
16. (1, −1)   17. (0, −5)   18. (0, 9)
19. (0, 3)   20. (0, 6)   21. (0, −1)
22. (0, 7)   23. (0, 3)   24. $\left(0, \frac{−5}{3}\right)$
25. $\left(0, \frac{1}{3}\right)$ 26. $\left(0, \frac{−16}{3}\right)$ 27. (−2, 2) 28. ±3

29. ±5   30. ±1   31. ±11   32. ±1
33. ±4   34. ±4   35. ±6

Exercise 11.3

1. −2, −1 2. −8, −1   3. −2, −6   4. −2, −5
5. −3   6. −4, −1   7. −2, −18 8. −5, −14
9. 2   10. 3, 9   11. 8, 7   12. 2, 11
13. 9, 4   14. 3, −2   15. 8, −6   16. −5, 6
17. 7, −1 18. −2, 7   19. −5, 10 20. 6, −1
21. −4, 3 22. −2, 1   23. −6, 3   24. −9, 6
25. 2, −7 26. −8, 3   27. 2, −8   28. 7, −15
29. −12, 2 30. 3, −13 31. 5, −4   32. 2, −4
33. −2, 7 34. −5, 1   35. −4, 6

Exercise 11.4

1. **(a)** 12, 8 **(b)** 9, 2 **(c)** 3, 7 **(d)** 5, 2
(e) 2, 7 **(f)** 2, 4 **(g)** 5, −1 **(h)** 4, 5
(i) 5, 3 **(j)** 2, 0 **(k)** −7, −56 **(l)** −5, −30
2. **(a)** −2, 4 **(b)** ±5 **(c)** 1, −7 **(d)** −2
(e) 0, −3 **(f)** 0, 5 **(g)** 0, −1 **(h)** 0, −5
(i) 0, −2 **(j)** 6, 0 **(k)** ±7 **(l)** ±11
3. **(a)** −1 **(b)** 1 **(c)** 5 **(d)** −4 **(e)** 2, 9 **(f)** 4
(g) −7 **(h)** 2, 1 **(i)** 2, 12 **(j)** −9, 4
(k) −4, −5 **(l)** −15, 2

Chapter 12

Exercise 12.1

1. **(a)** months of summer
   (b) multiples of 5 from 5 to 30
   (c) vowels
   (d) provinces of Ireland
   (e) whole numbers from 1 to 5
2. **(a)** {12, 14, 16, 18}
   (b) {odd numbers from 11 to 19}
   (c) {12, 15, 18}
   (d) {12, 18}
   (e) {15}
3. **(a)** {a, e, i, o, u}
   (b) {a, b, c, d, e, f, g}
   (c) {1, 2, 4, 5, 10, 20}
   (d) {11, 13, 17, 19, 23, 29}
4. **(a)** {M, T, W, Th, F, Sa, Su}
   (b) {Jan, Feb, Mar}
   (c) {Jan, Mar, May, Jul, Aug, Oct, Dec}
   (d) {6, 12, 18, 24, 30, 36}
5. **(a)** {last 3 months of the year}
   (b) {even numbers from 20 to 30}
   (c) {prime numbers less than 20}
   (d) {provinces of Ireland}
6. **(a)** T   **(b)** F   **(c)** T   **(d)** F
   (e) T   **(f)** F
7. **(a)** F   **(b)** F   **(c)** T   **(d)** T
   (e) T   **(f)** T
8. **(a)** $\notin$ **(b)** $\in$ **(c)** $\notin$ **(d)** $\notin$
   (e) $\in$ **(f)** $\in$ **(g)** $\in$
9. **(a)** $\notin$ **(b)** $\in$ **(c)** $\notin$ **(d)** $\in$
   (e) $\notin$ **(f)** $\in$ **(g)** $\notin$
10. **(a)** A = {Jan, Feb, May, July}
    B = {Jan ... Dec}
    C = {Jan ... Jun}
    D = {Sep ... Dec}
    (b) (i) {Jan ... Dec}   **(ii)** {Jan, Feb, May, Jul}
    (iii) {Jan, Feb, May}   **(iv)** {Jan ... Jul}
11. **(a)** {2, 4, 5} **(b)** {1, 2, 3, 4, 5, 7, 9, 10, 13}
    (c) {9}   **(d)** {1, 2, 3, 4, 5, 7, 8, 9, 10, 14}
    (e) {7}   **(f)** {2, 4, 5, 7, 8, 9, 13, 14}
12. **(a)** {e}   **(b)** {a, b, c, d, e, f, g, l, m, n, t}
    (c) {a, e}   **(d)** {a, b, c, d, e, f, g, i, o, u}
    (e) {b, c, d, f, g}   **(f)** {e}
    (g) {a, e, i, l, m, n, o, u, t}
13. **(a)** {1, 2, 3, 4, 6, 8, 12, 24}
    (b) {2, 4, 6, 8, 10}
    (c) {1, 3, 4} **(d)** {1, 2, 3, 4, 5, 6, 8, 12, 24}
    (e) {4} **(f)** {1, 2, 3, 4, 5, 6, 8, 10}
    (g) {2, 4, 6, 8}
    (h) {1, 2, 3, 4, 6, 8, 10, 12, 24}

Exercise 12.2

1. No
2. Yes

3. **(a)** {5, 6}   **(b)** {2, 3, 4, 5, 6, 7, 9, 12}
   (c) {2, 5, 9} **(d)** {3, 4, 7, 12}
4. **(a)** 3   **(b)** 6   **(c)** 4   **(d)** 3   **(e)** 2   **(f)** 3
5. x = T
6. 4 subsets of {4, 7, 3}
7. **(a)** {g, h, m} **(b)** {g, h, j, k, m}   **(c)** { }
   (d) {a, d, e, f, i, k, o, t, u, y}   **(e)** {j, k}
   (f) { }   **(g)** {d, f, k, t, y}   **(h)** {a, i, o, u}
8. D = G
9. **(a)** $\subset$ **(b)** $\not\subset$ **(c)** $\subset$ **(d)** $\not\subset$
   (e) $\subset$ **(f)** $\subset$ **(g)** $\subset$
10. **(a)** 5   **(b)** 1   **(c)** 21   **(d)** 3
    (e) 10   **(f)** 2   **(g)** 16
11. **(a)** {8, 9}   **(b)** {1, 2, 3, 4, 5, 6, 7, 8, 9}
    (c) { }   **(d)** {3, 8, 10}   **(e)** {9, 11, 12}
    (f) {1, 2, 3, 4, 6, 7, 8}   **(g)** {10}
    (h) {1, 2, 3, 4, 5, 6, 7, 8, 9}
12. K = M
13. **(a)** $\not\subset$ **(b)** $\subset$ **(c)** $\subset$ **(d)** $\subset$
    (e) $\not\subset$ **(f)** $\subset$ **(g)** $\subset$
14. **(a)** 9   **(b)** 2   **(c)** 1   **(d)** 2
    (e) 9   **(f)** 3   **(g)** 8

Exercise 12.3

1. **(b) (i)** {4, 5, 7} **(ii)** {6}   **(iii)** {3, 4, 5, 6, 7, 9}
2. **(b) (i)** {e, h, k} **(ii)** {f, g}   **(iii)** {a, b, e, f, g, h, k}
3. **(b) (i)** {1}   **(ii)** {1, 2, 5, 6} **(iii)** {2, 3, 4, 5}
   (iv) {3, 4, 6}   **(v)** {2, 3, 4, 5, 6}
4. **(b) (i)** {a}   **(ii)** {a, b, c, d, f}
   (iii) {d, e}   **(iv)** {b, c, e, f}   **(v)** {e}
5. **(b) (i)** {1, 2, 3, 6, 9, 18}   **(ii)** {4, 5, 12}
   (iii) {1, 2, 3, 6}   **(iv)** {4, 5, 9, 12, 18}
6. **(a) (i)** {e, g} **(ii)** {c, d, e, f}   **(iii)** {e}
   (iv) {c, d, e, f, g}   **(v)** {a, b, c, d, f}
   (b) (i) 2   **(ii)** 3   **(iii)** 3
7. **(a) (i)** {6, 7, 8, 9} **(ii)** {9, 10} **(iii)** {9}
   (iv) {6, 7, 8, 9, 10}   **(v)** {6, 7, 8, 11}
   (b) (i) 2   **(ii)** 3   **(iii)** 2
8. **(a)** F   **(b)** T   **(c)** T   **(d)** T   **(e)** F
   (f) F   **(g)** F   **(h)** T   **(i)** F   **(j)** F
9. **(b) (i)** {Down, Armagh, Antrim, Tyrone,
       Derry, Fermanagh, Cavan, Monaghan}
   (ii) {Antrim, Tyrone}
   (iii) {Donegal, Dublin, Cork, Laois, Leitrim}
   (iv) {Leitrim}
10. **(b) (i)** G   **(ii)** $\varnothing$
    (iii) Brazil, Germany, Italy, Japan
    (iv) Germany
11. **(a) (i)** {3, 6, 9, 12, 15}   **(ii)** {1, 2, 3, 6, 9, 18}
    (c) (i) {1, 2, 3, 6, 9, 12, 15, 18}
    (ii) {4, 5, 12, 15}   **(iii)** {1, 2, 18}

Exercise 12.4

1. **(a) (i)** {k, s, u, w, x}   **(ii)** {n, t, u, w}
   (iii) {w}   **(iv)** {k, s, x}   **(v)** {t}

(vi) {m, n, p, s, t, u, w, x}   **(vii)** {k, c, o, y}
(viii) {o, t, y}   **(ix)** {s, w, x}   **(x)** {k, o, y}
(b) (i) 2   **(ii)** 1   **(iii)** 3

2. **(b) (i)** {4, 9, 15}   **(ii)** {4, 15}
(iii) {4, 7, 8, 9, 11, 12, 14, 15}
(iv) {5, 8, 10}   **(v)** {8, 12, 14}
(vi) {8}   **(vii)** {8, 9, 12, 14}
(viii) {5, 6, 10, 13}

3. **(a) (i)** {2, 5, 8, 9, 10}   **(ii)** {1, 2, 7, 8, 10}
(iii) {2}   **(iv)** {1, 8, 10}   **(v)** {5}
(vi) {2, 3, 5, 6, 7, 8, 9, 10}   **(vii)** {3, 4, 6}
(viii) {1, 4}   **(ix)** {2, 9}   **(x)** {9}
(b) (i) 3   **(ii)** 1   **(iii)** 3

4. **(b) (i)** {e, f}   **(ii)** {f}   **(iii)** {b, e, f, m}
(iv) {a, d}   **(v)** {a, b, d, m}
(vi) {c, g}   **(vii)** {b, e}
(c) (i) 5   **(ii)** 2

5.
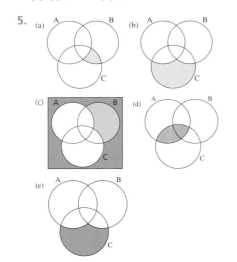

6. **(b) (i)** {11, 12}   **(ii)** {14}
(iii) {7, 8, 11, 12, 14, 15}
(iv) {8, 10, 13}   **(v)** {8, 15}
(vi) {8}   **(vii)** {8}
(viii) {7, 8, 9, 10, 11, 13, 15, 16}
(c) (i) 6   **(ii)** 2   **(iii)** 2

7. **(b) (i)** {a, b, c}   **(ii)** {a, c, e}
(iii) {b, f, g, k}   **(iv)** {d, h}

Exercise 12.5

1. **(a)** 5   **(b)** 7   **(c)** 3   **(d)** 4
   (e) 1   **(f)** 9   **(g)** 10
2. **(a)** 13   **(b)** 4   **(c)** 3   **(d)** 7
   (e) 6   **(f)** guitar only
3. **(a)** 3   **(b)** 9
4. **(a)** 220   **(b)** 40
5. **(a)** 5   **(b)** 2
6. **(a)** 18   **(b)** 6
7. **(a)** 5   **(b)** 23
8. 3   9. 16   10. 20
11. 0   12. 3   13. **(b)** 3
14. 20   15. 14

Exercise 12.6

1. **(a)** 30   **(b)** 14   **(c)** 13   **(d)** 7   **(e)** 10   **(f)** 5
   (g) 15   **(h)** 27   **(i)** 21   **(j)** 11
2. **(a)** 2   **(b)** 9   **(c)** 9   **(d)** 9   **(e)** 7   **(f)** 15
   (g) 23   **(h)** 20   **(i)** 10   **(j)** 34
3. **(a)** 16   **(b)** 1   **(c)** 23
4. **(a)** 0   **(b)** 17   **(c)** 5
5. **(a)** 7   **(b)** 23   **(c)** 8   **(d)** 5
6. **(a)** 7   **(b)** 9   **(c)** 2
7. **(a)** 8   **(b)** 9   **(c)** 16   **(d)** 43   **(e)** 21
8. **(a)** 32   **(b)** 5   **(c)** 10   **(d)** 12.5%

Exercise 12.7

1. **(a)** No   **(b)** Yes   **(c)** Yes **(d)** No
2. **(a)** ∈   **(b)** ∉   **(c)** ∈   **(d)** ∩   **(e)** ∪   **(f)** ⊂
   (g) ⊂
3. **(a)** {d, f}   **(b)** {d}   **(c)** {a, b, c, e}
   (d) {a, b, d, e, f}   **(e)** {a, b, e}
4. **(a)** {12}   **(b)** {6, 8, 10}   **(c)** {6, 10}   **(d)** {8}
5. **(a)** {4, 5, 6, 7}   **(b)** {7, 8}
   (c) {1, 2, 4, 5, 6, 7, 8} **(d)** {3, 9, 10, 11}
   (e) {3, 11}   **(f)** {5, 6}   **(g)** {5}
6. **(b) (i)** {4, 5, 6, 7, 8, 10, 11, 12} **(ii)** {3, 9}
   (iii) {3, 5}   **(iv)** {3}
   (v) {4, 6, 8, 10}   **(vi)** {3, 5, 7, 9, 11, 12}
   (c) (i) 5 **(ii)** 8   **(iii)** 3   **(iv)** 3
7. **(a)** 18   **(b)** 9   **(c)** 14   **(d)** 12   **(e)** 11
8. 5
9. **(b)** 4, 36, documentaries and soaps but not
   films
10. 7

Chapter 13

Exercise 13.1

1. **(a) (i)** 25   **(ii)** 29   **(b) (i)** July   **(ii)** April   **(c)** 27
2. **(a) (i)** 3   **(ii)** 3   **(b)** 7   **(c)** 7   **(d)** 5   **(e)** 17
3. **(a)** June, July, August **(b)** July **(c)** 6
   (d) Apr, May, Sept, Oct
4. **(a)** Holland **(b)** 44   **(c)** 10   **(d)** 8.8   **(e)** 14%
5. **(b)** 16   **(c)** 60   **(d)** 10%   **(e)** Oct, Nov
6. **(b)** Holland, Germany   **(c)** 7%
   (d) Holland, France, Germany
7. **(b)** 100   **(c)** 43   **(d)** 5%
8. **(b)** 420   **(c)** $\frac{2}{7}$ **(d)** 10%
9. **(b)** 65   **(c)** Chem
10. **(b)** 20%   **(c)** €780
11. **(b)** 60   **(c)** 50   **12. (b)** 50   **(c)** 40%

Exercise 13.2

1. **(a)** Feb **(b)** 50 cm **(c)** 64%
2. **(a)** Sat **(b)** €4400 **(c)** €2000 **(d)** 45%
   (e) Wed
3. **(a)** 120, 100, 80, 60, 50, 70 **(b)** 480
   (c) May **(d)** 62.5% **(e)** Jan, Feb
4. **(b)** 8 m **(c)** 20% **(d)** 1.2 m
5. **(b)** 29 **(c)** 11 – 12 **(d)** 15 – 16
6. **(b)** 2 **(c)** 300 g **(d)** 600 g
7. **(b)** year 3 **(c)** 60 **(d)** Fall
8. **(b)** Jan, Feb **(c)** €1000 **(d)** €167

Exercise 13.3

1.

Grade	A	B	C	D	E
Number	30	20	40	15	15

2. **(a)** 36°
   (b)

Type	P	WB	CF	RC
Number	6	20	16	18

3. **(a)** 60°
   (b)

Country	IRE	US	GER	SP	FR
Number	400	288	80	432	240

4. **(a)** 180°
   (b)

Subject	FR	ART	MUS	BIO
Number	24	8	2	6

5. **(a)** 120°
   (b)

Game	A	B	C
Angle	150	126	84

   (c) 42%

6. **(a)** 40°
   (b)

Fruit	Apple	Orange	Banana
Angle	144	90	126

   (c) 25%

7. **(a)** 1800
   (b)

Person	J	D	M	E	Jos
Angle	32	40	160	80	48

   (c) $\frac{4}{9}$

8. **(a)** 1
   (b)

Mode	Bus	Bike	Car	Train
Angle	160	100	80	20

   (c) 22%

9. **(a)** 30
   (b)

Sport	T	G	S	H	F
Angle	36	45	90	54	135

   (c) 12.5%

10. **(a)** 60
    (b)

Work in	H	F	Hot	O	R
Angle	60	90	96	42	72

    (c) $\frac{1}{4}$

11. **(a)** 7
    (b)

Activity	Sch	Home	Sleep	Leisure
Angle	105	30	120	105

    (c) 8.3%

12. **(a)**

Grade	A	B	C	D	E
Number	5	3	2	1	1
Angle	150	90	60	30	30

    (c) 25%

13. **(a)** 40
    (b)

Type	Com	Hor	SF	Soap
Angle	108	72	117	63

    (c) 20%

14. **(a)** 180
    (b)

Country	US	SP	ENG	IRE	FR
Angle	50	30	40	90	150

    (c) Ire, Fr

15. **(a)** 60
    (b)

Mark	A	B	C	D	E
Angle	42	90	120	72	36

    (c) 54 **(d)** 10% **(e)** 70%

Exercise 13.4

1. **(a)** 4; 3 **(b)** 1.7; 1 **(c)** 5; 2, 6 **(d)** 5; 5
   (e) 4; 2 **(f)** 7; 8
2. **(a)** 5, 3 **(b)** 6, 5 **(c)** 2.5, 3 **(d)** 2.2, $1\frac{1}{2}$
   (e) 3, $1\frac{1}{4}$
3. €22.33 4. 62 5
6. **(a)** 56 **(b)** 16 7. 108
8. 7 9. 3 10. 6
11. **(a)** 2, 4, 2, 3, 1 **(b)** 4 **(c)** 5.5
12. **(a)**

No. of goals	0	1	2	3	4
No. of games	5	3	4	6	2

    (b) 3 **(c)** 1.85 **(d)** 11 **(e)** 9 **(f)** 1.85
13. **(a)** 30 **(b)** €30 **(c)** €21 **(d)** 21
14. **(a)** 6 **(b)** €30 **(c)** €30
15. **(a)** 5 **(b)** 14 **(c)** 13 **(d)** 4

Exercise 13.5

1. 7 2. 5 3. 8 4. 6 5. 2

Exercise 13.6

1. **(c)** 120 **(d)** 20 **(e)** M, T, W, F **(f)** 27
2. **(c)** 20 **(d)** 38.3%
3. **(a)** $4\frac{6}{7}$, 3 **(b)** 6, 4 **(c)** 3, 2 **(d)** 4, 6

4. **(a)** 11 **(b)** 10.43 **(c)** 7
5. **(a)** 6 **(b)** 4 **(c)** 3.2 **(d)** 9
6. 2

Chapter 14

Exercise 14.1

1. **(a)** 22, 30 **(b)** 34, 70 **(c)** 32, 48
   (d) 38, 78 **(e)** 44, 112 **(f)** 36, 68.75
2. **(a)** 20, 25 **(b)** 36, 81 **(c)** 16, 16
   (d) 44, 121 **(e)** 56, 196 **(f)** 50, 156.25
3. **(a)** 34, 48 **(b)** 44, 56 **(c)** 44, 70
   (d) 60, 168
4. **(a)** 36 **(b)** 24 **(c)** 24
   (d) 30 **(e)** 21 **(f)** 9
   (g) 98 **(h)** 20
5. **(a)** 204 **(b)** 287 **(c)** 1100
   (d) 526 **(e)** 78 **(f)** 326.5

Exercise 14.2

1. **(a)** 30 **(b)** 22 **(c)** 24
   (d) 20 **(e)** 40 **(f)** 26
2. **(a)** 45 **(b)** 40 **(c)** 30
   (d) 24 **(e)** 40 **(f)** 42
3. **(a)** 7 **(b)** 9 **(c)** 4
   (d) 5 **(e)** 5 **(f)** 2
4. **(a)** 8 **(b)** 5 **(c)** 4
   (d) 3 **(e)** 5 **(f)** 6

Exercise 14.3

1. 8   2. 5   3. 9   4. 7
5. 5   6. 3   7. 5   8. 12
9. **(a)** 8 **(b)** 32
10. 9   11. 10   12. 3
13. 8   14. 5   15. 7

Exercise 14.4

1. **(i) (a)** 125.6 **(b)** 1256
   (ii) (a) 25.12 **(b)** 50.24
   (iii) (a) 62.8 **(b)** 314
   (iv) (a) 50.24 **(b)** 200.96
2. **(i) (a)** 44 **(b)** 154
   (ii) (a) 176 **(b)** 2464
   (iii) (a) 13.2 **(b)** 13.86
   (iv) (a) $75\frac{3}{7}$ **(b)** 452.57
3. **(a)** 13 **(b)** 81.64 **(c)** 530.66
4. **(a)** 30 **(b)** 188.4 **(c)** 2826
5. **(i)** 20, 62.83, 3.14 **(ii)** 50, 157
   (iii) 10, 31.4 **(iv)** 18, 56.52
   (v) 41, 128.74 **(vi)** 16.8, 52.75
6. **(a)** 324π **(b)** 36π

7. **(a)** 1225π **(b)** 70π
8. **(a)** 110.25π **(b)** 21π
9. 17   10. 50   11. 32
12. 7   13. 22   14. 70
15. **(a)** 56 **(b)** 9856
16. **(a)** 63 **(b)** 126
17. 14   18. 19   19. 100   20. 6
21. 20   22. 11   23. 30
24. **(a)** 33.5, 8.4, 24.4
   (b) 125.6, 20.9, 44.9
   (c) 205.1, 29.3, 57.3
   (d) 602.9, 75.4, 107.4

Exercise 14.5

1. **(a)** 84 **(b)** 88
2. **(a)** 64.5 **(b)** 94.2
3. **(a)** 353.25 **(b)** 77.1
4. **(a)** 357 **(b)** 76
5. 69.66
6. 87.92
7. 118.935
8. **(a)** 290.75 **(b)** 77.7
9. 119.25
10. 129.25
11. **(a)** 28 **(b)** 2464 **(c)** 376 **(d)** 15

Exercise 14.6

1. **(a)** 7 **(b)** 6.8 **(c)** 0.4
   (d) 29.2 **(e)** 6.492 **(f)** 9.5
2. **(a)** 4000 **(b)** 25 000 **(c)** 3250
   (d) 600 **(e)** 853 **(f)** 3 600 000
3. **(a)** 1920 **(b)** 10 080 **(c)** 1 080 000
   (d) 7 000 000
4. **(a)** 344 **(b)** 1476 **(c)** 127 800
   (d) 44 400
5. **(a)** 8000, 2400 **(b)** 4913, 1734
   (c) 1953.125, 937.5 **(d)** 216, 216
6. **(a)** 24 **(b)** 8 **(c)** 5
7. **(a)** 6 **(b)** €120
8. **(a)** 450 **(b)** 50 minutes
9. 11 340   10. 6 cm   11. 2.5 cm
12. 20 cm   13. 50 cm   14. 1080
15. 5 cm   16. 7 cm   17. 12 cm
18. 10 cm; 200

463

Exercise 14.7

1. 1470   2. 904   3. 113
4. **(a)** 69 300   **(b)** 9372
5. **(a)** 770   **(b)** 517
6. **(a)** 269 500   **(b)** 19 250
7. **(a)** 48 230   **(b)** 7636
8. **(a)** 7630   **(b)** 2204
9. **(a)** 70 650   **(b)** 10 127
10. 68 688 cm³   11. 7536   12. 3533
13. 4608π   14. 2300π   15. 1600π
16. 952π   17. 3014   18. 7 cm
19. 5.6 cm   20. 14   21. 20
22. 10   23. 14   24. 5
25. 20
26. **(a)** 9 947 520   **(b)** 9948   **(c)** 8455.80

Exercise 14.8

1. 267.9   2. 615.4
3. **(a)** 904.3   **(b)** 452.2
4. **(a)** 288π   **(b)** 144π
5. **(a)** 3052.1   **(b)** 1017.4
6. **(a)** 2143.6   **(b)** 803.8
7. **(a)** 121.5π   **(b)** 81π
8. **(a)** 36π   **(b)** 36π
9. **(a)** 11 498.7   **(b)** 2464
10. **(a)** 179.7   **(b)** 154
11. 9   12. 9   13. 6
14. 5   15. 9   16. 2
17. 4   18. 28   19. 13
20. 4   21. sphere   22. 4.2 cm

Exercise 14.9

1. **(a)** 36 π   **(b)** $2\frac{1}{4}$

2. 3   3. 4   4. 5

5. 2   6. 19.84   7. 8
8. 7   9. 6   10. 576 π
11. 235.7   12. 2512   13. 3

Exercise 14.10

1. **(a)** 4, 16   **(b)** 804.6   **(c)** 268.2
   (d) 268.2
2. **(a)** 4, 40   **(b)** 1106.3   **(c)** 2011.4
   (d) 268.2   **(c)** 670.4
3. **(a)** 36 × 36 × 36   **(b)** 7776
   (c) 24 438.9   **(d)** 22 217.1
4. **(a)** 12 000   **(b)** 9428.6   **(c)** 2571.4
5. **(a)** 4.5   **(b)** 954.6   **(c)** 2430
   (d) 520.8

Exercise 14.11

2. **(a)** 160   **(b)** 488   **(c)** 120
   (d) 21   **(e)** 248.52   **(f)** 264
3. **(a)** 44   **(b)** 80   **(c)** 38
   (d) 72   **(e)** 54   **(f)** 11.4
4. **(a)** 4, 40   **(b)** 1105.28   **(c)** 2009.6
   (d) 267.9   **(e)** 669.9
5. **(a)** 0.48 m²   **(b)** 3 m³   **(c)** €120
6. **(a)** 17.6   **(b)** 6   **(c)** 261
7. **(a)** 36 × 36 × 36   **(b)** 7776
   (c) 24 416.6   **(d)** 22 239.4
8. **(a)** 100.48   **(b)** 17 081.6
   (c) 341 632   **(d)** 153 734.40
9. 5
10. **(a)** 7500   **(b)** 5250   **(c)** 6352.20
11. **(a)** 16 × 4 × 4   **(b)** 256
    (c) 33.49   **(d)** 133.96   **(e)** 122.04
12. **(a)** 4019   **(b)** 2733   **(c)** 3307
13. **(a)** 7.234 560 cm³ = 7.23 m³   **(b)** 20
14. **(a)** 62.8 cm   **(b)** 10   **(c)** 22 cm

Chapter 15

Exercise 15.1

1. **(a)** 40, 140   **(b)** 60, 120   **(c)** 35, 145
   (d) 70, 110
2. **(a)** 45, 90, 45   **(b)** 70, 80, 30
   (c) 120, 30, 30   **(d)** 60, 60, 60
3. **(a)** 45   **(b)** 150   **(c)** 162
   (d) 32   **(e)** 144   **(f)** 113
4. **(a)** 55   **(b)** 35   **(c)** 50
   (d) 45   **(e)** 50   **(f)** 50
5. **(a)** H = 55; G = J = 125
   (b) L = 145, K = M = 35
   (c) P = 160, N = T = 20
   (d) X = 30, Y = 110, W = Z = 40
   (e) B = 90, A = D = 40, C = 50
6. **(a)** 36   **(b)** 30   **(c)** 15   **(d)** 20

7. **(a)** x = 18, F = 90, G = 36, E = 54
   (b) 60   **(c)** 50   **(d)** 40
8. **(a)** 10   **(b)** 10   **(c)** 20   **(d)** 12
9. **(a)** 16   **(b)** 40   **(c)** 13.9   **(d)** 18

Exercise 15.2

1. 6, 2, 6, 5, 3
2. **(a)** A = C = E = 110, B = D = 70
   (b) G = J = L = 115, F = I = K = H = 65
   (c) M = P = R = T = 57, N = S = Z = 123
   (d) Y = 119, W = X = Z = 61
3. **(a)** B = C = D = 109, E = F = G = 55
   (b) 122
4. **(a)** A = B = 45, C = 28, D = 107
   (b) E = F = 60, H = 40

(c) L = 65, J = K = M = P = 115
(d) R = S = W = V = 65; T = 115
5. (a) x = 18, A = C = 108, B = D = 72
(b) x = 15, W = T = 60, Z = 120
(c) x = 25, E = F = 80
(d) x = 40, H = 60
(e) x = 20   (f) x = 15, y = 45

Exercise 15.3

1. (a) 60   (b) 50   (c) 120   (d) 20
2. (a) 70   (b) 50   (c) 70   (d) 76
3. (a) 30   (b) 36   (c) 18
4. (a) 16   (b) 20   (c) $7\frac{1}{7}$
5. (a) A = 52, B = 76   (b) C = 47, D = 86
   (c) E = 62, F = 56   (d) G = 70, H = 40
6. (a) J = K = 46, M = 88
   (b) R = 96, N = P = 42
   (c) S = T = X = 34, W = 112
7. (a) A = B = 55   (b) C = D = 58
   (c) E = F = 78   (d) G = H = 47
8. (a) J = K = 57   (b) M = P = 71
   (c) S = T = 72, R = 36
9. (a) 56   (b) 68
10. (a) 43   (b) 43
11. (a) 62   (b) 118   (c) 31
12. (a) 45   (b) 135   (c) $22\frac{1}{2}$

Exercise 15.4

1. (a) A = 38, B = C = 142
   (b) D = 127, E = F = 53
   (c) G = 23, H = 110, K = 47
   (d) M = N = 95, P = 85
   (e) R = W = T = 46, S = 134
   (f) X = 83, Y = 54, Z = 43
2. (a) 60   (b) 30   (c) 30
   (d) 25   (e) 22   (f) 14

3. (a) A = 90
   (b) B = C = 45, D = 90
   (c) E = 117, F = G = 63
   (d) J = 64, H = K = 116
   (e) L = 33, M = 27, N = 120
   (f) P = 43, R = 100, S = 47
4. (a) 90   (b) 6   (c) 3   (d) 18
5. (a) 3   (b) 3   (c) 6
6. (a) 5   (b) 10   (c) 5   (d) 20
7. (a) 70   (b) 48   (c) 70   (d) 48
   (e) 70
8. (a) 80   (b) 60   (c) 72   (d) 48
   (e) 120
9. (a) 34   (b) 34   (c) 68   (d) 56
   (e) 90   (f) |kl| (g) |ok|

Exercise 15.5

1. (a) X = 90, Y = 68   (b) W = 16, Z = 90
   (c) E = 42, D = 90   (d) T = 55, S = 90
   (e) M = 59, R = 25, N = P = 90
   (f) G = 74, J = 20, H = F = 90
2. (a) C = 40, E = 100, D = F = 50
   (b) G = 22, H = 68, J = 44
   (c) M = 100, K = L = 50, N = 40
   (d) R = S = 45, P = 90
   (e) X = 60, T = W = 30
   (f) 36, 54
3. (a) A = 140, B = 60   (b) D = 70, C = 110
   (c) E = 80, F = 90   (d) H = 95, G = 105
   (e) J = 85, K = 106   (f) M = 88, L = 94
4. (a) 9   (b) 18   (c) 10
   (d) 30   (e) 45   (f) 10
5. (a) 90   (b) Y = 90, Z = 40
   (c) Y = 70, Z = 90   (d) X = 74, Y = 90
   (e) X = 30

Chapter 16

Exercise 16.1

5. (a) (i) $\vec{bc}$, $\vec{ef}$ (ii) $\vec{cb}$, $\vec{fe}$
   (iii) $\vec{cf}$, $\vec{ab}$, $\vec{bc}$, $\vec{be}$
   (iv) $\vec{gb}$, $\vec{ch}$, $\vec{he}$
   (b) $\vec{ce}$
6. (a) b   (b) f   (c) [cb]   (d) [cf]
   (e) bfc   (f) [ch]   (g) fhe
7. (b) $\vec{ba}$, $\vec{de}$
   (c) (i) a   (ii) [ae]   (iii) abe
   (d) (i) $\vec{db}$ (ii) $\vec{cd}$ (iii) $\vec{ab}$, $\vec{bc}$
8. (a) (i) c   (ii) g   (iii) e   (iv) [ef]   (v) cefg
   (b) (i) $\vec{dc}$, $\vec{ab}$, $\vec{gf}$ (ii) $\vec{cb}$, $\vec{da}$, $\vec{fe}$
   (iii) $\vec{ac}$, $\vec{cf}$, $\vec{dg}$

10. (a) F   (b) F   (c) F   (d) T   (e) T
11. (a) (i) $\vec{bc}$, $\vec{fe}$, $\vec{ed}$ (ii) $\vec{af}$, $\vec{cd}$
    (iii) $\vec{eg}$, $\vec{dh}$, $\vec{hb}$ (iv) $\vec{hd}$, $\vec{ag}$, $\vec{ge}$
    (v) $\vec{ab}$, $\vec{bc}$, $\vec{fe}$, $\vec{ed}$
    (b) (i) e   (ii) [bc]   (iii) [bh]   (iv) dhc
    (c) (i) $\vec{ec}$ (ii) $\vec{gb}$ (iii) $\vec{de}$
12. (a) (i) $\vec{dc}$, $\vec{ab}$, $\vec{ej}$, $\vec{hi}$
    (ii) $\vec{cb}$, $\vec{da}$, $\vec{eh}$, $\vec{ji}$
    (iii) $\vec{db}$, $\vec{ch}$, $\vec{fj}$, $\vec{ei}$
    (b) (i) $\vec{cb}$, $\vec{da}$, $\vec{eh}$, $\vec{ji}$
    (ii) $\vec{gf}$, $\vec{ce}$, $\vec{dc}$, $\vec{ej}$,...

465

(iii) $\overrightarrow{dc}$, $\overrightarrow{ab}$, $\overrightarrow{ej}$, $\overrightarrow{hi}$
(iv) $\overrightarrow{ca}$, $\overrightarrow{fc}$, $\overrightarrow{jh}$, $\overrightarrow{eb}$
(v) $\overrightarrow{de}$, $\overrightarrow{cj}$, $\overrightarrow{ah}$, $\overrightarrow{bi}$
(d) 20
(e) $\overrightarrow{ai}$, $\overrightarrow{dj}$

Exercise 16.2

3. (a) a　　(b) [ba]　　(c) o　　(d) [co]
   (e) aod　　(f) cdab
4. (a) a　(b) d　　(c) b　(d) [eb]　　(e) bcd
5. (a) t　(b) x　　(c) w　(d) a　　(e) [ym]
   (f) azr　(g) asym　(h) arzs　(i) xyzw　(j) zwx
6. (a) f　　(b) g　　(c) h　(d) i　　(e) f
9. (a) Yes　　(b) No　　(c) Yes　　(d) Yes
   (e) Yes　　(f) Yes　　(g) Yes

Exercise 16.3

4. (a) t　(b) b　(c) [wt]　(d) wbc　(e) bxy
5. (a) (i) e　　(ii) [dc]　　(iii) [ef]　(iv) [gi]
   (v) $\triangle$cia (vi) cbai
   (b) (i) c　　(ii) d　　(iii) [hg]　(iv) [gi]
   (v) $\triangle$gie (vi) gfei
6. (a) (i) c　(ii) d　(iii) [db]　(iv) dcb　(v) boa
   (b) (i) a　(ii) b　(iii) [db]　(iv) dab　(v) doc
7. (a) (i) y　(ii) o　(iii) [xw]　(iv) woz　(v) xwz
   (b) (i) z　(ii) o　(iii) [yx]　(iv) yox　(v) zwx

Exercise 16.4

1. (a) (i) c　(ii) [ed]　(iii) [cj]　(iv) fje　(v) cde
   (b) (i) h　　　　(ii) [de]　(iii) [hk]
   (iv) gkd　(v) hed
   (c) (i) d　(ii) [fc]　(iii) [dj]　(iv) ejf　(v) dcf
2. (a) $\overrightarrow{tr}$　(b) $\overrightarrow{pm}$　(c) S_{ts}　(d) $\overrightarrow{pt}$　(e) S_r
   (f) S_{wx}　(g) S_{ts}　(h) S_r　(i) S_r　(j) S_r
4. (a) (i) S_g　(ii) $\overrightarrow{hg}$　(iii) S_g　(iv) $\overrightarrow{fg}$　(v) S_{hi}
   (b) $\overrightarrow{im}$, $\overrightarrow{kg}$, $\overrightarrow{gf}$, $\overrightarrow{he}$　　(c) S_{kf}, $\overrightarrow{hi}$
5. (b) (i) $\overrightarrow{nq}$　(ii) $\overrightarrow{no}$　　(iii) $\overrightarrow{rp}$　(iv) $\overrightarrow{rq}$
6. (e) (i) $\overrightarrow{ux}$, $\overrightarrow{st}$, $\overrightarrow{tw}$　(ii) $\overrightarrow{ut}$, $\overrightarrow{xw}$　(iii) $\overrightarrow{yu}$, $\overrightarrow{tz}$, $\overrightarrow{zx}$
   (iv) $\overrightarrow{zw}$, $\overrightarrow{vy}$, $\overrightarrow{yt}$
7. (c) (i) d　(ii) o　(iii) boa　(iv) [ba]
   (d) (i) $\overrightarrow{bc}$　(ii) $\overrightarrow{dc}$　(iii) $\overrightarrow{oc}$　(iv) do
   (e) isosceles triangle
8. (b) egf, fgh　　　　　(c) $\angle$egf
9. (a) |xm| = |mj| = |mk|
   (c) (i) 25　(ii) 50　(iii) 65
10. (b) $\triangle$bgo　(c) $\triangle$ako　(d) $\triangle$ofb
    (e) (i) S_o　(ii) $\overrightarrow{cd}$ or S_{fh}　(iii) $\overrightarrow{cg}$ or S_{hg}
    (iv) S_{kg}　　　　　　　(v) $\overrightarrow{bf}$ or S_{hf}

Chapter 17

Exercise 17.1

1. (a) 5　　(b) 13　　(c) 20　　(d) 41
2. (a) 9　　(b) 8　　(c) 10　　(d) .24
3. (a) $\sqrt{149}$　(b) $\sqrt{51}$　(c) $\sqrt{80}$　(d) $\sqrt{57}$
4. (a) 4　　(b) 3　　(c) 5　　(d) 3
   (e) 4　　(f) 3　　(g) $\sqrt{15}$　(h) $\sqrt{7}$
5. (a) Yes　(b) No　(c) Yes　(d) Yes
   (e) Yes　(f) Yes　(g) No
7. $\sqrt{136}$　　8. 15　　9. 6
10. 9　　　11. 6.71　12. 5.39
13. (a) 10　　(b) 8
14. 19.5　　15. $\sqrt{80}$　16. 400

Exercise 17.4

1. (a) Yes　(b) Yes　(c) No　(d) No
2. (a) Yes　(b) No　(c) No　(d) Yes
3. (a) No　(b) Yes　(c) No　(d) Yes
4. (a) Yes　(b) No　(c) No　(d) Yes

5. (a) SSS　(b) SAS　(c) No　(d) ASA
   (e) ASA　(f) RHS　(g) ASA　(h) No
   (i) No　(j) SAS　(k) ASA
   (l) RHS or SSS
6. |ab| = |ab|, |bc| = |bd|, 90; SAS
7. ASA or SSS　　8. SAS　　9. SAS　　10. SAS

Exercise 17.5

1. (a) $\sqrt{193}$　(b) $\sqrt{95}$　(c) 5　　(d) $\sqrt{76.5}$
   (e) $\sqrt{31}$　(f) 4
2. (a) No　(b) Yes　(c) No　(d) Yes　(e) Yes
   (f) Yes
3. (a) 1.66
8. (a) No - not SAS　　(b) ASA　　(c) RHS
   (d) SSS　　(e) SAS　　(f) not SAS
9. (a) RHS
   (b) (i) 58　(ii) 32　(iii) 58　(iv) 64
10. SAS

Chapter 18

Exercise 18.1

1. **a** (2, 2), **b** (5, 0), **c** (−7, 4), **d** (−3, −5), **e** (2, −4), **f** (0, 4), **g** (7, −2), **h** (−4, −1), **i** (−7, −7), **j** (8, 5), **k** (3, −7)

2. **a** (−1, −1), **b** (−3, 2), **c** (−5, 0), **d** (6, −2), **e** (1, −5), **f** (3, −7), **g** (6, 3), **h** (4, 5), **i** (0, 5), **j** (−4, −5), **k** (−7, 4), **l** (−4, −5), **m** (−7, −3)

3. **l** (3, −7), **m** (6, −1), **n** (−3, −3), **o** (0, 0), **p** (3, 2), **q** (7, 5), **r** (9, 3), **s** (−4, 3), **t** (−6, 2), **u** (−6, −5), **v** (8, −3), **w** (−8, −7), **x** (3, 6), **y** (4, −3), **z** (2, 5)

4. **(a)** Gladiator **(b)** Alien Autopsy
   (c) Pulp Fiction **(d)** Schindler's List
   (e) Titanic **(f)** Forest Gump

5. **(a)** Coronation Street
   (b) EastEnders
   (c) Prime Time
   (d) Questions and Answers
   (e) Big Brother

6. **(a)** All for one and one for all
   (b) The opera ain't over till the fat lady sings
   (c) One small step for man, one giant leap for mankind

Exercise 18.2

1. **(a)** (5, 8) **(b)** (2, 3) **(c)** (1, 7) **(d)** (−1, −1)
   (e) (4, −3) **(f)** (2, 5) **(g)** (6, −2)
   (h) (4, 3) **(i)** (3, 4) **(j)** (−3, −1)

2. **(a)** (1, 1) **(b)** (−3, −3) **(c)** (−7, −4)
   (d) (1, −3) **(e)** (0, −8) **(f)** (−6, −3)
   (g) (−7, −5) **(h)** (−2, −8) **(i)** (−2, −4)
   (j) (−1, 3)

3. **(a)** (3, −6) **(b)** (11, −8) **(c)** (6, −4)
   (d) (12, −12) **(e)** (7, 0) **(f)** (7, −4)
   (g) (1, 0) **(h)** (3, −9) **(i)** (6, −3)
   (j) (7, 3)

4. **(a)** (−10, −1) **(b)** (−9, 4) **(c)** (−2, −2)
   (d) (−11, −7) **(e)** (−3, 3) **(f)** (−6, −1)
   (g) (−6, −2) **(h)** (0, −6) **(i)** (−5, −1)
   (j) (−5, 4)

5. **(a)** (2, 6) **(b)** (−1, 5) **(c)** (0, 0)
   (d) (−2, −2) **(e)** (−4, −4) **(f)** (4, 2)
   (g) (−4, 7) **(h)** (−3, 2) **(i)** (0, −5)
   (j) (−5, −1)

6. **(a)** (−4, −5) **(b)** (3, −4) **(c)** (4, 7)
   (d) (−5, 1) **(e)** (−7, −1) **(f)** (0, 4)
   (g) (4, 0) **(h)** (0, 0)

7. **(a)** (2, −3) **(b)** (3, 2) **(c)** (4, −6)
   (d) (−6, −1) **(e)** (−3, 2) **(f)** (0, −4)
   (g) (0, 5) **(h)** (3, 0)

8. **(a)** (−3, 2) **(b)** (4, −1) **(c)** (5, −1)
   (d) (−7, −4) **(e)** (6, −3) **(f)** (5, 1)
   (g) (−2, 0) **(h)** (0, −3)

9. **(a)** (−4, −3), (0, −5), (−2, −1)
   (b) (−1, −2), (−5, 0), (−3, −4)
   (c) (1, −2), (5, 0), (3, −4)
   (d) (−1, 2), (−5, 0), (−3, 4)

10. (−3, −2), (1, −1), (0, −5)

11. **(a)** (−3, −4), (−3, −1), (1, −1), (1, −4)
    (b) (−1, −2), (−1, −5), (−5, −5), (−5, −2)
    (c) (1, −5), (1, −2), (5, −5), (5, −2)

12. **(a) (i)** Sx **(ii)** So **(iii)** Sy
    (b) (3, 2) → (−6, 2) (6, 2) → (−3, 2)
    (3, 4) → (−6, 4)

Exercise 18.3

1. **(a)** √5 **(b)** √18 **(c)** √17 **(d)** √106
   (e) 5 **(f)** √32 **(g)** 5 **(h)** 5
   (i) √32 **(j)** 4

2. **(a)** √32 **(b)** √17 **(c)** √98 **(d)** √128
   (e) √40 **(f)** 5 **(g)** 5 **(h)** √13
   (i) √5 **(j)** √40

3. **(a)** Yes, √13 **(b)** Yes, √18 **(c)** No
   (d) No **(e)** Yes, √13

4. **(i)** √32, √8, √40 **(ii)** Yes

5. **(i)** √29, 5, 10 **(ii)** No

6. **(a)** √13, 2, 3 **(b)** 3

7. **(a)** 3, 4, 5 **(b)** 6 8. **(a)** 3 **(b)** √18

9. **(a)** 9, √20 **(b)** √137, √65

10. **(a)** √20, √20 **(b)** √40 **(c)** yes **(d)** rhombus

11. √98 = √32 + √18

12. √113 ≠ √61 + √8; not true

13. √97 = √20 + √29; not true

Exercise 18.4

1. **(a)** (3, 4) **(b)** (2, 2) **(c)** (1, 2)
   (d) (3, 3) **(e)** (2, 4) **(f)** $\left(4\frac{1}{2}, 3\frac{1}{2}\right)$
   (g) $\left(3\frac{1}{2}, 3\right)$ **(h)** (2, 3) **(i)** $\left(3, 5\frac{1}{2}\right)$
   (j) (3, 2)

2. **(a)** (2, −3) **(b)** $\left(2, -\frac{1}{2}\right)$ **(c)** (−4, −6)
   (d) (−2, 3) **(e)** $\left(-2\frac{1}{2}, 3\frac{1}{2}\right)$ **(f)** (−3, −2)
   (g) $\left(-2\frac{1}{2}, -2\frac{1}{2}\right)$ **(h)** (1, 1)
   (i) (1, 4) **(j)** (−5, 3)

3. (−1, 5)

4. **(a)** $\left(-2\frac{1}{2}, -3\right)$ **(b)** $\sqrt{4\frac{1}{4}}$

5. **(a)** (−1, 0) **(b)** (−1, 0)

6. (1, −1) 7. (−5, −3) 8. (−8, 5)

9. c(−3, 0), d(−11, −3)

10. c(−1, −2), d(−3, 1)

11. (−6, 8) 12. (7, −7)

Exercise 18.5

1. **(a)** -1 **(b)** 3 **(c)** 1 **(d)** $\frac{2}{3}$ **(e)** -1
   (f) vertical line **(g)** $\frac{3}{5}$ **(h)** 0

2. **(a)** $-\frac{3}{7}$ **(b)** $-\frac{1}{6}$ **(c)** $-\frac{1}{2}$ **(d)** 1 **(e)** $\frac{5}{6}$
   (f) vertical line **(g)** 1 **(h)** 0

3. **(a)** $\frac{3}{4}$ **(b)** $\frac{-4}{15}$ **(c)** 12 **(d)** $\frac{-3}{8}$
   (e) $-\frac{1}{2}$ **(f)** 1 **(g)** $\frac{11}{9}$ **(h)** $\frac{51}{40}$

4. $-1\frac{1}{2}$, parallelogram

5. 3   6. 2, $\frac{1}{4}$ 7. $-\frac{1}{3}$, -1

8. $\frac{1}{2}$, $\frac{1}{2}$ 9. 1, $\frac{2}{3}$; No   10. Yes; -4, $\frac{3}{5}$

22. 4   23. 2   24. 2   25. 4
26. 4   27. 2   28. -1 29. 2
30. 1   31. 0

Exercise 18.6

1. $2x - y - 10 = 0$ 2. $x + y - 8 = 0$
3. $4x - y + 1 = 0$ 4. $x - 2y = 0$
5. $3x - 4y - 7 = 0$ 6. $2x + 5y - 20 = 0$
7. $2x + 3y + 14 = 0$ 8. $y = 2$
9. $3x + 7y + 3 = 0$ 10. $x + y = 0$
11. $x - 3y + 2 = 0$ 12. $2x + 9y - 30 = 0$
13. $3x - 2y + 5 = 0$ 14. $2x - y + 6 = 0$
15. $x - y + 1 = 0$ 16. $3x + 10y - 31 = 0$
17. $x = 4$; vertical   18. $y = -3$; horizontal
19. $x - y = 0$

Exercise 18.7

1. $(4, 0)$ 2. $(8, 0)$ 3. $(3, 0)$ 4. $(3, 0)$
5. $(-3, 0)$ 6. $(3, 0)$ 7. $(0, 3)$ 8. $(0, -3)$
9. $(0, -3)$ 10. $(0, -10)$ 11. $(0, -2)$
12. $(0, 2)$ 13. $(0, 3)$ 14. $(0, -5)$
15. $(0, -2)$ 16. $(0, -6)$ 17. $(0, 6), (8, 0)$
18. $(0, -4), (4, 0)$ 19. $(0, -8), (4, 0)$

Exercise 18.8

1. **(b)** $\sqrt{73}$ **(c)** $\left(2\frac{1}{2}, 1\right)$ **(d)** $8x - 3y - 17 = 0$
2. **(b)** $\left(2\frac{1}{2}, 2\frac{1}{2}\right)$ **(c)** $\left(2\frac{1}{2}, 2\frac{1}{2}\right)$
   (d) $2\frac{1}{2}$ **(e)** $2\frac{1}{2}$ **(f)** parallelogram
3. **(b)** $-1\frac{1}{2}$ **(c)** $-1\frac{1}{2}$
   (d) $3x + 2y = 5$ **(e)** $3x + 2y + 13 = 0$
   (f) $\sqrt{52}$ **(g)** $\sqrt{52}$
4. **(a)** $\sqrt{8}$ **(b)** -1 **(c)** $x + y = 5$ **(d)** $(5, 0)$
5. **(a)** $(1, 4)$ **(c)** 1
   (d) $x - y + 3 = 0$ **(e)** $(0, 3), (-3, 0)$
6. **(a)** $(4, 0)$ **(b)** $(0, 3)$ **(c)** 5   **(d)** 5
   (e) $\sqrt{34}$ **(f)** $\sqrt{34}$ **(g)** $\left(3\frac{1}{2}, 4\right)$ **(h)** $\left(3\frac{1}{2}, 4\right)$
   (i) $\frac{5}{3}, -\frac{3}{4}$ **(j)** parallelogram
7. **(a)** $\sqrt{5}, \sqrt{5}, \sqrt{10}$
   (b) $(-1, -1), (-3, -2), (-2, -4)$
8. **(a)** $(2, 2), (7, -1), (4, 0)$ **(c)** $-\frac{3}{5}, \frac{1}{3}, -1$
   (d) same **(e)** $3x + 5y - 22 = 0$
9. **(a)** $(0, 13)$ **(b)** -1
   (d) $\sqrt{153}$ **(e)** $4x + y + 13 = 0$
10. **(a)** $(0, 6), (4, 0)$ **(b)** 3
    (d) $3x - 2y + 12 = 0$

Chapter 19

Exercise 19.1

1. **(a)** $D = \{1, 2, 3, 4, 5\} = R$
   (b) $D = \{1, 2, 3, 4, 5\}, R = \{-1, -2, -3, -4, -5\}$
   (c) $D = \{1, 2, 3, 4\}, R = \{a, b, c, d\}$
2. **(a)** $D = \{1, 2, 3\}, R = \{5, 7, 9\}$
   (b) $D = \{1, 2, 3\}, R = \{x, y, z\}$
   (c) $D = \{p, q, r\}, R = \{1, 2\}$
   (d) $D = \{$Dublin, London, Paris$\}$,
   $R = \{$Ireland, UK, France$\}$
4. $(2, 4), (2, 6), (2, 10), (3, 6), (3, 9), (7, 7)$
5. $(1, 1), (2, 4), (3, 9), (5, 25), (6, 36)$
6. $(16, 4), (25, 5), (36, 6), (49, 7), (64, 8), (81, 9)$
7. $(3, 0), (5, 2), (7, 4), (9, 6), (20, 17)$
8. **(a)** $(2, 2), (2, 5), (2, 6), (5, 2), (6, 4), (4, 4)$
   (b) $(a, a), (b, c), (c, b), (c, a), (d, b), (d, d)$
   (c) $(10, 20), (20, 10), (20, 25), (25, 25),$
   $(30, 10), (30, 20), (30, 30)$
   (d) $(7, 11), (11, 7), (11, 11), (11, 9), (9, 9),$
   $(9, 15), (15, 9), (15, 15)$
9. $(1, 2), (1, 3), (1, 4), (2, 3), (2, 4), (3, 4)$
10. $(2, 4), (4, 6), (6, 8)$
11. $(1, 6), (3, 6), (3, 12), (3, 9), (4, 12), (6, 12),$
    $(1, 11)...12. (2, 1), (5, 1), (7, 1), (10, 10),$
    $(1, 1), (3, 2), (5, 2), (5, 5)$
12. $(2, 7), (5, 10)$
13. $(5, 1), (7, 3), (11, 7)$

Exercise 19.2

1. $(0, 1), (1, 3), (2, 5), (3, 7)$
2. $(3, 5), (4, 6), (5, 7)$
3. $(0, -3), (1, -2), (2, -1)$
4. $(-2, -10), (-1, -7), (0, -4), (1, -1)$
5. $(-5, -25), (-4, -21), (-3, -17), (-2, -13)$

6. **(a)** (−3, 8), (−2, 7), (−1, 6), (0, 5), (1, 4), (2, 3)
7. **(a)** (−4, 11), (−3, 9), (−2, 7), (−1, 5), (0, 3), (1, 1), (2, −1)
8. **(a)** (2, 1), (4, 2), (6, 3), (8, 4), (10, 5)
9. **(a)** (2, 6), (3, 11), (4, 18), (5, 27)
10. **(a)** (1, −2), (2, 4), (3, 14), (4, 28), (5, 46)

Exercise 19.3

1. **(a)** yes **(b)** yes **(c)** yes **(d)** no **(e)** no **(f)** no
2. **(a)** no **(b)** yes **(c)** yes
3. **(a)** (1, 3), (2, 6), (3, 9) **(b)** yes
4. **(a)** (−2, 4), (−1, 1), (0, 0), (1, 1), (2, 4) **(b)** yes
5. **(a)** (−3, 11), (−2, 6), (−1, 3), (0, 2) **(b)** yes
6. **(a)** (−4, −13), (−3, −6), (−2, −1), (−1, 2), (0, 3), (1, 2), (2, −1) **(b)** yes
7. **(a)** (1, 2), (2, 4), (3, 6), (4, 8) **(b)** yes
8. **(a)** (0, 4), (1, 4), (2, 4), (3, 4) **(b)** yes
9. **(a)** (−3, −6), (−2, −1), (−1, 2), (0, 3), (1, 2), (2, −1), (3, −6) **(b)** yes

Exercise 19.4

1. **(a)** 7	**(b)** 8	**(c)** 5	**(d)** 1
2. **(a)** 3	**(b)** 1	**(c)** 11	**(d)** 9
3. **(a)** −4	**(b)** −3	**(c)** −8	**(d)** 0
4. **(a)** 10	**(b)** 4	**(c)** −20	**(d)** −2
5. **(a)** −1	**(b)** 1	**(c)** 7	**(d)** 6
6. **(a)** 3	**(b)** 7	**(c)** 5	**(d)** 13
7. **(a)** 4	**(b)** 9	**(c)** 1	**(d)** 0
8. **(a)** 15	**(b)** 3	**(c)** 0	**(d)** −1
9. **(a)** 34	**(b)** 4	**(c)** 6	**(d)** 24
10. **(a)** 12	**(b)** 36	**(c)** 12	**(d)** 4
11. **(a)** 19	**(b)** −5	**(c)** 4	**(d)** −8
12. **(a)** 3	**(b)** 6	**(c)** −9	**(d)** −2

Exercise 19.5

1. (1, 3), (2, 4), (3, 5), (4, 6)
2. (−1, −5), (0, −2), (1, 1), (2, 4), (3, 7)
3. (−3, −4), (−2, −2), (−1, 0), (0, 2), (1, 4), (2, 6)
4. (−2, −10), (−1, −7), (0, −4), (1, −1), (2, 2), (3, 5), (4, 8)
5. (−4, 20), (−3, 17), (−2, 14), (−1, 11), (0, 8), (1, 5), (2, 2), (3, −1), (4, −4)
6. (1, −5), (2, 0), (3, 5), (4, 10), (5, 15)

Exercise 19.6

1. (−2, 2), (−1, 3), (0, 4), (1, 5), (2, 6), (3, 7), (4, 8)
   (a) 6.5 **(b)** −4

2. (−2, 5), (−1, 4), (0, 3), (1, 2), (2, 1), (3, 0), (4, −1)
   (a) 3 **(b)** 4.5
3. (−3, −11), (−2, −8), (−1, −5), (0, −2), (1, 1), (2, 4), (3, 7), (4, 10), (5, 13)
   (a) −9.5 **(b)** 0.7
4. (0, −10), (1, −4), (2, 2), (3, 8)
   (a) −7 **(b)** 1.7
5. (−4, −8), (−3, −5), (−2, −2), (−1, 1)
   (a) −3.5 **(b)** −1.3
6. **(a)** f:(−2, −6), (−1, −3), (0, 0), (1, 3), (2, 6), (3, 9), (4, 16)
   g:(−2, 10), (−1, 9), (0, 8), (1, 7), (2, 6), (3, 5), (4, 4)
   (b) (2, 6)
7. **(a)** f:(3, 16), (4, 15), ... (8, 11):
   g:(3, 10), (4, 11), ... (8, 15)
   (b) (6, 13)
8. **(a)** f:(−1, −2), (0, −1), ... (5, 4):
   g:(−1, 4), (0, 3), ... (5, −2)
   (b) (2, 1)
9. **(a)** f:(2, 4), (3, 3), ... (7, −1):
   g:(2, −2), (3, −1), ... (7, 3)
   (b) (5, 1)
10. **(a)** f:(2, 3), (3, 2), ... (7, −2):
    g:(2, −1), (3, 0), ... (7, 4)
    (b) (4, 1)
11. **(a)** f:(−2, −9), (−1, −6), ... (3, 6), (4, 9):
    g:(−2, 1), (−1, 2), ... (3, 6), (4, 7)
    (b) (3, 6)

Exercise 19.7

1. (−3, 14), (−2, 6), (−1, 0), (0, −4), (1, −6), (2, −6), (3, −4), (4, 0)
2. (−4, 14), (−3, 6), (−2, 0), (−1, −4), (0, −6), (1, −6), (2, −4), (3, 0), (4, 6), (5, 14)
3. (−5, 14), (−4, 6), (−3, 0), (−2, −4), (−1, −6), (0, −6), (1, −4), (2, 0), (3, 6)
4. (−6, 7), (−5, 0), (−4, −5), (−3, −8), (−2, −9), (−1, −8), (0, −5), (1, 0), (2, 7)
5. (−7, 5), (−6, 0), (−5, −3), (−4, −4), (−3, −3), (−2, 0), (−1, 5), (0, 12)
6. (−4, 7), (−3, 0), (−2, −5), (−1, −8), (0, −9), (1, −8), (2, −5), (3, 0), (4, 7)
7. (−3, 3), (−2, 0), (−1, −1), (0, 0), (1, 3), (2, 8), (3, 15)
8. (−2, 10), (−1, 4), (0, 0), (1, −2), (2, −2), (3, 0), (4, 4), (5, 10)
9. (−3, −6), (−2, 0), (−1, 4), (0, 6), (1, 6), (2, 4), (3, 0), (4, −6)
10. (−5, −6), (−4, 0), (−3, 4), (−2, 6), (−1, 6), (0, 4), (1, 0), (2, −6)
11. (−6, 8), (−5, 13), (−4, 16), (−3, 17), (−2, 16), (−1, 13), (0, 8), (1, 1)
12. (−4, −6), (−3, 0), (−2, 4), (−1, 6), (0, 6), (1, 4), (2, 0), (3, −6)

13. (−5, −7), (−4, 0), (−3, 5), (−2, 8), (−1, 9), (0, 8), (1, 5), (2, 0), (3, −7)
14. (−4, 12), (−3, 4), (−2, 0), (−1, 0), (0, 4), (1, 12), (2, 24)
15. (−4, 36), (−3, 12), (−2, 0), (−1, 0), (0, 12), (1, 36)
16. (−5, 16), (−4, 6), (−3, 0), (−2, −2), (−1, 0), (0, 6), (1, 16), (2, 30)
17. (−4, 36), (−3, 20), (−2, 8), (−1, 0), (0, −4), (1, −4), (2, 0), (3, 8), (4, 20)
18. (−4, 36), (−3, 15), (−2, 0), (−1, −9), (0, −12), (1, −9), (2, 0), (3, 15), (4, 36)
19. (−4, 12), (−3, 0), (−2, −8), (−1, −12), (0, 8), (1, 0), (2, 8), (3, 12), (4, 28)
20. (−4, −9), (−3, 0), (−2, 5), (−1, 6), (0, 3), (1, −4), (2, −15)

Exercise 19.8

1. (−4, 5), (−3, 0), (−2, −3), (−1, −4), (0, −3), (1, 0), (2, 5),
   (a) −4 (b) −3.7 (c) x = −1 (d) −3, 1
2. (0, 6), (1, 0), (2, −4), (3, −6), (4, −6), (5, −4), (6, 0), (7, 6)
   (a) −6.5 (b) −5 (c) 1, 6 (d) x = 3.5
3. (−5, 14), (−4, 6), (−3, 0), (−2, −4), (−1, −6), (0, 6), (1, −4), (2, 0), (3, 6), (4, 14)
   (a) −3, 2 (b) −6.5 (c) 2.8
4. (−3, 12), (−2, 5), (−1, 0), (0, −3), (1, −4), (2, −3), (3, 0), (4, 5), (5, 12)
   (a) −1.8 (b) −4 (c) 3, −1
5. (−4, 14), (−3, 6), (−2, 0), (−1, −4), (0, −6), (1, −6), (2, −4), (3, 0), (4, 6)
   (a) −2.4 (b) −6.5 (c) −2, 3
6. (−2, −4), (−1, 0), (0, 2), (1, 2), (2, 0), (3, −4)
   (a) −1.8 (b) 2.3 (c) −1, 2
7. (−3, −6), (−2, 0), (−1, 4), (0, 6), (1, 6), (2, 4), (3, 0), (4, −6)
   (a) 6.5 (b) 3.2 (c) −2, 3
8. (−3, 48), (−2, 18), (−1, 0), (0, −6), (1, 0), (2, 18), (3, 48)
   (a) 7.5 (b) −1, 1 (c) −6
9. (−4, 23), (−3, 0), (−2, −13), (−1, −16), (0, −9), (1, 8), (2, 35)
   (a) 10 (b) −3, 0.6 (c) −16
10. (−6, −11), (−5, 0), (−4, 9), (−3, 16), (−2, 21), (−1, 24), (0, 25), (1, 24), (2, 21), (3, 16), (4, 9), (5, 0), (6, −11)
    (a) +10 (b) −5, 5 (c) 25 (d) x = 0
11. (−3, −15), (−2, 0), (−1, 9), (0, 12), (1, 9), (2, 0), (3, −15)
    (a) 12 (b) −4 (c) −2, 2 (d) x = 0
12. (−3, 66), (−2, 35), (−1, 12), (0, −3), (1, −10), (2, −9), (3, 0), (4, 17), (5, 42)

(a) −10 (b) 7.5 (c) 3, −0.25
13. (−2, −34), (−1, −12), (0, 0), (1, 2), (2, −6), (3, −24)
    (a) −10 (b) 2.5 (c) 0, 1.4
14. (−5, −6), (−4, 0), (−3, 4), (−2, 6), (−1, 6), (0, 4), (1, 0), (2, −6)
    (a) 6.5 (b) 2 (c) 1, −4 (d) x = −1.5

Exercise 19.9

1. (a) 20 km (b) 4 hr (c) 70 km (d) 14 km/h
2. (1, 100), (2, 200), (3, 300), (4, 400), (5, 500)
   (a) 350 km (b) $1\frac{1}{2}$ hrs
   (c) 500 km (d) 100 km/h
3. (0, 3.5), (3, 4.5), (6, 5.5), (9, 6.5), (12, 7.5)
   (a) 3.50 kg (b) 5.5 kg (c) 3 weeks (d) 7.5 kg
4. (0, 22), (1, 42), (3, 82), (4, 102), (5, 122), (6, 142) (a) €22 (b) €92 (c) 140 (d) €46
5. (0, 50), (1, 52), (2, 54), ... (9, 68), (10, 70)
   (a) €140 (b) €50 25
6. A: (0, 0), (0.5, 20), (1, 40), (1.5, 60), (2, 80), (2.5, 100), (3, 120)
   B: (1, 0), (1.5, 40), (2, 80), (2.5, 120)
   (a) 80 km (b) 1 hr (c) 40, 80 km/h
7. A: (0, 0), (7, 3500); B: (1, 0), (6, 3500)
   (a) 1750 km (b) $3\frac{1}{2}$ hrs (c) 500, 700 km/h
8. (a) 4° (b) 12 (c) −4 (d) 10 and 3
9. (−3, 3), (−2, −1), (−1, −3), (0, −3), (1, −1), (2, 3)
   (a) −3.5 (b) 1 p.m. (c) 8:40 a.m; 4:20 p.m.
10. (0, 0), (1, 48), (2, 64), (3, 48), (4, 0)
    (a) 64 m (b) 4 seconds
11. (0, 8), (1, 3), (2, 0), (3, −1), (4, 0)
    (a) 8 m (b) 1 m (c) 2 seconds

Exercise 19.10

2. (0, −6), (1, −3), (2, 0), (3, 3), (4, 6)
3. (a) $2a^2 − 6$ (b) −4 (c) −6 (d) $2(x − 1)^2 − 6$
4. (−3, −13), (−2, −10), (−1, −7), (0, −4) ... (3, 5)
5. (a) f:(−2, 0), (−1, 1), (0, 2) ... (3, 5);
   g:(−2, 6), (−1, 5), (0, 4), ... (3, 1)
   (b) (1, 3)
6. (−2, 40), (−1, 12), (0, 0), (1, 4), (2, 24)
7. (−3, −5), (−2, 0), (−1, 3), (0, 4), (1, 3), (2, 0), (3, −5)
   (a) 2, −2 (b) 4 (c) 1.8
8. (−5, 28), (−4, 12), (−3, 0), (−2, −8), (−1, −12), (0, −12), (1, −8), (2, 0), (3, 12), (4, 28)
   (a) 5.5 (b) −12.5 (b) −3, 2 (c) x = −0.5
9. (a) 14.2 m (b) 3.5 seconds (c) 13 m
   (d) 2 seconds, 5 seconds (e) 7 seconds
10. (0, 15), (1, 4), (2, −3), (3, −6), (4, −5), (5, 0)
    (a) 15 m (b) 6 m (c) $3\frac{1}{2}$ seconds

Chapter 20

Exercise 20.1

1. **(a)** b, a, c **(b)** c, a, b **(c)** a, c, b **(d)** b, c, a
2. **(a)** [xy] **(b)** [xz] **(c)** [xz] **(d)** [yz] **(e)** [yz]
4. **(a)** $\frac{48}{50}$ **(b)** $\frac{14}{50}$ **(c)** $\frac{48}{14}$ **(d)** $\frac{14}{50}$
   (e) $\frac{48}{50}$ **(f)** $\frac{14}{48}$

5. **(a)** $\frac{2}{5}$ **(b)** $\frac{\sqrt{21}}{5}$ **(c)** $\frac{2}{\sqrt{21}}$ **(d)** $\frac{\sqrt{21}}{5}$
   (e) $\frac{2}{5}$ **(f)** $\frac{\sqrt{21}}{2}$

6. **(a)** $\frac{24}{7}$ **(b)** $\frac{24}{25}$ **(c)** $\frac{7}{25}$
   (d) $\frac{7}{25}$ **(e)** $\frac{24}{25}$ **(f)** $\frac{7}{24}$

Exercise 20.2

1. **(a)** 0.8480 **(b)** 0.8290 **(c)** 0.7071
   (d) 0.5 **(e)** 3.4874 **(f)** 0.5299
   (g) 0.9848 **(h)** 0.9848
2. **(a)** 1 **(b)** 0 **(c)** 0 **(d)** 0 **(e)** 1 **(f)** 0.5
   (g) 1 **(h)** 0.5
3. All false 4. All true
5. **(a)** 45 **(b)** 28 **(c)** 27 **(d)** 55 **(e)** 8 **(f)** 76
   (g) 69 **(h)** 20 **(i)** 24 **(j)** 78
6. **(a)** 26 **(b)** 82 **(c)** 30 **(d)** 42 **(e)** 74 **(f)** 53
   (g) 72 **(h)** 81 **(i)** 8 **(j)** 46
7. **(a)** 45 **(b)** 60 **(c)** 45 **(d)** 60 **(e)** 90 **(f)** 30
   (g) 30 **(h)** 30 **(i)** 90 **(j)** 60

Exercise 20.3

1. 25   2. 15   3. 16   4. 2
5. 8   6. $\sqrt{50}$ 7. 7   8. 7
9. 60   10. 9   11. $\sqrt{11}$ 12. 1
13. 75   14. 25   15. 65   16. 12
17. 78   18. 72
19. 100; $\frac{96}{100}, \frac{28}{100}, \frac{96}{28}$ 20. 20; $\frac{21}{29}, \frac{20}{29}, \frac{21}{20}$
21. $\sqrt{2}, \frac{1}{\sqrt{2}}, \frac{1}{\sqrt{2}}$ 1   22. 18; $\frac{24}{30}, \frac{18}{30}, \frac{24}{18}$
23. 3; $\frac{5}{\sqrt{34}}, \frac{3}{\sqrt{34}}, \frac{5}{3}$ 24. 3; $\frac{\sqrt{40}}{7}, \frac{3}{7}, \frac{\sqrt{40}}{3}$

Exercise 20.4

1. 16.85   2. 18.84   3. 12.29   4. 44.78
5. 7.61   6. 14.06   7. 10.71   8. 13.21
9. 15.70   10. 17.60   11. 22.02   12. 20.65
13. 47.18   14. 28.90   15. 23.78   16. 62°
17. 71°   18. 24°   19. 58°   20. 12°
21. 65°   22. 15°   23. 66°   24. 25°
25. 18°   26. 32°   27. 77°
28. 24; A = 23°; B = 67°
29. 4.49; A = 26°; B = 64°
30. x = 13.16; y = 12.36; A = 70°
31. x = 13.5; y = 20.18; A = 48°
32. x = 16.96; y = 10.60; A = 32°
33. x = 8.05; A = 32°; B = 58°
34. x = 33.94; A = 19°; B = 71°
35. x = 11.97; y = 32.89; A = 20°
36. x = 8.72; y = 14.83; B = 54°
37. x = 26.41; A = 78°; B = 12°
38. x = 6.04; A = 51°; B = 39°
39. x = 8.75; A = 44°; B = 46°

Exercise 20.5

1. 17.32 m 2. 4 m   3. 54° 4. 6.93 m
5. 429 m   6. 41.95 m 7. 2007.5
8. 60 m   9. 75   10. **(a)** 1500 m **(b)** 6°
11. 39.1 m 12. **(a)** 30.14 m **(b)** 22.94 m

Exercise 20.6

2. **(a)** $\frac{8}{10}$ **(b)** $\frac{8}{10}$ **(c)** $\frac{8}{6}$ **(d)** $\frac{6}{8}$
3. **(a)** 0.8480 **(b)** 3.7321 **(c)** 0.9063
   (d) 1.4142 **(e)** 4.1302 **(f)** 3.8787
   (g) 0 **(h)** 0.5 **(i)** 1.7321
4. **(a)** 61° **(b)** 9° **(c)** 74° **(d)** 34° **(e)** 79°
   (f) 14° **(g)** 30° **(h)** 56° **(i)** 26° **(j)** 87°
5. **(a)** 10 **(b)** 39 **(c)** 51 **(d)** $\sqrt{117}$ **(e)** 10
6. **(a)** $\sqrt{20}$ **(b)** 10 **(c)** 6 **(d)** 5 **(e)** 9
7. **(a)** 2 **(b)** 6 **(c)** 6 **(d)** 84 **(e)** 13 **(f)** 58
8. **(a)** 32 **(b)** 32 **(c)** 57
9. **(a)** 30 **(b)** 45 **(c)** 60
10. 10.8   11. 1.56   12. 59
13. **(a)** 5.04 **(b)** 13.8   14. **(a)** 25.17 **(b)** 24

Chapter 21

Exercise 21.1

1. (i) e   (ii) l   (iii) h   (iv) a   (v) k
   (vi) i   (vii) b   (viii) d   (ix) c   (x) m
   (xi) g   (xii) f   (xiii) j
2. $x + 3$
3. $x - 1$
4. $2x + 5$
5. $x + 10$
6. $x - 6$
7. $x - 12$
8. $\frac{1x}{2}$
9. $4x$
10. $x - 55$
11. $2x + 4$
12. $3x - 10$
13. $4x$
14. $\frac{7x}{10}$
15. $\frac{x}{5}$
16. $2x$
17. $x - 14$
18. $2x$
19. $\frac{x}{9}$
20. $x - 1500$

Exercise 21.2

1. (a) $x + 7 = 12$ (b) 5
2. (a) $x + 3 = 7$ (b) 4
3. (a) $x + 12 = 15$ (b) 3
4. (a) $x - 4 = 2$ (b) 6
5. (a) $x - 10 = 15$ (b) 25
6. (a) $x - 11 = 5$ (b) 16
7. (a) $5x + 3 = 23$ (b) 4
8. (a) $2x + 5 = 17$ (b) 6
9. (a) $6x + 10 = 22$ (b) 2
10. (a) $2x - 8 = 10$ (b) 9
11. (a) $5x - 4 = 11$ (b) 3
12. (a) $3x - 6 = 15$ (b) 7
13. $x + 20$
14. $2x + 6 = 28$; 11
15. $4x = 48$; 12
16. $x + 15 = 4x$; 5
17. $x + (x + 18) = 184$; 63
18. $7x - 5 = 28$; $\frac{33}{7}$
19. 27; 54
20. $x + (x + 15\,000) + 2x = €105\,000$; €22 500

Exercise 21.3

1. (a) $x + y = 28$; $x - y = 12$ (b) 20, 8
2. (a) $x + y = 45$; $x - y = 15$ (b) 30, 15
3. (a) $x + y = 25$; $x - y = 3$ (b) 14, 11
4. (a) $x + y = 19$; $x - y = 11$ (b) 15, 4
5. (a) $x + y = 26$; $x - y = 16$ (b) 21, 5
6. (a) $x + y = 21$; $x - y = 3$ (b) 12, 9
7. (a) $x + y = 40$; $x - y = 8$ (b) 24, 16
8. (a) $x + y = 44$; $x - y = 2$ (b) 23, 21
9. (a) $x + y = 31$; $x - y = 3$ (b) 17, 14
10. (a) $x + y = 63$; $x - y = 5$ (b) 34, 29
11. (a) $2x + 3y = 19$; $x + 2y = 11$
    (b) €5, €3
12. (a) $3x + 4y = 548$; $4x + 3y = 474$
    (b) 36c, €1.10
13. (a) $2x + 5y = 85.50$; $5x + 2y = 93$
    (b) €14, €11.50
14. (a) $3x + 4y = 220$; $5x + 2y = 209$
    (b) €28, €34
15. 800 adults, 1400 children
16. 5500 adults, 6500 children
17. 50 000 adults, 30 000 children
18. 25, 35
19. 208, 32
20. 7, 5
21. 10, 16
22. 4 CDs, 4 DVDs
23. 90 tables, 60 chairs
24. 85c for apples, 55c for oranges
25. €1.10 for still, €1.30 for sparkling
26. cola = 80c, chocolate = 30c

Exercise 21.4

1. (i) h   (ii) e   (iii) j   (iv) a   (v) i
   (vi) b   (vii) c   (viii) f   (ix) d   (x) g
2. (a) 1   (b) 2   (c) 2   (d) 8   (e) 7
   (f) 2   (g) 6   (h) 4   (i) 5   (j) 14
3. (a) $2x + 5 = 9$ (b) 2
4. (a) $4x + 10 = 26$ (b) 4
5. (a) $5x - 8 = 12$ (b) 4
6. (a) $6x - 20 = 40$ (b) 10
7. (a) $x + (x + 5) = 28$ (b) €11.50
8. (a) $5(x - 5) = (66 - x) + 5$ (b) €16, €50
9. (a) $2x + 2(x + 8) = 56$ (b) 10, 18
10. (a) $60x + 80(12 - x) = 820$ (b) 7, 5
11. (a) 3, 1   (b) 2, 6   (c) 5, −2   (d) 5, 3
    (e) −4, 2   (f) −3, 8   (g) 3, 1   (h) −1, −3
    (i) 4, −3   (j) 3, 4
12. (a) $x + y = 15$; $x - y = 1$ (b) 8, 7
13. (a) $x + y = 31$; $x - y = 11$ (b) 21, 10
14. (a) $x + 2y = 5$; $3x + 2y = 9$ (b) €2, €1.50
15. (a) $x + y = 8$; $8x + 4y = 44$ (b) 3, 5